Interpersonal Conflict

seventh edition

William W. Wilmot

Joyce L. Hocker

McGraw Hill

Boston   Burr Ridge, IL   Dubuque, IA   Madison, WI   New York   San Francisco   St. Louis
Bangkok   Bogotá   Caracas   Kuala Lumpur   Lisbon   London   Madrid   Mexico City
Milan   Montreal   New Delhi   Santiago   Seoul   Singapore   Sydney   Taipei   Toronto

INTERPERSONAL CONFLICT
Published by McGraw-Hill, a business unit of The McGraw-Hill Companies, Inc., 1221 Avenue
of the Americas, New York, NY, 10020. Copyright © 2007, 2001, 1998, 1995, 1991, 1985, 1978
by The McGraw-Hill Companies, Inc. All rights reserved. No part of this publication may be
reproduced or distributed in any form or by any means, or stored in a database or retrieval
system, without the prior written consent of The McGraw-Hill Companies, Inc., including,
but not limited to, in any network or other electronic storage or transmission, or broadcast
for distance learning.

Some ancillaries, including electronic and print components, may not be available to customers
outside the United States.

This book is printed on acid-free paper.

4 5 6 7 8 9 0 FGR/FGR 0 9 8 7

ISBN   978-0-07-313554-0
MHID 0-07-313554-2

Editor in Chief: *Emily Barrosse*
Publisher: *Phillip A. Butcher*
Executive Editor: *Nanette Giles*
Senior Developmental Editor: *Jennie Katsaros*
Senior Marketing Manager: *Leslie Oberhuber*
Senior Media Project Manager: *Nancy Garcia*
Managing Editor: *Jean Dal Porto*
Senior Project Manager: *Diane M. Folliard*
Associate Designer: *Marianna Kinigakis*
Art Editor: *Katherine McNab*
Senior Production Supervisor: *Rich DeVitto*
Text/Cover Designer: *Pam Verros*
Cover Credit: *Getty Images/Andrea Rugg*
Composition: *10/12 Goudy by GTS, New Delhi, India*
Printing: *PMS Black, 45 # New Era Matte, Quebecor World Fairfield, Inc.*

Library of Congress Cataloging-in-Publication Data

Wilmot, William W.
    Interpersonal conflict / William W. Wilmot, Joyce L. Hocker.—7th ed.
        p. cm.
    Includes bibliographical references and index.
    ISBN-13: 978-0-07-313554-0 (soft cover: alk. paper)
    ISBN-10:   0-07-313554-2 (soft cover: alk. paper)
    1. Interpersonal conflict. 2. Conflict (Psychology) I. Hocker, Joyce L. II. Title.
HM1121.W56 2007
303.6'9—dc22

                                              2005050124

The Internet addresses listed in the text were accurate at the time of publication. The inclusion of a Web
site does not indicate an endorsement by the authors of McGraw-Hill, and McGraw-Hill does not
guarantee the accuracy of the information presented at these sites.

www.mhhe.com

This book is dedicated to:

Janice Lee Hocker Rushing

January 3, 1949–February 19, 2004

Contents

Chapter 8   Negotiating for Mutual Gains   243

Chapter 9   Third-Party Intervention   270

Preface

The core concepts of this book have been used by thousands of students and conflict practitioners in the United States and around the world since 1978. The resilience of the concepts has inspired us to keep learning about conflict and revising the book, now in its seventh edition. Our definition of conflict, crafted over many conversations and countless workshops and classes, is the most widely quoted definition of conflict in the communication literature. We are grateful for the continuing warm reception this work has received, and for the ongoing excellent help of the McGraw-Hill editors.

What is different? Long-time users of the book will continue to resonate with our philosophical stance, which has not changed. We have made significant changes as well. We added a new last chapter, changed the order of four chapters, and updated research emerging from various fields of study. We took the opportunity to make revisions to many of the chapters. Desiring to help those who teach the conflict course do so more completely and efficiently, we have added key terms and review questions at the end of each chapter. These will help students keep up with the concepts as they study. To enhance your class discussions, you can use the review questions and the new cases and applications added to each chapter. In response to your requests, we have produced an all-new Instructor's Manual to accompany the book; it contains not only a test bank but many useful teaching exercises and applications not in the text itself. The book's Web site, the Online Learning Center at www.mhhe.com/wilmot7, provides instructors with a downloadable Instructor's Manual and provides students with practice quizzes to help them review course concepts.

Chapter 1, "The Nature of Conflict," has been rewritten and reorganized. Reviewers let us know they would appreciate our getting right down to basics more quickly, so we have. We present the reasons for studying conflict, and then go quickly to the definition of conflict and its elements. We describe destructive conflict, power and self-esteem, and the importance of perception in conflict. Understanding destructive spirals sets the background for the following discussion of how to create a supportive climate for conflict. We introduce the key concepts of escalatory and avoidance spirals.

Chapter 2, "Perspectives on Conflict," was chapter 1 in several previous editions. Building on the core concepts in chapter 1, we discuss how each person's personal history of conflict, especially in the context of family, influences our responses to conflicts. We expanded the section on conflict metaphors by adding a section on transformative metaphors. These stimulate creative thinking about conflict resolution possibilities. We continue to use the lens model of conflict, showing how gender and cultural filters influence us all.

Chapter 3, "Interests and Goals," presents some of the material that readers have told us provides the "meat and potatoes" of the book. We changed the acronym in previous editions describing the four kinds of goals to the easy-to-remember TRIP, representing topic (content), relational, identity, and process goals. We show you how to analyze in depth every conflict interaction based on these four levels. We continue the popular discussion of prospective, transactive, and retrospective goals and end with a discussion of collaborative goals.

Chapter 4, "Power: The Structure of Conflict," while remaining essentially the same, has been updated. We have added a section on optimum power in interpersonal conflict. We added a short section on "designated power," to complete the section on kinds of power. We discuss the problems associated with both too much and too little power, and how to work toward balancing power.

Chapter 5, "Styles and Tactics," retains the comprehensive treatment of styles while updating and shortening it. We removed a confusing section on styles in systems. We highlight the two basic movements in conflict resolution: avoidance and engagement. We have added a new section on bullying as a natural extension of competitive tactics. We continue to use the familiar five styles descriptions, while advocating for flexible and adaptive styles depending on the conflict and the people involved.

Chapter 6, "Assessing Conflicts," is a practical chapter that gives many ways to diagram, understand, draw, think about, and observe conflicts. We removed one older assessment guide and added a new one based on the Harvard Negotiation Project's *Difficult Conversations* concept. This new guide supplements the Wilmot-Hocker guide, often used for the major paper in the course. With this new guide, we have provided another option for an in-depth conflict analysis for a major project. We hope you find it as intriguing as we do. Finally, we describe a new analysis of conflict stages.

Chapter 7, "Moderating Your Conflicts," has been moved to just before "Negotiating for Mutual Gains." In "Moderating Your Conflicts," we keep the popular emphasis on conflict in the midrange. We have added a new section on strong emotions in conflict, greatly expanded from the last edition. We end with the key skills of fractionating, reframing, and dialogue. A newly expanded section on communication formats provides guidelines for regulating conflict, ranging from conflict containment, to family meetings, to crisis management.

Chapter 8, "Negotiating for Mutual Gains," has been updated but the outline remains the same. We retained the popular competitive, collaborative, and principled negotiation approaches. The examples, however, now more closely relate to the interpersonal focus of the book, explaining negotiation as a key skill that bridges avoidance and "power-over" approaches. The chapter ends with a discussion of phases in negotiation and the useful "languages of collaboration" checklist.

Chapter 9, "Third-Party Intervention," has been reorganized. We begin with an expanded section on informal intervention for those times when you might be asked by friends or family to intervene. Then, formal interventions are charted, drawing clear distinctions between forms of third-party intervention. Important cautions to the third party are discussed. We added material on third-party practices across cultures, and removed several overly detailed charts.

Chapter 10, "Mending the Broken Branch: Forgiveness and Reconciliation," by guest author Gary W. Hawk, has been entirely rewritten. We are extremely pleased with this revision and think you will find it accessible, usable, and provocative. Forgiveness is defined, along with many misconceptions about the forgiveness process. The author takes the perspective that forgiveness is an option but is not required in many cases. New examples of forgiveness possibilities have been written, reflecting Gary's years of teaching in this area. Ways people get stuck along the process of forgiveness are discussed. An extensive new section on apology is presented in the chapter, with helpful lists to allow people to assess where they are in the process. Finally, reconciliation is discussed with its four "strands." Reconciliation is distinguished from forgiveness.

Self-forgiveness is discussed, and the chapter ends with an assignment on "reconciling conversations."

We have added an entirely new chapter, chapter 11, "Preventing Destructive Conflict." For quite a while, we have wanted to add material on the prevention of destructive conflicts in the first place. This new chapter defines prevention, gives a summary of core values that lead to best practices in conflict resolution, and again urges readers to learn from previous conflicts in order to prevent future conflicts. We present material on the overall cycle of conflict, along with warning signs and suggestions for avoidance spirals and escalation spirals. We give specific language that may be helpful for changing these pervasive spirals. We give post-conflict protocols for work and personal examples, and urge the use of post-conflict learning to help stop the recurring cycle of conflict. We include a section on personal change, especially in the areas of relationship and identity issues. We make specific suggestions to those who see themselves as habitually avoiding or escalating.

As always, we hope the book will inform and inspire you. We welcome any suggestions and invite you to communicate with us about any of your responses to this book. It has been a pleasure to continue working on this important topic through the years. Whether you are a long-time adopter or a student reading the book for the first time, we hope your lives are made richer by what you learn.

You can e-mail us at:

Bill Wilmot
wwwilmot@aol.com

Joyce L. Hocker
joyhocker@aol.com

❧Acknowledgments

To the Reader from Bill Wilmot

Life is quite a journey. We are all blessed to be here—and one life goal is to continually discover why. As our relationships ebb and flow, we move in and out of harmony with others. Even though I have been involved with this "conflict work" since 1976, I feel like a neophyte—continually learning and relearning important lessons.

I am blessed with "significant others" in my life, both personally and professionally. On the personal level, my wife Melanie Trost helps me stay connected and centered. As her own new career in hospice unfolds, she shares it and enriches me in the process. We pursue our interconnected Montana dreams in our log home in the mountains (with satellite Internet access!) and I greatly appreciate her presence. As a friend of mine said, "Bill, I can't believe you found a woman to live up there with you!" Melanie always leads with a kind heart and a sparkling intellect, never wavering from kindness toward others. Then there is Rosie (the dog) who is a true joy and never fails to get excited by my uttering the word "walk." Rosie, I apologize for all the absence on business trips. Maybe, in our next lives, I can be at home waiting for you to come back.

My family expanded this past year. My son Jason and his wife Kate, and my daughter Carina and her husband Alex, produced my first grandchildren just six days apart. It thrust me into the next generation with a bang. I now have a "favorite granddaughter," Sydney, and "favorite grandson," Evan. We share a family cabin in the Big Horn Mountains of Wyoming with my nephew Curtis and niece Pam. Thanks to all of you for your true collaboration on all our renovations and decisions. It is actually pleasurable to make decisions about Tepee for this and future generations. And Joyce Mangus, my "shisty," is a lifelong connection (she was here before I was). The funny thing is how she says, "I thought you said you were not going to write another book" whenever I express any frustration about writing deadlines. Thanks, Joyce, for continually opening your heart to your weird brother.

Friends are crucial. Elaine Yarbrough and Mike Burr have stayed the course for over 30 years, and it is a pleasure to be working professionally again with Elaine. If workshop participants can live through the two of us all at once, they are resilient! Mike's stroke has been a challenge, and I am humbled that he and Elaine allowed me into their lives in a small way to help. Roy Andes, who digs a wicked snow cave, is always ready to go on a trip, serve as a consultant, and be more like a brother than anyone. All I have to do is show up and he feeds me, makes me talk details on outdoor gear, and dream of future trips while packing for a current one. Curt Carlson is a model for how to treat people and never stray from one's ethical compass. We are writing our own book together (*The Discipline of Innovation*) that will bring his life work to fruition and help many organizations. My colleagues of the Collaboration Institute, Jacquie, Roy, Marc, and Julie (www.collaborationinstitute.com), are all wonderful professionals. Wouldn't it be nice if we weren't all so busy and could get together more often without all the "schedule wars"? I continue to learn from all of you about facilitation, mediation, and intervening to help people in organizations.

Life is precarious, and the loss of a number of close family and friends over the past few years brings this message home in a way that one has to actually attend to it. My parents Vi and Wally are now gone, as is my sister Jeri, who was only 13 months older than me. My family of origin continues to slowly disappear—highlighting the importance of good relationships with those left. Janice Hocker Rushing and I had an almost 30-year relationship, first as an in-law and later as a resilient friend. This book is dedicated to Janice, a truly sweet soul. More than anyone over the years, she gave us insightful critiques and support. My friend Wes Shellen left a very positive mark on his students and family and allowed me into his life. I always tell stories in conflict workshops about Wes and me and how we went from enemies to friends—showing that working at conflict can transform relationships. When he and I were once debriefing how that all happened, he came up with the line of a lifetime. He said, "Bill, this transformation happened when you stopped worrying about my karma and began working on your own."

My incremental disengagement and early retirement from the Department of Communication Studies at the University of Montana has been difficult but rewarding. My very last class on conflict was one of the best—a great way to go out. Thanks to my students. As I continue doing workshops on conflict management and mediation, I have to admit I rather like not reading papers from the participants. As professor emeritus, I go back frequently, use the library, hang out at the student union, and consult and intervene in trouble spots with staff and faculty. I am pleased that university people find my conflict management and facilitation skills to be of some help.

As you might surmise, this revision would not have happened without my verbally talented co-author Joyce Hocker. We have fine-tuned our working relationship so well that it is almost tempting to take on another book project. Even in spite of the Microsoft

Word difficulties, we persevered and got it done. Your counseling work combines with my organizational work and enlivens the book with real world applications. Thanks Joyce, especially given all the personal losses you have borne in the past year; you managed to step up and never fail.

And thanks to Nanette Giles and Jennie Katsaros of McGraw-Hill. You have been more supportive than most editors and we really appreciate your prompt responses to all sorts of questions and queries. Our reviewers were extremely helpful. While we can never take all your suggestions, we very much appreciate your assistance.

Finally, as life goes on for all of us, we sometimes find that our spiritual path is a necessary source of support and centering. I am deeply appreciative of His Holiness the Dalai Lama, and all of the teachers in the Tibetan Buddhist and Zen lineages. Two nuns in particular, Ven. Thubten Chodron and Ven. Robina Courtin both teach with incredible clarity and challenge. I highly recommend Chodron's book, *Working with Anger*. She will help you see the "identity" issues that we all bring to our disputes. I had the privilege of traveling with Ven. Courtin to sacred sites in India for a month. Both of these teachers are models for how to do spiritual growth in the midst of life's turmoil. I remain hopeful that someday Tibetans can return to their sovereign homeland, free of Chinese control. The dispossessed people of the world, in Tibet and elsewhere, have incredible obstacles. May you all be free from suffering.

To my students over the years, thanks. You have been an absolute joy. Thank you for all of your hard questions, pressing me always for practical application. And sometimes you even agreed with me. Probably more than any discipline, the study of communication and conflict is enriched beyond measure by always grounding it in real life experiences. Finally, a deep apology to my English teachers in Upton, Wyoming. Had I known that I would actually write books some day, I would have treated you more kindly, challenged you less, and maybe even heeded your advice.

To the Reader from Joyce Hocker

In 1971, when I began the research for my dissertation on conflict resolution at the University of Texas, I could never have imagined that in 2005 I would still be investigating, practicing, and writing about peacemaking in personal lives. Yet, through 15 years as a professor and 19 years as a clinical psychologist and organizational consultant, I remain convinced that we can trust the principles we write about.

This seventh edition is dedicated, as were editions two through six, to Janice Hocker Rushing, my beloved younger sister, who was Professor of Communication at the University of Arkansas. Janice created a climate of openness and excitement in the classes she taught on conflict; the rhetorical study of film, myth, and criticism; and rhetorical studies. Janice was the most involved and perceptive reviewer of this book, from the first through the sixth editions. She taught from it; gave us excellent, considered feedback; and had the most organized set of teaching files for the course I have ever seen. In this edition's dedication we are forced into the past tense because Janice died in February of 2004, shortly after finishing a brilliant book about her life and the lives of women in the academic world. As Bill and I wrote in the dedication of the third edition, "Janice, your presence was the gift." I could not have known that the year of book revision would also revise my personal life so thoroughly. Our mother, Jean Lightfoot Hocker, died in July 2004 at our family cabin in Colorado. Then our father, the

Rev. Lamar Hocker, slipped away in January of 2005, as I was in the middle of this revision. My brother Ed and I were privileged to be with each of our dear family members as they made their transition. I am deeply grateful for Ed's love and support through this time. He is a remarkable man and brother, thoughtful, peaceful, and full of integrity.

Despite the losses, grace infused the year and the revision process. For a while I was not sure I could think and write while in the grip of grief. I found that many people helped me in ways that leave me full of gratitude. First, Janice's voice lives and evolves as an inner dialogue in my life. I hear my father's words and cadence in his impassioned, reasoned speech. I feel my mother's pragmatic, calm, factual, optimistic approach. She believed in "us," we three siblings, and was our first writing teacher. Thank you with all my heart to my hospice support group—Sharon, Rob, Cathy, and Roberta—who held me up through this time. Thank you to the "Divine Ensemble," so named by our good friend Gale Young, who pointed out how we each played our parts to support Janice and each other in those terrible days in early 2004. My husband Gary Hawk played the flute, prayed, and built a stone wall with my brother Ed when it was not their turn to be a part of the interior vigil in Janice's study. Thanks beyond measure to Paula, Joel, Jean, Gale, and Tom. My brother of the heart, Janice's husband, Tom Frentz, has supported and encouraged my writing, told me I could do it, read drafts, and unfailingly, gently urged me on. I am very grateful, Tom. I am also grateful to Art Bochner and Caroline Ellis, who encouraged me to write and to reconnect with the communication profession. One day Bill and I read a brilliant, detailed review for the present edition. It seemed only Janice could have written it; later we discovered that Jane Elvins, at the University of Colorado, a former student and colleague of Janice's, had written this most helpful review. Thank you, Jane.

My assistant Sally Brown helped make this revision possible. She organized all the references, developed the index, provided technical support, kept my business running, and did research for my other projects so I could focus on writing and revising. Sally, you provide essential ongoing assistance and you are a grand friend. Thank you. Likewise, Bill Wilmot has again been a great team member for revising this book. Bill's consulting experience and immersion in hands-on conflict resolution has again enlivened the writing and revision process. Bill is always helpful in answering the "how does this work?" question. His enthusiasm for the project helped me when my concentration faltered. I am proud of our long collaboration.

Gayle Younghein, my long-time friend and partner in leading women's retreats, gave me her open-hearted friendship in Costa Rica last year when I wondered whether I should have remained in Arkansas with Janice. Later she persuaded me to go to France with her and a group of friends and *then* come home and tackle the revision. You were right, Gayle. In Missoula, my women's group supported me with love, cards, and prayers. Members of University Congregational Church have poured out support and love, and my professional colleagues have helped me focus on both my clients and my own need for rest and exercise. Thank you to Britt Finley, Patricia Hennessy, Marianne Spitzform, Victor Lieberman, Linda Kastelowitz, Diane Haddon, John and Rita Sommers-Flanagan, and Nancy Errebo for your loving listening—and Diane, thanks for all those workouts, Thai lunches, and soaks in the hot tub. I continue to be grateful to the staff of the Division of Diabetes Treatment and Prevention of Indian Health Service, especially Kelly Acton, M.D., Lorraine Valdez, and Cheryl Wilson, for giving me the opportunity to consult with them on communication and conflict resolution. I am also grateful for my therapy clients, their stories, their courage, resilience, and trust.

In the swirling currents of this past year I am grateful for Missoula, Montana. I can walk in the back door of Butterfly Herbs and get my morning coffee on the way to work, go see the people downstairs at the bank who greet me by name, and stop off at Scotty's Table after a long workday where the staff treats me like one of the family. The staff at the Women's Club reminds me to work out, no matter what. The web of this community supported me in this last year. I love you, Missoula—but remember, readers, it's dark and gray in the winter and you don't want to move here!

I continue to give thanks for the wholeness of this life, that seasons of sorrow turn round to seasons of joy. Gary and I now have a granddaughter, Emilia Jane, born to her wonderful parents, Andy and Heather Hawk. My hope for "EJ" is that she will live in a world that becomes more peaceful each year. Kyle Hawk and Samantha Wood care for trees, orchids, raptors, and the life of the heart in their adopted Pennsylvania. I am blessed by my extended family and I love you all.

At home, two special "beings" enrich my life. Our aging but still handsome tuxedo cat, Lightfoot, let me know when late-night writing had gone on long enough. He knows he is more important than the computer. He continues to bring joy and lightness to our home. My husband, Gary Hawk, has provided much more than the usual support during this writing process. He has supported me through four editions of this book. After reading his chapter 10, I simply said, "Wow." Gary talks with me about the ideas in the book, especially the deeper challenges of dialogue, reconciliation, and truth-telling. He shares his experiences teaching at the Davidson Honors College, where he explores many of these ideas with his students. He is my partner in life and in all of these practices. Janice always said that Gary is "deep as a well." Thank you, Gary, for being the anchorite this year when I could not be, for loving me and listening to me, and for being patient while I finished this project. And thank you for loving and supporting my family. I cannot imagine this year or this life without you.

From Both of Us

Thanks to our reviewers Thomas Downard, Northeastern University; Jane P. Elvins, University of Colorado; Jennifer A. Samp, University of Georgia; R. Jeffrey Ringer, St. Cloud State University; Dewey Hemphill, Crichton College; Amy Bippus, California State University, Long Beach; Isabel C. Botero, University of Minnesota, Duluth, for your insightful comments. Of course, we take all the blame for any of your suggestions that we passed up, but about 90 percent of them have been incorporated. We both feel gratitude for the competence and professionalism of Nanette Giles and Jennie Katsaros, our editors at McGraw-Hill. You made this a pleasure. We are especially grateful for the expert, timely, and gracious help of Diane Folliard, our production manager, who helped in innumerable ways as the manuscript was prepared for production.

Part One

Conflict Components

Chapter 1

The Nature of Conflict

Conflict happens.

Why Study Conflict?

Conflict is a fact of human life. It occurs naturally in all kinds of settings. There is no less need for conflict management now than there was 30 years ago when we began this project. Nations still struggle, families fracture in destructive conflicts, marriages face challenges and often fail, and the workplace is plagued with stress.

The study of conflict is a basic human requirement and the practice of constructive conflict is an essential set of interpersonal skills. We have confidence that your lives will be enriched by what you will learn in this course, and what you will continue to learn for the rest of your lives. Welcome to the process!

The study of conflict can pay big dividends in your personal relationships. If you are an adolescent or a parent of an adolescent, it will come as no surprise to you that it takes about 10 years after an adolescent leaves home for parents and children to negotiate roles that bring them closer to equality than they were in their earlier parent–child relationship (Comstock 1994). At the heart of this negotiation is the conflict process. The study of conflict can assist in this process of redrawing family boundaries, letting you see which styles backfire, and which ones work best.

Family relationships provide the most intense laboratory for conflict resolution. You may have a long-standing conflictual relationship with one of your siblings. When you begin to see each other much less frequently, the daily irritations may well subside, giving you an opportunity to approach each other differently. Yet, hurts and fights from the past may make it difficult to create a new relationship. The ideas in this book will give you some starting places for finding new ground with your families.

Mental health improves with a constructive conflict process. The National Institute of Mental Health funded a decade of studies of depression as one of the major public health problems of our time. Depression affects one's personal relationships and results in millions of dollars lost in the workplace due to missed days; then there are the medical and counseling costs. Effective conflict management is one aspect of interpersonal therapy, a well-researched counseling technique for dealing with depression. When people experience conflicts, much of their energy goes into emotions related to those conflicts. They may be fearful, angry, resentful, hopeless, or stressed. Adding to one's repertoire for resolving conflicts reduces a common stressor. Ineffective resolution of interpersonal disputes adds to depression and hopelessness. Eating disorders, physical and psychological abuse of partners (O'Leary et al. 1989), and problem drinking (Murphy and O'Farrell 1994) also are associated with destructive conflict environments.

We all know that romantic relationships provide a rigorous test of our skills. Siegert and Stamp (1994) studied the effects of the "First Big Fight" in dating relationships, noting that some couples survive and prosper, whereas others break up. These communication researchers tell us quite clearly that "the big difference between the non-survivors and survivors was the way they perceived and handled conflict" (357). As Wilmot (1995) notes, "What determines the course of a relationship . . . is in a large measure determined by how successfully the participants move through conflict episodes" (95).

One of the ultimate testing grounds for romantic relationships is marriage. Almost all spouses report "occasional marital disagreement" (Bolger et al. 1989; Metz, Rosser, and Strapko 1994). For many spouses the disagreements may be very brief, whereas for others they may continue over many days. It is common and normal for partners to have conflicts or disagreements, and in fact, managing conflict is one of the central tasks of maintaining a marriage (Gottman 1994). Gottman found, after decades of research on conflict in marriage, that couples who stay together enter conflict gently, make repairs along the way when they wound each other, avoid criticizing and blaming, and avoid criticizing each other where they know it hurts. Even in conflictual interactions, trust must be maintained (1999). Constructive conflict skills can be learned, but many people have never seen these conflict approaches modeled at home. As you might guess, learning to constructively resolve conflict is clearly and directly linked to marital satisfaction. (Kurdek 1995, 153).

One key skill in all long-term committed relationships is conflict management—certainly, the data on marriages suggest this is true (Gottman 1994). The presence or absence of conflict does not determine the quality of a marriage; rather, how the couple handles conflictual situations determines the quality of the relationship (Comstock and Strzyzewski 1990). Even beliefs about conflict are more important to marital happiness than whether or not the two partners actually agree with one another (Crohan 1992).

How you handle conflict spreads to other members of your family. For example, it has been noted that adult children who are taking care of their parents usually have high levels of conflict with siblings (Merrill 1996). Learning effective skills for dealing with your younger brother or sister is far better than engaging in a family dispute that will affect your children and subsequent generations as well.

Our family of origin socializes us into constructive or destructive ways of handling conflict that carry over directly into how romantic relationships are later handled (Koerner and Fitzpatrick 2002). For example, step families' conflicts are destructive 95 percent of the time (Baxter, Braithwaite, and Nicholson 1999).

Severe parental conflict predicts both internal and external conflicts for adolescents (Turner and Barrett 1998). Many parents try to protect their children from exposure to their marital conflicts, but when children are present, often the conflicts are even worse and more destructive than when the parents fight alone (Papp, Cummings, and Goeke-Morey 2002).

Family research is quite clear about the systemwide effects of destructive marital conflict. First, negative conflict between the parents reduces the family's network of friends and creates more loneliness (Jones 1992). Conflict between the parents tends to both change the mood of household interactions and shift the parents' attention to the negative behaviors of their children (Jouriles and Farris 1992). Parental conflict has a direct negative impact on the children. Communication patterns between fathers and their young adult children seem to have a circular relationship—the young adults treat their fathers the way they were treated (Dumlao and Botta 2000). Conflict between parents predicts well-being of the children, with more conflict associated with maladaptive behavior on the part of the children (Dunn and Tucker 1993; Garber 1991; Grych and Fincham 1990; Jouriles, Bourg, and Farris 1991). Finally, the effects of destructive conflict patterns suggest that "ongoing conflict at home has a greater impact on adolescent distress and symptoms than does parental divorce" (Jaycox and Repetti 1993, 344). Parents who either avoid conflict or engage in negative cycles of mutual damage directly influence the children's subsequent lives. A modest relationship exists between mothers who avoid conflict and their daughters' marital satisfaction (VanLear 1992). On the other end of the continuum, children who are exposed to harsh discipline practices at home (which coincide with a negative and hostile relationship between the parents) are more at risk for aggression, hyperactivity, and internalizing by withdrawing, having somatic complaints, and experiencing depressive symptoms (Jaycox and Repetti 1993). The family effects also reach beyond the immediate environment. One study demonstrated that children from high-conflict homes had much stronger negative reactions while watching a video of angry adults than did children from low-conflict homes (El-Sheikh 1994).

While married individuals are generally healthier than unmarried persons, if you are married and in conflict, your health is likely to be poorer than that of single people (Burman and Margolin 1992). Hostile behavior during conflictual interactions seems to relate to changes in one's immune system, resulting in poorer overall physical health (Kiecolt-Glaser et al. 1996). Wives appear to suffer more from hostile conflictual situations than do husbands (Kiecolt-Glaser et al. 1996).

Simply stated, the level of conflict and how destructive it is affect all areas of family well-being. If you, as a present or future parent, change your own conflict resolution skills, you will affect everyone in your families, present and future. As you look back on your own family history, you probably know the truth of this statement.

Children and adults who were physically and sexually abused as children face significant difficulties in their later conflicts. It is not possible to generalize completely, because many people exhibit remarkable resilience and effectiveness in their lives despite terrible abuse. Yet common responses to abuse, including the verbal abuse of yelling and the silent treatment, are hypervigilance; difficulty relaxing; withdrawal at the first sign of tension or conflict; floating away, or dissociating; and not knowing or expressing what one really wants. Children's own attitudes toward marriage are directly affected by the conflict between their parents. If their parents have frequent conflict, children have a much less favorable attitude toward marriage (Jennings, Salts, and Smith 1991). A child's general feeling of self-worth are directly affected by interparental conflict (Garber 1991). This means that it isn't primarily a question of whether parents divorce or not that affects the children; rather, it is the level of conflict present in either the intact family or the restructured family that impacts the children.

The skills of conflict management are not intuitively obvious. For example, it isn't just the people who call one another names who have relationship difficulties deriving from conflict. It has been clearly demonstrated that "couples who never engage in conflict are at long-term risk" (McGonagle, Kessler, and Gotlib 1993, 398). In conflict, we must learn to "do what comes unnaturally." If we do what we have always done, we will keep getting the results we have always gotten—results that may keep us mired in the same old patterns. Who would imagine, for instance, that moving toward bad news, instead of away from bad news, is often the better strategy? How many of us intuitively know to tell more and more of the truth when a conflict is becoming destructive rather than keeping quiet or yelling? How many of us know how to tell the "truth under the truth" in a way that protects ourselves and the relationship and yet furthers the dialogue? These nonintuitive skills will be presented in detail in this book.

Unresolved conflict has a tremendous negative impact. It directly affects the parties themselves. In personal relationships, unresolved conflict leads to drifting away from one another and sometimes jettisoning the relationship entirely.

Therefore, we need to study conflict in personal relationships for the following reasons:

- How you engage in conflict will directly affect your romantic relationship.
- The long-term satisfaction of your marriage may hinge on how well you manage conflict.
- Your mental health will be improved as you learn to deal with conflict constructively.
- People around you will benefit from your improved skills.
- The overall health and mental health of your families depend partly on successful conflict resolution.
- Many people have experienced abuse and have no positive models for resolving conflicts. Studying the topic can help remedy past misuses of power.
- Conflict resolution skills are not "just common sense." They are complicated sequences of relational skills that most people don't know.

So far, we have presented the reasons for studying conflict in personal relationships. In addition, conflicts at work present important challenges that affect your career development. "Conflict is a stubborn fact of organizational life" (Kolb and Putnam 1992, 311). One study surveyed workers and found that almost 85 percent reported conflicts at work (Bergmann and Volkema, 1989). With an increasing awareness of cultural diversity and gender equity issues, it is imperative that we become familiar with issues surrounding promotions and harassment. In fact, one can see communication training in organizations as a form of preventive conflict management (Hathaway 1995). Managers must learn conflict skills to intervene in disputes in their organization (Yarbrough and Wilmot 1995).

Ongoing, unresolved workplace conflict also has negative effects that reach far beyond the principal parties. If the executive director of a nonprofit agency and her board cannot get along, employees tend to take sides, fear for their jobs, and, like those above them, wage a campaign discrediting the other group. Health care environments present the probability of damaging conflicts. For instance, when doctors and nurses engage in destructive conflict, the patient suffers. When nurses, who often are the person who knows the patient's situation most intimately, withdraw, patient illness and death rises (Forte 1997).

Ignoring workplace conflict sets destructive forces in motion that decrease productivity, spread the conflict to others, and lead to lessened morale. In one organization, the president and CEO was on the verge of reorganizing the structure, affecting 600 people, so that two vice presidents would not have to talk to one another!

Some of the advantages to studying organizational conflicts follow:

- As an employee, you can learn how to get along with

    Fellow employees

    Your manager

    The public

- As a supervisor, you can begin to

    See conflicts coming

    Learn productive responses

    Get more cooperation from employees

    Help employees resolve their disputes with one another

    Keep interpersonal conflicts from spreading to other parts of the organization

As you will see in chapter 9, "Third-Party Intervention," you might study conflict so you can be of help to others experiencing interpersonal conflict. To be of most help you will need specific intervention skills, but understanding conflict dynamics is an absolute prerequisite for being an effective helper to others—children, friends, family, and work associates.

We study conflict because life is full of paradox. When we allow two or three different ideas to be true all at once, we are exercising first-rate intelligence. When opposing ideas enter into our consciousness or conversation, and we are able to juggle all these ideas without "dropping" the most inconvenient ones, we make ourselves resilient and adaptable to life's challenges. Holding onto paradoxical thinking means you can help mediate conflict in groups, families, and the world. People who feel compelled to rush to judgment contribute little to conflict resolution. People who accept that many things are true at once add to the world's store of sanity.

Why study conflict? Because if we don't, we are more likely to repeat the damaging patterns we see on the job and in our homes. Examining the dynamics of conflict will allow us to unpack those dynamics, see what brings on destructive moves, and build more productive options for ourselves both at work and at home. Since the first edition of this book was published in 1978, much more interest in the process of conflict as a natural, inevitable part of communication has been apparent in research and the popular press. Most writers now know that conflict is not different from "regular" communication but is a part of the ongoing flow of the communication between human beings. We might define ourselves as being "in conflict," of varying intensities, many times a day or week. Even people who vastly prefer peace, harmony, and calm interaction find themselves involved in situations that are tense, escalating, and uncomfortable. Truly, we do not have the option of staying out of conflict unless we stay out of relationships, families, work, and community. Conflict happens—so we had best be prepared for it.

❧A Beginning Example

The following dialogue may be familiar to you in tone, if not in content:

> Son: My graduation expenses cost a lot more than I thought they would. I had to pay for the senior trip, the dinner, and all kinds of things I didn't know would come up. I don't know how I'm going to pay for my car insurance this summer. Could you help me out?
>
> Mother: I thought you were going to pay for all those things out of your work earnings this summer. I haven't budgeted for this at all.
>
> Son: I haven't been able to find a job yet. You know I've been looking. I can't drive if I don't have insurance, and if I don't have a car I can't work.
>
> Mother: This is not what we agreed on. The payments would be your responsibility after graduation. We've been clear on this all along.

The mother and son are engaged in interpersonal conflict. Their conflict results from their particular communication choices. The son asks for extra help; the mother makes a decision first rather than asking questions. The next few interactions may well escalate toward damage of an important ongoing relationship. The son may be uncertain how he will look for work if he can't drive. He may want to save money he was given for graduation for other purposes. Yet he also wants his mother's recognition of him as an adult, and he wants to be seen as responsible. The mother wants, presumably, to help her son find work, to teach him to manage money, and to preserve a give-and-take relationship between them. She doesn't want to alienate her son, but she doesn't want to feel taken advantage of or to go against an agreement. Their individual and relational goals can only be met through creative conflict interactions. When conflict is viewed as a problem to be solved instead of a battle to be won or interaction to be avoided, creative solutions can be found.

In the Chinese language the character for conflict is made up of two different symbols: one indicates danger whereas the other indicates opportunity. As you think about these two approaches, decide whether you respond first to conflict as a dangerous, obstructive dilemma or whether you experience conflict as a welcome opportunity for change. The *I Ching* teaches that the wise person in conflict remains clearheaded, inwardly strong, and ready to meet his or her opponent halfway (Wilhelm 1977). At the beginning of your study of conflict, we ask you to consider the possibilities inherent in conflict. By the end of the course, we hope you come to experience the activity as an important means of growth rather than a failure or a negative event to be avoided at all costs. Ask several people important to you how they would rate themselves. What are the differences? Do you have conflict over *whether to have conflict*? Discuss your findings with class members.

8   Part 1   Conflict Components

Application 1.1	My Basic Approach to Conflict

Where are you on the following ratings describing your approach to conflict?

I love peace and harmony and will go to great lengths to avoid conflict.

I sometimes will willingly engage in conflict, but only if I can see no other good choice.

I like the give-and-take of a good verbal conflict and am not particularly wary of getting involved.

I enjoy constructive conflict. My adrenaline gets going and I like to see what can come of it. I even seek out conflict at times.

I count on conflict to help clear the air, solve problems, and get us to a "different plane."

By studying this book and participating in class exercises, you will be able to understand your present conflict behavior, make choices to engage in new behavior during conflicts, and thus act as a change agent in times of crisis and turbulence. People can change their conflict behavior. Your approach to conflict is not an inborn set of responses but rather a developed repertoire of communication skills that are learned, refined, and practiced. You don't have to remain the way you have been in the past.

❧Conflict Defined

All interpersonal conflicts, whether they occur between family members, romantic partners, students and teachers, employees and supervisors, or groups, have certain elements in common. One of the popular definitions of conflict, offered by Coser (1967), asserts that conflict is "a struggle over values and claims to scarce status, power, and resources in which the aims of the opponents are to neutralize, injure, or eliminate the rivals" (8). Note that this definition grew out of the cold war, in which conflict between the United States and the former U.S.S.R. dominated Western approaches to conflict. Conflict was definitely viewed as a win-lose situation. In 1973 Deutsch maintained that "conflict exists whenever incompatible activities occur . . . an action which prevents, obstructs, interferes with, injures, or in some way makes (resolution) less likely or less effective" (156). Mack and Snyder (1973) suggested that two parties must be present, along with "position scarcity" or "resource scarcity," in addition to behaviors that "destroy, injure, thwart, or otherwise control another party or parties, . . . the parties can gain (relatively) only at each other's expense" (36). All of these early social science definitions help us distinguish conflict from simple "strain," "disagreement," or "controversy" (Simons 1972; Schmidt and Kochan 1972). Conflict varies in intensity and range. At least two continua have been advanced to describe the intensity of conflict. It may be seen as a (1) mild difference, (2) disagreement, (3) dispute, (4) campaign, (5) litigation, or (6) fight or war (Keltner 1987). Another continuum (Moore 1996) shows conflict ranging from avoidance to violence.

For purposes of this book, **conflict** is defined as follows:

> *Conflict is an expressed struggle between at least two interdependent parties who perceive incompatible goals, scarce resources, and interference from others in achieving their goals.*

Transforming a conflict depends on perceptual and/or conceptual change in one or more of the parties. **Perception** is at the core of all conflict analysis. In interpersonal conflicts, people react as though there are genuinely different goals, there is not enough of some resource, and the other person actually is getting in the way of something prized by the perceiver. Sometimes these conditions are believed to be true, but sorting out what is perceived and what is interpersonally accurate forms the basis of conflict analysis.

Careful attention to the elements that make up conflict will help you understand an apparently unresolvable conflict. When conflicts remain muddled and unclear, they cannot be *re-solved*, or solved a different way.

An Expressed Struggle

An *interpersonal* approach to conflict management focuses on the communicative exchanges that make up the conflict episode. **Intrapersonal conflict**—internal strain that creates a state of ambivalence, conflicting internal dialogue, or lack of resolution in one's thinking and feeling—accompanies **interpersonal conflict.** One may endure intrapersonal conflict for a while before such a struggle is expressed communicatively. If you are upset with your father yet you do not write him, or you phone him less often and avoid expressing your concern, do you have a conflict?

Application 1.2	My Intrapersonal Conflicts

Think of an intrapersonal strain you may be feeling right now, or felt for a while in the past. What is the struggle you feel? Have you ever lived through an intrapersonal conflict that did not ever become expressed? If you answered yes to this question, ask yourself if you might have expressed the conflict ever so slightly in some way.

People involved in conflicts have perceptions about their own thoughts and feelings and perceptions about the other's thoughts and feelings. Conflict is present when there are *joint communicative representations* of it. The verbal or nonverbal communication may be subtle—a slight shift in body placement by Jill and a hurried greeting by Susan—but it must be present for the activity to be interpersonal conflict. Therefore, although other conditions must also exist before an interaction is labeled "conflict," Jandt (1973) asserts, "Conflict exists when the parties involved agree in some way that the behaviors associated with their relationship are labeled as 'conflict' behavior" (2). Often, the communicative behavior is easily identified with conflict, such as when one party openly disagrees with the other. Other times, however, an interpersonal conflict may be operating at a more tacit level. Two friends, for instance, may both be consciously avoiding the other because both think, "I don't want to see him for a few days because of what he did." The interpersonal struggle is expressed by the avoidance. **Intrapersonal perceptions** are the bedrock upon which conflicts are built; but only when there are communicative manifestations of these perceptions will an "interpersonal conflict" emerge.

Communication is the central element in all interpersonal conflict. Communication and conflict are related in the following ways:

- *Communication behavior often creates conflict.*
- *Communication behavior reflects conflict.*
- *Communication is the vehicle for the productive or destructive management of conflict.*

Thus, communication and conflict are inextricably tied. How one communicates in a conflict situation has profound implications for the residual impact of that conflict. If two work associates are vying for the same position, they can handle the competition in a variety of ways. They may engage in repetitive, damaging rounds with one another, or they may successfully manage the conflict. Communication can be used to exacerbate the conflict or to lead to its productive management.

The following example explains how to move a conflict from an internally experienced strain to an interpersonal communication:

Leslie: (To new husband, Greg, referring to Greg's 15-year-old son.) I've noticed Brennan is using my towels and other stuff from my bathroom instead of the things from his bathroom. Do you think he's annoyed because he can't share our bathroom any more? Or he is just being thoughtless? I don't want to share our bathroom and I can't stand it when he leaves damp towels all over the place!

Greg: I don't know. He hasn't said anything. Do you want me to check it out, or do you want to?

Leslie: (Sigh.) Well, I'm uncomfortable, but it's my job to check it out. I won't make assumptions. I'll just ask him.

This situation could have escalated into a "war of the towels," or been handled unproductively by the stepmom leaving curt notes, the stepson avoiding contact, and both building up negative assumptions about the other. As it happened, the boy did admit to his new stepmother that he was irritated. He and his father had lived together for years without bothering much about which towel was whose, and he resented being told which bathroom and towels to use. Leslie had a chance to say what privacy and neatness meant to her. The three of them talked it through, defusing what could have been a big conflict that would have been over the wrong things (towels instead of the new relationships).

Most **expressed struggles** become activated by a *triggering event*. A staff member of a counseling agency is fired, setting off a series of meetings culminating in the staff's demand to the board that the director be fired. Or, in a roommate situation, Carl comes home one night and the locks are changed on the door. The triggering event brings the conflict to everyone's attention—it is the lightning rod of recognition.

Interdependence

Conflict parties engage in an expressed struggle and interfere with one another because they are **interdependent.** "A person who is not dependent upon another—that is, who has no special interest in what the other does—has no conflict with that other person" (Braiker and Kelley 1979, 137). Each person's choices affect the other because conflict is a mutual activity. People are seldom totally opposed to each other. Even two people who are having an "intellectual conflict" over politics are to some extent cooperating with each other. They have, in effect, said, "Look, we are going to have this verbal argument, and we aren't going to hit each other, and both of us will get certain rewards for participating in this flexing of our intellectual muscles. We'll play by the rules, which we both understand." Schelling (1960) calls strategic conflict (conflict in which parties have choices as opposed to conflict in which the power is so disparate that there are virtually no choices) a "theory of precarious partnership" or "incomplete antagonism." In other words, even these informal debaters concerned with politics cannot formulate their verbal tactics until they know the "moves" made by the other party.

Parties in strategic conflict, therefore, are never totally antagonistic and must have mutual interests, even if the interest is only in keeping the conflict going. Without openly saying so, they often are thinking, "How can we have this conflict in a way that increases the benefit to me?" These decisions are complex, with parties reacting not in a linear, cause–effect manner but with a series of interdependent decisions. Bateson (1972) presents an "ecological" view of patterns in relationships. As in the natural environment, in which a decision to eliminate coyotes because they are a menace to sheep affects the overall balance of animals and plants, no one party in a conflict can make a decision that is totally separate—each decision affects the other conflict participants. In all conflicts, therefore, interdependence carries elements of cooperation and elements of competition.

Even though conflict parties are always interdependent to some extent, how they perceive their mutuality affects their later choices. Parties decide, although they may not be aware of this decision, whether they will act as relatively interdependent agents or relatively independent agents. Both or all may agree that "we are in this together," or they may believe that "just doing my own thing" is possible and desirable. A couple had been divorced for three years and came to a mediator to decide what to do about changing visitation agreements as their three children grew older. In the first session, the former husband seemed to want a higher degree of interdependence than did the former wife. He wanted to communicate frequently by phone, adopting flexible arrangements based on the children's wishes and his travel schedule. She wanted a monthly schedule set up in advance, communicated in writing. After talking through their common interest in their children, their own complicated work and travel lives, the children's school and sports commitments, and their new spouses' discomfort with frequent, flexible contact between the former partners, they worked out a solution that suited them all. Realizing that they were unavoidably interdependent, they agreed to lessen their verbal and in-person communication about arrangements while agreeing to maintain written communication about upcoming scheduling. They worked out an acceptable level of interdependence.

An example of negotiating independence occurred with Katie, a junior in college, and her mother, Sharon. Katie wanted to set up a 30th anniversary party for her parents, who live just two hours from her college. Her mother, Sharon, kept saying on the phone, "Don't bother. Don't go to any trouble. It's not worth it." Katie persisted that she and her younger sister really wanted to do this (she insisted that they were interdependent). Mom stopped answering the phone and returning e-mails. Katie drove home the next weekend and asked Mom to talk the whole thing through with her. Katie learned that Mom was so angry with Dad for ignoring the upcoming event that she wanted to withdraw. She couldn't imagine enjoying a party that came only from her kids while she was simmering with resentment at her husband. So Katie talked to Dad about helping plan the party. Mom told her husband that she had been feeling hurt and slighted. They all got involved and had a good time. Now, notice that it was *not* Katie's role to play therapist with her parents—but she helped by asking them to talk to her and to each other. In a healthy family, everyone can talk to every other member. This builds healthy interdependence.

Sometimes parties are locked into a position of mutual interdependence whether they want to be or not. In some cases, interdependent units do not choose to be interdependent but are so for other compelling reasons. Some colleagues in an office, for instance, got into a conflict over when they were to be in their offices to receive calls and speak with customers. One group took the position that "what we do doesn't affect you—it's none of your business." The other group convinced the first group that they could not define themselves as unconnected, since the rest of the group had to be available to fill in for them when they were not available. They were inescapably locked into interdependence. If a working decision was not made, the parties would have almost guaranteed an unproductive conflict, with each party making choices as if they were only tenuously connected.

Most relationships move back and forth between degrees of independence and interdependence. At times there will be an emphasis on "me"—what I want—and on separateness, whereas at other times "we"—our nature as a unit—becomes the focus. These are natural rhythmic swings in relationships (Frentz and Rushing 1980; Galvin and Brommel 1982; Baxter 1982; Stewart 1978). Just as we all need both stability and change, conflict parties have to balance their independence and dependence needs.

Relationship and interdependence issues precede other issues in the conflict. Actually, these negotiations over interdependence permeate most conflicts throughout the course of the relationship, never becoming completely settled. A helpful practice is to address the interdependence issue openly in ongoing, highly important relationships. In more transient and less salient relationships, the interdependence may be primarily tacit, or understood.

Perceived Incompatible Goals

What do people fight about? (We use the word *fight* to mean verbal conflict, not physical violence.) People usually engage in conflict over *goals that are important to them*. One company had an extreme morale problem and asked for our help. The head cashier said, "All our problems would be solved if we could just get some carpet, since everyone's feet get tired—we're the ones who have to stand up all day. But management won't spend a penny for us." Her statement of incompatible goals was clear—carpet versus no carpet. But as the interviews progressed, another need emerged. She began to talk about how no one noticed when her staff had done good work and how the "higher-ups" only noticed when lines were long and mistakes were made. There was a silence, then she blurted out, "How about some compliments once in a while? No one ever says anything nice. They don't even know we're here." Her stated needs then changed to include not only carpet but self-esteem and increased attention from management—a significant deepening of the goal statement. Both goals were real, carpets and self-esteem, but the first goal may have been incompatible with management's desires, whereas the second might not; the need for recognition may have been important to both the cashiers and management.

We do not support the overly simple notion that if people just worked together, they would see that their goals are the same. Opposing goals are a fact of life. Many times, people are absolutely convinced they have opposing goals and cannot agree on anything to pursue together. However, if goals are reframed or put in a different context, the parties can agree. Recently a student teacher's supervisor outlined her goals for the student. Included in the list was the demand that the student turn in a list of the three most and least positive experiences in the classroom each week. The student asked to be transferred to another teaching supervisor. The chair asked why, saying, "Ms. Barker is one of our best supervisors." The student said, "That's what I've heard, but I can't be open about my failures with someone who's going to give me my ending evaluation. That will go in my permanent files." In a joint discussion with the supervisor and the student, the chair found that both were able to affirm that they valued feedback about positive and negative experiences. Their goals were more similar than they had thought; the means for achieving them were different. The supervisor agreed to use the list as a starting point for discussion but not to keep copies; the student agreed to list experiences so the supervisor would not feel that the student was hiding her negative experiences. Trust was built through a discussion of goals. Perceptions of the incompatibility of the goals changed through clear communication.

Goals are perceived as incompatible because parties want (1) the same thing or (2) different things. First, the conflict parties may want the same thing—for example, the promotion in the company, the one available scholarship, or the attention of the parents. They struggle and jockey for position in order to attain the desired goal. They perceive the situation as one where there "isn't enough to go around." Thus, they see their goal as incompatible with the other person's because they both want the same thing.

Second, sometimes the goals are different. Mark and Tom, for example, decide to eat out. Mark wants to go to Bananas and Tom wants to go to Pearl's. They struggle over the incompatible choices. Sometimes the goals are not as opposed as they seem. Two roommates would like to move out of the dorm and into an apartment. After looking around, Janet tells Allison that she thinks she'd "better just stay put." Allison was, naturally, hurt. As they talked about the situation, Janet told Allison she was afraid Allison wanted to spend more than Janet was able to. They found an acceptable budget and agreed to stick with it, thus resetting their goals more clearly. Of course, many times the content goals seem to be different (like which restaurant to go to), but beneath them is a relational struggle over who gets to decide. Regardless of whether the participants see the goals as similar or different, **perceived incompatible goals** are central to all conflicts.

Perceived Scarce Resources

A resource can be defined as "any positively perceived physical, economic or social consequence" (Miller and Steinberg 1975, 65). The resources may be objectively real or perceived as real by the person. Likewise, the scarcity, or limitation, may be apparent or actual. For example, close friends often think that if their best friend begins to like someone else too, then the supply of affection available to the original friend will diminish—a **perceived scarce resource.** This may or may not be so, but a perception that affection is scarce may well create genuine conflict between the friends. Sometimes, then, the most appropriate behavior is attempting to change the other person's perception of the resource instead of trying to reallocate the resource. Ultimately, one person can never force another to change his or her valuing of a resource or perception of how much of the resource is available, but persuasion coupled with supportive responses for the person fearful of losing the reward can help.

Money, natural resources such as oil or land, and jobs may indeed be scarce or limited resources. Intangible commodities such as love, esteem, attention, and caring also may be perceived as scarce. A poignant example concerns dropouts in the school system. By watching videotapes of classroom interactions, researchers could predict by the fourth grade which students would later drop out of school. The future dropouts were those students who received very limited eye contact from the teacher, either by their own doing or the teacher's. They became nonpersons, at least nonverbally. The glances, looks, smiles, and eye contact with the important person in the room became a scarce resource upon which the students were highly dependent. Often children fight with one another over this perceived scarcity—teacher attention. Or they fight with the teacher, resulting in a gain of that resource. A child would rather get negative attention than none. When rewards are perceived as scarce, an expressed struggle may be initiated.

In interpersonal struggles, two resources often perceived as scarce are **power** and **self-esteem.** Whether the parties are in conflict over a desired romantic partner or a change in work hours, perceived scarcities of power and self-esteem are involved. People engaged in conflict often say things that may be easily interpreted as reflecting power and self-esteem struggles, such as in the following scenarios:

"She always gets her own way." (She has more power than I do, and I feel at a constant disadvantage. I'm always one down.)

"He is so sarcastic! Who does he think he is? I don't have to put up with his mouth!" (I don't have ways to protect myself from biting sarcasm. It feels like an attack. I feel humiliated. The only power I have is to leave.)

"I refuse to pay one more penny in child support." (I feel unimportant. I don't get to see the children very often. I've lost my involvement with them. Money is the only way I have to let that be known. I don't want to feel like a loser and a fool.)

"I won't cover for her if she asks me again. She can find someone else to work the night shift when her kids get sick." (I feel taken advantage of. She only pays attention to me when she needs a favor.)

Regardless of the particular subjects involved, people in conflict usually perceive that they have too little power and self-esteem and that the other party has too much. Of course, with each person thinking and feeling this way, something needs to be adjusted. Often, giving the other person some respect, courtesy, and ways to save face removes the need to use power excessively.

Interference

People who are interdependent, perceive incompatible goals, and want the same scarce resource still may not meet the conditions for conflict. *Interference*, or the perception of interference, is necessary to complete the conditions for conflict. If the presence of another person interferes with desired actions, conflict intensifies. Conflict is associated with blocking, and the person doing the blocking is perceived as the problem. For instance, a college sophomore worked in a sandwich shop the summer before her junior year abroad. She worked two jobs, scarcely having time to eat and sleep. She was invited to a party at a cabin in the wilderness, and she really wanted to go. She worked overtime on one day then asked for a day off from the sandwich shop, but the employer was reluctant to say yes, since the student was the only one the employer trusted to open the shop and keep the till. For an angry moment, the employer, who was interfering with what the student wanted to do, seemed like the main problem. Goals appeared incompatible, no one else was available to open (scarce resource), and the two parties were interdependent because the student needed the job and the owner needed her shop opened and the cash monitored. She was about to say, "No. I'm sorry, but I can't cover you." The student volunteered to train someone else, on her own time, to cover for her. The problem was solved, at least for this round, and the conflict was avoided. But if the student had quit in disgust or the employer had said no, both would have sacrificed important goals.

Another example of **perceived interference** involves Kelly, who prizes time alone in a lookout tower each summer. She plans for the weeks and looks forward to that solitude each year. When her two college-age daughters asked to join her, Kelly hesitated, saying she didn't think there was enough room. The daughters were disappointed and hurt, since they had been away at college and thought this would be a wonderful way to all be together. Mom could have told them she loved solitude and asked whether they could figure out some way so they could be together, but her quiet time could be maintained. For instance, the daughters love to hike and might have been glad to plan several days of hiking. Instead, the situation stayed unresolved and hurt feelings simmered.

Being blocked and interfered with is such a disturbing experience that our first "take" is usually anger and blame. We will discuss the difference in *intent* and *impact*. For now, we suggest you adopt this radical idea:

You do not know what other people are thinking unless you enter into honest dialogue. You don't know their intention without dialogue. You can't read minds. Conversation is the best approach.

❧Destructive Conflict

Conflicts move from episode to episode in a continually unfolding pattern of interaction between the prime parties. The moves and interpretations of each party influence those of the others. Nowhere can we more clearly see the interlocking effects of moves and countermoves than in **destructive conflicts.**

Conflict interaction can be productive or destructive depending on many factors, including the context in which it occurs (Camara and Resnick 1989) and the kinds of communication used. Conflict is potentially costly to all parties; these costs can exceed the gains if the conflict is drawn out before some kind of settlement is reached (Boulding 1989). If all participants are dissatisfied with the outcomes of a conflict and think they have lost as a result (Deutsch 1973), then the conflict is classified as destructive.

Often the parties cannot predict during a conflict whether it is going to end up as a destructive or constructive conflict. However, several characteristics of spiraling destructive conflict can be identified. Participants can sometimes rescue a destructive interaction, making the overall effect more positive, but if the interaction continues to be characterized by the following descriptions, the overall result will be a destructive, win-lose experience for all parties. Gottman (1999) refers to the following four communication practices as the "**four horsemen of the apocalypse**," meaning that when these four behaviors "ride in" to a relationship, the end is near (see figure 1.1).

Critical Start-Up Sets the Tone for Any Conflict

The first moments of a conflict interaction—the **critical start-up**—can set the scene for a constructive or a destructive conflict. In fact, in Gottman's research (1999) the first minute of conflict with married couples predicts for 96 percent of the couples studied whether they will stay together or divorce. This amazing finding results primarily from the way the conflict is entered, or engaged. Criticism makes a harsh start-up. When wives escalate from neutral feeling to negative feeling quickly, right at the beginning, the outlook for the marriage remains bleak. Women criticize more than men do

Figure 1.1   The Four Horsemen of the Apocalypse

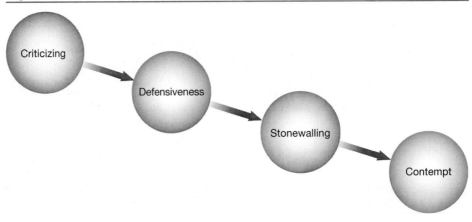

in marital conflicts. (We'll get to what men do that is equally destructive!) When a conflict begins with a critical statement, the conflict is likely to escalate quickly. Any conflict that begins with "you always" or "you never" is likely to have a destructive effect. For instance, the following example shows a harsh start-up:

Pamela: You are the most selfish man I know! My mother is sick, maybe terminally, and you can't stir yourself to drive 30 miles for her birthday. Great. Now I get to tell my Mom that I'm married to a narcissistic jerk! Could you think of someone else for a change?

Many times, one person will criticize to get the other person's attention, to indicate how awful she or he is feeling, to try to make the conflict important enough to resolve, or to vent frustration or despair. However, none of these reasons, though understandable, is a good enough reason to begin conflictual interaction with criticism. Instead, a complaint can be used.

A Constructive Complaint

- Use an "I" statement.
- Describe the undesirable behavior.
- Use neutral, not judgmental, language.
- Ask for a specific, behavioral change.

A constructive complaint can be helpful. A destructive complaint includes blame and the attribution that there is something wrong with the other person, not just the behavior. The following is an example of a *constructive complaint:*

Pamela: I am upset that we are not going to see my Mom together. I have asked you three times to clear your weekend so we could both go see her. Next weekend is her birthday. She is sick and I want to see her, and I want you to come with me. I am frustrated and impatient with the excuses you've given me. I hope you will come. I don't want to have the kind of marriage where I have to see my folks by myself.

Application 1.3
From Criticism to Constructive Complaints

In your small group, practice changing criticisms to complaints. Think of destructive criticism, maybe that you have used, or that others have used against you, and practice brainstorming about how to change these critical comments to legitimate complaints. Don't be afraid to make the complaints strong and assertive—they need not be soft and wishy-washy. Remember—complaints avoid blame, use I statements, describe instead of judging, and leave the door open for change. Practice transforming criticism into descriptive complaints, while remaining honest.

Defensiveness Characterizes Destructive Conflict

When people use defensive communication, they are communicating a desire to protect themselves against pain, fear, personal responsibility, or new information. In an emotionally charged issue, if a person can listen to learn about oneself and the other, defensiveness drops away (Paul and Paul 1987). When defensiveness predominates, many destructive outcomes occur, such as power struggles, boredom and deadness, lack of fun and joy, chronic fighting, emotional pain and distance, and a desire to retaliate (Paul and Paul 1983, 1987). Defensiveness implies that one is warding off an attack. Notice that the metaphor for conflict that underlies the need to defend is a negative metaphor, *war* or *attack*. When you are defensive, you might whine, deflect, attack, and further defend. The interaction can get to look and sound like Ping-Pong.

> Barbara: Every time I try to talk to you about my day, you launch off into complaints and whining about how bad life is for you. You never listen to me. [Notice that Barbara is in fact attacking, criticizing, and blaming.]
>
> Mark: If I didn't get my two cents' worth in you'd talk all evening. All you ever do is complain. I decided weeks ago that every time you come home with some "poor me" tale, I'll match you. Besides, I have a right to be heard too. You aren't the only important one in this family.
>
> Barbara: If things are so rotten for you in this relationship, why are you sticking around? All I'm asking for is a little empathy, but I guess that's beyond you.

You can easily see that neither Barbara nor Mark is the least bit interested in learning, only in attacking and defending. This interaction will undoubtedly escalate or lead to hostile withdrawal. Defensiveness comes from a misguided sense of righteous indignation, expressed poorly. Another word for defensiveness might be *contrariness*. Some people seemingly can't help adopting a devil's advocate or contrary point of view. For them, conversation is a battle of wits. They enjoy the game of "batting ideas around" and are often very good at the performance. The pursuit of mutual understanding may seem boring and unchallenging (Yankelovitch 1999, 141). Contrariness and defensiveness impede constructive conflict.

Creating a Supportive Climate Rather Than a Defensive Climate

One of the best descriptions of defensive communication was written by Jack Gibb in 1961. It is so useful we suggest you memorize the categories. This schema will help you moderate your own defensiveness very effectively—if you pay attention to your own language. **Defensive climates**—rather than **supportive climates**—are created when people use the following kinds of language:

- *Evaluation rather than description.* Judgmental and evaluating language leads to a defensive response in the other person. No one enjoys being "graded," especially as inadequate. Instead, use neutral and nonblaming language. Rather than saying, "You are closed-minded on this . . ." say "You really like the idea of going camping instead of kayaking. Are you open to some other options?"

- *Control rather than problem solving.* When you try to control the other person, you might insist on details, shut down communication, or simply say, "No way I'm going to do that." Instead, say, "We can solve this problem. I'll listen to you; I ask you to listen to me." "Let's generate several possibilities."

- *Strategy rather than spontaneity.* In strategic communication, the other person feels manipulated and managed. When you are communicating spontaneously, you are free of deception and are communicating honestly, in a straightforward way. Rather than saying "I'll get back to you on that," say, "I'm not comfortable with that idea. Let's keep talking."

- *Neutrality rather than empathy.* No one likes to feel like a "case" or a "type." When a doctor says to a patient with cancer, "That's the protocol we use in this kind of cancer," the patient will feel dismissed or made into an object. Instead, the doctor could say, "This is my best advice based on my experience and the research. What do you think? Will this work for you?"

- *Superiority rather than equality.* No one likes to be talked down to. If you indicate that you are more powerful, smarter, or more experienced than the other person, you will create defensiveness. Rather than "You'll see that I'm right when you have more experience," say, "I feel strongly about this. What is your experience?"

- *Certainty rather than provisionalism.* Dogmatic, inflexible statements create defensiveness. Openness creates a supportive environment. Rather than "I am never going to drive at Christmas again," say, "Driving at Christmas is something I'm not wanting to do. I still want to see our family, but I hate being on the highway at Christmas. Let's talk about other options."

Stonewalling Occurs When One Person Withdraws from the Interaction

Usually, when people are engaged in conversation, they give all kinds of nonverbal cues, as well as verbal cues, that indicate their involvement. They give eye contact, head nods, changes in facial expression, brief vocalizations, and so on (Gottman 1999). Turn taking is regulated in a refined dance of interaction that shows that the other person is "there." Stonewallers don't do any of this. They show in every possible way that they are not "there." They glance only to see what the other person is doing, then glance away. They maintain a stiff neck and frozen facial features. They try to conceal what they are thinking and feeling. Men consistently stonewall more than women. In fact, in Gottman's study (reported in 1999), 85 percent of stonewallers were men. The combination of criticism and stonewalling predicted divorce quite easily. Most women find this kind of "I'm not here" behavior on the part of men highly upsetting. Stonewalling is more than avoidance of conflict. It is an attempt to signal withdrawal from communication while, in fact, still being present in the conversation, but in a destructive way. Stonewalling also can mean a refusal to engage in a topic no matter how the other person brings it up. You can probably imagine the frustration and fury that accompanies stonewalling. A less destructive form of stonewalling might be called *holding back*. When Yankelovitch (1999) asked people why they were not more forthcoming in group discussions, they said they had to be comfortable enough to speak, or that they wanted to see what developed before they got involved. Men hold back in public discussions more than women do, although women also feel reserved when the trust has not been built. People hold back when they sense hostility in a group or in the other.

Contempt Contributes to Destructive Conflict

"Contempt is any statement or nonverbal behavior that puts oneself on a higher plane than one's partner" (Gottman 1999). Contempt often involves a nasty kind of mockery, put-downs, hostile corrections, and nonverbal expressions of contempt. The contemptuous look (mouth pulled over to one side) is "powerfully corrosive," according to Gottman and our own experience. Many times we have heard people say the right words, but with an expression of contempt, which leads inevitably to more destructive communication. Often contempt is accompanied by sarcasm, ridicule, and outright hostile joking. In healthy relationships contempt is almost never present. Contempt is never justified in a long-term, important relationship, since it functions as a powerful attack on the personhood of the other.

Application 1.4	Four Horsemen

Look back over the explanation of the "four horsemen." Answer the following questions, then discuss.

Which of the four communication modes has been used against you in harmful ways?

Which of the four do you use, and in what circumstances?

Choose an example of your own use of one of the four destructive modes explained above. What fear or anger underlay your use of this approach?

Can you think of a way you could communicate more honestly and constructively? Give one example. Practice changing your communication when you are tempted to use one of the four horsemen. If you want, keep track of your attempts for a paper on your communication style.

Inflexibility, or Rigidity, Characterizes Destructive Conflict

When parties are unable or unwilling to adapt to changing circumstances, instead following rules "to a T" or "going by the book," potentially constructive conflict often deteriorates. One manager refused to discuss reprimands with employees, instead recording the incidents in letters that could later be used as part of a paper trail in case an employee needed to be fired. As a result, trust plummeted to zero in the office, and employees formed coalitions to protect each other from the inflexible boss. The supervisor, in addition to creating a hostile working environment, received "pretend change" instead of genuine change in employees' behavior. Everyone lost as the cycle of distancing and inflexible communication intensified.

A Competitive System of Dominance and Subordination Results in Destructive Conflict

"Authenticity and subordination are totally incompatible" (Miller 1986, 98). Dominant groups tend to suppress conflict, minimizing and denying its existence. This works reasonably well for those in power since they can make and enforce the rules. In fact, a measure of the dominant group's success and security is often its ability to suppress conflict, to keep it hidden, unobtrusive, and unthreatening to the group's position of power. In a situation of unequal power, in which a myth of harmonious relationships is set forth, the subordinate person is put in charge of maintaining that harmony. Then any recognition of differences is treated as insubordination (Miller 1986; Jordan 1990).

Escalatory Spirals

In the previous section we explored some of the most negative communication behaviors that lead to destructive conflict. Now, we will describe patterns of destructive conflict that require interaction.

Escalatory Spirals Pervade Destructive Conflict

Often conflict gets out of hand. What begins as a careful exchange of opposing views deteriorates into an emotion-laden, careless interchange in which strong feelings, usually anger and fear, are aroused. This causes the primary intentions of the parties to shift from a useful exchange to damaging the other person (Baron 1984). Escalatory conflict spirals have only one direction–upward and onward. They are characterized by a heavy reliance on overt power manipulation, threats, coercion, and deception (Deutsch 1973). In an **escalatory spiral,** the relationship continues to circle around to more and more damaging ends; the interaction becomes self-perpetuating. Its characteristics are misunderstanding, discord, and destruction (Wilmot 1987). Figure 1.2 illustrates the runaway dynamics that occur in a typical destructive conflict spiral.

In this example, two roommates begin with a misunderstanding that accelerates each time they communicate. Brad begins complaining about Steve's messiness. At each crossover point in the spiral, thoughts and actions might occur as they do in this version of an actual conflict:

1. Brad says to Steve, "Hey, why don't you do your part? This place is a hole."

2. Steve says, "Out of my face, dude!" (He then leaves the apartment.)

3. Brad, still upset about the messy apartment, finds Steve's ex-girlfriend and says, "Has Steve always been such a slob? I can't stand living with him."

Figure 1.2   Conflict Spiral

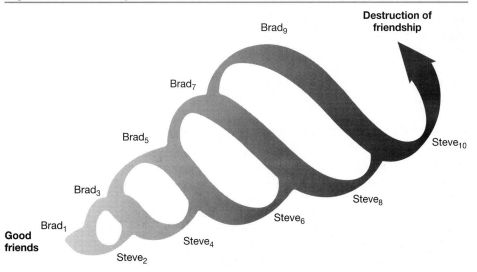

4. Steve, hearing from his ex-girlfriend that "even Brad knows that you are a slob," decides that he will get back at Brad for his meanness. So Steve begins deliberately messing up the bathroom, knowing that it will drive Brad crazy.

5. Brad comes home, sees the messy bathroom, and puts an ad in the campus newspaper that says, "If anyone sees Steve K., tell him to clean up his half of the apartment—it's a pigsty."

6. Steve, angered at the public announcement, comes home late one night and, while Brad is sleeping, lets the air out of Brad's tires.

7. Brad runs into a mutual friend the next day and hears that Steve is the one who let the air out of his tires. So Brad goes home, moves all of Steve's belongings into the hall, changes the locks on the door, and puts a sign on Steve's belongings that says, "Help yourself."

Brad and Steve's conflict escalated without much direct communication between the two of them—they let their actions speak instead of words. A destructive conflict in an intimate relationship, between spouses, for example, may be characterized by the above features, in addition to "hitting below the belt" (Bach and Wyden 1968). Each person uses hit-and-run tactics to damage the other person where it hurts most, emotionally. For instance, a woman may ridicule her husband for making less money than she does when she knows he is extremely sensitive to this issue. She may be trying to bring up an important topic, but the attempt will surely fail. The injunction "don't fight unless you mean it" is ignored in a destructive conflict, and the interlocking, damaging moves occur repeatedly. In a destructive conflict, one party unilaterally attempts to change the structure of the relationship, restrict the choices of the other, and gain advantage over the other.

Probably the best index of destructive conflict is that one or both of the parties have a strong desire to "get even" or damage the other party. When you hear a friend say, "Well, she may have gotten me that time, but just wait and see what happens when I tell some things I know about her!" you are overhearing one side of a destructive conflict in action. Wilmot (1995) observes, "if the conflict is responded to in destructive ways . . . it starts sequences of episodes that detract from relational quality" (95). The conflict continues unabated, feeds upon itself, and becomes a *spiral of negativity* (see figure 1.3). The three parts—the behaviors, the perceptions of others, and the perceptions of the relationship—mutually reinforce each other. As behavior becomes more destructive and one's view of the other and the relationship goes downhill, each person continues to perceive himself or herself as free from blame (i.e., "It is all his or her fault"). In an organization, for example, one person on the verge of firing an employee said, "Well, I'm a good supervisor. He just won't cooperate. It is all his fault. Besides, he will probably be better off if I fire him."

Escalatory spirals bring about a cascade of negative effects, self-perpetuating dynamics in which the (1) behaviors, (2) perceptions of the other, and (3) perceptions of the relationship continue to disintegrate (with each party viewing one self as not responsible for any of it). Beck (1988) aptly summarizes the later stages of the process:

> When a relationship goes downhill, the partners begin to see each other through a negative frame, which consists of a composite of disagreeable traits ("He's mean and manipulative"; "She's irresponsible") that each attributes to the other. These unfavorable

Figure 1.3   The Spiral of Negativity

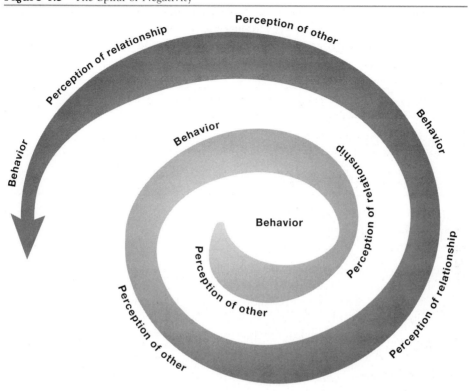

attributions color how the offended mate sees the partner; negative actions are exaggerated and neutral actions are seen as negative. Even positive acts may be given a negative coloring. (207)

Declines happen in all kinds of relationships—between social groups, among marriage partners, between roommates, within the work setting, and with families.

Avoidance Spirals

Avoidance Patterns Reduce the Chance for Productive Conflict

Escalatory spirals can be called "fight" patterns. Conflict parties also manifest "flight" patterns of avoidance of the conflict. For now, be aware that patterns of avoidance also create and reflect destructive conflictual interaction. One form of avoidance is an active attempt to lessen dependence on each other. By making such an attempt, each party reduces the influence of the other on his or her choices. Both parties then become less invested in the relationship. Many long-term marriages, for example, become devitalized, with the spouses expecting less and less of one another. This is often the natural consequence of lessened interaction. Spouses who are prevented from enriching daily interaction by the pressure of jobs, children, and other stresses become estranged. The barrier between them becomes harder and harder to breach. **Avoidance spirals** occur in other contexts as well. The child who is not picked for the soccer team and says, "I didn't want to be on your team anyway," is withdrawing, as is the employee who says, "I don't care if they fire me—who needs them anyway?" The basic dynamics of all avoidance spirals are

- *Less direct interaction.*
- *Active avoidance of the other party.*
- *Reduction of dependence.*
- *Harboring of resentment or disappointment.*
- *Complaining to third persons about the other party.*

Whereas escalatory spirals are characterized by overt expression of the conflict, avoidance spirals demonstrate covert expression. At least one of the parties tries to impact the other through lack of cooperation. If you are mad at your small group, your late report may serve to get everyone into difficulty with the professor. Any form of withholding from someone who depends on you can bring negative consequences to the other. For example, when you withdraw, the other party does not know what you want or are thinking. Often the other will say something like, "What is wrong?" Then you say, "Nothing," covering up anger, resentment, or disappointment.

Oddly enough, sometimes people want destructive conflict in their relationships (Neimeyer and Neimeyer 1985). Although escalatory and avoidance spirals may appear to be totally negative to outsiders, the conflict party may be getting something valuable from these spirals. For example, if John can stay locked in an overt struggle with Bill, the impasse may give John a sense of power and self-esteem: "I refuse to cooperate because I'll never forgive him for what he did. He was a sneak." Or, if you are in an avoidance spiral, complaining about your supervisor, employee, spouse, or friend to others builds closeness between you and your listener. For example, a husband and wife may both complain about the other to the children, each thereby building a close bond with the child who is the chosen listener. One can get locked into a position of complaining bitterly about a spouse or co-worker but not take any steps to alter the relationship directly. In short, people may be invested in not moving past the destructive conflict.

The Attack/Withdraw Pattern, or The Pursue/Flee Pattern

This pattern is a destructive dance usually manifested in intimate relationships. It destroys chances for productive conflictual interaction. In the pursue/flee pattern, described in detail in Lerner's *Dance of Intimacy* (1989), one partner specializes in initiating conversation, commenting on the lack of closeness between the partners, bringing up feelings and issues to get them resolved, and drawing the other partner out by asking questions like "You seem preoccupied—what's going on?" or "We don't seem close these last few weeks. Is something bothering you?" Then the "dance" of distance is engaged in as the other partner minimizes the problems, denies anything is wrong, promises to do better, comments on content problems only, avoids discussion of any relationship issues, or gives excuses such as "I've just been really busy," or "I'm distracted by what's going on at work," or "I'm just premenstrual. Don't take it personally." The conflict remains frustratingly unresolved because each partner specializes in a role that is so prescribed, whether initiating or fleeing, that the issues remain unexplored. These dynamics will be addressed in chapter 5, "Styles and Tactics." For now, as you begin to watch and analyze conflicts around you, pay attention to who initiates and who withdraws, or flees. One way to arrest this pattern is to make a comment about communication such as "I notice that I'm the one who brings up problems, and you feel defensive. We need to do something different." The one who flees can own up to the discomfort caused by the pursuit by saying something like "I feel pounced on, especially about my feelings. I need time to sort out what's going on. I will talk to you; I just need to do it at a time when I'm not exhausted or frazzled."

Gottman (1994) discovered that the avoidance sequence described as attack/ withdraw, or pursue/retreat, leads to relationship breakup because of its negative impact. Avoidance, or stonewalling, comes after some preliminary episodes. For the marriages Gottman studied, the destructive sequence consisted of criticizing, defensiveness, stonewalling, and contempt. Thus, avoidance can be viewed within the overall spiral of conflict as leading to eventual dissolution of a relationship. One other feature of Gottman's work is noteworthy: If avoidance is accepted by both partners ("conflict- avoiding couples"), it can stabilize the marriage. When avoidance is coupled with dissatisfaction and disagreement, with one person pursuing and the other fleeing, that is damaging.

Reciprocity of Negative Emotion Can Lead to Destructive Conflict

Three kinds of reciprocity can be identified in communication: (1) low-intensity emotion is responded to in kind (e.g., anger is met with anger), (2) high-intensity emotion is met in kind (e.g., fury is met with fury), and (3) low-intensity emotion is met with high-intensity emotion (e.g., hurt is met with rage). Gottman and Krokoff (1989) found that the escalation of negativity by husbands predicted divorce. When men refused to accept influence from their women partners, the relationship went downhill. It's important to understand just what is being reported by this finding. Gottman and his researchers are not saying that men should do what women want, but that meeting negative emotion with more negative emotion predicts relationship breakup. Why would this be? *Escalating negativity on the part of men can lead to violent interactions.* A team of researchers watched videotapes of violent men interacting with their partners. They likened the experience to that of baseball players at automatic pitching machines who bat back every pitch. These violent men refused to be influenced by anything their wives had to say. Small requests or complaints were "batted back" regardless of their merit. In a companion study of 130 nonviolent couples, 80 percent of the men who did not accept any influence from their wives ended up divorced! Most women accepted influence from their husbands, and that acceptance did not predict anything about their marriages (Gottman, 1994). The violent relationship is a one-way power struggle gone wild; the escalating spiral of negativity ends in verbal or physical violence. We will have more to say about the cycle of violence, but the important thing to note at this point is that meeting negative emotion with more, especially more destructive, negative emotion leads to big problems in relationships.

Retaliation Runs Rampant in Destructive Conflicts

Conflict participants destroy chances for change when they pile up grievances, hold grudges, and wait for opportunities to retaliate. "Don't get mad—get even!" is the watchword for this urge to get back at the other person. Retaliation often becomes paired with covert avoidance. One person acts as though everything is just fine while planning a payback move for later. You can probably think of many retaliatory moves that have either been made against you or been made by you yourself. Some examples of retaliatory moves are letters to someone's supervisor complaining about or pointing out some indiscretion that the employee committed; a snub such as not inviting someone to a function; a blatant move such as emptying out a partner's savings account, running up phone bills, and then moving out; and so on. Dirty tricks inevitably ruin the conflict atmosphere.

Humans in various cultures distinguish between the kind of aggression that can be directed against members of their own population and that directed toward other human groups. Stevens (1989) cites a tribe in Brazil, the Mundrucus, who distinguish between themselves, whom they call "people," and the rest of the world population, whom they call "pariwat." These in-group and out-group distinctions allow them to refer to others in the way they would refer to huntable animals (40–41). In North American and Western European cultures, the use of verbally demeaning and abusive communication serves a similar function (Evans 1992). Whole groups of minorities receive demeaning descriptions, and individuals in low-power positions in relationships suffer from pervasive demeaning, shaming, and blaming communication.

~A Note of Encouragement

Conflict brings both danger and opportunity, and the dangerous aspects are well known. Changing our usual behavior, learning to "do what comes unnaturally," requires an examination of one's most deeply held values and spiritual beliefs. At its most effective, conflict resolution can never be simply a set of techniques, put on or cast aside at will. You will want to think and feel through your own principles as you study this subject.

If people are to survive and thrive, working together is not an option but a necessity. Principles learned at the interpersonal level lead to collaborative principles at the global level. Because of this, what you learn about collaboration within relationships will affect a much larger plane of well-being. Breggin (1992) reminds us:

> In every aspect of life . . . we need better principles for resolving conflict and promoting harmony within ourselves and others. We need approaches that make personal and political sense, that connect us in a rational and caring manner to ourselves as individuals and to the world around us, including people and nature. We need a viewpoint that helps us understand and heal the pain of human conflict. (3)

We are connected human beings who must balance our need for personal autonomy with our need for connection. We can no longer live by the myth that somewhere out there is a place where we can be completely independent and do what we wish. More than 40 years ago, Martin Luther King stated this imperative: "I can never be what I ought to be until you are what you ought to be, and you can never be what you ought to be until I am what I ought to be. This is the interrelated structure of reality" (King, 1989).

In conflict, no one set of principles will always work, and no one set of behaviors avoided can keep you out of conflict altogether. Yet, people do change their orientation to conflict and amaze themselves with their ability to transcend formerly destructive situations. If enough of us are willing to weave webs of connection with others, all our shared hopes for the world can be realized. Long-standing stereotypes can be dissolved, mistrust can be overcome, understanding can be achieved, people previously at odds can work together on shared objectives, new levels of creativity can be reached, and bonds of community can be strengthened (Yankelovich 1999).

In order to find creative solutions, we must be willing to take our conflicts seriously. We need to find ways to manage our worst reactions and call on our best communication. Combs (2004) summarizes four stages of conflict that come from many cultures, traditions, and spiritual backgrounds. She describes four key stages:

- *The appearance of conflict.*
- *The absence of hope.*
- *The occurrence of creativity.*
- *The emergence of stability.*

When you have experienced many conflicts that actually turn out better than you might have feared, you will become more hopeful and encouraged. For many years, we have believed in and observed these positive values of conflict that is humane and well done. We know that conflict resolution is a set of skills that can be learned, and that we would all be better off learning these skills. You can change your approach, and you can be a force for change in others.

~Summary

Conflict happens. It is part and parcel of all our interactions—with romantic partners, at work, and with our families. As you study conflict, you learn new responses to these inevitable situations that arise.

Conflict is defined as "an expressed struggle between at least two parties who perceive incompatible goals, scarce resources, and interference from others in achieving their goals." We express conflict through our communication, we need others and they need us (interdependence), and we see us and the other as having incompatible goals (and so do they). Finally, in all conflicts the two parties interfere with what the other wants.

Destructive conflict damages the parties and their relationship. In marriages, one common destructive pattern is criticizing, defensiveness, stonewalling, and contempt. One way to deal with conflict is to create a supportive rather than a defensive environment, and we detail the specifics of how to do that.

The two main destructive patterns are (1) escalatory spirals and (2) avoidance spirals. After describing these, we give a note of optimism. Conflicts can be productive if handled properly.

Key Terms

Use the text's Online Learning Center at **www.mhhe.com/wilmot7**
to further your understanding of the following terminology.

conflict 9	interdependent 11	destructive conflicts 16
perception 9	perceived incompatible	four horsemen of the
intrapersonal conflict 9	goals 14	apocalypse 16
interpersonal conflict 9	perceived scarce resource 14	critical start-up 16
intrapersonal perceptions 10	power 14	defensive-supportive climate 18
expressed struggles 11	self-esteem 14	escalatory spiral 21
conflict parties 11	perceived interference 15	avoidance spiral 24

Review Questions

Go to self-quizzes on the Online Learning Center at **www.mhhe.com/wilmot7** to test
your knowledge of the chapter concepts.

1. Give reasons why we need to study conflict.
2. In what contexts do conflicts arise?
3. Define conflict.
4. What are common responses to abuse in one's history?
5. What are the interpersonal expressions of conflict?
6. What is the purpose of dialogue?
7. What do we depend on others for?
8. What do they depend on us for?
9. What is the role of perception in conflict?
10. How do power and self-esteem function in conflict?

11. What is the relationship between perceived incompatible goals, scarce resources, and interference?
12. How can you create a supportive climate?
13. What are intangible resources?
14. What characterizes destructive conflict?
15. What is a "good complaint"?
16. What is a spiral?
17. What is an escalatory spiral?
18. What is an avoidance spiral?
19. Give an optimistic answer to "conflict always happens; therefore . . ."

Chapter 2

Perspectives on Conflict

❦Your Personal History

Think of the most disturbing conflict you have experienced in the past half-year or so. What was your emotional response to this conflict? What is your usual response to conflicts? Do you generally like to get everything out in the open, even if such an effort creates tension and strong feelings? Or do you usually seek peace, harmony, and reduction of strong emotions? How would you describe yourself?

Keep these recent interactions in mind as you read this chapter, reflecting on your own philosophy and experience of conflict.

In your family of origin you may have learned that to "blow up" was a normal, natural way for people to show they cared about each other. Perhaps your family was quiet, calm, and restrained. Fighting, if it happened at all, went on behind closed doors. Maybe you were punished for raising your voice, physically hurt for talking honestly to an adult, or told to keep your opinions to yourself. Maybe you experienced, as Joyce did, hours of sitting around the family dinner table, catching up on the events of the day, talking over what was happening, and being asked how you felt and what you thought about your life's happenings. If so, you might bring a "we can work this out" perspective to conflict. Maybe you learned, as one of the authors did, that conflict was not talked about and that "actions spoke more loudly than words." You may have been taught not to dwell on problems but to just move on.

Think about how your **personal history** has taught you either to jump right into conflict or to strenuously attempt to reduce or avoid it. For most of us, the choice to avoid or confront a difficult conversation is, well, *difficult*. We all weigh the costs and benefits of bringing up something that may well be awkward, unpleasant, or frightening. Far before we are actually engaged in interpersonal conflict, we make choices every day about what conversations to avoid and what conversations to attempt to have. We struggle about these choices, knowing that if we avoid a tough topic we might feel taken advantage of and experience resentment. If we confront a problem, we might make matters worse. Researchers at the Harvard Negotiation Project have written an excellent guide to *Difficult Conversations* (Stone, Patton, and Heen 1999.) Their work guides us into the choice whether to avoid or confront, and gives encouragement to those who prefer to avoid.

None of the ideas in this book is more important than coming to terms with your own life's learning—what to keep, what to challenge, what to change, and what to discard because it no longer fits your needs. Think also about your role in your family of origin. You may have been raised in a blended family or be raising children in a blended family right now. If so, you may fill several roles depending on which family you are in at the moment. Do you want to change your usual role? Do you need to learn more about getting along rather than automatically challenging authority? Maybe you want to learn to speak up in your own clearly heard, authentic voice if you are usually silent or have been silenced by others.

We ask our students to choose which of the following descriptions best describes their family of origin: (1) **avoidant family,** that is, family members avoided most conflict; (2) **collaborative family,** that is, family members used collaboration; or (3) **aggressive family,** that is, family members engaged in a lot of overt yelling, calling of names, and similar aggressive moves. While there is an artificial nature to these distinctions (for example, some families will avoid, then be aggressive, then avoid again), what emerged were family "rules" for handling conflict that are quite distinct. Here are some of them:

Avoidant Families

- Conflict doesn't exist, and if it does, don't recognize it.
- If there is a conflict, figure out what to do about it on your own.
- Don't tell anyone else if there is a struggle.
- Walk away if something starts to brew.
- Don't ever raise your voice.
- Snide comments are fine.
- Sulking and the silent treatment are necessary strategies.
- If someone has a concern, don't respond to it.
- Don't express strong feelings.

Collaborative Families

- Have a family meeting or mealtime chat to discuss issues.
- Use good listening skills when someone has a concern.
- Deal with people directly.
- Say openly what you are feeling.
- Parents need to help resolve their children's conflicts.
- Regular interaction is important.
- Dirty tricks such as sulking are not allowed.
- Strong feelings are seen as normal and are allowed.

Aggressive Families

- Survival of the fittest describes the general climate of the family.
- Be brutally honest regardless of the impact.
- Show your emotions strongly even if that hurts someone.

- Establish your position early.
- Have an audience present when you engage someone.
- Don't back down—hold your ground no matter what.
- You have to take it if someone attacks you.
- People who don't engage are weak.

While these lists will vary from family to family, notice how different the three lists are from one another. If you grew up in an avoidant family and your roommate grew up in an aggressive family, it would not be too surprising if a conflict between the two of you was difficult to resolve—each of you would break the rules of interaction the other expected you to follow. So our personal history in our families of origin will have a big impact on what we choose to do when conflict starts to rumble below the surface in our relationships.

One family exemplifies the way approaches to conflict may change over time. Karen and Len are parents of Rachel, who suffered a serious head injury while riding a horse when she was 14. Up until that time, the parents seldom raised their voices and life at home was fairly peaceful. Since Rachel's accident, Mom feels stress because of numerous medical appointments and very little time to get her work at the family business and at home completed. Len has decided that Rachel should help out more; he has begun yelling at Rachel to "pitch in and do something to help your mother," while Karen yells back, "You expect too much. She's only 14 and she's doing the best she can." Rachel alternates between placating her father by working hard, then disappearing to avoid the yelling. The family could now be described as aggressive, but this approach has developed recently because of stressors.

Our personal history also includes all of our interactions with others up to the present. What we experience as a preschooler, in school, with friends on the playground, and in all of our adult exchanges influences our expectations. Some of us have experiences of working through difficulties with others and life; thus, we willingly engage in what might prove to be a difficult talk. Others of us expect (and thus receive) constant tension, turbulence, and strife. These people are more likely than others to react to daily challenges with self-criticism and criticism of others, blame, negativity, defensiveness, irritability, or selfishness (Heitler 1990). Of course, these approaches invite a reciprocal response. Think about your current beliefs and expectations about human interaction. Are you primarily hopeful and optimistic, or cynical and pessimistic?

If you grew up in a family in which verbal, physical, or sexual abuse was part of the environment, you definitely will have very strong reactions to conflict. You may be very watchful, careful to smooth over any signs of discomfort. You may have learned to take the abuse to protect others in the family. You may feel guilt at the inevitable failure of that strategy. Maybe you waited until you were old enough and then left, to go to work, get married, or go to college, the armed forces, or a friend's apartment. Perhaps you learned to escape, either physically, or by numbing out, not caring, thinking of something else, or forgetting the conflict. Alyssa, who grew up with ongoing verbal and physical violence, learned to take her horse out for all-day rambles, coming back after dinner and making herself busy with grooming her horse and cleaning the stalls. Then she would grab a snack when no one was looking and take it to her room. Josh, now 25, started to use drugs at 11, which enabled him to mentally tune out while the yelling and hitting was going on. Some kids hung out at friends' houses until they absolutely had to go home. Children of violent homes have developed many strategies for dealing with their dangerous backgrounds. Some victims of violence learn to use violence in a "first strike capability" mode. They intend never again to be taken by surprise.

Application 2.2   My History With Violence

It is important to begin to think about the influence of violence on your life. Answer these questions in your own journal, notebook, or with a small group. What influence, if any, does violence have on your conflict responses? What experiences have you had with violence, whether verbal, physical, or sexual? If you have not experienced violence directly, what violent experiences of others have affected you?

Your particular age group is subjected to unique influences that may shape how you view conflict. If you were raised in the Great Depression you are not likely to view the open expression of conflict as positive (Krokoff, Gottman, and Roy 1988), while the younger generation is beginning to learn about constructive conflict in school—a topic not even considered a couple of decades ago.

Your current living situation certainly influences your methods of handling conflict. If you are with people with whom you feel safe and supported, you can experiment with new styles. If not, you will experience less freedom, possibly relying on what you already know how to do. Similarly, some work situations encourage constructive (or destructive) conflict, whereas others reward people for silence and withdrawal. All of these factors of our own personal history feed into our expectations and actions when we are in conflict situations.

Application 2.3   My Influences

List the 10 most important influences on your personal response to conflict, in order of importance. Keep this list for later discussion of "My Personal Style of Conflict."

Throughout this book we will encourage you to understand yourself and your history while you are learning to understand conflict, change conflicts, and gain confidence in your new repertoire of interpersonal conflict skills. The authors of this book often undertake what we call a *life review*, or self-review of conflict influences. These influences change in importance over our lives. For Joyce, the major influences on her approach to conflict were the experience of her father's positions being terminated because of conflict over social justice issues, and the way her parents coached the three siblings to talk things out and never fight. Her early training in leadership development quickly placed her in a coaching and teaching role as early as junior high. She gained humility when intimate relationships ended or changed even when good skills and good will were employed. For Bill, some of the major influences on his approach to conflict are that he grew up in a family that totally avoided all conflict, so he thought avoidance was the only option. Then in college, he became an intercollegiate debater and developed the ability to argue with others. Now, he practices a value of neither avoiding nor attacking—but pushing himself to collaborate with others in all situations, work and private.

❧Negative Views of Conflict

Prior to a training session to be held for a large corporation, a revealing dialogue took place. The agreed-upon topic was "Conflict on the Job: Making It Work Productively." Three days before the training was to take place, a worried manager called. He said the proposed topic "certainly sounded interesting," and he was "sure everyone needed help in the area," but he wondered if the leader would take a more "positive" approach to the subject. He urged a title change to "Better Communication in Business," and explained that his company didn't really have "conflicts," just problems in communicating. He felt conflict was such a negative subject that spending concentrated time on it might make matters worse. The executive's apprehensions about conflict were mirrored by a participant in a course called "Managing Conflicts Productively," who said she came to the course because she had never seen a productive conflict—all the conflicts she had witnessed were destructive. Further, her statement suggested that such a thing as a helpful conflict probably did not exist.

Several well-known cultural clichés present a fairly clear picture of how many of us were taught to think about conflict. Parents may tell their children, "If you can't say anything nice, don't say anything at all"; "Pick on somebody your own size"; "Don't hit girls"; "Don't rock the boat"; "Children should be seen and not heard"; "Act your age!" (which means act my age, not yours); "Be a man, fight back"; and "Sticks and stones may break my bones, but words will never hurt me!" All of these sayings give a bit of philosophy about conflict, regarding with whom to fight, permissible conflict behavior, when to engage in conflict, and the power of words in conflict behavior. All of the sayings make assumptions that are not helpful to persons who want to learn to carry out productive conflict behavior.

If you were asked to list the words that come to mind when you hear the word *conflict*, what would you list? People commonly give the following responses:

destruction	anxiety	threat
anger	tension	heartache
disagreement	alienation	pain
hostility	violence	hopelessness
war	competition	stress

Many people view conflict as an activity that is almost completely negative and has no redeeming qualities. Some take the attitude that "what the world needs now is good communication," that if people could just understand each other better, they wouldn't have to experience conflicts. While there is an increasing awareness of the potentially positive features of conflict when done skillfully, many widely accepted assumptions continue to work against a positive view of conflict. Some of the most common **negative views of conflict** are presented here.

1. *Harmony is normal and conflict is abnormal.* Years ago Coser (1967) and Simmel (1953) supported the idea that conflict is normal in a relationship that endures over time. They described conflict as cyclical, or rising and falling. No one expects relationships to be in a constant state of upheaval, or they would reach the "critical limit in a degenerative communication spiral and disintegrate" (Wilmot 1995, 70). Observation of people in relationships shows that conflict is not a temporary aberration. It alternates with harmony in an ebb and flow pattern. But common expressions such as "I'm glad things are back to normal around here" or "Let's get back on track" express the assumption that conflict is not the norm. You can expect conflict, even in vibrant, enduring relationships.

2. *Conflicts and disagreements are the same phenomenon.* Often people in conflicts assure each other that "this is really just a disagreement." Simons (1972) notes the extensive use of the term *communication breakdown* to describe conflict situations. This term seems to mean that in conflict, one is not communicating. A problem with equating conflicts and disagreements is that people assume that if a discussion is "just a disagreement," it can and should be resolved by reaching a better understanding or by communicating better. As explained in chapter 1, conflicts are more serious than disagreements. They require more than a clarification of terms or more careful listening, although those two communication skills greatly speed the process of conflict management.

3. *Conflict is a result of personal pathology.* Conflict is often described as "sick," and conflict participants may be labeled as "neurotic," "hostile," "whining," "paranoid," "egomaniacs," "antisocial," "dependent" or "codependent," or "enabling." Labels offer no substitute for a careful analysis of the elements of the conflict. Conflict results more often from a lack of appropriate personal power and too little self-esteem than from someone with a sick personality. In studying conflict, people's *behaviors* should be described, *not their personalities*. Of course, people do get stuck in pathological patterns because of learning or emotional disorders. Sometimes people are so stuck in a destructive pattern that they cannot change and they cannot participate in collaboration. But the process of conflict itself should not be viewed as pathological. People engage in conflict for understandable reasons. If someone is "rigid," they may have too much or too little power. If someone is "defensive," they may be under attack or expect to be threatened.

4. *Conflict should never be escalated.* The term *conflict process* better describes the various options in conflictual interactions than *conflict resolution*. Sometimes, the most productive choice is to temporarily make the conflict larger so it can be seen, dealt with, and given importance. Sometimes an escalation—not a runaway upward spiral but an emotionally intense expression—is unavoidable and cannot be suppressed without relationship damage (resentment, silent hostility, despair, hopelessness, and private decisions to leave). Conflict skills include learning to make enough noise to be heard and to make conflict big enough to be seen.

Justice is often served by people of lower power banding together to confront higher-power people. Sometimes people with higher power take a stand to make a conflict larger because it is the right thing to do.

5. *Conflict interaction should be polite and orderly.* Overly nice communication of any kind ensures a lack of authentic interchange. Productive conflict management often is chaotic and confusing. Private arguments, especially, seldom conform to public standards of reasonableness, consistency, or relevance in argumentation. Sillars and Weisberg (1987) note that conflicts do not follow rules of polite conversation. Unlike college debaters, conflict participants do not have to respond directly, or in order, or even with relevant expressions. "As conflicts intensify, conversations become increasingly less orderly, clear, relevant, and goal-directed, and increasingly impulsive, emotional and improvisational" (149). With intensity, communication becomes less strategic and rational and more emotionally expressive and personal. A good conflict is not necessarily a nice conflict, although the more people use productive communication, the more likely that the conflict will both solve problems and help the relationship go forward.

6. *Anger is the predominate emotion in conflict interaction.* Another misconception is that the primary emotion associated with conflict is anger, or hostility. Instead, many emotions accompany conflict. We are more familiar with the heated, angry, gut-wrenching feelings accompanying conflict than we are with the aching, lonely, sad, anxious, disappointed, uncertain, resentful, and forlorn feelings. Adults are not encouraged in our society to acknowledge fears, loss, feelings of abandonment, and loneliness. When people talk about their conflicts, the experience expressed is most akin to heartbreak or loss. In conflict the emotional connection is broken between people. As the relationship changes to one of distance, the natural give-and-take that used to come easily is lost. In the experience of brokenheartedness, people turn to avoidance, bitterness, anger, denial, or retaliation. The loss of the emotional bond remains one of the most painful experiences of humankind. The poet Robert Frost has expressed this loss well:

Fire and Ice

Some say the world will end in fire
Some say ice.
From what I've tasted of desire
I hold with those who favor fire.
But if it had to perish twice,
I think I know enough of hate
To say that for destruction ice
Is also great
*And would suffice.**

Application 2.4	Emotions in Conflict

What emotions are most common for you when you experience conflict? Think of three areas of conflict: family, romantic, and work. In each area, list your most common emotions. If there doesn't seem to be a set of common emotions, think of one conflict as an example in each area. How did/do you feel? Be sure to use words of feeling, not judgment or description.

7. *There is one right way to resolve differences.* Americans tend to resolve disputes, at least in public, in one of four ways: fight, vote, litigate, or appeal to various authorities (Stulberg 1987). These approaches assume that someone will win and someone will lose and that all will accept the process and abide by its outcome. In a local church whose members were trying to employ new forms of decision making, great disagreement arose over the idea of using collaborative, consensus-based forms of decision making. In one conflict over whether homosexual people should be given full rights and privileges in the church, the debate at the large public meeting centered primarily around whether it was possible to make decisions that were binding without a vote and how to vote without automatically creating "winners and losers." Many appeared more threatened by the change in process than by the possible outcome of the decision. In everyday life, subordinates subvert managers, children disobey parents, and coalitions form after a vote is taken, essentially changing the meaning of the vote. People assent with half a heart then fight against the agreement with all their strength. Sometimes the best method for resolving disputes is not apparent, which leads to a struggle over how to struggle. Rather than being viewed as a waste of time, conflict should be viewed as multilayered. Many productive ways to resolve differences can be employed.

Positive Approaches to Conflict

The above set of common assumptions probably reflects the predominate mode of thought in the contemporary West. However, one cannot just say "that is how people see conflict." Many societies, including our own, express contradictory views of conflict—sometimes it is bad, sometimes it is good. Therefore, we may grow up with a confusing perspective on when conflict is helpful or when it should be avoided. We learn few strategies for changing conflict situations from harmful ones into productive ones. Children may receive confusing messages about their conduct of conflict. Sports are all right, but violence outside a sports framework is not. Conflicts with peers are all right if you have been stepped on and you are a boy, but talking back to parents when they step on you is not all right. Having a conflict over a promotion is acceptable, but openly vying for recognition is not. Competing over a girl (if you're a boy) is admirable, but having a conflict over a boy (if you're a girl) is catty. And so on. Persons in power send two different messages: (1) fight and stand up for yourself, but (2) only when it is acceptable (Bateson 1972). Thus, people develop mixed feelings about conflict, and many simply learn to avoid it altogether.

Yet, there are some **positive approaches to conflict** worthy of our examination. For example, would you list the following words after hearing the word *conflict?*

exciting	intimate
strengthening	courageous
helpful	clarifying
stimulating	opportunity
growth producing	enriching
creative	energizing

One of the assumptions of this book is that conflict can be associated with all of the above words. Conflict does receive some positive endorsement in legal challenges and competition in business. In games, children learn that "hitting hard" and "fighting to win" are positive virtues. Strategizing, scheming, and maximizing your gains are also necessary. Conflict can be approached from a potentially positive perspective. Consider the following advantages and functions of conflict:

1. *Conflict is inevitable; therefore, the constructive way to approach conflict is as "a fact of life."* Too often, people blame others for conflict, assuming, as we saw above, that harmony is the norm. If you can accept that conflict is inevitable, you can calm down and use your problem-solving skills rather than expending effort in blame and avoidance.

Application 2.5   An Important Interpersonal Situation

Think of any situations you may have experienced over more than a few months' period of time. You can think of your family, a summer job, a roommate situation, or a sports or extracurricular experience. Discuss with your small group whether any of these situations was conflict free. If so, was anything lost? If there was indeed conflict, what might have been gained? Did anything positive come from the conflict? If the conflict was destructive, can you think of positive results that might have occurred if the conflict had been handled differently?

---

2. *Conflict serves the function of "bringing problems to the table."* In intimate relationships, conflict can make clear that there are problems to be solved. Many times in couple relationships, conflict emerges over division of labor (Kluwer, Heesink, and Van de Vliert 1996) and over the distribution of power (Kurdek 1994). When couples report high levels of problem severity, they are more likely to divorce (Amato and Rogers 1999). One rule of thumb we have developed is that "If a conflict occurs three times it isn't about the content." It may be about power, self-esteem, division of labor, or resentments and hurts from the past.

    Don and Heather have been married for two years. They have a nine-month-old son. Heather works three days a week out of their home, running an environmental consulting business. Before their marriage, she worked for various nonprofit environmental groups. She is also an artist who sells her work to environmental organizations. Don is a mechanical engineer with a full-time job at a small firm. They reported a conflict over tasks at home. Here is a summary of their dilemma:

> **Heather:** Don and I have agreed that I will work three days a week, and in the other two days, take on most, but not all, of the home responsibilities. But since our child is home some of the day, every day, I often am doing many things at once—laundry, playing with or caring for Nathan, answering e-mails about work, and trying to write up reports and initiate contacts with clients. That's all right with me, since I like to have a lot going on, except for one problem. When I want to go out with my women friends some evenings, after being home all day, Don gets upset if I leave household and child care tasks for him to do. He doesn't understand that I can't just neatly divide my work into three days of business and two days of home and child care. I can't stand feeling stuck and controlled.

> **Don:** I thought Heather and I worked out a good plan. I would work full-time out of the home, and she would work three-fifths' time at home, leaving her time to do most of the home tasks. I don't think she organizes very well. I resent being left with housework when she goes out in the evenings. It's not what we agreed. We need to change something.

Application 2.6   Don and Heather

What problems, specifically, do Don and Heather face? What are some of the areas that could derail them? In other words, applying the "three times" rule, what is the conflict *not* about? What is the conflict more likely to be about? How could they begin to solve the problem and make their relationship better?

---

3. *Conflict often helps people join together and clarify their goals.* Many times people keep on doing things "the same old way" until there is a conflict. When conflict arises, they must decide what their priorities are and how to use their resources. In one organization, a group of nurses were told they must function without a nursing supervisor. They were told by upper management to work out their own schedules and assignments as a team. As they struggled with more work and fewer paid hours available, after a period of several months of blaming and complaining, they met together as a team and worked out their problems. While the initial reduction in resources was not at all desirable, they now work effectively as a team.

4. *Conflict can function to clear out resentments and help people understand each other.* In a conflict, one cannot continue to go along as though one's own perspective is the only one. When others speak up and say what they need, want, think, and feel, the circle of understanding is often expanded beyond the individual. Even though it may be difficult, conflict can help people pay attention to other points of view.

To continue the examination of views of conflict, we will present an overview of everyday metaphors people use when describing conflict.

Metaphors Make a Difference

Metaphoric and imaginative language pervades everyday speech in informal, formal, spoken, and written contexts. When people spontaneously describe conflict as something else, they use a metaphor, which is a way of comparing one thing to another by speaking of it as if it were a different object or process. Arnie, an Army colonel, described his office as a windmill, with people going around in circles, not knowing that the pipe connecting the mechanism to the underground well had been disconnected. Through this metaphor, one can picture the pointless confusion and chaos of the office. Karen described her family as a movie scene in which a train is rushing across a bridge on the point of collapsing. Father, as the engineer, is unaware of the danger since no lookouts are posted to warn of hazards, so he speeds on. Arnie and Karen used extended metaphors to describe rich scenes.

Our cognitive system itself is fundamentally metaphoric. Imaginative speech makes up much of language (Lakoff and Johnson 1980; Hayakawa 1978; Ortony 1975; Weick 1979). Hayakawa writes that metaphors are not "ornaments of discourse" but are "direct expressions of evaluation and are bound to occur whenever we have strong feelings to express" (109). Conflict brings up such strong feelings that metaphoric analysis, of both the process of conflict and specific conflicts, aids in understanding, intervention, and lasting change. The use of metaphoric analysis of specific conflicts will be explained in chapter 6, "Assessing Conflicts." Aristotle understood analogy or metaphor to be the source of truths, a mark of genius. A metaphor or analogy "can take its creator, as well as its hearers, quite by surprise" (Rushing 1983, 2). We continue to listen for spontaneous metaphors for the process of conflict. When conflict itself can be described with a transformative, living metaphor, the process of a specific conflict will much more likely be transformative and creative. **Conflict metaphors** reflect and create expectations.

In the following section, common metaphors for conflict interaction will be explained. The way a conflict is characterized metaphorically creates a certain perception of what can happen, what will happen, what should happen, and with what kind of feeling actions might take place (McCorkle and Mills 1992). As you read this book, studying conflict and learning how to manage conflict productively, pay attention to how people express thoughts and feelings about conflict through metaphors.

Application 2.7	What Is Conflict Like?

Before you read further about metaphors and conflict, take a moment to think of how you generally describe conflict. Finish the sentence "Conflict is like . . ." Then respond to this open-ended sentence, "Conflict in my family could best be described as . . ." What are the underlying assumptions of your metaphor(s)?

Win-Lose Metaphors

Many images and expressions of conflict cast such a negative tone around the process that creativity is stifled. Win-lose metaphors imply that the outcome is predetermined with little possibility for productive conflict management. Conflicts that are viewed in this way are generally called *win-lose conflicts*, or *distributive conflicts*. In conflicts of this nature, what one person wins, the other person, by necessity, loses. A scarce amount of resources is distributed, usually unevenly, among the participants. One of the main reasons conflict brings up so much emotion is that people assume that they have so much to lose. Sometimes, that is true. Sometimes, as you will see, that assumption can be changed.

Conflict Is Warlike and Violent

War, with its violence, is the central metaphor of conflict in the United States and Western Europe. Conflict often is characterized as a battle. The following phrases regarding conflict reflect the metaphor of war and violence:

> Your actions are completely indefensible.
>
> He attacked me where I was most vulnerable—through my kids.
>
> That criticism is right on target.
>
> OK, shoot!
>
> I feel beaten down and defeated after our talk.

When conflict is envisioned as warlike, certain actions seem natural. In a staff meeting, for instance, if accusations are "hurled back and forth" as if by primitives bashing each other with stones, if arguments are felt to be "right on target," then the whole melee is structured as a battle. The scene is that of a battlefield; the actors are people of warring groups who are committed to wiping each other out since the other is perceived as being threatening. The acts are those that aim to produce an advantage by killing or reducing the effectiveness of the opponent. The resolution possibilities are reduced to offense and defense, and the purpose or outcome is inevitably harm, vengeance, a reduction of players, and a repetition of the argument/battle. The war metaphor influences the entire perception of the conflict. Both winning and losing sides feel incomplete; victors desire more power, and losers shore up their defenses for the next attack. Perhaps you work in an organization whose workers act as if conflicts were large or small wars, and fights were battles in the ongoing war. If your organization uses a "chain of command," gives people "orders," "attacks competitors," "wages advertising or public relations campaigns," "fires traitors," "employs diversionary tactics," or "launches assaults," then the organization may well have evolved a military metaphor for conflict management (Weick 1979). If so, conflict is likely to be solved the way it would be if one were on a battlefield.

"He Is Killing Me"

In a large technological research firm, military metaphors abound. The program directors are under a lot of stress with high-stakes external negotiations, which involve millions of dollars. When they have a meeting with someone who shouts or stomps out of the room, they find it very unpleasant. Between rounds of negotiation, they might tell another program director that "he is killing me." Everyone immediately knows what this metaphor means: (1) this negotiation is very important, (2) I'm concerned that we won't "make a deal" on this contract, and (3) he is acting in ways that make me uncomfortable.

Couples talk in warlike terms, too. They may say:

- I just retreat. I fall back and regroup. Then I wait for an opening . . .
- He slaughters me when I cry and get confused.
- When I don't want it to come to blows (laughs), I launch a diversionary tactic, like telling him the kids are calling me.

"She's Squeezing the Life out of Me"

A divorcing couple, Kent and Jeannie, were at odds over the division of their property. Most of the big items had been decided, and they were down to the smaller but more symbolic things such as music, art, family pictures, and gifts to one another. In describing their negotiations, Kent said in the mediator's office, "She's choking me," "These are my lifeblood," and "These things are my life." Jeannie saw the items as "just stuff, for heaven's sake." The metaphors the couple used revealed the degree of importance they put on the items.

Chronic use of military or violent metaphors severely limits creative problem solving. People overlook improvisation, alternative actions, and opportunities to contradict the norms instead of following orders. The military image saves us the trouble of inventing new ones. However, "other metaphors are needed to capture different realities that exist right alongside those military realities" (Weick 1979, 51).

Conflict Is Explosive

Perhaps you experience "explosive" conflicts, using phrases like the following to describe the process:

He's about to blow up. Any little thing will set him off.

Larry's got a short fuse.

The pressure's building up so fast that something's gotta give soon!

I just needed to let off steam.

She really pushed my button.

Put a lid on it!

Phrases like these indicate a perception of conflict as being made up of flammable materials (feelings), trigger issues, and an ignition of the explosion that, once started, can't be stopped. Maybe the pressure builds "under the surface," like in a volcano, or "in a pressure cooker," such as an overcrowded office. People often say they "blew their stacks" in response to an event. If people act out explosive conflicts, they often see them as somehow out of their control ("He touched it off, not me"). Explosions blow away familiar structures, often requiring a period of rebuilding and cleanup. The "exploder" may feel better after a release of pressure; the people living in the vicinity may feel blown away.

The explosion metaphor limits creativity in conflict because the only way participants can imagine resolving the issue is by "blowing up" or by avoiding "touching it off." This image denies personal responsibility for the pressure and mistakenly urges only two avenues for resolution. Additionally, people with "explosive tempers" are often relieved of their own responsibility to do something about the buildup of tension before they have to blow up. Family members are taught to keep from making Dad or Mom mad, thus learning that conflict can be avoided by not provoking someone, thus keeping the peace. Family systems theorists have labeled this pattern as one of the destructive patterns of codependence—of taking too much responsibility for the actions of others.

Conflict Is a Trial

The legal system provides a regulated, commonly accepted system for managing social conflict. The system has evolved over hundreds of years and serves our culture well in many instances. However, Western society has come to rely too much on the legal system, partly as a result of the breakdown of community and personal modes of managing conflict. Thus, legal terms creep into personal or organizational conflict metaphors, since at least the legal system has firm rules and expectations. Phrases like the following indicate that legal metaphors may be shaping conflict behavior:

- He's got the best case.
- The jury's still out on that one.
- You're accusing me.
- She's the guilty party.

Even in conflicts between romantic partners or friends, one person might take on the role of the accusatory prosecuting attorney, one the role of the defender of the accused. Friends might get informally brought in as jury; one might say to friends, "Should I let him off on this one?" Arguments between interdependent people often go back and forth as if there will be a judgment of guilt or innocence, but often the jury stays out, no judge appears, and the case remains unresolved, to simmer through the system until another suit (interpersonally) arises. Courts maintain clearly delineated processes, basing decisions on law and precedent. Interpersonal situations, however, admit feelings as evidence, do not bind parties to the outcome of a conflict, and maintain no systems of law and order to back up a decision. Few "trials" settle underlying issues in the conflict in personal relationships. Instead, romantic partners or friends keep "going back to court" (keep arguing). The legal metaphor doesn't fit the usual interpersonal situation, but the participants act as if it does, then remain bitterly disappointed that their understanding of the case doesn't carry the day.

Conflict Is a Struggle

People experience conflict as a hopeless or difficult struggle like "being on a sinking ship with no lifeboat," traveling "a rocky road," working with "a checkbook that won't balance" (McCorkle and Mills 1992), or "arm wrestling." Sometimes conflict is expressed as a power struggle, or a struggle to get "one up." The "conflict as a struggle" metaphor implies that the process takes a lot of emotional and physical energy and may indeed turn out to be fruitless. Sometimes people say, "It was a struggle, but we finally made it," indicating some form of conflict resolution that worked out reasonably well.

Conflict Is an Act of Nature

Conflict is expressed as a negative natural disaster, or at least an uncontrollable act of nature, such as a tornado, a hurricane, an avalanche, being swept away by a flood, or an earthquake, or a fire raging out of control (McCorkle and Mills 1992). One telling phrase was that experiencing conflict felt like being "a rowboat caught in a hurricane." McCorkle and Mills note that those who feel powerless may "(a) take little or no responsibility for their own actions that sustain the conflict, (b) feel that the other participant has all the choices, or (c) believe that no one involved has any choices" (64). The best course of action, then, would be to avoid conflict, since no positive outcome can be expected.

Conflict Is Animal Behavior

Human animals often characterize conflict as something done by other members of the animal realm—not themselves. People may be called "stubborn as a mule" or described as "butting heads," or in a very common phrase, conflict is called "a zoo" (McCorkle and Mills 1992). You may hear phrases like "tearing his throat out," "slinking around," "stalking," or entering into a "feeding frenzy."

Conflict Is a Mess

Another intriguing image is that of conflict as a mess or as garbage. You'll hear "Let's not open up that can of worms," "They got all that garbage out in the open," "Things are falling apart around here," or "Everything's disintegrating." People will ask to "tie up some loose ends." Another clear expression of the "mess" metaphor emerges when people say, "This is a sticky situation," or "Something stinks around here."

Messes are difficult to manage because they spill over into other areas and can't be contained easily without making a bigger mess. A messy conflict usually means one that is full of personal, emotional attachments. This metaphor limits creativity to the extent that feelings are judged to be messy or not amenable to rational treatment. If the opposite of a messy conflict is a clean, or straightforward, one, involving only facts and rationality rather than messy feelings, then only part of the conflict can be resolved. The feelings will go underground and "create a stink."

Conflict Is a Communication Breakdown

A "breakdown in communication" is one of the most popular designations of conflict. McCorkle and Mills (1992) refer to this breakdown as "one-way communication," in which people "talk to a brick wall" or "argue with someone from another planet." Referring to the process as a breakdown implies a telephone line that is down, a computer that won't communicate, a car that won't run, or a sound system that won't amplify sound. The implication that a breakdown can be "fixed," however, often turns out to be inaccurate. Many times people communicate clearly in conflict interactions—only to find out that they are in an intractable conflict. Clarity of communication usually improves the process of conflict management greatly, but it is a mistake to assume that clarity removes conflict.

Conflict Is a Wound

Conflict may be described as a wound, or as something that hurts or is painful. Others may be accused of "gouging me" or "raking me over the coals," or "beating me up" or "hurting me." After a repeated series of messages that hurt, one may say, "I'm immune."

She can't hurt me any more" (Vangelisti 1994). In this way, the wound of conflict functions almost like a disease to which one might become immune.

Neutral or Objective Metaphors

A few metaphors—**neutral or objective metaphors**—indicate that conflict is neither negative nor positive but embodies possibilities for either, depending on how skillfully the conflict is enacted.

Conflict Is a Game

The game, especially the ball game, image is popular. While it is true that games end in victory or defeat, making the overall metaphor win-lose, the process of "playing the game" can be viewed as neutral. People "bat around ideas," "toss the ball into his court," "strike out," go "back and forth," and "make an end run." Some people are judged to be "team players." Images of referees, an audience, or coaches are popular. In this media age you'll hear "Would you do that again on instant replay?" which may mean "I can't believe you said that." The game image assumes the existence of rules defining the game and defining interaction among the players. Rules define fouls, out-of-bounds behavior, winning, losing, and when the game is over. An even more interdependent game is chess, which requires the players to keep in mind at all times the predicted moves of the opponent. Chess is a game that can only be won by a highly developed prediction of the strategy of the other player. If one doesn't take account of the opponent, one loses immediately. In chess, everyone plays by the same rules.

The game metaphor is limiting when people won't "play fair" or don't see the conflict as having gamelike qualities at all. Many men are raised to feel comfortable with the game image, accepting wins and losses as "all part of the game." Many women are less comfortable with the structure, insisting on talking about what is going on, which men see as not playing by the rules. In an extended study of women engineers, Fletcher (1999) was told again and again that solving high-visibility problems was the way to get ahead. People solving problems of this type were referred to as "hitting a home run," as opposed to being "singles hitters," who were seen as slow, steady contributors, but not the kind of team players that win the promotion game. "Real work" was defined as the kind of problem solving that involved team playing. Men consistently were ranked higher in this skill than were women (Fletcher 1999, 91). Game metaphors may be positive for men and potentially limiting or negative for women. Game metaphors work poorly in intimate conflicts, since most games provide a winner and a loser. In intimate conflicts, if anyone wins, the relationship loses.

Conflict Is a Heroic Adventure

The hero image is endemic to conflict images. The superheroes of Western movies, science fiction, myths, and our own childhoods are used even in adult life. This archetypal imagery describes a process in which slightly scared people appoint a leader who is "bigger and better" than they are, then pledge loyalty to that leader, who is bound to protect them. The hero or heroine is one who has found or done something beyond the normal range of experience. "A hero is someone who has given his or her life to something bigger than oneself" (Campbell 1988, 123). The question is whether the hero or heroine is really a match for the task at hand, can really overcome the dangers, and has the requisite courage, knowledge, and capacity to serve.

This desire to follow a heroic leader emerges in all cultures. In social or political movements, leaders organize the energies of many people who overcome many obstacles to reach a common goal. Many contemporary films focus on the actions of a hero or heroine who saves large numbers of people (Rushing and Frentz 1995). The limit to this heroic metaphor in conflict resolution is that one can become used to passively watching events happen on TV or elsewhere. The spectator feels helpless or unimportant. And if the right leader does not emerge, a wonderful chance for change may be lost. Additionally, people often get stuck in certain roles in the heroic drama, such as damsel in distress, knight in shining armor, lieutenant or helper to the "great one," or victim.

Many of the heroic roles specify men as actors. Roles such as king, dragon slayer, the lone Western gunslinger, the sports hero, or the action hero of adventure movies are more often filled by men than women (Gerzon 1992). However, Rushing and Frentz (1995) indicate that films, especially Westerns and science fiction, are providing more and more heroic roles for women, such as Ripley in the *Aliens* series.

Conflict Is a Balancing Act

Conflict is referred to as a delicate balancing act, like that of a tightrope walker, or that of a rock climber, who must find just the right handholds or fall to sure death. Often negotiations in the formative stages are referred to as "in a very delicate" stage, in which one "false move" will scuttle negotiations. Satir (1972) refers to a family as a mobile, which can be unbalanced by one member's having too much weight or getting stirred up, thus making the whole mobile swing and sway. Working toward balance is seen as a positive process.

Transformative Metaphors

Some metaphors for conflict help us envision ways to transform the conflict. By picturing conflict in a transformative way—that is, using **transformative metaphors**—we may use our imagination to move out of the negative perspective of conflict into understanding conflict as an opportunity to change the *way* interactions proceed.

Conflict Is a Bargaining Table

A collaborative approach to conflict is exemplified by the common metaphor of "the table." Diplomacy, labor negotiations, and parliamentary procedure all use this image. The conflict structure and procedure depend on the table as a central feature. Families are urged to sit down to dinner together, labor and management officials "come to the table," and diplomats struggle over the shape of actual tables at conferences. These real or imagined tables communicate information about who the conflict participants will be, how they will act, and what their placement will be in relationship to each other. The table is a spatial metaphor defining the relationships.

King Arthur, in historical legend, created a round table to symbolize equal discussion, with each knight having one vote. The idea of "Right makes might" substituted, for a time, for "Might makes right." When the federation disintegrated, the round table, smashed to pieces by dissident knights, became a symbol of the disintegration. Other examples of "table" imagery in conflict management include the following:

In parliamentary procedure, "tabling a motion" stops movement toward a decision, and "bringing a motion off the table" indicates a readiness to decide. "Under the table" refers to hidden or secretive agreements. "Turning the tables" comes from a medieval custom of turning from one dinner partner to another to begin conversation. It was done in response to the king's or queen's gesture. If the "tables are turned," a person feels a sudden lack of contact or support, or loss of an ally.

The table metaphor continues to help us think about power, especially uneven power. Conflict resolution remains difficult if people are "negotiating at an uneven table" (Kritek 1994). People may be metaphorically seated at an uneven table if they do not have the skills to negotiate, come from the nondominant culture, hold unequal positions in an organization, or do not have the freedom to come and go from "the table" (the conflict resolution process).

Conflict Is a Tide

A second transformative metaphor for conflict is the tide. Tides ebb and flow within predictable parameters based on the phases of the moon, the climatic conditions, the shape of the shoreline, and the currents of the ocean. The tides are predictable only through observation and careful record keeping. They must be seriously considered by those on land and sea or they can become life threatening. Every sailor knows the folly of going out on the ocean without knowing the tidal patterns. Tides can be destructive, but they also wash in nourishment and unexpected flotsam, sometimes even treasure. Debris is washed out, exposing new features of the coastline. Tides are repetitive, powerful, and inescapable.

Thinking of conflict as a tidal rhythm in relationships may help to reduce fear. If the relationship is equal and trusting, conflict will develop its own rhythm that will not wash away the foundation of the relationship. Conflict will ebb, as well as rise. For example, many families experience more conflict than usual when a college student comes home for the summer to work. After being on their own for several years, possibly in both dorms and apartments, many students experience too many restrictions at home, and parents experience what appears to be too little family involvement and accountability on the part of the student. Many times, several "high tide" conflict experiences prompt a family to reset the expectations and boundaries. Then for the rest of the summer, conflict episodes recede to "low tide." Thinking ahead about this possibility helps many family members navigate well through a potentially stormy time.

Conflict Is a Dance

Another potentially positive image is conflict as a dance. People speak of "learning to dance to the same music." In a dance, both or all participants have to learn how close and how far to move, how to regulate distance, when to slow down and when to speed up, how to maintain contact with partners so you know where they will be, and how to end the dance (Lindbergh 1955). Different flourishes and steps can add to the grace and beauty of the dance. Dancing can be energetic, stimulating, and exhilarating. Sometimes one's partner steps on one's toes, can't dance very well, is awkward, or doesn't know the steps yet. But the whole idea of dancing with partners is to create something beautiful, graceful, and inspiring that depends on each person's skill, training, and individual expression. Dance can give collaborative images of conflict on which to build. Conflict envisioned as dance is reflected in the following statements:

"I feel hurried. I need more time." (The person is not saying, "I need a different partner.")

"Quit dancing around, and come over here
may be saying, "I don't know these steps, a

"They're just do-sa-do-ing [a square-dancir
though they are doing something togethe
other and their arms folded—a fairly non

Conflict Is a Garden

Conflict can be like a carefully cultivated gard
gardening, seeds are planted for future growth
the garden is watered when needed. Sun and
the most fruitful outcomes occur when the c
tive conflict can be seen as a garden, many positive outcomes
good gardening, poisons are not put on the ground—thus, rage, and attacks, w..
son an ongoing relationship, become as unthinkable as putting dry-cleaning fluid on rose-
bushes. In good gardens, individual plants are given room to grow. Some plants are
thinned to make room for mature plants. In human relationships, people learn to leave
space for others, to give them room to grow, and to plant compatible varieties together.
As a child you may have learned that no amount of watching beans or carrots in a garden would make them grow any faster. Human relationships, especially when conflict has
recently been part of the environment, need time to grow slowly, to recover from stress,
and to put down roots. We can "harvest" the fruits of careful labor (Kritek 1994, 275).
The "garden" image thus holds a lot of promise, especially as world understanding shifts
to encompass environmental realities, and we begin to understand our Earth as a single
garden.

Conflict Resolution as Quilt Making

One metaphor that many women relate to is the vision of making a quilt (Kritek 1994)
or "piecing together a solution." We may speak of putting together a "patchwork
of ideas." When making a quilt, people have to decide on the basic color scheme
(tone or emotional climate), the design, and what kind of fabric to use. Many individuals work together to create something beautiful and useful. While quilts can be made
by individuals instead of groups, the more common experience is for women to gather
together to sew and solve relational problems. Recently, quilt making has been studied
as an art form pioneered by women. Not only did women gather together to make a
quilt out of scraps and remnants, they also engaged in informal conciliation around the
quilting activity. Such activities still flourish. Community groups have made quilts for
AIDS projects, for relief activities, and for fund-raising for various programs.

Conflict as Musical Improvisation

Conflict can reflect artistry, as in jazz or drumming. In certain kinds of music, individual musicians follow the lead of one soloist, picking up on the theme or the rhythm and
extending the music. The solo passes around in the ensemble. In drumming circles the
rhythms grow out of the shared experience of the rhythm. Interpersonal conflict can be
like this. Someone gets a good idea, expresses it, and the others, rather than insisting
on a different melody or rhythm, "add in" to what has begun. Dissonance and harmony
make interesting music.

Mixing the Metaphors

Since the images used in conflicts are central to the conflict process, problems occur when people envision conflict in completely different ways. One person may think of conflict as war, with all the attendant warlike images, while the other assumes that conflict is more like a chess game—strategic, careful, thoughtful, and planned. The following case presents an example of problems arising from different images of conflict.

Case 2.1	Is It a Mess or an Explosion?

Lynn and Bart are married to each other. Lynn sees conflict as a mess, something sticky and uncomfortable, even slightly shady or dirty. People in her family believe that husbands and wives who love each other don't have conflict very often. Conflict is distasteful to her. She is likely to say, "I don't want to talk about it now. Let's just leave the whole mess until this weekend. I can't handle it tonight." Bart sees and feels conflict as an explosion—his stomach tightens, his pulse races, and his heart begins to pound. He likes to reduce the pressure of all this emotion. He's a feelings-oriented person, while Lynn is more likely to use a reasoning process if she has to deal with an issue. Bart is likely to say, "I am not going to sit on this until Saturday morning. I'll burst. You can't expect me to hold all this in. It's not fair, you always . . ."

In addition to their specific conflict, Bart and Lynn are fighting over how to fight; indeed, they are fighting over what conflict is and how they experience it. Each assumes that the other thinks about the conflict the way he or she does. They could not be farther from the truth, as they probably will find out. The following case presents another example of different views of conflict within an organization.

Case 2.2	The Trial Begins

Charlotte, the district manager, sees conflict as a trial. She plays various roles when she is in conflict with the assistant managers. Sometimes she asks them to bring in facts to back up their opinion; sometimes she accuses them of not doing their homework. Sue is assistant district manager. She sees conflict as a process of bargaining around an imaginary table. She keeps trying to find areas of compromise, while Charlotte acts as judge or jury, deciding which ideas are best supported. Charlotte later fires Sue for not being able to take a stand, for being indecisive, and for not being aggressive enough in developing her own program. The two managers thought conflict was a different kind of process, and they made no provisions for their differing expectations.

Other images of conflict can be detected in ordinary conversation. Listen to the way you and others talk, scrutinize news reports, and pay attention to images in public speeches. See if you can determine the metaphor that shapes a particular conflict in a family, an agency, a social group, the general public, or even the nation. What might it mean, for instance, if conflict is seen as an irritant, as in "She bugs me," or "Get off my back," or "He's just trying to get a rise out of you"? Do you think conflict takes on a life of its own, as when it "snowballs out of control" or is "a runaway train"? Many people experience conflict as an endless circle of repetition, going nowhere, as exemplified by phrases such as "We're just going round and round," "We're on a merry-go-round," or "Here we go again!" The tedium of conflict is reflected in "Same song, second verse." People refer to conflicts as "a drain," "a lot of grief," "a heavy burden," or "poison." Attending to these vivid images can unleash your creativity and help you to sort out which images of conflict are limiting and which are helpful.

Application 2.8	Reframing Your Conflict

Think of a conflict you have observed or experienced—possibly one you thought about earlier in the chapter. First, determine whether any negative conflict metaphor applies to this conflict. You can think of a negative metaphor of your own, or use one we have presented. If you stay in the negative framework, what options are available to you for resolving the conflict? List at least three. Now choose a transformative or neutral metaphor for "framing" the same conflict. List at least three options that might be available to you if you envision the conflict in this way. Discuss your results.

The Lens Model of Conflict

As you have seen, the metaphors we use to comprehend conflict illuminate our personal ways of viewing conflict interactions. While each conflict episode is unique, common elements underlie all conflicts.

The building blocks of conflict are represented in figure 2.1, the **lens model of conflict.** For the sake of simplicity, the lens model will be illustrated with just two conflict parties, though many times there will be more than two parties involved. Two fundamental aspects are important in all conflicts: (1) *communication behaviors* and (2) the *perceptions of those behaviors*. We can think of the study of conflict as a view through a lens, like the lens of a camera, or through prescription glasses. The lens model specifies that each person has a view of (1) oneself, (2) the other person, and (3) the relationship. These perceptual pieces form the fundamental "views" of all conflicts, and combine together to form the mosaic of a particular conflict. Figure 2.1 shows these central features.

Figure 2.1   The Lens Model of Conflict Interaction

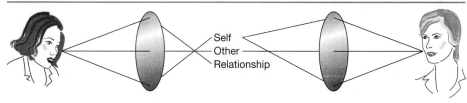

Self
Other
Relationship

As you can see from figure 2.1, the minimal features of all conflicts are as follows:

- The *communicative acts* (behaviors) of each person
- The *meanings* (attributions) attached to those acts by each person:

    each person's view of self

    each person's views of the other

- The *meanings* (attributions) the two people ascribe to their relationship:

    past events

    current events

    future projections

Note that each person has a "lens" that gives that person a particular perspective, just as people use different types of glasses to see. There are multiple views of conflict, yet each looks "real" to the one seeing it.

In the Far East, this notion of lens is captured when people speak of two sides of seeing something. In Nepal and Tibet, for example, a person in conflict might say, "Well from my side, I guess I am getting tired of waiting for him, but from his side I don't know what is going on." The notion of "side" captures just how different two perceptions will be. One side usually does not understand the other side—your lens and my lens distort the events in different ways.

Have you noticed how easy it is to focus on what your "opponent" does in a conflict? She leaves you out of a meeting, cuts you off in the middle of an explanation, or takes a position and sticks with it even though you have perfectly reasonable grounds for what you think. How easy it is to tell your friend, "her actions say it all." However, actions do not "speak for themselves"—the impact of someone's actions depends on how the behaviors are interpreted by the other people involved. For example, Amber and Aaron are attorneys married to each other. At home, Amber interrupts Aaron a lot; both push for airtime. Yet Aaron likes Amber's involvement and passion and doesn't take her interruptions personally. Behaviors usually do not carry meaning by themselves—meaning is created through the interactions. Intent and impact are different. All behavior is up for interpretation.

Behaviors do not occur in a relational vacuum. Perceptions of and attributions about behaviors are at the heart of the conflict process. Research on attribution theory shows quite conclusively that we make different attributions about ourselves than about others. Attribution research shows the following:

- We try to make sense out of behavior by looking for causes.
- We attribute causes of *our* behavior to external factors (e.g., "I was under extreme time pressure.")
- We attribute causes of *others'* behavior to internal dispositions (e.g., "She always wants her own way.")

Clearly, we use a different lens for viewing ourselves than we do for viewing others. When we are exposed to conflict (which has many negative features for most of us), we tend to attribute the negative effects to the other rather than to ourselves. This tendency explains the familiar refrain of "It's his fault!" Sillars and Parry (1982) found that as the stress of conflict increases, blame of others also increases. We begin with an attribution of blame, then choose our next conflict move based on our perception that the other is at fault. Confounding the problem, we attribute our successes to our own efforts and our failures to external factors. The other party does the same thing. No wonder conflict is so difficult.

The lens model illustrates that people's views of self, other, and relationship are always, to some degree, distorted. We all have "filters" influencing our experience. As we will see in chapter 3, often in U.S. culture we "save face" for ourselves and "damage face" of the other. The other is probably doing the same thing. If you have ever known both individuals of a broken-up romance, you see the two sides very clearly. Where they once had only good things to say about the other ("she is just so perfect"), they now see only the negative features. When you talk to both of them after the breakup, their filters are so strong it doesn't even sound as though they were in the same relationship! Indeed, they were not, since each saw the relationship through his or her own lens.

The following conversation between two people occurred with two listeners present. As you can tell, the people conversing are in conflict with one another. Notice the different internal filters they automatically use that give them their opposing perspectives. The two of them work together and had just hosted a special event. They coordinated a series of public meetings for 13 people outside their organization.

Program coordinator:	The executive director does not listen to me, does not include me in decisions, reluctantly agrees to include me, then goes her merry way without consulting me. This happened five times this week during the visit of some important people. She is just too controlling. I don't see that I have a future here.
Executive director:	The program coordinator is too passive and does not remember when I talk to him. Further, he is being power hungry and wanting to run things himself. I specifically remember inviting him to participate on most of these occasions. What is his problem?

The two of them then began a round of "did too," "did not." Slowly, they began to work their way through this dispute. Both remain involved in the organization, with the program coordinator taking more responsibility and the executive director sharing more information.

Outsiders to a dispute, whether they are social scientists or friends, also have their own **attributions** and lenses—adding still other sides to the conflict equation. Whereas the parties in the example above see the issues as inclusion, power, control, and assertiveness, an outsider might focus on other issues. For example, during the exchange between the program coordinator and executive director, one of the outsiders was thinking, "Hmmm, if the coordinator doesn't dampen this outburst, it will blow this relationship sky high, and the executive director is looking a bit smug—maybe she excluded him on purpose and is glad she did."

These three lenses offer very disparate pictures of the unfolding dispute. Notice how different the starting observations are for all the people present in the discussion. The lenses are operating at full force. And when the categories become rigidly defined, you can see how people get locked into intense struggles.

In a conflict interaction, you often hear the principal participants say, "Yeah, well that is just your perception," as if the other's view isn't relevant. At the heart of all conflicts are the perceptions of the parties—they fuel the dispute engine. Research illuminates the importance of perceptions. For example, one consistent finding about married couples is that if they believe they are similar to one another, they are happier. Whether or not they are similar is actually irrelevant—their lenses determine their happiness (Acitelli, Douvan, and Veroff 1993). On the other side of the coin, when you come to see your work relationship (or personal relationship) as "having no hope," that belief alone predicts dissolution (Wilmot 1995). As a relationship declines, the individuals make fewer dyadic and more individual attributions (Lloyd and Cate 1985). The dissolution of a marriage is speeded up if the two players see it as emanating from individual factors (Siegert and Stamp 1994, 358). If during the first big fight the individuals develop a shared view of what happened, their relationship is more likely to survive.

One study on environmental organizations and the timber industry found that each side responds to, anticipates, and often copies the moves they think the other will make (Lange 1993). This same dynamic is present in personal and workplace conflicts as well. If you are not in communication with the other party, much like the environmentalists and timber industry representatives in Lange's study, then you mull over the conflict in your own mind. Without interaction with the other, the only "information" you have is what is going on in your own mind—your filter doesn't have a chance to get corrected. The result? "Prolonged thinking about disputes in the absence of communication focuses individuals on their own perspective and enhances biases toward seeing disputes as serious and holding partners responsible for conflicts" (Cloven and Roloff 1991, 153). When we run our own stories in our minds, then our view gets even more distorted. Cloven and Roloff found that only 1 percent of the time, individuals reported that they had thought about the conflict from the partner's view (136).

As you can see, the distorted lens can become even more warped in time. Here is an example of such thinking:

Joan

- Why is Jack late?
- He must be tied up.
- He was late last week, too.
- Hmmm, he is moving into the "irresponsible zone."
- I wonder if he wants to tell me something about our relationship.
- It has now been 25 minutes—he is so inconsiderate.
- I knew he would be like this—Sandy warned me about him.
- Jack is a real jerk.

Jack

- Hi, Joan. Sorry I'm late. I was counting on Kevin to bring my car back on time and he was late. Driving over I realized my cell phone was out of power. I am very sorry—you must have thought I was not coming.

Application 2.9	"That's Not What I Meant!"

Think back to a difficult issue that was made more difficult by perceptions that colored the experience. Remember a time when you were certain that the other person's motivation was harmful to you. How did you react as a result of this assumption? What was the outcome? Was the other ever able to say, "That's not what I meant at all. I was trying to tell you . . . ?" What happened to the relationship as a result of these different perceptions?

~Gender Effects and Gender Filters

Gender Effects

Membership in the "gender club" remains exclusive for all of your life, exerting one of the several powerful, pervasive influences on your developing conflict repertoire. Your own gender and the gender of those with whom you engage in conflict affects (1) your behavior and (2) your views.

One of the primary ways to view the role of gender in conflict interaction comes from the *communication differences tradition*, made popular by scholarly work in communication and linguistics. This tradition has taken a "separate but equal" way of viewing communication differences. Rather than presenting women as deficient in "general" (male) communication skills or males as lacking important relational skills that women are assumed to possess, both gender-based preferences are studied openly. Given the scope of that work, only that directly pertaining to conflict interactions will be summarized here. (See Ivy and Backlund 2003, Wood 1997, Tannen 1994, and Pearson, Turner, and Todd-Mancillas 1991 for comprehensive reviews of gender differences and similarities.)

Current research does show that in some circumstances there are female/male differences—that is, **gender effects**—in enacting conflict. In laboratory exercises, men will often exhibit dominating and competitive behavior and women exhibit avoidant and compromising behavior (Papa and Natalle 1989). In real-life observations of young girls and boys (at age 11), it has been noted that adolescent girls use indirect means of aggression, whereas the boys use more physical aggression. Interestingly, both sexes used direct verbal aggression equally (Bjorkqvist, Osterman, and Lagerspetz 1994). Tannen summarizes her research on gender differences in conflict by concluding that women are more likely to avoid conflict. Men are more likely than women to take control of the conversation to lead it in the direction they want. However, they expect their (female) conversational partners to mount some resistance to this effort, as men would be likely to do. Women often remain in the "listening" role rather than "lecturing," which puts them at a disadvantage in having their voices heard (Tannen 1994, 11). In organizations, women are more likely to leave than men are when there is ongoing, pervasive conflict.

Before we decide that "men are like this and women are like that," we need to examine the similarities among men's and women's conflict behaviors. In a comprehensive examination of sex differences, researchers concluded that "no meaningful gender differences in positive affect behavior, influence strategies, autocratic behavior, democratic behavior communication, facilitation and leader emergence" were found. They report, "in both survey and observational studies, we discovered more similarities than differences between men's and women's conflict behaviors" (Canary, Cupach, and Messman 1995, 131). However, the question of gender differences remains highly complex. In an approach called **social learning theory,** individuals are assumed to learn to be male or female based on communication and observation. They learn gender roles in same-sex groups. Woods (1997) explains that through imitation, young children imitate almost anything they see and hear. However, only gender-consistent communication is rewarded by important others around the child. Children slowly learn how to be a girl and how to be a boy.

Culture plays an important role in gender development. Macoby points out that when she and Jacklin published *The Psychology of Sex Differences* in 1974, they were looking for differences in individual abilities. They found few differences. When they examined the behavior of boys and girls in interactive situations, important patterns of difference became evident. Gender is "framed" in the overall cultural context, and is best understood as being imbedded in a particular culture. Different valuing of autonomy and dependence is reflected in common cultural roles (Young-Eisendrath 1998). In Western culture, girls and women are seen as valuing connection with others, the communication of care and responsiveness, and the preservation of the relationship (Gilligan 1982; Jordan et al. 1991). Boys and men are seen as valuing **autonomy and independence** more highly, learning to communicate in ways that preserve their independence from others (Kohlberg 1976). Research that is focused on individual abilities to communicate in a certain way misses the cultural point that boys and girls are socialized to act in certain ways. One of the main hopes we have as we explore conflict, gender, power, and culture is to give each of you the opportunity to choose from a wide range of communication behaviors, whether you are female or male. The more choices you have, the more likely you are to be able to resolve disputes intelligently and constructively.

One difference that should concern each of us is the way that self-esteem is influenced by one's gender. Current research clearly identifies a major slump in self-esteem for girls in early adolescence (Sadker and Sadker 1994). They may not experience a major climb in their self-esteem until midlife, when family roles are less stringent and their career development is more in place. Boys typically feel more self-esteem earlier in their lives but suffer from a sense of failure and disappointment in midlife when they do not reach their (unrealistically) high personal goals (Barnett, Marshall, and Pleck 1992, 79). One of the tenets of this book is that all conflicts are about two issues: power and self-esteem. Both genders are limited by self-esteem issues, perhaps at different times in their lives. One finding seems clear on a worldwide basis, however. Men have more power culturally, even in highly educated countries such as the Scandinavian countries (Young-Eisendrath 1993). Therefore, women and men often sit at an uneven table. Later, we will discuss in detail ways to balance power effectively for long-term conflict resolution, especially in intimate relationships.

Gender differences depend partly on maturity and experience. One study shows experienced managers manifesting no gender differences in style, but "among participants without managerial experience, women rated themselves as more integrating, obliging, and compromising than did men" (Korabik, Baril, and Watson 1993, 405). Likewise, in a negotiation context, "Women are not necessarily more fair-minded or compassionate" than men (Watson 1994, 124). In the workplace, Gayle (1991) notes that on conflict strategy selection, the effects of gender are "minuscule" compared to the effects of a host of other, unidentified factors. It may well be that most of the effects ascribed to gender are due to other relationship factors such as power, gender of the opponent, prior moves of the other, and so on.

Gender Filters

In addition to potentially directing behaviors, gender often affects how one sees conflict behaviors. As we have seen, males and females tend to differ in terms of seeing self and other as connected. Even when actual behaviors may seem identical, for instance negotiating competitively, men and women often conceptualize the relationship differently. Women tend to see the **self-in-relationship,** with everyone affecting everyone else. One's self is formed and enacted in various relationships. Men are more likely to see the self as independent, not as connected to specific relationships. For effective conflict management, we must have both separate voices and a view that we are connected. When we see the self-in-relationship as a theoretical starting point, it allows us to concentrate on the following dimensions of conflict:

- Interdependence rather than power over others.
- Mutual empathy as the basis for understanding and communicating.
- Relational self-confidence instead of separate self-esteem (autonomy).
- Constructive conflict instead of domination.
- Staying engaged with others while in conflict.
- Valuing separate knowing and connected knowing.
- Utilizing both report talk and rapport talk.
- Continuing dialogue when there is disagreement.

New models of constructive conflict are being built on the ideas of partnership and self-in-relationship (Tannen 1990; Young-Eisendrath 1993; Belenky et al. 1986; Jordan et al. 1991; Goodrich 1991; Brown and Gilligan 1992; Jordan 1992; Wilmot 1995; Gottman 1999). These ideas underlie the development of constructive conflict practices as it has been presented in all the editions of this book. The constructive practices will be developed more in depth in subsequent chapters.

The filters based on gender have two effects on our understanding of conflict. First, many of the studies trying to pinpoint conflict behaviors are based on differences as perceived by the respondents of surveys. For example, most of the studies that find male-female differences in conflict choices ask college students to answer "in general" rather than for a particular conflict. College students have a stereotyped belief that there are gender differences, and as a result, they report "behavior" differences when they may not be present. They may also answer according to how they would like to see themselves, or how most women and men their age see themselves. Their filters for seeing self and other influence the studies looking for behavior differences in women and men.

Gender filters also affect our understanding of conflict because our filters may affect our behaviors. When feeling powerless, males tend to "state their position and offer logical reasons to support it." Women's approaches depend on the gender of their opponents

(Watson 1994). As another researcher put it, "Men may use a more independent criterion for managing conflict and women a more interdependent one" (Miller 1991, 28). Women will choose responses based on interpersonal obligations, and men based on the offended person's rights. As a result of their focus on relationships, females in conflict seem to exhibit fewer self-presentational actions (Haferkamp 1991–92). In preschool children ages three to five, for example, Sheldon (1992) notes that young girls' expressions of self-interest are often meshed with "an expression of communal interests." Research also indicates that women in lesbian relationships may benefit from both being female in that they have "more optimism about conflict resolution" (Metz, Rosser, and Strapko 1994, 305). The filters we use, based on gender, affect how we enact conflict behaviors.

Cultural Effects and Cultural Filters

Who knows but one culture, knows no culture.
—Augsburger, *Conflict Mediation Across Cultures: Pathways and Patterns*

Cultural Effects

Application 2.10   Your Cultural History

The United States is culturally diverse. Think about your own cultural history and roots, whether you and your family have been in the United States for generations or whether you are recent immigrants. To gain a sense of how pervasive cultural differences are, think about the neighborhood in which you spent part of your childhood, your fourth-grade classroom, your experience making a geographical move, or your experience getting to know friends or new family members from a different cultural background from your own. Share the results of your reflections with someone from a different culture or geographical background in your class.

Each of us experiences cultural diversity at some level. About 150 different languages are spoken in the United States. The southern part of the United States becomes more influenced by Hispanic cultures each year. U.S. culture is becoming less of a Western European offshoot in many ways, making the recognition of **cultural effects** essential. Changes in the workplace demand that we become sensitive to different ways to process conflict. "Consider the increasing diversity, for instance. The often quoted Hudson Institute Report on Workforce 2000 predicts that 85 percent of those entering the workforce in this decade will be women, minorities and immigrants" (Yarbrough and Wilmot 1995, 4). Augsburger (1992) states:

> What comprises a conflict in one culture is a daily difference of opinion in another. A serious insult in one setting—crossing one's legs or showing the sole of one's foot, for example—is a matter of comfort in another. An arrogant challenge in one culture—putting one's hands on one's hips—is a sign of openness in another. A normal pathway for de-escalating a conflict in one society—fleeing the scene of an accident—constitutes a serious

offense in another. Human boundaries are cultural creations—social boundaries, legal boundaries, and emotional boundaries are all drawn according to each culture's values, myths, and preferences. (23)

Cultural Effects Depend on Many Factors

Conflict behavior is not easily predicted by country of origin. In general two kinds of cultures exist: **individualistic** and **collectivistic.** See Gudykunst and Yun Kim (2002), for an overview of intercultural communication. As these authors explain, communicating across cultures is a kind of intergroup communication. One of the problems we encounter is that communicating with "strangers" (their term for persons from other cultural groups than one's own) becomes more and more the norm as our worldwide communication becomes more rapid and frequent. Those of us in the largely Western, individualistic cultures must come to an understanding about the values and expectations of those in collectivistic cultures. For instance, prevention of serious conflict is much more likely to occur in Japan and China (collectivistic cultures) than in individualistic cultures (Moran et al 1994). But each culture uses a very wide variety of ways of conflict. These ways are taught from childhood to persons in the culture, so that they become the expectations for how conflict is conducted (Tinsley 2001). Yet, these cultures—for instance, Nigeria (a non-Asian collectivist culture) and Canada (an individualistic society)—do not teach their members to take neatly predictable, opposite approaches (Gire and Carment 1993).

Westerners now understand that in many Asian cultures, self-expression is frowned upon if it does not further the needs of the group. In the West, in general, autonomy and self-expression are regarded more highly. Therefore, for Westerners to assume that individual expression is of higher value than harmony in the larger group is to remain in a Western, **ethnocentric** mode. Culturally, it may be for Westerners that harmony is achieved by explicit expression of individual emotion. Avoidance, which is prized in some other cultures, may escalate conflict in the United States.

The United States, generally, is an individualistic culture. A person is supposed to say what he or she means and resolve disagreements through the use of power (as in competition) or by working things out together (collaboration) (Wilson 1992). In this type of culture, things are discussed and spelled out, rather than supported by culturally defined, subtle nuances of interaction. This approach to resolving differences and communicating relies on assertiveness, relatively equal power, and freedom from fear of reprisal. Since these attributes are seldom present, however, U.S. culture rewards actions that are, for some people in the culture, stressful or even impossible. For example, Barnlund notes, "One of the most frequent shocks experienced by Japanese in coming to America is the resilience of friendships in the face of such strong clashes of opinion: Friends are able to confront each other, to vigorously argue contradictory views and to continue to be close friends in spite of their differences" (1989, 157). In situations in which people enjoy approximately equal power and understand the rules of interaction easily and well, the ideal of clarity and expressiveness works well. But when there is not a common base of assumptions, one's assertiveness can backfire.

In less individualistic, more collective cultures, discrepancies abound between what is meant and what is actually said. Disagreements are resolved through avoidance or accommodation, resulting in considerable face saving (discussed at length in chapter 3).

Table 2.1   Characteristics of Conflict in Two Types of Cultures

Key Questions	Individualistic Cultures	Collectivistic Cultures
Why?	Analytic, linear logic	Synthetic, spiral logic
	Instrumental-oriented	Expressive-oriented
	Dichotomy between conflict and conflict parties	Integration of conflict and conflict parties
When?	Individual-oriented	Group-oriented
	Low-collective normative expectations	High-collective normative expectations
	Violations of individual expectations create conflict potentials	Violations of collective expectations create conflict potentials
What?	Revealment	Concealment
	Direct, confrontational attitude	Indirect, nonconfrontational attitude
How?	Action and solution-oriented	Face- and relationship-oriented
	Explicit communication codes	Implicit communication codes
	Line-logic styles	Point-logic style
	Rational, factual rhetoric	Intuitive, affective rhetoric
	Open, direct strategies	Ambiguous, indirect strategies

Source: Reprinted, by permission of the publishers, from W. Gudykunst and S. Ting-Toomey, *Culture and Interpersonal Communication* (Beverly Hills, CA: Sage, 1988), 158.

Nuances of communication take on major importance, along with expected ways of behaving and working out problems. People do not confront others assertively and directly; to do so is considered rude and ignorant. In collectivistic cultures, members rely heavily on inferred meaning, whereas in individualistic cultures, members strive for an understanding of the literal meaning (Borisoff and Victor 1989, 141). Communication researchers have provided a clear summary of some of the differences between individualistic and collectivistic cultures. Table 2.1 portrays the differences in communicative strategies—direct and open compared to ambiguous and indirect. No wonder cross-cultural communication is getting more and more attention; we certainly need all the help we can get!

Similarly, Triandis (1980) notes some of the salient differences between the two orientations. In individualistic cultures

many individuals are high in internal control, who emphasize private goals, who pay attention to what the person does rather than who the person is . . . and where one finds more alienated and rootless individuals, where people think that decisions made by individuals are better than decisions made by groups . . . where going one's way and not paying attention to the view of others is acceptable, where personal enjoyment is emphasized, where friendship is a matter of personal choice. (65)

However, in collectivistic countries

there is an assumption that maintaining a strong group is the best guarantee of individual freedom, there is a strong emphasis on doing what the in-group specifies . . . shame and loss of face are mechanisms of social control, there is sometimes the tyranny of the group, interpersonal relations are an end in themselves, there are narrow in-groups, there is a concept of limited good, there are more people under external control or motivation, people tend to think that planning is a waste of time, goals tend to be group rather than individual goals, who does something is more important than what she/he does. (66)

Some of the specific differences in styles will be explored in more depth in chapter 5, "Styles and Tactics."

We live in a cobweb of relationships. When you die you are finally free of this cobweb of relationships—which you leave to your children to carry on.
—Hiroko Takada, from Japan

In addition to bridging the gaps between cultures, we need much more exploration of cultural diversity within the United States. For example, many cultural groups share some of the features of mainstream U.S. culture yet are distinct in ways that make conflict management and mediation of their disputes challenging to someone from the dominant culture. Buitrago (1997) outlines some of the key features of Hispanic cultures that require careful consideration, and we need detailed exploration of many other cultural groups as well, ranging from Native American to African American cultures.

Whatever set of assumptions you choose to use, each framework places boundaries on constructive conflict management. Sometimes effective management requires people to be clear, direct, and assertive. Yet, at other times, deferring until the time is right, focusing primarily on the relationship components, and thinking of indirect ways to manage the dispute are the best approaches. To solve the most difficult problems, we cannot rely solely on the teachings of one culture. One major problem encountered in individualistic cultures is that we receive little training in the search for commonly acceptable solutions. If three people want different things, often the problem is resolved by competing to see who is the strongest ("We'll play it my way or not at all!"), or a person has to have enough power to persuade others to go along with a search for a collaborative solution. Therefore, many potentially collaborative ideas generated by low-power people are dismissed as unimportant.

In the United States, even in communication studies departments, students are often taught that directness, ease in public, clarity of expression, assertiveness, and the ability to argue well are prerequisites to participation in conflict management. Indeed, in many contexts these skills are essential. However, for people who hold low-power positions in society, this is a very difficult set of skills to be learned. To correct this imbalance, we need to focus also on *indirect* communication skills for people in high-power positions. Both high- and low-power people contribute to the tangles that occur in personal conflict, and both must participate in better conflict management. Finally, cultural considerations include nonverbal communication; concepts of time (such as lateness or promptness); place of meetings or talks; whether content, relationship, identity, and process issues can be separated or not; and face saving (Borisoff and Victor 1989). As you begin to pay attention to the structure of conflict interactions, include these cultural and power issues in your analysis. Conflicts usually are not at all simple. If someone opens a conflict interaction by saying, "It's simple. We just have to do what makes sense . . . ," you can be sure that, if the conflict is ongoing or has raised a lot of emotion, the solution is not simple at all.

Cultural Filters

As you would expect, your filters based on your culture influence how you interpret others. If you come from an individualistic culture, and have a friend from Asia who rarely speaks, in public agrees with everything everyone says, and never has an overt struggle with someone else, you might see that person as having "no backbone." Or, conversely, if you come from a culture that prizes indirectness, to hear someone argue with a parent is almost offensive. Such a person seems rude and insensitive to you. Each **cultural filter** influences our perceptions of others' behavior, and therefore is a key to attributions we make.

If we want to make more accurate attributions and meaning of others' behavior, we need to translate, interpret, and become fluent in several "conflict dialects." For instance, if you find it difficult to express hostility, then when your new friend begins to rage at the cashier, you will have difficulty dealing with it. For you he is "off the scale," yet for him he is "letting them know how to treat customers."

While this book cannot cover all facets of cross-cultural communication, some working acquaintance with your own filters absorbed through your cultural background will allow you to have more conflict management options. Without such an awareness, one remains ethnocentric and trapped within the assumptions of one's own culture and biased against people from other groups with different assumptions about behavior (Ruhly 1976).

~Summary

Conflict is an important area of study because we all face it as we move through our interpersonal, family, and work lives. Your personal history, such as your family of origin and other influences, makes a difference in how you respond to conflict. Perceptions about conflict, whether it is an activity to be avoided or sought out and whether it is a negative or positive activity, develop over one's lifetime. In this process, refined images or metaphors develop in one's imagination and language that give shape and meaning to conflict episodes. The lens model of conflict provides a framework for viewing how both gender and culture (1) shape behaviors and (2) influence perceptions of others' communicative behavior. Gender often plays a key role in the behaviors one chooses in conflict, and also influences how one sees others. Finally, one's culture (such as being individualistic or collectivistic) affects one's behaviors and one's perceptions of others in a conflict.

~Key Terms

Use the text's Online Learning Center at **www.mhhe.com/wilmot7** to further your understanding of the following terminology.

personal history 29
avoidant family 30
collaborative family 30
aggressive family 30

negative views of conflict 34
positive approaches to conflict 37
conflict metaphors 39

neutral or objective metaphors 44
transformative metaphors 45
lens model of conflict 49

～Review Questions

Go to the self-quizzes on the Online Learning Center at **www.mhhe.com/wilmot7**
to test your knowledge of the chapter concepts.

1. What is your own personal history with conflicts?
2. Is your family avoidant, collaborative, or aggressive?
3. Has your family approach to conflict changed?
4. What are some negative views of conflict?
5. Describe some positive views of conflict.
6. What do conflict metaphors tell us?
7. What are some examples of win-lose metaphors?
8. What are some neutral or objective metaphors?
9. Can you come up with a new transformative metaphor?
10. Chart the elements of the lens model of conflict.
11. What are some persistent gender effects?
12. What does it mean to say there are gender and cultural filters?
13. How does your culture affect how you view and do conflict?

Chapter 3

Interests and Goals

> ## "Winning or Losing?"
>
> An American father and his 12-year-old son were enjoying a beautiful Saturday in Hyde Park, London, playing catch with a Frisbee. Few in England had seen a Frisbee at that time, and a small group of strollers gathered to watch this strange sport. Finally, one homburg-clad Britisher came over to the father: "Sorry to bother you. Been watching you for a quarter of an hour. Who's winning?" (Fisher and Ury 1981, 154).

Our interests and goals are sometimes hard to identify. Not only do outsiders usually misperceive our interests, we are often confused about them ourselves. This chapter describes the types of interests we struggle over with others. We treat "interests" and "goals" as different terms for the same things—what we want from others.

All conflicts at some level hinge upon the fact that people perceive that there are *incompatible goals* held by at least two people who are *interfering* with what the other person wants. Whether a sister and her older brother are struggling over limited parental attention, two managers are competing for a coveted promotion in the organization, or a seller and buyer are arguing over the price of a car, the perception of incompatible goals fuels the conflict. In every conflict the interdependence of the parties is built on both common and disparate goals, but the parties often perceive only the disparate goals. Conflict intensifies as people think they want different things; often the dawning awareness of conflict's existence comes when people say to each other, "What you want is not what I want." Conflict is more than a disagreement; it is when people believe that another interferes with their interests and goals.

Our goals are different in diverse relationships. In a friendship, for example, your main goal might be affinity—wanting the other to like you (Bell and Daly 1984). On the job, you may primarily want to gain information from colleagues or to persuade them about something. Our goals range from obtaining money, goods, services, love, or status to getting information. In a conversation, your primary goal might be to express your feelings (Argyle and Furnham 1983). Coleman, Fine, Ganong, Downs, and Pauk (2001) found that the majority of conflicts in stepfamilies involved resources (e.g., possessions, space, time, attention, privacy, money), divided loyalty, perceptions that the parents were showing favor to their "own" children, and conflicts with members of the extended family.

Many times, especially in emotionally charged conflict situations, we may be unaware of what goals we want to achieve. If you are angry at your roommate, you might not know whether (1) you want to punish her for being sloppy; (2) you want to have her like you, but you still want to influence her cleanliness standards; or (3) you want her to get angry and move out, so you can get a new roommate. Most conflict participants initially lack goal clarity; participants only discover their goals through experiencing conflict with the other participants. As we will see later, the goals will probably shift during the course of the conflict. What you want to achieve in the conflict also affects the tactics you choose during the conflict. For example, if you are "defending yourself," you are likely to use self-oriented tactics—being competitive and looking out only for yourself. On the other hand, if you want to improve a relationship, you are more likely to use conflict moves that are integrative—taking account of the others' needs as well as your own (Canary, Cunningham, and Cody 1988). One fact emerges from studying goals in personal and organizational settings—effectively functioning teams have a clear understanding of their objectives. The more clearly individuals or groups understand the nature of the problem and what they want to have occur, the more effective they will be in solving problems (Larson and LaFasto 1989; Hilgerman 1994).

Types of Goals: TRIP

People in conflict pursue four general **types of goals:** (1) *topic* or *content* (2) *relational*, (3) *identity* (or *facework*), and (4) *process*. The acronym TRIP stands for these major types of goals, which overlap and shift during disputes. These types of goals will be examined one at a time (Wilmot and Andes 2004).[1]

The Four Types of Goals Pursued During Conflict

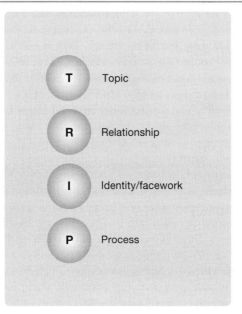

[1] In earlier editions of this book, we used "content" following the influence of Watzlawick, Beavin, and Jackson (1967). We have found, following the work of Wilmot and Andes (2004) that the TRIP acronym is much easier for students to recall; thus, we have changed the label "content" to "topic." Throughout this book, "content" and "topic" are used interchangeably.

Topic Goals: *What* Do We Want?

The key question when looking at a conflict is "What does each person want?" **Topic,** or content, **goals** emerge as different ideas about what to do, what decisions to make, where to go, how to allocate resources, or other externally objectifiable issues. Topic goals can be listed, argued, supported by evidence, and broken down into pros and cons. For example, Amanda might tell her supervisor, "I have been here six months, and I would like to have a raise." Other examples of topic goals are

securing a student loan	a clean apartment
more free time	meaningful work
a new pair of skis	fashionable clothing
space to work	a different job
a vacation overseas	reliable transportation
to sell a house for $80,000	a digital video recorder

In different contexts, the topics change. For example in the workplace here are some typical topics that emerge that cause disputes.

promotion	efficiency	getting to work on time
title	how hard you work	job assignments
accuracy	salary	new computer
office location		

In friendships, people might struggle over

loans from friends	what holiday plans to make
sharing a ride	how welcome friends are in a shared apartment
where to recreate	
what music to listen to	whether to share possessions
movies to see	

Application 3.1   My Topic or Content Goals

Select three different relationship contexts such as school, work, friendship, and romantic relationship.

1. For each relationship, list the "topics" that typically arise in disputes.
2. Compare the list of topics across the three relationships.

Most of us have topics that are distinct in each relationship type as well as some that cross all three categories. You might, for example, have cleanliness as an important topic regardless of the situation, or it might be restricted to only your living environment.

Topic goals can be easily seen and talked about; they are external to us—we can point to them and say, "I want that." Yet, although they are objective, people often feel very deeply about them.

Topic or content struggles are of two types: (1) people want different things (I want to get the most for my car, and you want to pay the least for it); or (2) people want the same thing (same job, same romantic partner, same room in the house). In either case, what happens is a struggle over the goals. The perception that there is not enough to go around—a perception of a scarce resource—intensifies the conflict. More examples of struggles over content goals follow:

- A divorcing couple tries to construct a visitation schedule that allows each parent access to their young children but that also fits with each parent's work schedule. The specific visitation schedule is the topic goal (at this point, separate goals) of the couple. Mom may state, "I want the kids on Sundays," or "I want to see them one night a week when they are at your house." Dad might say, "I want them on alternate weekends."

- A romantic couple talks about the pros and cons of either being together for the summer and both working in a restaurant, or one going to Glacier Park to be on trail crew and the other to work as a biologist in the River of No Return Wilderness Area. They want to spend the summer together, but both also want to advance their respective careers.

- Three mid-level managers must come to agreement about which benefits would motivate their employees to stay with the company the longest. Jill favors educational benefits, in addition to a basic benefits package, whereas Chuck favors increased insurance options, while Jim wants to increase flextime options. All three managers want to keep employees longer but disagree on how to do that.

- Mary is going to put her house up for sale because she will be moving to a different region. She asks $195,000 for the house, knowing that this price will pay for both her relocation and three months of living while she finds a new job. In addition to this amount of money, she wants to sell the house quickly—also a topic goal.

Usually, when you ask people what they want in a conflict, you will hear a topic goal from at least one of the parties—"I just want a different office." For most people, topic goals are the easiest to identify and tell others about. The topic, although important and the beginning point to understanding all disputes, is just one part of the conflict mosaic. Some writers refer to topic goals as "substantive" or "realistic" goals, but we believe the following kinds of goals are also real and substantive.

Relational Goals: *Who Are We* to Each Other?

The key question when assessing the **relational goals** of a conflict is "Who are we in relationship to each other during our interaction?" Relationship goals define how each party wants to be treated by the other and the amount of interdependence they desire (how they define themselves as a unit). Additionally, the amount of influence each will have with the other is worked out through relational interaction.

Differing relational goals lead people into conflict just as differing topics do. People often experience deep disagreement about the question of who they are to each other. The following statements, expressed during actual conflicts, are relational goal statements:

How You Want to Be Treated by the Other

What I need here is some respect.

So, what happened to our collegial relationship?

What I want is for you to support me when we are in public.

I won't put up with that kind of abuse.

Well, you don't have to be nasty about it.

I want to be included on projects that affect me.

I expect professional conduct from everyone on this team.

You told Sandra the report would be in by the due date. Then you called in sick and left me holding the job. This hurts my trust that you will do what you say.

I was hired at the same time Jim was, and now he's receiving extra training. I want access to training as well so I can grow in this job.

The Amount of Interdependence You Want (Are We a Unit?)

I thought we were best friends.

I can't help if I don't know if you want to stay on the project with me.

We both have our separate lives to live now, so let's get on with it.

What I do is none of your business.

I just don't know who we are to each other anymore.

Relational goals will emerge in any ongoing dispute and must be recognized and managed. For example, Donohue, Drake, and Roberto (1994) note that "the more mediators ignore disputants' relational concerns, the more difficulty they will experience in reaching agreement" (261). Yet, relational goals seldom become open, spoken messages (Wilmot 1995). Relationship definitions might instead be communicated by who talks first, who talks the most, nonverbal cues such as eye contact, and many other factors. For example, if an employee asks for a raise and is told no, the supervisor might be warning, on the relational level, "Don't push too far. I have the right to tell you what we can afford and what we cannot afford." If the employee says, "Why not? This is the best year we've ever had!" the relational message might be, from the employee's perspective, "I have a right to challenge what you say." Much of the communication regarding relational goals remains tacit and unspoken. Productive conflict interaction sometimes requires that a third party or a participant make overt the tacit relationship definitions. The following are some examples of relational goals:

- A second wife decides not to go to a big family gathering of her husband's relatives. She resents the expectation that since his family gathers at Labor Day every year, she is expected to attend. She prefers to visit with her family at that time of year. If the husband and wife have a conflict over this issue, the content goals may be fairly clear: the husband wants the wife to go to the gathering, whereas the wife wants to visit her family and not attend the big gathering. The wife's relational goals might be varied: to establish equity in the time she spends with her family, to establish her independence from the new family group, or to protect herself from comparison to the first wife. The husband's relational goals might be to please his family, to introduce his second wife to the family in a relaxed setting, or to spend more time with his wife. Each argues about how much influence they will allow the other to have, about what kind of a unit they are, and about many other relational issues. If the couple argues about content goals only, they will get stuck on issues about plane fares and what they can afford, or the weather in Georgia around Labor Day, or the accommodations provided. In ongoing relationships such as this one, the goals surrounding who the participants are to each other need to be given priority. Most people argue content when they ought to be talking about relational goals.

- In a staff meeting, Joan insists that "before we decide on the reorganization, I need to know how committed you all are to staying with the organization." She needs some clarity on how people define their relationship to the larger group before plunging ahead with an extensive reorganization plan.

- Two teenage girls currently are "on the outs" with each other. Jennifer talks about how JoAnn is "high and mighty," then JoAnn complains to another friend that Jennifer has "an abnormal need to be in on everything." The conflict erupted the day after JoAnn canceled her plan to go shopping with Jennifer and went with another friend instead. The content, whether to go shopping together, was not the issue; the relational strain was.

Relational goals *are at the heart of all conflict interactions* yet are difficult to specify from the outside (and sometimes from the inside as well). That is because each person translates the same event into his or her own relational meaning. A conflict is interpreted differently by each participant. Just as we have no success in translating Ukrainian unless we speak the language, conflict parties must learn the relational language of their conflict partners. For example, a father and daughter fight many evenings when she comes home from school and he arrives home from work. Mother gets pulled into playing peacemaker, trying to urge them to get along better. The following example demonstrates how an event can trigger such a conflict.

Daughter scatters books, shoes, and lunch box in the living room while she gets a snack. Father comes home an hour later, sees the mess, and explodes. Daughter says, "I forgot," and Father says, "You always forget."

Content messages: "I forgot." "You always forget."

Daughter's translation: It's not important. I wish he'd pay attention to something that is more important to me.

Father's translation: She doesn't listen. She is getting too independent to care what I think.

The difficulty with relational issues is that we never ultimately know the other person's translations. Just as the daughter and father have different translations for these events, usually the conflict parties cannot accurately guess what the other's translations will be, or if they can, they try to dismiss them. The friend who says "you shouldn't be bothered by not being invited to the picnic" is not accurately tuning into your translations. One technique in conflict management, therefore, is to have conflict parties *share their relational translations* of the content issues.

Other examples of incorrect or incomplete translations of each other's messages are illustrated by the following:

- A couple argues over who should fill the car with gas each week—each feels she or he is doing more work than the other and wants credit for what is already being done. But the man argues that he shouldn't have to do all the work on the car, and the woman argues that he doesn't notice now much work she does for him, such as taking clothes to the cleaners. Not only are they arguing about content, but they are mistranslating the crucial relational goals (which remain unstated).

- Co-workers bicker each day about whose turn it is to lock up the business, which requires staying longer at the end of the day. None of the procedures developed seem to work—people have doctor's appointments, or have to pick up a child, or have a racquetball court reserved, so they have to leave early. This conflict is becoming a big issue. So far, the only way people resolve the issue is by coming up with creative excuses for leaving work. Resentments grow daily, factions are created, and pretty soon, the boss will have to step in and make a new rule, which will displease everyone. No new procedure (content solution) will work until leftover resentments are explained and attended to (relational issues). Then new, shared goals can be developed that have a chance of finally working.

Relational goals are often reactive. What I want from you is the result of what I think you think about me. Once a conflict is triggered, each party reacts to what he or she thinks the other is doing or wanting. When Sandy says, "I won't take that kind of treatment from Jason," she is reacting to her guess about how Jason will act in the future, too. Once the conflict spiral begins, each person responds to an image of the other that may not be accurate. When Jason replies, "You are just trying to control me," he states his relational reaction to Sandy. In this manner, relational goals escalate into polarized states.

Application 3.2   My Relational Goals

Take two important relationships to you, for example, a parent, romantic partner, life-long friend, or other personal relationship. Think of a time you were upset at how he or she treated you. Then, list the "relational issues" that arose. For example, look at the samples of relational issues and amount of interdependence examples we gave above and see if you can identify your key relational issues.

Let's summarize some principles about relational interests and goals.

- Every statement carries a relational message.
- We each translate or interpret relational messages differently.
- Relational interests carry more urgency than topic interests.
- Our relational interests are triggered in reaction to the other's behavior.

Good relationships make the topic issues much easier to resolve, bring synergy to a conversation and enhance our positive identity.

Identity, or Face-Saving, Goals: *Who Am I* in This Interaction?

The key question in assessing **identity,** or **face-saving, goals** is "Who am I in this particular interaction?" or "How may my self-identity be protected or repaired in this particular conflict?" As conflicts increase in intensity, the parties shift to face saving as a key goal (Rubin 1996). Face saving, or identity protection, occurs throughout the conflict but will be highlighted more at certain times than at others.

In addition to content and relational goals, interaction goals include specific desires to maintain one's sense of self-identity. Identity needs have been extensively discussed as face work or saving face (Folger, Poole, and Stutman 2004; Wilson 1992; Goffman 1967; Brown and Levinson 1978). Often people will say, with frustration, "What are we fighting about?" or "I don't know what is going on!" Many times, a puzzling or maddening interaction can make sense if one analyzes whether one or more of the parties is primarily trying to present a positive face by claiming one's need to be approved of, to be included, and to be respected (Lim and Bowers 1991). When face saving becomes an issue, people are less flexible and engage in destructive moves (Folger, Poole, and Stutman 2004). According to Brown (1977), "In some instances, protecting against loss of face becomes so central an issue that it swamps the importance of the tangible issues at stake and generates intense conflicts that can impede progress toward agreement and increase substantially the costs of conflict resolution" (175).

Many times we express our identity or face-saving goals openly. The athlete who says, "I don't use drugs because I'm not that kind of person" or a friend who says to you, "I'm really good with verbal retorts" is telling you about their preferred identity. Or the teenager who says, "I don't have premarital sex because it violates my beliefs" is giving a clear identity statement. Simply listing the answers to "who am I" will be a good start for identifying your identity. These identity statements often arise when people are talking about themselves.

competent	likeable	responsible	trustworthy
best friend	logical	enthusiastic	well-organized
reliable family member	friendly	expert	leader

Another way to find your identity concerns is the exercise in Application 3.3.

Application 3.3   My Criticism Log

Keep track of all the negative thoughts you have about people in your world over a few days and jot them down in your notebook or diary. You don't need to track the type of relationship, who the other is, or anything else—just list the negative thoughts you have or comments you make. Some examples are "he is so stupid," "I can't believe how incompetent she is," "he is so mean to everyone," and "she is just power hungry."

1. List all these criticisms of others, then in groups of three or four, just read them aloud to others (don't worry about how you sound; just say them even though they are sometimes difficult to share).

2. Members of your group help you identify your two or three main "themes" for your criticisms of others. Most of us have two or three main identity dimensions that arise in criticisms of others. Put these "themes" in nonjudgmental or positive terms.

   For example, medical doctors often say things about their colleagues such as "he isn't the sharpest knife in the drawer," "she didn't do very well in medical school," "I just don't know how he became a doctor given his inability to process all the details," and "he isn't very bright." The theme of "intelligence" is clear.

3. Discuss with the group your main identity "themes" and how they predict with whom you will have conflict or struggles.

The importance of identity, or saving face, can be seen when large corporations or individuals are sued in court. In some circumstances, they can enter an "Alford Plea," which means "we don't admit guilt, but based on the evidence presented we think we would be convicted." Thus, we read news reports of organizations saying, "we didn't do it, and we paid the plaintiff $15,000,000." On one hand this seems absurd, but on the other it helps sensitize us to the importance of saving face. The issue is no longer "did I break the law," but "how can I protect how I see myself and others see me?"

In each conflict interaction, individuals either save face or lose or damage face. Self-esteem has been discussed as a scarce resource. This is another way of saying that people's sense of self is often tenuous, not fixed. Few people are so full of self-esteem that they do not care about looking good in conflicts, or being seen as intelligent, honorable, correct, or justified. Likewise, when your opponent begins to perceive that you are damaging his or her sense of self, the stakes get higher. Face work occurs for each party throughout the conflict (see figure 3.1). In face-saving conversations, people often give accounts of what has happened, or what the interaction meant, as a way to "repair" one's identity after a personal attack (Buttny 2000).

Since people often act out of self-interest, what normally happens as a dispute progresses is that people protect their own face, or identity, while damaging the other's face, or identity. Productive conflict management demands that we attend to neglected quadrants. One study analyzed communication in three cases of hostage negotiations. The cases involved three different people: (1) an armed, suicidal man barricaded inside a TV station; (2) a man suffering extreme emotional instability who was barricaded in a house; and (3) an armed man holding his children hostage. What

Figure 3.1   Dimensions of Saving and Damaging Face

emerged in the taped FBI transcripts was the necessity to let the men save face while working to get the hostages released. The outside negotiators had to restore the armed men's face, by saying such things as "I think you are an extremely strong person for how you have handled this so far," "You've got a whole lot of people who care about you," and "The people you are trying to help, they need you" (Rogan and Hammer 1994). Sometimes face is saved ahead of time, and other times it is restored after there has been some loss, like in the hostage situation.

Figure 3.1 also shows how someone can damage one's own face. Though it seems unlikely, people often say negative things about themselves. When you say, "I'm just a terrible parent," or "I'm a lousy student," or "What does someone my age think he/she is doing going back to school?" those statements are damaging to one's own face, or identity. In the hostage situation, the armed men were, in effect, saying, "I'm just crazy," and the job of the outside negotiators was to get the men to start to see their own behavior as not quite so damaging to their view of themselves. Once face is restored, one is more free to give up extreme defensive tactics, such as holding hostages.

People try to avoid loss of face by defending their self-images against humiliation, embarrassment, exclusion, demeaning communication, or general treatment as unimportant or low-power individuals. Attempts to solve a problem or stop a conflict by causing another person to lose a sense of dignity and worth never work in the long run. Remember the four horsemen discussed in chapter 1, and how many destructive conflict cycles result from this kind of destructive communication. Overuse of power may temporarily solve a problem. When losers are created, however, the losing group or individual waits for a time and place to "make it right," either by getting back at the winners, by subverting the ongoing process, or by leaving the relationship, work setting, or group. Demeaning communication creates ongoing pain and dissatisfaction, and the conflict remains unresolved at a deep level.

Face saving and giving others face are extremely important in all cultures but often take precedence over topic issues in Asian cultures. It is now well known in the business community that entirely different kinds of negotiations are required in Asian cultures. Attempting to give others face and avoiding at all costs the loss of face of the other are part of the requirements of polite interaction among many Pacific Rim cultures. One would never pin an opponent down or attempt to prove him or her wrong.

The box labeled "Going Public," from a newspaper column about mediation in different types of disputes, briefly treats the necessity of saving face, even in Western cultures.

Going Public: Like Dirty Laundry, Gripes Are Best Aired in Private

"ASK A MEDIATOR"

by William Wilmot, PhD, and Roy Andes, MA, JD

Reader: I'm an employee of a business that's falling apart. We have a high profile in the community and could easily pressure the management by going public with our complaints. Should we?

Mediators: We are a society addicted to two values at odds with one another: privacy and public disclosure. Nowhere more than in conflicts do those values collide. Although the public likes to know what's going on, and the press likes the pizzazz of conflict, people whose relational dirty laundry gets hung out in public suddenly become more positional, more intransigent and more likely to use lawsuits and other formal or hostile procedures.

Why? The answer is privacy and face saving. We all want people to feel good about us, to like us, and to give us strokes. We feel that if we are completely open about our dilemmas and conflicts people are less likely to give us the things we want. How many of us tone down, postpone or even entirely avoid family arguments in public? How many of us in conflicts with friends or co-workers prefer to talk "privately" rather than in the presence of strangers? ALL of us, of course, do so. It's only natural. It's just as true for public officials and corporate executives as for the rest of us. People want privacy when they have to confront strong feelings and disagreements.

Destroying that privacy is as much an escalation of a conflict as throwing a bomb into the room. In response to such a "bomb," most people respond aggressively. They are certainly less likely to be cooperative, and less willing to try to work collaboratively to help you get what you want and need.

If you want to solve problems rather than preach about them, do it in private. If you want sincerity and openness, privacy is the best way to go. This is why mediators provide absolute confidentiality of mediation discussions. It's also why good negotiations take place out of the glare of press attention. Collaboration and problem-solving take mutual commitment, safety, patience, and thoughtfulness. None of those virtues emerge in a 30-second sound bite.

You can tell that attempts to save face are being employed when you or others engage in the following kinds of communication (adapted from Folger, Poole, and Stutman 1993):

1. *Claim unjust intimidation.* Topic goals take second place to this specific kind of relational goal—to stand up to another's attempt to take over. People accuse

others of taking advantage, declare their resistance to unjust treatment, and often seek support from outside parties when they are being treated unjustly.

2.   *Refuse to step back from a position.* A person who no longer feels comfortable with an earlier position may choose to stay with it, even in light of new information, because looking foolish or inconsistent results in losing face. Thus, topic and larger relational goals are set aside to avoid looking weak, ill informed, or incompetent. In a community in a Western mountain state, water rights became a major conflict for a group of summer home owners in the mountains. A city tried to claim water rights to a small creek that flowed through the home owners' property. One man resisted the efforts of a majority to build a legal defense fund because he had said at a meeting, "I'm not going to pay some lawyer to fritter away my money on something we can't stop anyway!" As several summers wore on, this embattled individual refused to step back from his position of "no money to lawyers" and "we can't make any difference anyway." He wrote letters to others in the home owners' group, bitterly protesting the intimidation of the majority group in assessing a fee for each home owner to build the legal fund. Clearly, as new information came in strongly supporting the efforts to fight the city's water claim, as when the district court judge supported the summer-home group, the man who was fighting to avoid losing face found himself in a dilemma—to fight further might be to lose face even more. Eventually, he pretended he had supported the legal efforts all along but just thought the fees were too high. This was a face-regaining effort, and the home owners' group wisely dropped the issue so the man could be part of the community again. For him, the content and relational goals had become temporarily unimportant.

3.   *Suppress conflict issues.* People also try to save face by refusing to admit that a conflict exists, since to acknowledge the conflict might mean that events are out of control, which might make people feel uncomfortable and incompetent. In the water rights conflict discussed previously, several longtime friends of the dissident home owner said things like, "Well, Kent is just cantankerous. He'll get over it," or "Well, these things bring up strong feelings." The association had few effective means of conflict resolution. Many felt that to acknowledge conflict at all would mean that their group was in danger of losing a sense of camaraderie and community spirit. One board member tried to schedule a meeting that the dissident individual could not attend because of his travel schedule—an attempt to suppress or avoid the issue of face, or identity, needs.

In productive, ongoing relationships, several kinds of communication will help people restore their lost face or prevent further loss of face. You can increase flexibility and problem solving if you

1.   *Help others increase their sense of self-esteem.* Treat others with goodwill, giving them the benefit of the doubt even when they have been belligerent or unproductive. You might say things like "Everyone gets upset sometimes. We can get past this," or "You must not have had all the information I had. You couldn't have known about the Grandview project yet, as I did." Even saying something

like "I know you were doing what you thought was best" gives the other person the benefit of the doubt and is usually true. People do tend to do what they think is best at the time.

2. *Avoid giving directives.* Parents can tell their teenage children, "I want you to honor the house rules we've discussed. I want to be able to trust you and not worry about monitoring you—you're almost grown and can make decisions for yourself." This approach is much better than "If you don't follow the rules we've set up you can find somewhere else to live!" As will be discussed later, it's better to avoid direct threats and to use persuasion and face-saving communication instead. No one wants to be pushed around. Even if you have "right on your side," it may not always be wise to be "right," as this creates winners and losers.

3. *Listen carefully to others and take their concerns into account.* Even when you don't have to listen because you have the power to make a decision independently, listening and taking care of others' concerns as best you can helps them feel included, approved of, and respected.

4. *Ask questions so the other person can examine his or her goals.* By asking questions instead of attacking, you give the other person a chance to change in the interaction instead of entrenching or digging in (note the warlike metaphor).

In conclusion, helping others protect their self-identity as a good, worthy and competent human being goes far toward helping resolve conflict by allowing people to focus on other goals than self-protection.

Process Goals: *What Communication Process* Will Be Used?

The key question when assessing **process goals** is "What communication process would work best for this conflict?" Many times people disagree about how to formally or informally conduct a conflict. A group might argue over the merits of consensus versus voting. Intimates often disagree about whether strong emotions hurt the process of conflict or not, or whether the partners should stay up and talk when one is sleepy or wait until morning. Work groups go back and forth about whether to send out opinion questionnaires, talk informally in a series of meetings, delegate certain decisions, or put off deciding certain issues. All these relate to the process of conflict interaction and will impact content, identity, and relational goals.

Some examples of process goals are

giving each one equal talk time	talking informally before deciding	not allowing the children to speak
consensus	having high-power person decide	voting
decisions made by subgroup	secret ballot	

Different processes of communication may change the relationships involved. For instance, minorities may be given more power with a free flow of communication, whereas higher-power people might maintain their power with a more tightly organized form of interaction, such as one that relies heavily on written communication. One of the current trends in the workplace is that people want more processes that enhance equality and open participation. People struggle in organizations and small groups over the pros and cons of consensus, informal discussion, information gathering, delegated decisions, written summaries, voting, and parliamentary procedure. Women, more so than men, are more comfortable soliciting everyone's opinion (Brown and Gilligan 1992). Process goals also vary in different cultures, with some being quite authority oriented and others relying on equal participation. In Native American tribal politics, a long process of consensus building is often required before a decision is considered valid by the tribe. The tribal members delegate less to their elected officials than do Western European cultures.

In addition to changing the levels of influence, different processes encourage or discourage creative solutions. Quick, well-defined processes help you move forward but may decrease creative, innovative solutions. Longer, sometimes confusing processes that build in time for reflection and evaluation improve the chances for creativity. Thus, different processes affect the outcome of a conflict interaction as well. For instance, one couple began to struggle over when to buy a house. The wife wanted to buy a house in the next few months, whereas the husband wanted to save more money before they looked seriously. The husband suggested that they first discuss with each other their financial goals and then talk about the house. This discussion resulted in the wife's decision that she, too, wanted to wait at least a year so that they could better their financial situation. By changing from content issues, such as the interest rate, the availability of houses in the desired neighborhood, or the likely tax consequences, to a different process, such as talking about other goals, the couple changed the relational conflict ("I've got to get her/him to listen to me") to a mutually acceptable process.

Large public meetings are arenas for process conflict. In one conservation organization, the planning group struggled over whether to have a symposium of speakers presenting their ideas on biodiversity or whether to break the participants up into small groups to discuss different ideas and then bring questions back to the resource people. The executive group, anxious to present their organization's views on the importance of biological diversity, decided on a process they could control, the symposium of carefully chosen speakers. This led to a clear but noninvolving presentation.

Conflicts over process involve face-saving or face-giving goals as well. People who know they are in the minority often argue over correct parliamentary procedure, which provides more options for hearing from the minority than does, for instance, informal large-group discussion followed by voting. Often, process conflicts change as individuals are heard. People drop their obstruction to a certain process if they are assured of being heard and counted (face/identity issues) and when they see that their content and relational goals are being protected. As in struggles over differing content, relational, and identity goals, process conflicts blend into the other conflicting goals. Shifting from one level to another often helps parties avoid becoming stuck in an unproductive conflict.

❧The Overlapping Nature of TRIP Goals

Now that each type of goal has been explained and illustrated, we can deepen our analysis of goals in conflict. A number of features about conflict goals need to be highlighted.

Figure 3.2   Content Goals Paramount

Feature 1: Not all types of goals emerge in all disputes. Raging disputes go on in which no process, or procedural, issues emerge. In the workplace, for example, there may be a heated disagreement between two supervisors, yet neither wants to change any of the processes used, how frequently they meet, or who is included. Similarly, many examples of conflicts can be cited in which there are no content issues. Two friends may be locked in a struggle over how responsive they are to one another, a relational issue that doesn't involve content. It is often puzzling to parents how their children can fight for hours over "nothing"—no identifiable content issues. But rest assured, if there is a struggle and no content issues are apparent, the struggle is about something. The dispute rests on identity, process, and/or relational grounds.

Feature 2: Interests and goals overlap with one another and differ in primacy. When you begin a dispute over your grade (the topic goal), you also want to be treated well by the professor (the relational goal) and want to think that you tried hard (the identity, or face-saving, goal). Figure 3.2 demonstrates how this might look from your side.

As you can see, you begin a discussion with the professor with the topic issue paramount in your mind; the relational and identity issues are there but not as important to you. Note therefore that even though they differ in prominence, different goal types emerge. The professor, on the other hand, may be most concerned that she be seen as a fair and kind person, so a diagram of her goals at the beginning of the conversation might look like figure 3.3. She may be most concerned about relational issues, such as others seeing her as a fair person who treats students equally, and identity issues ("I'm doing this job the way it should be done; I like how I respond to student concerns"). Her primary goals, then, are relational and identity goals. The topic goal of the student's grade is much less significant, unless the student feels he or she is being treated unfairly.

A second example illustrates how a process or procedural goal might be utmost in one party's mind. You are a member of a departmental student group and would like to run for president. You were out of town last weekend, and this Tuesday in class someone said, "Hey, what do you think about Stan being president of the student club? We had an election last night." For you, the procedural issue of not being notified of a meeting when others knew you wanted to run for president is the paramount issue, as shown

Figure 3.3 Relational and Identity Goals Paramount

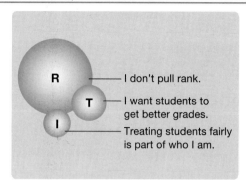

in figure 3.4. Note that in this case, the procedural issue looms largest, followed by identity and relational issues of equal weight.

The examples illustrate that for each party, the paramount interests probably differ from those of another person in the same situation. Notice that all of these examples included relational and identity goals because it is rare to have a conflict that does not involve identity and relational issues.

Feature 3: Identity and relational issues are the "drivers" of disputes; they underlie topic and process issues. As you listen to people describe conflicts, you begin to notice a pattern—at the core of the disputes are their concepts of who they are and how they want to be treated in relationships. In most business disputes, for example, regardless of the topic issue, someone is concerned about trust, treatment, or communication—relational issues. Further, the face saving discussed earlier is a key element in all disputes. Because we are human beings, our inherent subjectivity drives disputes. Think back to when you were not chosen to play as a kid or were excluded from some high school activity, and you may remember just how important relational and identity issues are. As discussed under Feature 1, relational and identity concerns will almost always overlap—*who you are* with others is related to *how* the relationship is conducted. Figure 3.5 illustrates which goals are almost always present and, in fact, drive almost all disputes.

Figure 3.4 Process Goals Paramount

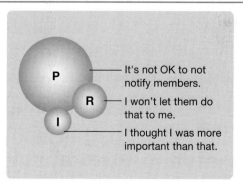

Figure 3.5   Relational and Identity Goals Propelling a Dispute

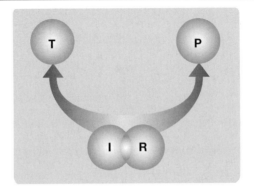

Note that the relational and identity issues are the subjective forces that propel the topic and process issues into focus. Even though the identity and relational issues are the most difficult to talk about, they are the most potent issues in conflicts. One interesting feature of how people operate, given that relational and identity issues are the foundations of all conflicts, is that sometimes identity and relational interests may be met indirectly. For example, it may not be common in your family to say, "I feel excluded," but rather, family members may watch others at the family picnic, see who is left alone, and seek them out for a talk. In an organization, it may not be within the cultural norms to say, "I don't feel very valued here," but the president may give you access to the boardroom for meetings if he or she guesses that you are feeling pushed aside. Similarly, watch little kids at play. One of the kids may be left out, and another may turn to that child and say, "Want to play dolls with me?" Such a move is both a relational and identity tactic. When Bill, one of the coauthors of this book, was 12 and not getting any time with his dad, he was hyperactive and on the verge of delinquency. An observant neighbor, Francis Cowger from Upton, Wyoming, noticed him, and offered him a summer job driving his tractor. Many relational and identity needs were filled for Bill on a John Deere tractor. If Francis had approached Bill's dad and said, "I think your kid needs some attention, but I know you are working 14 hours a day, so how about I give him a job on my ranch this summer?" Bill's dad would have been insulted. But the indirect offer to help, by giving Bill a job, avoided a conflict with the father and allowed Francis to give neighborly assistance. By being alert to the "relational translations" someone else might make, you can serve both relational and face-saving needs indirectly through content. Indirect, topic-only solutions do not work in intense conflict situations, however. The more severe and strained the conflict, the less satisfying the content approaches will be. This leads to the fourth feature of conflict goals:

Feature 4: In a serious dispute, topic-only solutions are rarely satisfying to conflict parties. If you know someone who has ever won a lawsuit, ask him or her, "How do you feel about the other party and the process you went through?" You probably will hear anger, frustration, and exasperation, with the person usually launching into a tirade about both the other party and the other party's attorney. That is because (unless it is a very unusual case) only topic issues have been addressed, and the needs to save face, to be listened to, and to be told that you aren't crazy have not been attended to. During the dispute there is often so much threat to each person's identity that content solutions alone are not satisfying. In this type of situation, if an outsider says, "You got $150,000; what more do you want?" the plaintiff will usually answer, "An apology."

Feature 5: Conflict parties often specialize in one kind of goal. Conflict parties in on-going struggles often highlight one type of goal and limit themselves to it, as in the following dialogues:

In the Family

Grandfather:	My daughter is just not a good mother to her kids—she needs to learn how to be a better mother. The kids need to be cleaner, and they are always late to school. Those kids need a better mom. (topic specialization)
His daughter:	[the mother of two small boys] I am just not willing to have the kids spend time at their grandparents' house until Dad learns how to treat people better. He only criticizes me and the kids and never says anything positive. (relational and identity specialization)

In the Organization

Faculty member:	This is a ridiculous place to work. I put in a lot of hours and no one notices. I'd just once like to get some credit for what I do here. (relational specialization)
Chair of department:	Dr. Samuels just doesn't do a very good job in the classroom. I can't support him for promotion until he begins to get higher marks from the students. I'll have to have some hard-hitting sessions with him outlining how a professional person does a job like his. (topic specialization, then a shift to relational specialization)

In these conflicts, the participants separate and specialize—one party on topic goals and the other on relational goals. This split tends to keep the conflict going—as the topic specialist continues to expect better "performance" from the other, the relational specialist becomes more and more critical of the treatment he or she receives.

Specialization in either topic or relational goals often reflects the parties' relative power. All too often, high-power parties are the ones who focus exclusively on topic. Failure to acknowledge relational goals may be due to a lack of skill or can show hostility, lack of caring, or even a desire to compete. Focusing only on topic devalues the other person and his or her concerns. The most powerful group member usually wins by structuring the conflict and ignoring troubling relational issues from lower-power people. Topic discussion is simpler and requires less investment in the other person. Similarly, lower-power members may wish to bring in goals other than topic goals as a power-balancing mechanism. If a lower-power person can get the higher-power person to agree that relational process, and identity goals, are important, the lower-power person is "empowered" and becomes a legitimate party in the conflict.

Feature 6: Goals may emerge in a different form. Sensitivity to the different types of goals allows you to recognize when one type of goal is being acted out in terms of another. Any one of the four can come to the surface in a different form. Topic goals emerge as relational, identity, or procedural goals. Relational goals can emerge as topic,

Figure 3.6 Relational Goals Emerging in Topic Form

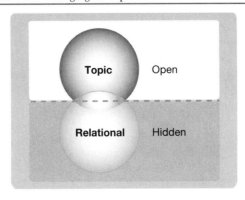

identity, or procedural goals, and so on—there are 12 possible substitutions. One of the most common is illustrated in figure 3.6: a relational goal carried by topic.

Many times conflict parties are simply unable to identify their relational goals. Instead, they act them out at the topic level. For example, you may feel devalued by your boss, so you wage an ongoing, persuasive campaign to change the performance evaluation system used by the organization. Or you think your brother does not respect you, so you argue that he doesn't have the training to handle your aging mom's finances. In "Stay for Dinner," notice the shift in goals.

"Stay for Dinner"

Connie, Sharon, and Janene, seniors at a university, share an old house near campus. They have known each other for years; they grew up in the same town. Their roommate relationship has, thus far, been fairly smooth, although recently an issue has emerged. Janene eats two meals a day on campus at the food service. Connie and Sharon like to cook, so they prepare their meals at home. They have invited Janene to share their evening meal several times, and Janene has occasionally accepted. It's Thursday night, Janene is rushing to get to the food service before it closes, and the following dialogue takes place:

Connie: Hey, Janene, you might as well stay and eat with us. It's late—you'll never make it.

Janene: No big deal. If I miss it, I'll get a hamburger or something. [She rushes out the door.]

Connie: [to Sharon] That's the last time I'm going to ask her to eat with us. She thinks she is too good to be bothered with staying around here with us.

A few weeks later, Connie and Sharon find someone who is willing to room with them, share cooking, and pay a higher rate. So they approach Janene and say, "We are struggling with finances, and we have someone who will eat here, share expenses, and save us all money on food. Would you rather pay a higher rate or move out?"

Figure 3.7   Identity Goals Emerging in Topic Form

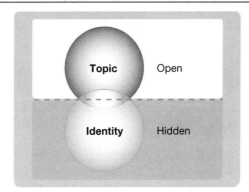

As you can see, this dispute began with two people feeling excluded and quickly degenerated into a topic-only conflict. Because relational issues were ignored, a long-time friendship was lost.

Identity conflicts, as well, often erupt on the topic level, as shown in figure 3.7.

"I'm right/Are not/Am too" is an example of an identity-driven dispute that gets played out on the topic level. Each person starts by wanting to feel right (identity, or face saving). Watch what quickly happens.

"I'm Right/Are Not/Am Too!"

Duane and Kathy are going to a movie. Duane is driving, and they both notice a red car passing them.

Duane: That's a Subaru, like the kind I was telling you about.

Kathy: No, I think it was a Toyota. But it's pretty.

Duane: No, it was a Subaru!

They argue back and forth about the rightness of their claims. Neither is a car expert, but both are adamant, using sarcasm and biting humor.

Kathy: Well, you may be right, but I still think it was a Toyota.

Duane: Look, I know I'm right!

Kathy: You never think I know anything!

Duane: You don't know anything about cars. Blow if off. It's not important.

Kathy sits silently for 10 minutes.

The couple will continue to argue about identifying cars, but both have stated relationship concerns. Kathy feels she is not given credit as a knowledgeable person. Duane states that he needs to be right on things he knows more about. The couple appear to be negotiating about who has preeminence in certain areas of expertise. They haven't worked out how to "call off the conflict" or how to ask for more respect from each other. They are likely to find other topics to fight over until the relationship is addressed directly. The following box presents two openings that might start them off more productively.

Duane: I get bothered when you challenge me about something I know a lot about. I start thinking you don't think I'm very smart.

or

Kathy: Duane, I'm not that interested in Toyotas, or Subarus either. But I've been thinking that you get the last word on most topics we discuss. It makes me want to never give in—even if I know I'm wrong.

✺Goals Change in Interaction

TRIP goals are like a lava lamp, glowing, changing, altering, and always moving.
—Leanne Eleff, 2001

Goals don't stay static but undergo transformation before, during, and after disputes. They will emerge as one type and, during the course of the dispute, flower into another type. Even after the struggle is over, goals will shift and change.

Take the case of Eleanor, a senior in a class. She felt the grade on her last essay was too low.

The Bad Grade	
Eleanor to her friend:	That instructor has it in for me. He continues to ignore me in class and on the last assignment, he really cheated me. I'm simply not going to put up with that any longer.
Eleanor thinking to herself as she waits to see the instructor:	Ok, when I go in there, I'm going to get him to apologize to me for causing me such grief. I want him to see just how much he has ruined my senior year.
Eleanor in the office:	Mr. Jones, I would like it if you would re-grade the first essay question. I don't think you understood what I was trying to write.
Mr. Jones:	Sure, glad to. I'll give it back to you on Tuesday after class.

Note how her goals changed. She began with bad treatment and being ignored (relational goals) and a content goal (being cheated) to a relational goal (I want him to apologize to me) to a pure content goal (reevaluate one question). Such change and flow are typical in conflict situations.

One way to look at this flow of goals is to specify how goals change across time from (1) prospective (before interaction with the person), to (2) transactive goals (during the interaction itself), to (3) retrospective (after the conflict is over). It is important to be able to track the changes in both your and the other person's goals—they continue to evolve over time.

Prospective Goals

The word *goals* most commonly connotes intentions people hold before they engage in conflict. For instance, Sally might say to Dorothy, "What do you hope to accomplish at the board meeting? The last one was awful—so much confusion and disorganization." Dorothy might reply, "I want to sort out who's in charge of the budget decisions and how we're supposed to come up with $5,000 more next year than we took in this year. I don't want to take responsibility for more fund-raising." Dorothy has stated her **prospective goals**—those she can identify before the board meeting begins. Simply stated, she hopes that the board will decide who makes budget decisions and delegate fund-raising to some responsible party. Most of the other board members will come to the meeting with their own prospective goals. An effectively managed meeting will take account of all the prospective goals members bring, whether they are readily stated or not.

Taking the time to clarify what you want from a particular interaction lays the groundwork for more effective conflict. The expectation of collaboration establishes a positive tone for the discussion.

When you clarify your prospective goals, you

- Gain clarity about what you want from a meeting.
- Prepare yourself for a discussion.
- Get a sense of "I can do this."

Of course, as we have the actual conversation with the person, we usually change in their presence like Eleanor did. During the discussion, your goals continue to shift and change during the transaction itself.

Transactive Goals

In many conflicts "goals are quite complex and ephemeral" (Sillars and Weisberg 1987), and they only become clear as the conflict unfolds. For example, during a struggle with your housemate over financial misunderstandings, you discover that what you really want is to move—which you did not know you felt until the argument began. You have just stumbled onto a **transactive goal**—one discovered during the conflict itself.

Transactive goal development takes place during conflict episodes rather than before or after. You may have been absolutely certain that you wanted an assistant to carry out the new project your boss assigned to you, but during a staff meeting you may change your demand for an assistant. You now say that you can do the work without an assistant for at least six months. What happened? Did you back down? Did the boss win? Did you have "no guts"? More likely, you became aware of the interdependent nature of your work team and decided to change your demand, given the needs of the entire group. You may have been given recognition for the difficulty of your job. Maybe your boss said in front of the group, "I'd like to give you an assistant, but I don't have the money in the budget and don't know where I can get it" (a face-saving message). Your conflict goals changed because of the communication event.

A school board member was trying to decide how to handle her strong opposition to the closed, or "executive," sessions of the board that her colleagues on the board supported. She discussed the incipient conflict with friends ahead of time, rehearsing what she was going to do (prospective goal). When the next board meeting arrived, she did not give her prearranged speech. She compromised and agreed with her colleagues that some closed meetings, in limited circumstances, were acceptable. This change is an example of transactive goal development.

The concept of transactive goals developed from the conviction that communication, itself, is transactional. To describe communication accurately, we must look at what happens when people are together instead of looking at each person's separate experiences (Wilmot 1987; Laing, Phillipson, and Lee 1966). Relationships are interpenetrative, with each person influencing and being influenced by the other (Wilmot 1995). To say that the board member in the example was persuaded by the other board members is simplistic. Neither did she persuade them to adopt her point of view. They all influenced each other, creating new, transactive goals through the process of a board meeting.

You may have noticed that your goals change in conflicts as you get a chance to express your feelings, be heard, and talk through your opinions and wishes (while the other party does the same). If you are a person who says, "I don't know what I want until we get a chance to discuss it," you understand transactive goals. The following box exemplifies the way new goals develop as a conflict progresses. Note that the two friends see themselves as interdependent and that they value their relationship as well as solving the immediate topic issue (finding the lost object).

Verbal Communication	Goal Analysis
First phone call:	
Amy: You know that silver star pendant I loaned you? I guess you didn't return it with the rest of the jewelry, because I can't find it.	Amy's #1 prospective goal is to *get the pendant back from Janice.*
Janice: I don't have it. I remember that I didn't borrow it because I knew it was valuable to you. You must have misplaced it somewhere. But I'll look.	Janice's #1 prospective goal is to *convince Amy that she is not responsible for the disappearance of the necklace,* a goal that is incompatible with Amy's prospective goal.

(continued)

Verbal Communication	Goal Analysis
Second phone call:	
Amy: I still can't find it—I'm getting panicky. I'll hold while you go look. Please check everywhere it might be.	Amy maintains prospective goal #1 by escalating her previous goal statement. Amy and Janice still have incompatible goals.
Janice: You're upset about the necklace, and I don't know what I can do since I honestly don't think I have it. But what really concerns me is that you are upset with me. You mean a lot to me, and this hurts.	Transactive goal #2: *Affirm the relationship in spite of the loss of the necklace.*
Amy: I know. I really don't want to put it all on you. I'm glad you understand, though. You know, John gave me that necklace.	Amy reaffirms transactive goal #2, making it mutual. She agrees to discuss, affirming the relationship as a new, additional goal.
Janice: Well, what can we do to get this solved? I feel awful.	Janice restates transactive goal #2 and offers transactive goal #3: *Find the necklace together without damaging the relationship.*
Amy: I'll hang up and we'll both go look everywhere and then report back.	Amy advances transactive goal #4: *Share the responsibility with a new plan of action.*
Janice: OK. And then we'll come up with something if we don't find it right away. Cross your fingers.	Janice accepts transactive goal #4 and advances transactive goal #5: *We will keep working until we solve this problem.*

We shift to negative goals when we can't "get what we want." It is only when we get frustrated that we belittle, injure, or try to damage the other. This shift from the original topic or content goal to a negative relationship or identity goal characterizes the destructive conflict. In diagram form, the goal change occurs as follows:

1. You want a promotion:
   You ⟶ Promotion

2. When you ask her for a promotion, your supervisor says, "No way. You aren't going to get a promotion as long as I'm the boss here. Your work has been substandard, not worthy of promotion." Your boss interferes with your original goal, and you begin to focus most of your attention on her interference and your attempts to gain power.

3. You then begin to lose sight of your original goal and spend energy trying to get even with the boss. You talk to people at home and at work about her, tell others how biased she is, spread rumors at work, and do other things to undercut her authority.

This example describes a typical pattern of goal shifting in a conflict. What began as a topic goal, getting a promotion, turns into a relational contest between the two of you—you shift from a positive content goal to a negative relational goal.

Such shifts occur often and can be either spontaneous or strategic (Infante and Wigley 1986). Two business partners, for example, who begin by wanting to help each other earn sizable amounts of money, experience a misunderstanding over a contract and then spend the next two years trying to one-up each other during board meetings and to get others in the organization to side with them. The partnership begins to flounder as each member thinks the other is more trouble than he is worth.

One other type of goal shifting occurs in conflicts. Often, a person who is frustrated over the content of a conflict (the vote doesn't go your way; you can tell the outcome of the discussion will be unfavorable) will shift from content to process. Concerns about fair process, equal treatment, and other process issues often surface when one has not been successful at attaining a desired content goal. The teenager who launches an appeal to use the family car and is turned down may resort to arguing that "you listened to Steve, but you didn't let me tell you why I needed the car. You treated me unfairly." She is switching from the unsuccessful content attempt to a discussion of process. Similar process concerns arise in many conflicts after the participants realize their content goals have been thwarted. A change in any type of conflict goal spills over to the other types of conflict goals. Often, as in previous examples, identity issues become intertwined with relational goals. When you feel powerless in relationship to another person, your sense of effectiveness or worthiness is challenged. Thus, identity goals rise in importance.

Conflict parties also *sacrifice content for relationship goals* or relationship goals for content. When the spouse never argues, avoids expressing any disagreement, and always says, "whatever you want, dear," he or she is sacrificing content goals in order to maintain the relationship. Acquiescing to others and never telling them what you really feel are types of content goal sacrifice. Alternatively, if you are intently set on your content goal (making money, negotiating the best possible contract, or always winning), you may be sacrificing the relationship in order to win the content. If you never consider the wishes of the other and always try to win, you are probably destroying valuable relationships in order to accomplish your goals.

In conclusion, conflict goals change over time. As one goal is frustrated, others assume more importance. You may not know which goals, topic, relational, identity, or process, are the most important, for they are in flux. Goals change during the transactions we have with others.

Retrospective Goals

Retrospective goals emerge after the conflict is over. People spend a large part of their time and energy justifying decisions they have made in the past. They need to explain to themselves and others why they made the choices they did. This process often happens with intimates who, for example, have an intense conflict over discipline of the children. After the first triggering comment, they may say, "Let's decide what's best for the children, not just what fits our own upbringing" (prospective goal). During subsequent conflicts over specific instances of discipline, they discuss everything from how the individual children react, to whether Mom and Dad should support each other's choices, even if they don't agree. If they decide that discipline is to be handled differently from the way it was in past episodes, Mom might say retrospectively, "I mainly wanted to see whether you would begin to share the discipline with me." Dad might say, "All along I was really trying to get you to see that you need to loosen up with the kids." Assuming that the couple comes up with a wise agreement they can follow in future episodes, the retrospective sense making helps them to define who they are and to make meaningful statements about the place of the conflict in their lives. Monday morning quarterbacking is important in ongoing relationships as well as in sports.

Since we do not know the implications of a conflict until we look back on it, retrospective goals give us clarity. Weick (1979) explains this sense-making process as the reverse from the usual way of looking at goals. He explains organizational behavior as "goal interpreted." People act in an orderly fashion, coordinating their behavior with each other, but with little notion of how this is accomplished until after the fact. Then they engage in retrospective meetings, conversations, paper writing, and speeches to explain why they did what they did. Talking about what happened after an important conflict is as important as talking about what will happen before a conflict episode. In these retrospective accounts, your prospective goals for the next episode are formulated. Thus, we learn from experience.

Retrospective sense making also serves the function of face saving. Visitors to the United States often comment on our lack of face-saving social rituals as compared to the situation in Japan, China, and other countries. Even if you have been involved in a competitive conflict and have won, rubbing it in or gloating over the loser will only serve to alienate and enrage the person, perhaps driving him or her to devious actions in retaliation. If you give respect to the person, even if you did not agree with the position, the person's "face" will be saved, and you will lay the groundwork for collaboration in the future. Following are some face-saving comments:

> Employer to job applicant: We looked very highly on you and your application. Our offer to Ms. Shepherd was based on her experience in our particular kind of operation. Even though you and I have been at odds for some time over organization of the new program, I want you to know that your new ideas are always sound and well organized. I just have different priorities.

> Mother to teenage daughter: I know you didn't want to cause us worry. You couldn't have known how upset we'd be that you were four hours late. But since you did not follow our agreement, we are grounding you for a week, as we said we would if the rule was not followed.

∾Goal Clarity

As noted above, how conflict parties formulate, alter, and explain their goals in a conflict determines to a large degree the success of the conflict experience. This section
gives suggestions for better articulating and working with goals to improve your
conflicts.

Clarify Your Goals

Goals that are unclear or hard to specify usually produce more conflict. One study
demonstrated that in organizations, unclear and ambiguous goals produced more conflict between employees (Schnake and Cochran 1985). A careful specification of everyone's goals lets you decide which ones to abandon, which ones to trade, and which ones
to maintain (Hermone 1974). Further, as Papa and Pood (1988a) demonstrated, **goal
clarity** before the conflictual interaction results in increased satisfaction with the discussion with the other party.

Sometimes, however, a discussion of goals in interpersonal conflict elicits the same
avoidance reaction mentioned in earlier chapters: "I don't want to be manipulative. If
I figure out what I want ahead of time, I'm being pushy and presumptuous—I'll let the
chips fall where they may." However, all effective communication is goal directed
(Phillips and Metzger 1976). This means that communication is purposive, not that it
is manipulative, and that people communicate for reasons and to reach goals. Since no
one can avoid being goal directed, especially in conflict communication, productive
conflict management depends on parties' taking open responsibility for their goals. In
other words, know what your goals are, state them clearly to yourself, and communicate them in a flexible manner to your conflict partners. Advantages of clarifying your
goals follow:

1. *Solutions go unrecognized if you do not know what you want.* If parents are not clear
   about whether they want their 18-year-old to live at home or to board in the
   dorm at a local college, they will not know how to manage the conflict with the
   son who wants to live in the dorm but does not have a job. If saving money is
   the primary goal, the parents might allow the son to live in the dorm and get a
   job. If the parents have decided that they do not want him to live in the dorm
   under any circumstances, the son's offer to get a job may trigger a covert conflict
   that is unclear and unproductive for all parties.

2. *Only clear goals can be shared.* Since people cannot read your mind, you must
   clearly communicate your goals. An example of this kind of goal sharing occurred
   in an academic department. The chairperson complained that the faculty was not
   paying enough attention to university politics. He made several statements over a
   period of a week or so, urging more attendance at meetings, more discussion of
   long-term budget and curriculum plans, and voluntary participation in activities
   around campus. Since all this happened at the beginning of a semester, when
   the rest of the faculty were feeling busy, hassled by bureaucratic demands, and
   underappreciated, the response from the faculty was negative. A genuine conflict
   began to brew. Finally, the chairperson said, "Since keeping us involved in the
   university is my job, I feel really down when nobody supports what I'm doing.

I need some feedback on what you think so I'm not just floundering around." Because he changed his goal statement from "Why don't you people work more?" to "I need support for what I'm doing," the conflict was reduced and productively managed.

3. *Clear goals can be altered more easily than vague goals.* One agency was embroiled in conflict over whether to fund and provide staff support for a new program to aid recently unemployed families. The three staff members who had been charged with setting up the new program did not know whether the agency director wanted to support that particular new program or whether he wanted to demonstrate to the funding sources that the agency was committed to being responsive to families in general. When the director clarified that the specific program should serve an underserved population, the staff members altered their previous goals so that the new program would assist with community problems of child abuse that were receiving little funding at that time. The change in staff goals was possible because the larger goals were clarified for the staff members, along with their important role in reaching the goals.

4. *Clear goals are reached more often than unclear goals.* Having a map helps travelers reach a destination. Similarly, Raush et al. (1974) found that 66 percent of the conflicts in which the issue was clearly stated were successfully resolved, whereas only 18 percent of the conflicts in which the issue remained vague and nonspecific were resolved. For example, a couple is considering where to move after college. If they choose the first option, "We will stay in the same city no matter what," they will have made a significantly different choice than if they choose the second option, "We will both get the best jobs we can." Those with shared individual and relational destinations are more likely to arrive at some desired point together. Clarifying goals has one risky outcome: it may make seriously incompatible goals apparent. However, they will become apparent sooner or later. Additionally, when goals are "stated explicitly and directly there is control of escalation" (99). When one's goals are unclear, they often promote overreaction from the other person, who misjudges the nature of the conflict. We are remarkably poor at second-guessing the goals of our conflict partners.

Often people create difficulty by assuming that their goals cannot be attained—that the other party will stand in their way. How many times have you planned and schemed for days, only to find that others were perfectly willing to give you what you wanted? A friend was miserable because her children would not give her any free time on the weekends. She began to believe they did not respect her needs. Finally one night she said in tears, "If I don't have some time alone, I'll go crazy." The teenagers were glad to make plans to give her time with no responsibilities. She simply never had asked. Even if the goal is a difficult one, allotting time to accomplish a clear goal allows for its attainment (Neale and Bazerman 1985).

In conclusion, clarifying goals is a key step in conflict management. People assess the conflicts in which they participate by making decisions about which goals are worth pursuing. In common language, they get a "grip" on the situation before deciding how to proceed.

Estimate the Other's Goals

Once a destructive conflict begins spiraling, *all our behavior is* **reactive.** We make choices based on what we think the other is thinking and intending. While not as elaborate as chess moves, all conflicts share a structure similar to chess—knowing the other has "moves," you try to counter his or her moves. Our **estimate of the other's goals**—about "what the other wants"—propels our own choices.

When you talk to two parties to a dispute individually, you will be struck by their misjudgments of the other's goals. Here are some samples from real disputes:

Party #2 Estimate of #1's goals	Party #1 Goals
He wants to control me	I need some predictability
She is trying to fire me	I want to restructure the unit
He wants favored treatment	I want to be recognized
He doesn't value our input	This crisis demands action
She is getting ready to break up with me	I need just a little more space

One of the patterns in disputes is that as you get more convinced you *know* what the other wants, you are less accurate. Figure 3.8 demonstrates this relationship.

Becoming convinced we know absolutely what the other wants sets the stage for misinterpretation. As Sillars (2002) notes in his research on married couples in conflict, "I have been struck by how confident people seem to be when making very tenuous inferences about others" (8). One dramatic example comes from Catholics who were abused. They had this to say about their goals:

> Most survivors do not want to receive money from the church as compensation for what was done to us. Most of us merely want to ensure that our perpetrators are removed from being able to abuse others in their position as trusted priests. We'd like some apology for what we've endured. Sometimes we want an apology or acknowledgement given to our parents (Survivors 2004).

Now, of course, this doesn't mean that the legal system will respond to these goals. In American culture we often substitute money for other goals, since legally it is easier to do that and also pay for your lawyer.

Figure 3.8   Confidence and Accuracy about the Other's Goals

Confidence and accuracy about the other's goals

Your confidence   Your accuracy

In most personal conflicts where you know the other for a long time, your inferences about the other are "well informed but also quite biased" (Sillars 2002, 2). We all assume we "know" someone well, but the research is quite clear that we don't! For one thing, when individuals are asked to report their thoughts during a video recall, only 5 to 7 percent of the time are they thinking about their partner's perspective (Sillars 2002). Further, while one person focuses on the topic (content), the other focuses on the relationship—they tend to see only their part of the TRIP issues and not the other person's.

Given that there is misunderstanding about the other, this by itself feeds negative conflict spirals and the descent into destructive conflict. In addition, however, *both parties feel misunderstood by the other*. They somehow know the other is misunderstanding their goals, and, in fact, feeling misunderstood then moves the conflict to a more destructive level. As you feel misunderstood, you will choose destructive conflict moves to get back at the other.

No wonder we get into such difficulties in conflict. We misunderstand the other, react to what we think he or she is intending, feel very confident in our assessments, and then justify our damaging moves.

No magic process untangles these intertwining misperceptions. Communication itself is fraught with difficulties, but one revolutionary thing to do is ask the other what he or she needs. Many years ago, Bill, one of the coauthors, had an ongoing struggle with a colleague. Finally, after many days of tug-of-war in meetings, Bill stomped into Wes's office and said (not in a good tone of voice), "Wes, what do you want?" Wes calmly replied, "For you and me to go to lunch." Bill, taken aback, said, "What are you saying? We are arguing about a tenure case." Wes said, "Well, that is what I want." So, against his better judgment, Bill went to lunch with Wes and survived it. Not only that, but their relationship began to slowly transform. What was driving the dispute from Wes's side was feeling that Bill didn't value him. They had lunch every three weeks from then on, and as a result, their conflicts subsided. Sometimes all you have to do is (1) ask and (2) listen!

Collaborative Goals

The best goals are clear, as explained previously, and help conflict interactants collaborate on resolving the conflict while protecting their ability to work, live, or interact with each other in important ways. The following statements characterize **collaborative goals** and may be used as a checklist for "good goals":

1. *Short-, medium-, and long-range issues are addressed.* Many times people engage too forcefully with others at the beginning of a conflict because they are afraid their ideas will not be heard. Collaborative goals build in ways for people to be involved in the process as it unfolds. To form collaborative goals, plan for evaluations along the way. Give as much attention to a few weeks or months from now as to "right now." Looking at longer-range goals helps de-escalate the importance of initial, prospective goals. One city council, meeting in a retreat, specified which goals, over a time line, were important to them. They set up a plan to specify who would do what by when and with what evaluation process. A year later, only those goals that had been broken down into a specific time line were achieved. Goals that are set up on a time line are less overwhelming than global goals such as "Let's

change the way we get along as a family" or "I want more say about the financial structure of our family."

2. *Goals are behaviorally specific.* Doable goals (Phillips and Metzger 1976) can be checked. "I'll try to do better" might become a doable goal with specification; at present, it is a positive statement but not a collaborative goal. Terms used in intimate relations are often more vague than statements in business relationships. A corporate vice president could not get away with telling the president, "I will try the best I can to remember to turn the monthly reports in on time," but intimates make such vague promises frequently. Specificity helps the parties know when a goal has been accomplished. The following examples illustrate how to make vague statements more specific:

   • Instead of saying, "Please respect my things more," say, "I want you to ask me before you borrow any of my clothes. I'm usually glad to oblige, but I want you to ask me, all right?"

   • Instead of saying, "Let's get this show on the road" (and then showing nonverbal impatience during a meeting), say, "I need to leave this meeting at 5:00 sharp."

   • Instead of saying, "This time, young lady, you're going to listen to what I say!" a parent might say, "Last time we talked about your messy room I wasn't pleased with where we got. This time, I want you to listen to me, and I will listen to you, and then I want us to decide on what is reasonable. OK?"

3. *Statements orient toward the present and future.* The language of change uses what can be done now instead of what should have been done in the past. Hopeful statements instead of blaming statements set the expectation that agreements can indeed come about. A department head might say, "I want our program group to increase services to clients without increasing hours worked by our counselors," instead of, "We have got to be more efficient than we were last year."

4. *Goals recognize interdependence.* In all conflicts, tension arises between serving self-interest and serving the interests of the other party. In Western cultures we have overemphasized self relative to community interest, whereas Eastern cultures tend to focus on the interests of the group, or community (Dien 1982). Research consistently indicates, however, that when conflict parties operate with both concern for self and concern for others, the agreements that emerge serve the parties best (Tutzauer and Roloff 1988; Holloway and Brager 1985). This does not mean that you give in to the other; you can remain firm in achieving solutions that work for you while simultaneously seeking to please the other (Tutzauer and Roloff 1988). When one has low concern for the other coupled with a high demand for one's own goals, however, coercion and manipulation result (Kimmel et al. 1980). High concern for self and the other coupled with high demand that one's own goals remain important gives the parties an opportunity to develop creative, integrative solutions to the conflict.

5. *Collaborative goals recognize an ongoing process.* An overriding goal of constructive conflict is to remain committed to the process of constructive conflict. The particular content can be transcended by adhering to a collaborative process.

Fisher and Ury (1981) remind conflict managers that goal setting begins with the participation of all conflict parties. "Give them a stake in the outcome by making sure they participate in the process" (27). For collaborators, "the process is the product" (29).

The outcome of constructive conflict should be wise agreements. Wise agreements are fair and durable and take the interests of all parties into account (Fisher and Ury 1981, 4). The struggle for wise agreements is exemplified by a couple with children that goes to court for a divorce. The agreement should be representative of both sides; should be fair to all parties, including the children; should keep the couple out of court in the future; and should set up care for the children if they are too young to care for themselves. The process should be efficient, involve all parties' interests, and improve or at least not damage the relationship between the parties.

When conflict parties work together to clarify goals and specify what the conflict is and is not about, destructive conflicts subside. Collaboration is a high-energy alternative to avoidance, violence, coercion, frustration, despair, and other forms of destructiveness. Collaboration is not always possible, but when it is, destructive conflict is transformed into constructive problem solving.

The participants can come to see themselves as working side by side on a problem, attacking the problem instead of each other. The overarching process goal is "We, working together, can solve this problem that is confronting us." Part of the self-interest of conflict parties is preserving a workable relationship, focusing on the problem instead of each other. Relational preservation becomes a superordinate goal, as in the classic Sherif and Sherif (1956) study where groups of boys were placed in situations that aroused conflicts of interest between the two groups. The researchers then introduced a common enemy, thus stimulating the two groups to work together, which reduced their intergroup hostility. In interpersonal conflicts, long-term relational, process, and identity goals can reduce conflict over short-term goals.

❧Summary

As a conflict unfolds, topic, relational, identity, and process goals emerge (TRIP). Topic goals are the "objective," verifiable issues that people talk about. Relationship goals are those pertaining to the parties' influence on each other. Who gets to decide, how they treat one another, and other aspects of their communication are relationship goals. Identity, or face-saving, goals have to do with the needs of people to present themselves positively in interactions and to be treated with approval and respect. Process goals refer to parties' interests in how the interaction is conducted.

Although most conflict parties center their discussions on content and process goals, the relationship and identity components often fuel the feeling in a given conflict.

Goals change in the course of a conflict. Prospective goals are those identified before interacting with the other parties. Transactive goals emerge during the communication exchanges. Transactive goals often shift; a destructive conflict is characterized by a shift from original goals to a desire to harm the other party. Retrospective goals are identified after the conflict episodes have occurred. Unregulated, unplanned, fast-paced con-flicts keep many people from understanding their goals until they later have time to reflect on the transactions.

Productive conflict management is enhanced by clarifying your goals, better estimating the other's goals, and working to build collaborative goals. Working against or without consulting the other party often sets destructive forces in motion that preclude integrative management of the conflict.

Key Terms

Use the text's Online Learning Center at **www.mhhe.com/wilmot7** to further your understanding of the following terminology.

types of goals 63

topic goals 64

relational goals 65

identity, or face-saving, goals 69

process goals 74

prospective goals 83

transactive goals 83

retrospective goals 87

goal clarity 88

reactive behavior 90

estimating the other's goals 90

collaborative goals 91

Review Questions

Go to the self-quizzes on the Online Learning Center at **www.mhhe.com/wilmot7** to test your knowledge of the chapter concepts.

1. Define the four types of goals (TRIP).
2. How do goals shift over time?
3. How do goals overlap and influence one another?
4. When do conflict parties shift their goals?
5. What does it mean to sacrifice one kind of goal for another?
6. What happens to goals in interactions with others?
7. What happens when we experience change in prospective goals?
8. Give an example of a transactive goal.
9. What are common identity themes?
10. How do retrospective goals change?
11. What does it mean to "specialize" in a type of goal?
12. What are the advantages of goal clarity?
13. Do conflict parties accurately estimate the other's goals?
14. What determines if goals are collaborative?

Chapter 4

Power: The Structure of Conflict

The stick, the carrot and the hug may all be necessary, but the greatest of these is the hug.
—Kenneth Boulding, *Three Faces of Power*

What Is Power?

Just as energy is a fundamental concept in physics, **power** is a fundamental concept in conflict theory. In interpersonal and all other conflicts, perceptions of power are at the heart of any analysis. Hundreds of definitions of power tend to fall into three camps. Power is seen as (1) *designated* (power given by your position), (2) *distributive* (either/or power), or (3) *integrative* (both/and power). *Designated* power comes from your position, such as being a manager, the mother or father of a family, or the leader of a team. Your power is conferred by the position you hold.

Distributive power comes from your ability to achieve your objective "over the resistance of another . . ." (Dahl 1957, p. 3). Distributive power focuses on power over or against the other party. For example, if you see dominance as the key to power, you see power as distributive. You would see the situation as either "I dominate you or you dominate me" (Burgoon, Johnson, and Koch 1998).

Integrative definitions of power highlight power *with* the other. Integrative views stress "joining forces with someone else to achieve mutually acceptable goals" (Lilly 1989, 281). Integrative definitions focus on "both/and"—both parties have to achieve something in the relationship. As we shall see, it is not what outsiders say about power, but the views the conflict parties have that determine the outcomes of their conflicts.

This chapter examines the role of power in conflict by examining common assumptions people have about power. We then further develop orientations to power, analyze currencies or resources that lead to power, and propose a relational theory of power. We conclude with ways to judge, or assess, power, and give ideas about how to rebalance power so constructive conflict can take place. Sometimes all we can do in conflicts is keep the destruction from spiraling out of control, or negotiate an uneasy "balance of terror." Often, thankfully, alternatives to the top-down exercise of power emerge when people commit themselves to finding them. Constructive use of power solves problems, enhances relationships, and balances power, at least during interaction. When that happens, the hard work that goes into learning about conflict management is worth it!

❧Orientations to Power

In chapter 1, the lens model of conflict was outlined. You learned that your particular views of self, other, and relationship are the key ingredients in a conflict (along with the other's perceptions of these). When a dispute occurs between two people, they often talk about power, and their perspectives will predispose them to engage in certain communicative moves. People feel passionately about power—who has it, who ought to have more or less, how people misuse power, and how justified they feel in trying to gain more power for themselves. This orientation toward power seems to be true for many reasons.

We each need enough power to live the life we want. We want to influence events that matter to us. We want to have our voices heard, and make a difference. We want to protect ourselves against perceived harm. We want to hold in high esteem ourselves and those we care about. We do not want to be victimized, misused, or demeaned. No one can escape feeling the effects of power—whether we have too much or too little.

When people struggle with each other, they almost never agree on anything having to do with power. For example, if you are a student intern in a real estate firm and you feel that brokers have all the power, you are likely to keep silent even when you disagree—giving the impression that you agree when you don't. If, on the other hand, you feel that both you and the brokers have sources of power, you will be more likely to engage in discussion to work through issues. As an intern, you may have sources of power such as your close connection to others in the office, your ability to help the brokers do their jobs, and your knowledge of the real estate business you gained working last summer. If you think of yourself, however, as "just a lowly intern," you may miss many opportunities to be a team member because you have assessed your power incorrectly. We will discuss these issues later in this chapter.

You probably have an emotional response when you hear the word *power*. Kipnis notes, "Like love, we know that power exists, but we cannot agree on a description of it" (1976, 8). The following exercise will help you think about how you respond to the *idea* of power.

Application 4.1	Meaning of "Power"

Respond quickly to the word *power,* as you did with the word *conflict* in chapter 2. What comes to mind? The following are common associations: Mark the ones that fit for you, and add connotations of your own:

power play	power source	power corrupts
high powered	power behind the throne	devious
bullheaded	run over	authority
power politics	powerhouse	overpower
low powered	sneaky	strong-arm
bulldozed	powerful	influence

(continued)

Application 4.1   Meaning of "Power"

Discuss what you were taught about the use of power. List three explicit or implicit "learnings" about power from your personal history, then discuss these with your small group. Some examples from students include

"When people gang up on you, there's nothing to do but get away. You can't go up against a group."

"The most important kind of power is your own character."

"Stay connected to people in power; they can help you."

"Using power with those you care about is despicable."

"We don't talk about power. Power isn't nice."

"Your father/mother has the say around here. Don't cross him/her."

"It's safest to get in a coalition with someone older and stronger."

"I learned to gain power by manipulation, deception, sneaking, or lying."

"As a pretty young girl I learned to gain power by flirting and playing with boys and men."

As reflected by this list, people have different views of power, some positive and some negative. One group of researchers (Cavanaugh et al. 1981a, 1981b; Goldberg, Cavanaugh, and Larson 1983) classified views of power. Using samples of salespeople, government employees, corporate executives, and law enforcement personnel, they concluded that the prime *orientations toward power* were varied. Some people viewed power as good—that the responsibility and challenge of power are exciting and that they would like to be powerful. Others saw power as instinctive—something we all possess innately. Still others saw power as consisting of valued resources, such as political skill; as a charismatic thing that people have within themselves; or as being reflected in control over others and autonomy of the self. We respond to conflict differently based, in part, on our different orientations to what power itself consists of, and whether it is a positive, negative, or benign characteristic.

Either/Or Power

Take a look at the list of words associated with power—most show an either/or association. You have power in order to move others against their will; it becomes a contest of the wills when you are in a "power struggle." When you examine typical newspaper stories about power, you read about the either/or (distributive) notions of power. In fact, it is difficult to even find examples of any other orientation toward power in the popular press. Many people think that power is only "force"—pushing others around against their will. When you read about nations using military might against other nations, you see **either/or power** in operation.

Once a relationship begins to go downhill, concerns with power increase. As any relationship deteriorates, the parties shift to a more overt focus on power—and this shift

Figure 4.1   Power Emphasized in a Distressed System

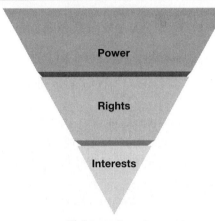

Distressed system

is reflected in their discourse (Beck 1988). In fact, a characteristic of destructive conflict is that parties start thinking and talking about power. Almost no one thinks that he or she has more power than the other power, at least when emotions run very high. We think the other has more power, which then justifies dirty tricks and our own attempt to gain more power. We often see ourselves as blameless victims of the other's abuse of power. When partners are caught in this destructive cycle of either/or power, their communicative interactions show a lot of "one up" responses, or attempts to demonstrate conversational power over each other (Sabourin and Stamp 1995). Partners might say, "She is just trying to control me," or "I'm not going to let him push me around." People, whether married couples or work colleagues, try to "keep score"— watching the "points" they have vis-à-vis the other party (Ross and Holmberg 1992). When partners develop an overt concern with power, their struggles over power are directly related to relationship satisfaction (Kurdek 1994). Figure 4.1 demonstrates how concerns rank in a distressed relationship.

As Ury, Brett, and Goldberg (1988) so aptly note, the focus for a dispute becomes power—who has the right to move the other. The teenager who says, "You can't boss me around," the spouse who shouts, "Just who do you think you are?" and the co-worker who states, "Well, we'll see who the boss is around here!" are all highlighting power and giving it center stage in the dispute. These struggles often escalate. Dissatisfied couples are more than three times as likely to escalate episodes and focus on power than satisfied couples (Alberts and Driscoll 1992). Using the terms we developed in chapter 3, power becomes the overriding relationship concern. Getting more power becomes the overriding *relationship issue.* We are not suggesting that power shouldn't be an issue. Rather, we suggest that when power itself becomes the main focus of thinking and discussion, parties are likely to be involved in an escalating power struggle, and may well have temporarily lost sight of interests and solutions.

Figure 4.2 Power De-emphasized in an Effective System

Effective system

Source: From William Ury, Jeanne M. Brett, and Stephen B. Goldberg, *Getting Disputes Resolved: Designing Systems to Cut the Costs of Conflict.* Copyright © 1988 Jossey-Bass Inc., Publishers, San Francisco, California. Reprinted by permission.

Notice in figure 4.1 that disputes also involve "rights" and "interests." Rights, similar to our idea of core concerns, include not being discriminated against, being free from physical harm, and other constitutional and legal guarantees we have as citizens. Sometimes it is more appropriate that disputes get settled on the basis of rights rather than power or interests. For example, if the famous *Brown v. Board of Education* case in 1954 outlawing segregation in public schools had been settled on the basis of power, it would have resulted in a struggle in the streets. If, on the other hand, it had been settled on the basis of interests, Brown might have negotiated her way into school, but the country's social policy would not have changed. When we solve a dispute based on interests, the goals and desires of the parties are the key elements. For instance, if you don't want your teenage son to use the car, you can (1) tell him it is not OK as long as you pay the bills in the house (power); (2) let him know that you own the car and have all the rights to its use (rights); or (3) let him know that you are dissatisfied with how he drives, and until you are convinced he will be safe, you will not lend the car (interests). Thus, disputes can occur on any one of the three levels. When power becomes the only personal goal, the dispute is harder to resolve.

Figure 4.2 illustrates an effective system in which the emphasis is on interests with rights and power playing smaller but still important roles. As you can see by comparing figure 4.1 with figure 4.2, an overemphasis on power is symptomatic of a distressed system.

Both/And Power

Rather than always seeing power as distributive, you can view it as (1) both/and or (2) designated. Boulding (1989) notes that "the great fallacy, especially of political thinking in regard to power, is to elevate threat power to the position of dominance" (10). Interpersonal relationships reflect the same fallacy—many people just can't envision power in terms other than "either/or," or "win/lose." Yet a study of the dynamics of successful disputes and ongoing relationships reveals that power functions on a broader basis than either/or thinking. Disputes become power struggles if the parties allow them to be defined as such. Conceptually, the alternative to framing disputes as power struggles is to place power in a position subordinate to rights and needs.

To help us understand the cultural basis of our assumptions, Augsburger (1992) details the lack of verbal fighting in some other cultures. In these cultures, power is activated as both/and or designated power, discussed in the next section. In Japanese and Javanese cultures, for instance, to name two obvious examples, harmony and cooperation are basic values, and verbal contradiction is not the automatic first choice in conflict. A more accepted process is to affirm the strengths of each other's position, let them stand without attack, and then join in exploring other options. Both parties search for superior options (59).

Both/and power is often the first choice of women in our culture. Researchers at the Jean Baker Miller Center at Wellesley have spent two decades explicating "relational theory" in an attempt to balance the traditional male orientation that permeates United States culture. In their view, relational theory is a belief system that describes how growth and effectiveness occur (Fletcher 1999). Masculine theories, which until the last 20 years or so have been accepted as the only psychologically sound theories, often assumed that maturity and competence depend on autonomy, or separation from constraints, other people, and group identity. Boys, for instance, learn to relate to power through games and competition more than girls do. Boys learn to be comfortable with the hierarchy of teams, captains, coaches, and bosses. Girls learn to play with less focus on hierarchy. Many girls' games are cooperative in nature, with girls taking roles to play out, after discussing together what to do. As Heim and Galant (1993) notes, "There's no boss in dolls." For boys, conflict means competition, which often enhances relationships. For girls, competition is often painful and damages relationships. Girls often prefer to look for a win/win situation (Heim and Galant, 1993, 27).

Relational theory and practice offer the idea that maturity and competence depend on growth-in-connection and mutuality. The ability to develop relationally depends on mutual empathy, mutual empowerment, responsibility to both oneself and others, and the ability to experience and express emotion, to experience and learn from vulnerability, to participate in the development of another, and to enhance each other's efforts (Fletcher 1999; Jordan et al. 1991). This approach does not need to be seen strictly as a female approach. Many effective forms of conflict resolution depend on a relational approach. Some situations in which power is heavily unbalanced also require a level of competition and assertiveness that does not come naturally for many women. If competition remains the dominant approach, however, constructive conflict resolution is unlikely to occur, except temporarily.

For instance, when people work in teams, a major skill required is the ability to use the kind of mutual power described above. Making the project work, moving toward mutual goals, and getting a new effort up and running require skills very different from those used with either/or power. Yet, this kind of mutuality often is not valued as much as the more masculine either/or power. Fletcher (1999) explains how relational work disappears in organizations since it is not categorized as "real work." For instance, preventing problems is not seen as being as important as solving problems in some work environments. Mothers who coordinate highly complex family activities sometimes are seen as "not working" because their efforts involve interaction among all the family members instead of major attention being given to their own schedules and needs. Fletcher's (1999) research with engineering firms showed that in a culture of independence and self-promotion, which prizes individual achievement and winning at competition—coming out on top—voluntarily helping others was seen as naïve and powerless (95). The following case illustrates the difference between either/or and both/and power.

Application 4.2   The Case of Lynn and Daniel

Lynn and Daniel are a married couple in their 30s. Daniel is employed as a smoke jumper supervisor. This work requires him to be ready literally at a moment's notice to get in a plane and direct safety activities for firefighters from various regions when a fire breaks out. Lynn and Daniel have two small children, ages two and four. They have decided that for now, the family needs are best served by Lynn's being the primary parent, and taking care of the children, especially since Daniel is sometimes gone for weeks during fire season. Here's where the problem comes in. Daniel was raised in a family in which the person making the money had the power. He believes that since Lynn is not making much money (she works part-time as a piano teacher), she should not make major purchases without his permission. He expects Lynn to pay the necessary bills, but to ask him for money, when she needs it, for household expenses. Lynn is angry and sometimes feels defeated since, in her view, Daniel does not know the needs of the household. She thinks she should be able to make expenditures as she sees fit. When she wants to plan a trip, or buy something out of the ordinary, Daniel says, "Make the money, then. I'm working as hard as I can." Lynn believes that Daniel completely devalues her work at home.

How can this couple change their orientation to power in order to solve their problems and enhance their long-term relationship? Specifically, how might they move from *either/or* power to *both/and* power? See what ideas you can generate.

Designated Power

The third kind of power is **designated power,** giving *power* to some other group or entity. In earlier editions of this book, we referred to this kind of power as being similar to a "relational savings account." People place "power" into an "account" that they can then draw on when their individual reserves are not sufficient to solve a problem. Many examples of designated power can be noted. As citizens, we delegate power to law enforcement officers, elected politicians, heads of regulatory agencies, teachers, administrators, and even employers. We do not assume that we have or should use our independence without restraints in our civil society. At work, by agreeing to work in a retail outlet, agency, or other organization, we delegate power to others. For instance, someone else may be in charge of your schedule, place of work, tasks, and pay. Yet, you are not powerless, since the employer needs your services and, we hope, wants to create a productive work environment. Even though power is inherently unbalanced in an employer–employee dyad, the low-power person has delegated personal power to the employer. They still maintain interdependence. In a couple situation such as the case of Lynn and Daniel above, the couple could designate power to "the needs of the family," which both would then define. In a marriage, threat power works poorly, since threats build resentment and distance. In fact, if Lynn and Daniel continue on their present course, they will probably divorce or have to live with a very unhappy and distant marriage. When people designate power to a greater entity, they are giving up power over, or distributive power, for the larger good of the interdependent relationship.

Application 4.3	Types of Power

List as many kinds of designated power (*"power to"*) relationships as you can. Think of educational, family, couple, work, friend, and recreation contexts. See if you can think of several *either/or* power relationships that could be improved by being made a *"power to"* relationship. Not all distributive power relationships can be changed in this way; we are, however, urging you to think creatively at this point. Many of the later conflict resolution strategies in this book depend on creative thinking about power.

Power Denial

Some people are so "antagonized by any discussion of power" (Madanes 1981, 217) that they may deny that power and influence are appropriate topics for discussion. We often try to convince others and ourselves that control is not part of our interpersonal patterns. One student wrote that in her relationship with her boyfriend, "No one has to have power—we just listen to each other, try to respond with love, and always put the relationship and each other first." She seemed to think that acknowledging any use of power would destroy her perfect relationship with her boyfriend.

Many people view power as negative and find "explicit references to power . . . in bad taste" (Kipnis 1976, 2). Cahill (1982), conducting research on married couples, encountered this view when he interviewed them about their relationships. When he asked them about decision making, persuasive techniques, and disagreements, the discussion flowed smoothly. But when he asked about their relative amounts of power, he encountered long silences, halting answers, obvious embarrassment, and reluctance to speak of the topic. Similarly, McClelland (1969) noted that when people were told they had high drives to achieve or affiliate, they derived great satisfaction from the feedback, but people who were told they had a high drive for power experienced guilt.

In its extreme form, reluctance to talk about power emerges as **power denial.** Haley (1959) listed four common attempts people use to deny that they exercise power. These four forms of denial are presented in the following box.

Denying Power Use

1. Deny that you communicated something.
2. Deny that something was communicated.
3. Deny that you communicated something to the other person.
4. Deny the situation in which it was communicated.

The speaker can deny *he or she is communicating* by using a number of common ploys, such as saying, "I'm not myself when I drink," or "It's just the pressure I'm under that's making me act like such a grouch." You may hear the claim "I can't help it. I told you I was jealous. I'm not responsible for what I said." To say that you are not responsible for your communication lets you exercise control (if others accept your claim) while denying that you are doing so.

Denying that a *message was communicated* is another way to ignore the existence of power. The simplest way to deny communication is to say, "I did not say that." Since this kind of denial usually gets you in trouble after a while, another form develops, such as, "I forgot I said that. Did I really say that? I didn't mean to." For example, a supervisor might consistently forget to include the new members of a staff in the lines of communication in an agency. As a result, the newer, less powerful members are often late for meetings or miss them totally, having to reschedule other meetings at the last minute. When confronted by those left out, the supervisor said, "Oh, my administrative aide is responsible for scheduling meetings."

Denying that a message was communicated *to a particular person* is another way of expressing discomfort with the exercise of power. For example, a salesperson rings the doorbell of an apartment complex, and the following dialogue ensues:

Salesperson: Hello, I'd like to take this opportunity . . .

Apartment dweller: People are bothering me too much! Oh, I'm not talking about you. It's just that everyone bugs me day in and day out. I get no peace of mind. I wish the world would calm down and leave me alone.

Salesperson: Maybe I can see you another time. I'm sorry I bothered you . . .

The person who was bothered is exercising considerable control in the communicative transaction and at the same time is denying that control by pretending that the remarks are not meant for that particular salesperson. Another common way of denying that your comments were addressed to the other person is to claim that you were "just thinking out loud" and did not mean to imply anything toward the other person. For instance, a boss might say, muttering under his or her breath, "If I could count on people . . ." Then when a subordinate asks what is wrong, the boss might say, "What? Oh, nothing—just a hard day."

The last way to deny communicative power attempts is to *deny that what has been said applies to this situation*. Saying, "I'm used to being treated unfairly by others; I probably always will be" denies the clear implication that you feel the other is treating you in a demeaning manner. One employee left work without notifying her supervisor. She had been working extra hours in order to finish a report due to their funding agency. As she left, she was heard to say, "Let's just see how everyone can get along without my help since they seem to ignore my suggestions." When her supervisor confronted the employee on the overheard statement, she said, "Oh, I was just under stress from working all weekend. I didn't mean anything about the rest of the team. They're doing the best they can." The employee who left denied that she used her power to withhold her expertise under deadline pressure. She also denied the importance of what she said.

All of the preceding examples are ways that people can deny exercising power in a relationship when, in fact, they really are exercising power. Whenever you communicate with another, what you say and do exercises some communicative control—you either go along with someone else's definition of the conflict, struggle over the definition, or supply it yourself. Even if you would rather be seen as a person who does not exert power, you exercise influence on how the conflict interaction is going to be defined.

The fact that power is central to the study of conflict does not mean that people are always sneaky and try to get power illegitimately. Rather, the productive exercise of personal power is crucial to your self-concept. Without some exercise of power in your interpersonal relationships, you would soon feel worthless as a person. As you read this chapter, do a "power profile" of your own behavior—the way you really communicate, not just the way you might want to be seen. Sometimes there is a difference! Remember that just as one cannot not communicate (Watzlawick, Beavin, and Jackson 1967), one does not have the option of not using power. We only have options about whether to use power destructively or productively for ourselves and relationships.

❧A Relational Theory of Power

A common perception is that power is an attribute of a person. If you say, "Lynn is a powerful person," you may, if she is your friend, be referring to such attributes as verbal facility, intelligence, compassion, warmth, and understanding. Or you may refer to a politician as powerful, alluding to her ability to make deals, call in favors, remember names and faces, and understand complex economic issues. In interpersonal relationships, however, a **relational theory of power** explains status more effectively. Excluding situations of unequal physical power and use of violence, power is a property of the social relationship rather than a quality of the individual. Lynn, for instance, has power with her friends because she has qualities they value. When she suggests something to do, like going on an annual women's backpacking trip, her friends try to clear their calendars because they like her, have fun with her, and feel understood by her. Lynn has a way of making a group feel cohesive and at ease. But if an acquaintance hated backpacking, did not like some of the other people going on the trip, and was irritated at Lynn because of a misunderstanding that had not yet been cleared up, Lynn's power with the irritated acquaintance would lessen considerably.

Power is not owned by an individual but is a product of the social relationship in which certain qualities become important and valuable to others (King 1987; Rogers 1974; Harsanyi 1962a; Deutsch 1958; Dahl 1957; Soloman 1960). Deutsch (1973) states the case well: "Power is a relational concept; it does not reside in the individual but rather in the relationship of the person to his environment. Thus, the power of an agent in a given situation is determined by the characteristics of the situation" (15). Rather than residing in people, "power is always interpersonal" (May 1972, 23). In the strictest sense, except when violence and physical coercion are used, power is given from one party to another in a conflict. Power can be taken away when the situation changes. Power dynamics are fluid, changing, and dependent on the specific situation. Each person in a conflict has some degree of power, though one party may have more compared to the other, and the power can shift during a conflict.

Power is based on one's dependence on resources or currencies that another person controls, or seems to "possess." Emerson (1962) specified that a person's power is directly tied to the nature of the relationship. In terms of two people, A and B, person A has power over person B to the extent that B is dependent on A for goal attainment. Likewise, person B has power over person A to the extent that A is dependent on B. The following box expresses this simple formula.

$$PAB = DBA$$

(the power of A over B is equal to the dependence that B has on A), and

$$PBA = DAB$$

(the power of B over A is equal to the dependence that A has on B).

Your dependence on another person is a function of (1) the importance of the goals the other can influence and (2) the availability of other avenues for you to accomplish what you want. As Emerson (1962) states, "The dependence of Actor B upon Actor A is directly proportional to B's motivational investment in goals mediated by A, and inversely proportional to the availability of those goals to B outside of the A-B relation" (31). In a mutually beneficial relationship, power is not fixed, but shifts as each becomes dependent in a positive way on the resources the other person may offer. This process builds a relationship and takes time to accomplish (Donohue and Kolt 1992).

Increasing another's dependencies on you can be constructive or destructive. In the following case, we see an example of mutual dependence at the beginning of the case, but in the end, a destructive outcome based on too much dependence that was not worked out to the parties' mutual satisfaction.

Application 4.4   Power Play

In a medical clinic in a rural town, a conflict over flextime had been brewing for several months. Many of the staff wanted the option of flexible time. The doctor in charge of the clinic traveled frequently since she often had to give presentations elsewhere. The administrative assistant especially wanted the option of flexible time. She was unhappy with the way the office policies were set up, believing them to be unfairly weighted toward professional staff and against hourly employees. When the assistant had problems with child care or needed to go to an appointment, she was not allowed to leave if the director was gone. The physician in charge also was a working mother, but she was able to work out her own schedule. The administrative assistant used tactics that a person stuck in a low-power position would typically use—calling in sick, forgetting, making mistakes, losing files, promising and then not following through, and complaining to other staff members. The director had begun a process of documenting her poor work. When the doctor went to a professional meeting in another state, she discovered that no hotel reservations had been made, the conference fee had not been paid, and the materials for her presentation to the conference had not arrived. When the doctor arrived back at the office, ready to fire the assistant, she found that the assistant had resigned without notice.

In "Power Play," a seemingly unequal power situation was suddenly balanced by the resignation of the assistant—a classic "got you now" move on the part of the low-power person. Each of the participants in this conflict attempted to exercise power. When the administrative assistant assured the physician that she would take care of the arrangements for the conference and then did not, she destructively increased (temporarily) the doctor's dependence on her. If the physician had rethought the flexible-time needs of the office staff and then given desired resources (flexible time off), this change would have been an example of constructively increasing dependencies.

One way to reduce power others have over you is to change your goals. If after a few years in a job a person is not valued by an organization, a change of goals is likely to occur. The disenchanted employee might remark, "It is not important to me what they pay me for this job. I'll just do the minimal amount of work and expend all my creative energy on my hobbies." By altering the importance of the goal, you reduce the power the other has over you. The often-heard remark "There are other fish in the sea," used when a person has been dropped in a love affair, is just another way of saying that you have alternative sources for accomplishing your goals. (Or at least you hope you do, and you want other people to think you do!)

Communication plays a very important role in working out interdependence. People try to persuade others that they are valuable, that they need to be connected, and that the other's needs can be met best in a constructive relationship with the person doing the persuading. Communicating about the value you offer another is one way of increasing your power; the other becomes more dependent on you, and thus you have more power in that relationship. For example, recently Cheryl moved to a new state, and she immediately began going out with Jon, who had lived there for a long time. Jon took Cheryl on trips, introduced her to his wide circle of friends, and introduced her to cross-country skiing, rafting, and rock climbing. When Cheryl became disenchanted with Jon and made one attempt to break up with him, he reminded her of all the plans they had made for the future, and that he was going to include her on a big rafting trip Cheryl wanted to do. Jon was attempting to persuade Cheryl of the importance of what he provided her—he tried to influence her perception of his positive power. Unfortunately for Jon, Cheryl was unhappy enough that she had already investigated other ways to raft and climb, and decided a mediocre relationship was not what she wanted. His influence attempt failed, and they broke up.

☙Individual Power Currencies

You may have had the experience of traveling in a foreign country and trying to adapt to the use of different currencies. Euros used in Greece are worthless in India, where rupees are used to buy items of value. A pocketful of rupees is worthless in France unless you exchange it for the local currency. Just as money depends on the context in which it is to be spent (the country), your **power currencies** depend on how much your particular resources are valued by the other persons in *a relationship context*. You may have a vast amount of expertise in the rules of basketball, but if your fraternity needs an intramural football coach, you will not be valued as much as you would be if they needed a basketball coach. Power depends on having currencies *that other people need*. In the same manner, if other people possess currencies you value, such as the ability to edit your term paper or give you a ride, they potentially maintain some degree of power over you in your relationships with them. Conflict is often confusing because people try to spend a currency that is not valued in a particular relationship.

Power currencies are classified in many different ways by researchers. Raven and French (1956) label the bases of power as reward, coercive, legitimate, referent, and expert. Kipnis (1976) maintains that influential tactics are best classified as threats and promises, persuasion, reinforcement control, and information control. May (1972) notes five types of power: exploitative, manipulative, competitive, nutrient, and integrative. Folger, Poole, and Stutman (1993) supply this list: special skills and abilities, expertise about the task, personal attractiveness and likability, control over rewards and/or punishments, formal position in a group, loyal allies, persuasive skills, and control over critical group possessions. Regardless of the various labels, everyone has potential currencies that may be used to balance or gain power in a relationship. Even when you devalue your own currency, a careful analysis can show you areas of wealth. The following box presents a list of general power currencies.

R

Resource control: Often comes with one's formal position in an organization or group. An example is the controlling of rewards or punishments such as salary, number of hours worked, or firing. Parents control resources such as money, freedom, cars, and privacy for teenagers.

I

Interpersonal linkages: Your position in the larger system, such as being central to the communication exchange. If you are a liaison person between two factions, serve as a bridge between two groups that would otherwise not have information about each other, or have a network of friends who like each other, you have linkage currencies.

C

Communication skills: Conversational skills, persuasive ability, listening skills, group leadership skills, the ability to communicate caring and warmth, and the ability to form close bonds with others all contribute to interpersonal power. All people need to be related to others, to matter to others, and to be understood by others. Those who communicate well gain value and thus interpersonal power.

E

Expertise: Special knowledge, skills, and talents that are useful for the task at hand. Being an expert in a content area such as budget analysis, a process area such as decision-making methods, or a relational area such as decoding nonverbal cues may give you power when others need your expertise.

Resource control often results from attaining a formal position that brings resources to you. The president of the United States, regardless of personal qualities, will always have resources that go along with the job. Leadership and position, by their very nature, place a person in a situation in which others are dependent upon him or her, thus bringing ready-made power. Whatever your position—secretary, boss, chairperson, teacher, manager, or volunteer—you will be in a position to control resources that others desire. Many resources are economic in nature, such as money, gifts, and material possessions. Many people try to be close and supportive to those around them by buying gifts. They trade on economic currencies in order to obtain intimacy currencies from others. Their gifts are not always valued enough to bring them what they want, however. Not surprisingly, people who give gifts to each other often try to work out an agreement, probably implicitly, about the amount of money that can be spent to keep the dependence (and power) equal. If an inordinate amount of money is spent by one person, then typically the other person feels overly indebted. As Blau (1964) writes, "A person who gives others valuable gifts or renders them important services makes a claim for superior status by obligating them to himself" (108). People with little money usually have limited access to these forms of power. College graduates who cannot find jobs must remain financially dependent on parents, thus limiting independence on both sides. Elderly people whose savings shrink due to inflation lose power; mothers with children and no means of support lose most of their choices about independence, thus losing most of their potential power. Economic currencies are not the only important type of power currency, but they operate in personal conflicts as well as in larger social conflicts.

Another cluster of power currencies comes from one's *interpersonal linkages*, a set of currencies that depend on your interpersonal contacts and network of friends and supporters. People often obtain power based on whom they know and with whom they associate. For instance, if you have a good friend who has a mountain cabin you can share with others, then you have attained some power (if your family or friends want to go to the cabin) because of your ability to obtain things through other people. Young children try to trade on their linkage currencies when they say such things as "My Uncle Ben is a park ranger, and he will give us a tour of the park."

Interpersonal linkages help one attain power through coalition formation. Whenever you band together with another (such as a good friend) to gain some sense of strength, this coalition can be a form of power (Van de Vliert 1981). The small boy who says, "You better not hit me, because if you do, my big sister will beat you up" understands the potential value of coalitions. Similarly, Jason, a four-year-old boy, invented a friendly ghost, Karsha, who would come and help him in times of difficulty. After one particularly trying day with his younger sister (who was two years old), Jason recited to his father the virtues of Karsha. Karsha was "bigger than a mountain, a giant, who comes in the mornings and kills spiders with his hands. Karsha also makes electricity and has long hair. And Karsha is mean to babies that bite little boys." Interpersonal linkages are a source of power when people check out their network for what classes to take, where jobs might be available, where rentals might be found, and other kinds of information. "Who you know" is often a source of power.

One's *communication skills* also serve as potential power currencies. If you can lead a group in a decision-making process, speak persuasively, write a news release for your organization, serve as an informal mediator between people who are angry with each other, or use tact in asking for what you want, you will gain power because of your communication skills. Many times, students who have developed their communication skills are sought by employers because of their skills. Likewise, if you can facilitate the social process of a group, serve as the fun-loving joker in the family, or get conversations started at work, others typically will value you. It is not only the qualities, per se, that bring power but that these currencies are valued by others.

Communication skills also include the ability to form bonds with others through love, sex, caring, nurturing, understanding, empathic listening, warmth, attention, and other characteristics of intimate relationships. If a father provides genuine warmth and understanding to his teenage daughter who is going through a tough time at school, his support is a currency for him in their father–daughter relationship. Some people draw others to them because they listen attentively, remember what is important to others, and ask questions that show the importance of the others. These qualities should not be viewed as manipulative because if one's words and actions are not sincere, the phony quality of the communication becomes evident and power is not enhanced. Conflict management skills depend on a thorough grounding in communication skills. One cannot become an effective conflict manager without excellent interpersonal communication skills. These skills provide a positive base for the exercise of power with others, or relational power.

Expertise currencies are involved when a person has some special skill or knowledge that someone else values. The worker who is the only one who can operate the boiler at a large lumber mill has power because the expertise is badly needed. The medical doctor who specializes in a particular area has expertise power because her information and skills are needed by others. Almost all professions develop specialized expertise valued by others, which serves as a basis of power for people in the profession. Family members develop expertise in certain areas that others within the family come to depend on, such as cooking, repairing the car, or babysitting.

We limit our own power by developing some currencies at the expense of others. For example, women have traditionally been most comfortable providing more warmth and affection than men do (Johnson 1976). If this particular communication skill is developed at the expense of the ability to clarify a group discussion, a woman unnecessarily limits her power potential. The person who trades on currencies of interpersonal linkages, such as access to the boss, may neglect the development of expertise. The person who gains power by controlling resources, such as money or sex, may neglect the development of communication skills, resulting in a relationship based on coercive instead of shared power; withdrawing warmth in intimate relationships too often substitutes for good communication skills. A worker who focuses on the development of expertise in computer programming and systems analysis may ignore the power that can be developed through interpersonal linkages, thus furthering a tendency toward isolation in the organization. The most effective conflict participant develops several forms of power currencies and knows when to activate the different forms of power. A repertoire of currencies is a better base for sharing power than exclusive reliance on one form of power, which too often leads to misuse of that power.

Clarifying the currencies available to you and the other parties in a conflict helps in the conflict analysis. People are often unaware of their own sources of productive power, just as they do not understand their own dependence on others. Desperation and low-power tactics often arise from the feeling that one has no choice, that no power is available. Analyze your power currencies when you find yourself saying, "I have no choice." Usually, you are overlooking potential sources of power.

Application 4.5   My Sources of Power

Think of a particular relationship in which there is conflict, strain, or the potential for struggle. List your own sources of power, using the *RICE* acronym explained above. Then list sources of power that the other person has in this particular relationship. Are there any that you (1) might be overlooking or (2) have under- or overdeveloped? What did you learn from looking at your own and the other's sources of power?

❧Assessing Power: A Relational View

Since power is a dynamic product of shifting relationships, the amount of power parties have at any one time cannot be measured precisely. One maxim to remember when you are in the middle of a conflict is this: *"Each person firmly believes that the other person has more power."* Many of the pathologies or misuses of power arise because the image people have of their power (and others') is unrealistic (Boulding 1989, 65). Because each person in the conflict so often believes that he or she is in the low-power position, the conflict escalates. People use devious and manipulative tactics, since they truly think they have no choice. This **perception of power** is almost always inaccurate. In this section, ways of assessing power more accurately are presented. Remember that in emotionally involving conflicts, we usually feel out of power. Therefore, feelings are not the only, or even a very accurate, guide.

What might be a better way to assess the various power issues when your emotions are involved? Thinking about power, with the use of concepts and assessment instruments, can help engage your objectivity instead of subjective feelings only. As you think through what is happening, what has happened in the past, and what you would like to have happen in future interactions, you can gain a healthy distance on a current conflict.

The most common way to measure power is to compare the relative resources of the parties in a conflict (Berger 1980; Galvin and Brommel 1982; McCall 1979). For instance, in organizational work, it is generally agreed that power accrues to "those departments that are most instrumental in bringing in or providing resources which are highly valued by the total organization" (McCall 1979).

People have power in the organization when they

- are in a position to deal with important problems;
- have control over significant resources valued by others;
- are lucky or skilled enough to bring problems and resources together at the same time;
- are centrally connected in the work flow of the organization;
- are not easily replaced; and
- have successfully used their power in the past (McCall 1979).

This method of assessing power places high reliance on the resources controlled by a person or group on whom the organization is dependent. Although it provides a useful starting point, this method has two limitations:

1. It defines resources too narrowly (Berger 1980).

2. It puts too much emphasis on the source of the influence. Overemphasis on the source is characteristic of most studies of power, such as the "bases of power" work of Raven and French (1956) and the research of Kipnis (1976). Most assessments of power view the relationship as one-way. Person A is seen as exerting influence on person B. In diagram form, the relationship looks like this:

$$A - - - - - - - - - \to B$$

The relational perspective presented thus far characterizes the communication as two-way: each participant has power *with the other*. The relationship looks like this:

$$A \leftarrow - - - - - - - - - \to B$$

As power is designated to a partnership or other entity, the relationship might look like this:

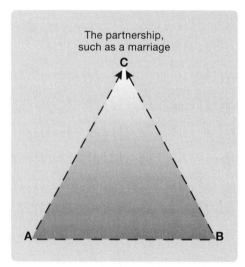

Most research presents power as a static property and disregards the dynamic elements of power. Resources are treated as possessions rather than as a changing part of the relationship process. One would assess power, using this perspective, by examining the resources that one party possesses. Many popular books on power take this individualistic approach. We have already discussed the serious limitations of this "one-way" approach.

Research on power has also focused on decision making or conversational control within the family unit. Decision-making approaches began with the classic Blood and Wolfe (1960) study of Detroit housewives. They asked wives questions such as "Who decides where the family will take a vacation?" and "Who decides what job to take?" Researchers in subsequent years tried to analyze power similarly by asking "Who has the last say about spending money?" (Safilios-Rothschild 1970), "Who is the real boss in the family?" (Heer 1963), and "Who would decide how you would spend $300?" (Kenkel 1957). It seemed reasonable that the most powerful member of a family would be the one who made most of the important decisions; unfortunately, there were difficulties with this popular method of measuring power. First, the researchers did not ask both spouses the questions. They might have received different answers if they had asked each partner separately. Second, the questions asked for "perceived authority"—who the participants thought made most of the decisions rather than who actually did (Bochner 1976; McDonald 1980). As a result, the participants may well have answered according to who they thought *should* have been making decisions. Given the sex-role stereotypes of that time period, a woman may have not wanted to tell a researcher that she was "the real boss." Whether it was accurate or not, women usually reported that their husbands made most of the decisions (Turk and Bell 1972).

In other cases researchers have studied decision making in the laboratory by presenting decision-making tasks such as responding to conflict stories or trying to match subtly different colors (Olson and Straus 1972; Olson and Rabunsky 1972). The problem with this approach was that many times the people completing the decision-making tasks together were strangers to each other. Obviously, people act differently with strangers than they do with intimates. In an extensive review of the decision-making assessments of power, McDonald (1980) says, "After twenty years of studying marital decision making, we actually may know little more than the authority expectations of couples" (850). He then argues that more research should focus on the "powering processes," or the interaction between the parties (Sprey 1972; Scanzoni 1979).

Looking at conversational control is the other main way researchers have attempted to study power (Millar and Rogers 1987, 1988). At one time or another, you have probably judged someone as powerful because he or she controlled the conversation. Many researchers have studied conversational control in couples (Mishler and Waxler 1968; Rogers and Farace 1975; Rogers-Millar and Millar 1977; Ellis 1979). Assuming that conversational control and power were the same thing, these researchers studied who talked the most, who interrupted the most, who changed topics the most, and who engaged in more "one up" moves. These two measures of power, decision making and conversational control, do not measure the same concept. If you look at different measures of power, you will probably reach different conclusions about who is most powerful (Olson and Rabunsky 1972; Turk and Bell 1972; Bochner 1976; Berger 1980; McDonald 1980).

Application 4.6
Who Has The Power?
An Observation and Assessment

With a group of people serving as the audience, try this experiment: watch a movie, role-play, or video presentation of two people in conflict. Or have two class members take on a problem-solving task or role-play an argument. They might argue about where to go for spring break, whether to ask a roommate to leave a living arrangement, or how to fairly assign grades to a group project. The audience makes notes throughout the conversation about who has the most power, and why. Then discuss your observations and your assessment.

You will probably find that almost everyone in the audience has a different way of deciding who really is more powerful. For some it may be nonverbal dominance; for others, vocal quality; for still others, amount of time spent in overt argument, or who "wins" at the end, or who appears to "let the other win." In essence, no single validating criterion for assessing power has been discovered by researchers; such a specific technique may not exist (Gray-Little 1982; Berger 1980).

Power is especially difficult to assess when influence is exercised covertly, or in hidden ways. Most of us have trouble deciphering covert power, or choices made based on another person's potential influence. For example, Will is an outdoorsman who would like to take a weeklong fishing trip, but he knows that his wife will not like being left alone for such an extended period of time since she works and would have to assume all the care of the children. Will proposes a two-day trip and, in the process, talks more and controls the discussion. An observer might guess that Will was in control of both process and outcome, since he and his wife agree that he will go on the two-day trip. Yet Will's conversation was structured around his estimate of his wife's reaction. Her power was important to his decision, yet an outside observer could not have known that without asking.

People who look the most powerful to outsiders often are less powerful than they appear. In fact, without knowing the structure of a relationship, you cannot guess who has the most power, since people balance their power currencies in complex ways. For instance, if one person "lets" the other do the talking for the group, the person who gives tacit permission for the other to talk is actually controlling the situation. Gender issues come into play, since women in our culture cannot usually become the powerful aggressor without facing social disapproval or physical danger. Many women learn to seek safety and power by hiding, becoming invisible, or becoming relationally oriented. Whereas a woman's safety and power needs are often met by becoming smaller and less visible, the traditional masculine style of seeking safety is by becoming the feared individual, by becoming bigger and more visible (Kaschak 1992, 126). A woman's overt use of power often exposes her to denigration and attack, whereas a man's overt use of power may be viewed as evidence that he is a good leader. Overt use of power by men at home is judged differently than in some work situations.

Power is exercised in ways that look weak. Sometimes the most powerful behavior is to appear to submit, yet resist, or act in a nonresistant way. An example of this form of power was Martin Luther King Jr.'s civil rights tactics, based on Gandhian principles, in which civil rights workers were trained to sit down when confronted by powerful persons, to protect their bodies if attacked but not to attack in response, and to use nonaggressive verbal responses. As happened in India, weakness in the face of strength made stronger persons question their use of force and coercion. A less productive "weak" way of exercising power is that of the apocryphal Army private who, when ordered to do KP duty, does as sloppy a job as possible while asking constantly, "Is this the way? Am I doing it right?" This "reluctant soldier" example can be seen in offices, in families, and on work crews where one person is "trying" (but failing) to get it right. The supervisor, parent, or crew boss then gets disgusted and does the job himself or herself.

Another indirect way to gain power is to refuse to cooperate when other people are depending on you. When this tactic is used in conjunction with unexpressed anger, it is labeled *passive aggressive behavior*. In passive aggression, a person acts aggressively (in

one's own self-interest, without much regard for the other) by being passive, or uncon-
cerned, when the other person needs a response. Passive aggression is displayed when
people feel they have a low level of power, whether they do or not, since it appears to
be a safer way of expressing anger, resentment, or hostility than stating such feelings
directly. Additionally, "nice" people (Bach and Goldberg 1974) may use passive aggression instead of direct conflict statements because they have been taught that it is not
nice to engage in conflict. Bach and Goldberg's (1974) list of common passive aggressive behaviors has been expanded to include the following:

- Forgetting appointments, promises, and agreements.
- Slipping and saying unkind things, then apologizing.
- Acting out nonverbally, such as by slamming doors and banging objects, but
  denying that anything is wrong.
- Getting confused, tearful, sarcastic, or helpless when certain topics come up.
- Getting sick when you've promised to do something.
- Scheduling two things at once.
- Evading situations so that others are inconvenienced.

The following case presents an example of passive aggressive communication.

Application 4.7

Deteriorating Roommate Relationship

Two college roommates have a practice of borrowing each other's possessions. When
Jan and Cheryl first moved in together, they decided it would be inconvenient to ask
each time they wanted to use a CD or borrow an article of clothing. Cheryl has been
keeping Jan's things longer than Jan wants her to, however, often causing Jan to have
to look for her CDs, textbooks, car keys, sweaters, skis, and gloves. Recently, Jan lost
several of Cheryl's possessions, including a CD she took to a party. She feels justified
since Cheryl has been misusing the privilege, too. They are avoiding the issue and
spending time away from each other. Role-play a direct instead of indirect way for Jan
to ask for change. Remember to verbalize content and relationship concerns, specific
goals, and face-saving techniques. Show listening and problem solving. Try the role-play
two ways: (1) Both people cooperate and (2) Cheryl does not cooperate at first. She
instead becomes defensive, attacks, withdraws, or acts in any other way you want to
play out a destructive conflict. Show how she and Jan might finally resolve the conflict
(realistically!).

The "cure" for passive aggression is to confront angry feelings directly instead of
indirectly. The college professor who double-schedules may feel overloaded and underappreciated but could tell people directly that too many appointments are interfering
with the rest of his or her work.

Power Imbalances

In most relationships, there are times when the participants become aware of discrepancies in their relative power with one another. If one party has more power than the other, the conflict is unbalanced; many of the choices the parties then make are attempts to alter these imbalances. Keep in mind that who has power is always a relative judgment—each party has sources of power even during times of **power imbalance.** Such power asymmetries have predictable effects on both the higher- and lower-power parties, and the imbalance produces systemwide effects on the relationship.

High Power

The exercise of social power for most people in Western culture is satisfying and even produces joy (Bowers and Ochs 1971; May 1972). **High power** is often a goal that people strive for; those with less power often feel, "If I were just the boss, things would be a lot better around here." The major difficulty with having a higher power than someone else is that it may corrupt you. Corruption is more than a word that describes a crooked politician. Corruption means moral rottenness, and inability to maintain the integrity of the self. A constant high level of power may "eat into" one's view of self and other, forming a perceptual distortion that may take on monstrous proportions. Higher-power persons, organizations, or nations may develop altered views of themselves and other parties. Constant feelings of higher power can result in these consequences:

1. A "taste for power" and the restless pursuit of more power as an end in itself.

2. The temptation to illegally use institutional resources as a means of self-enrichment.

3. False feedback concerning self-worth and the development of new values designed to protect power.

4. The devaluing of the less powerful and the avoidance of close social contact with them (Kipnis 1976, 178).

The undesirable consequences of a power imbalance can take many forms. For instance, studies show that if a teacher uses strong power over a student, the relationship disintegrates into the exclusive use of coercive strategies (Jamieson and Thomas 1974; Raven and Kruglanski 1970). Or the person highest in power may claim benevolence, that harmful actions are actually "for the good of the other person," thereby dismissing the negative consequences to the lower-power person. When someone is fired from an organization, it is common to hear, "It was for her/his own good—he/she will be better off spending time doing X." According to Guggenbuhl-Craig (1971), persons in helping professions, such as ministers, teachers, health workers, and others, can lose touch with their need to exercise power in order to feel valued and needed. Although helpers undoubtedly are in their professions in order to help, they also must have "helpees," or they have no function. How can a physician be a physician without people who need healing? How can teachers teach if no one values learning? If helpers do not understand that helping also contributes to their own sense of self-worth and personal fulfillment, the act of helping can become a high-power move. Just as during the Inquisition, when the learned scholars were sure that they were helping the persons accused of heresy, an unrestrained high power may make the powerful party blind to the havoc wreaked on the less powerful party. You may have had times in your personal relationships when power became unbalanced; if so, you know the harm that unrestrained power can bring, whether you were the one with too much power or the one without enough power.

Striving for higher power can destroy even the best of relationships. For example, in intimate relationships, the person who is least invested in the relationship has the most power (the "Principle of Least Interest," Waller 1938). Paradoxically, decreasing the investment for the purpose of gaining higher power is ultimately self-defeating, since you have to continue your decreasingly fragile investment in order to remain more powerful. And the lessened dependence can lead to the demise of the relationship. If you convince yourself that "I don't have to put up with this," then you don't usually stay in the relationship.

Finally, persons or nations with higher power can deny that power is exercised; they may deny that there is a conflict (it is a "minor disagreement") or use any of the other forms of denial mentioned earlier. Unrestrained higher power can corrupt the power holder's view of the self and view of the other, and it can set the stage for continued unproductive interaction.

Low Power

If absolute power corrupts absolutely, does absolute powerlessness make you pure?
—Harry Shearer

Just as power can corrupt, *powerlessness can also corrupt* (May 1972). If lower-power people are continually subjected to harsh treatment or lack of goal attainment, they are likely to produce some organized resistance to the higher-power people. When one reaches the stage where "nothing matters" (one cannot attain his or her goals through accepted means), violence or despair is spawned. It is the person who feels powerless who turns to the last resort—giving up, aggression, or violence (Richmond et al. 1984; Kipnis, Schmidt, and Wilkerson 1980; Falbo and Peplau 1980). Too much losing does not build character; it builds frustration, aggression, or apathy. A typical example of how perceived unequal power results in aggression is the relationship between students and teachers. In one study, when students were asked what they considered doing to resolve conflicts they had with more powerful teachers, they replied on paper, "Use a .357 magnum," "Blow up his mailbox," "Sabotage him," and "Beat him up" (Wilmot 1976). At the very least, asymmetry in perceived power can lead to coercion in an attempt to "get even" (Jamieson and Thomas 1974; Raven and Kruglanski 1970). Most examples of retaliation occur because the person doing the retaliating perceives himself/herself to be in a low-power situation.

In severe, repetitive conflicts, **both** parties feel **low power,** and they continually make moves to increase their power at the other's expense. Since, as noted, the assessment of power is problematic, it is very difficult to determine the exact levels of power in a conflict. However, if each party believes she or he has less power than the other, a destructive, escalating spiral of conflict usually results. Each party attempts to increase power at the other's expense, with the next round bringing yet more destructive moves. Each person feels "behind" and justified in engaging in dirty moves because of what the other did.

Application 4.8   The Case of an Escalating Spiral

Tom and Paula were a married couple with two small children. Tom felt the financial pressure of providing for the young family since he and Paula had decided that Paula would work at home, caring full-time for the children until they were at school. Tom, a dentist, scheduled more patients during each day and arrived home later than he used to. To release the increased stress, he set up golf games with friends on the weekends, something he and Paula used to do together. Paula felt lonely and upset that Tom was spending more time at work and with his friends. She let Tom know that she needed more help at home and asked him to pitch in with some of the chores around the house and with getting the children bathed and put to bed. Tom resented being asked to do more at home, since he felt his financial contributions to the family were unappreciated. Paula felt taken for granted and tired of being alone with the two children. Both felt low in power but acted in ways that communicated to each other that they were really higher in power than the other. Both felt justified in their escalating anger at each other. Both felt lonely, unappreciated, misunderstood, and scared. They were only a few weeks away from "dirty tricks" when they sought professional help.

As in the previous case, role-play this situation with different strategies for constructive change, using what you have learned so far. You might have three different small groups set up a role-play, with the class judging which seems most constructive, and most realistic.

Often, as with Tom and Paula, even if the lower-power person wants to act aggressively, there are restraints against that person's doing so. The powerless will try to restore equity, and if that fails, they have few options; one option is to use passive aggressive behavior, as discussed previously. In addition, Madanes (1981) notes that developing severely dysfunctional behavior is an exercise of power that affects all close associates. Lower-power parties will sometimes destroy a relationship as the ultimate move to bring about a balance of power.

The combination of denigration from the higher-power person and destructive power-balancing moves from the lower-power person contributes to a system of interactions that is not productive for either party. A cyclical, degenerative, destructive conflict spiral characterizes the ongoing interactions. The power disparity promotes struggles over power, increases the underlying bases of the conflict, and leads to lessened involvement in the relationship for both parties. When the four horsemen enter a spiral, nobody wins.

Application 4.9   Nobody Wins

Craig is a supervisor in a community agency, and Marilyn is a staff member who works part time. Craig coerces Marilyn into taking on a community volunteer program—a job she neither wants nor has time to develop at a competent level. Marilyn resists working on the program, and deadlines are looming. Craig, noticing her avoidance, humiliates her in a public meeting by pointing out what has not been done, and asking her to agree to

(continued)

work hard on the program. Marilyn accedes (on the surface) but talks to her friends about how poorly she is treated. After two months of Craig's disapproval of her progress and of her seeking social support and a new job elsewhere, she resigns.

Answer the following questions about Craig and Marilyn:

How might Marilyn have changed her passive aggressive stance into a constructive one?

How might Craig have changed his "power over" stance into a constructive one?

What might a beginning dialogue that is constructive sound like?

Craig did not accomplish his original goal of starting the community program, and Marilyn left her job. They achieved a power balance in an unproductive manner, much like in a game of leapfrog. When one person is behind, he or she then jumps into the lead, and the other person, sensing that he or she is "losing," does the same. Pretty soon the relationship is suffering, and neither person has achieved any of the original goals. In cases of power disparity, agreements are "basically unstable since they are grounded on unilateral threats rather than on mutually established norms" (Apfelbaum 1974, 151). The ever-accelerating unproductive moves are the result of attempts at power balancing through counterproductive means. The alternative is to balance the power through productive avenues and recognize that with extreme power asymmetry, effective long-term management is not likely.

A concise visual summary of our view of power and its effects is in Figure 4.3. Cameron and Whetton (1995) inspired this graph, which we adapted to an interpersonal

Figure 4.3   Interpersonal Power

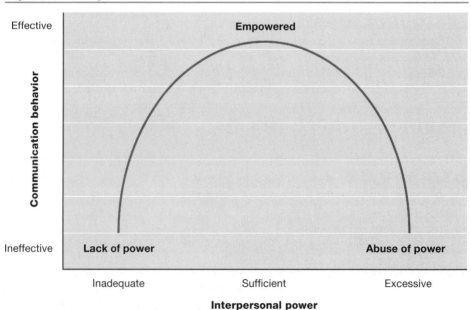

orientation. As you can see, both lack of power (low power) and excessive power (high power) lead to ineffective communication behaviors. When you have sufficient power, your interpersonal behaviors are at their best.

☙Constructive Power Balancing

Integrative power depends very much on the power of language and communication, especially on the powers of persuasion.
—Kenneth Boulding, *Three Faces of Power*

Up to this point, various words have been used almost interchangeably—*integrative power, both/and power, power with, power to a partnership, collaboration,* and *sharing power.* What is the rationale for viewing power in such terms? Is it actually possible to develop practices in which power isn't used against people but is used for mutual benefit?

We believe that *collaboration and the constructive realignment of power* is usually best for all concerned, with the following conditions:

* The high-power person is not abusing power in a way that takes away all possibility of influence by the lower-power person or persons.

* One person is not lying, distorting, or suffering from a disorder of character, such as sociopathy. A sociopath is a person who has no conscience and is not moved by the plight of others.

* The long-term gains are worth the expenditure of energy.

Competitive power has its place, too. We view competitive power as being useful when the following conditions are in place:

* Crucial needs of one party are at stake—needs the person is not willing to compromise about unless no other option exists. These might be economic or personal survival, protection of children, avoidance of harm, or protection of a crucial sense of self.

* Competition can lead to collaboration—when the playing field becomes more level.

Since destructive conflicts are often set off by struggles over power, and given that power is relational, power always is in a state of change. The only question is how one goes about changing power. If you struggle with someone because "you won't give in," you are trying to block their exercise of power—and they are probably doing the same thing. The paradox is that the more you struggle against someone, the less power you will have with that person. From a both/and perspective, the more powerful we feel, the more we are setting ourselves up for resistance from the other party. Put bluntly, power against is usually eventually blocked and diminished. Boulding (1989) says it well: "Power over human beings is very complex. Other human beings can answer back, fight back, obey or disobey, argue and try to exercise power over us, which a tree never does" (53). We must recognize that while we need to exercise appropriate power and influence, the other person needs to exercise influence as well, so we might as well cooperate with each other so we can both be effective. The both/and perspective as well as the "power to the partnership" perspective assumes that you all want to accomplish your goals and that you need each other to do that. Since it is the other who is blocking you (and you blocking him or her), integrative power moves beyond the tug-of-war and to a new plane of relationship.

Whereas destructive struggling for power leads to a downward spiral of more thwarting and interference and to a lessened ability to accomplish your goals, shared power leads to a synergy of power creation through productive communication. As you work with each other, each of you stops directly interfering with the other and actively assists the other in getting what he or she wants, and the communication between you serves a transcendent function (Wilmot 1995). With cooperation you actually *create more power* than the two of you could have created separately. Shared power is not a weak, tentative approach—it is powerful and energetic, and it requires great skill.

Collaboration depends on a model of shared power. Rarely will you be in a life situation in which all the power resides with the other, so collaboration is almost always possible. Research makes this clear. Alberts and Driscoll (1992) demonstrated that satisfied couples will "pass, refocus, mitigate or respond" to the other rather than struggle over power. The sense of "we-ness," of working together, pulls romantic couples through their first big fight (Siegert and Stamp 1994). Gottman (1999) makes it clear that successful couples work together to "repair" their relationship instead of making the other wrong. If they do not learn to seek repairs as a matter of course, they do not stay together. Any relationship in which power is not shared ultimately will end, in divorce, abandonment, withdrawing, retreat into mental illness, or the continuation of a grim, joyless relationship.

Analyze the success of the change described in this case. What made the change possible? Specify how the power-against model changed to a power-with model. Take

---

Application 4.10   It's Their Fault

Bruce is the production manager of a large electronics manufacturing facility, and Lenny is the engineering manager. Each supervises a five-person team of managers. Lenny's engineers are responsible for (1) designing systems for production and (2) quality control. Bruce's production employees are responsible for output—they have to get the product out the door and shipped to customers. Over a two-year period, the two teams seemed gridlocked. Engineering staff members complained, both in their staff meetings and to the plant manager, saying, "Those production people—we design good systems for them to follow; they don't follow them, and then quality slips. What is their problem?" Meanwhile, production employees openly criticized the engineers on the manufacturing floor by saying, "They think they are so hot—yet their elaborate designs don't work, they treat us like slaves, and they don't know or care how we are being held to a minimum number of units produced." Finally, the plant manager had to ask for outside help. The production and engineering managers met, as did the work teams. They agreed to (1) shift quality control to the production side, (2) have the engineers provide training to the production employees so they could enforce quality control, (3) not make any more negative public comments about the other team, and (4) require the production and engineering managers to attend each other's staff meetings. What was a "power-against" situation became, over a period of a month, a "power-with" situation. The plant manager was very pleased that his two key players in engineering and production were now helping each other accomplish their goals rather than interfering with one another. Production output and quality both improved. A new system of rebalanced power made collaboration possible.

these steps and apply them to another power-against situation. What are some general principles you can use in the future?

Conflict participants are more likely to make a long-range relationship work if they move toward equality in power. Models for productive power balancing, although scarce, do exist. In everyday life, individuals can learn to cooperate and to reach agreements if power is distributed equitably, or fairly (Apfelbaum 1974, 138). For relationships to work over time, people must continually realign the power balance as the situation warrants.

What can friends, co-workers, family members, or intimates do when they discover power asymmetry in their relationships? They can (1) work to make the relationships more equal, (2) try to convince themselves and their partners that the relationships are more equal than they might seem (by restoring psychological equality), or (3) eventually abandon the unbalanced relationships (Hatfield, Utne, and Traupmann 1979). For instance, family members negotiating household tasks may say, "I should get more credit for taking out the garbage than you do for cleaning the counters because I hate to take out the garbage and you don't mind doing the counters." The person who hates taking out garbage is trying to balance power by restoring psychological fairness. We are all too familiar with friendships that fail because of inadequate power balancing.

An interpersonal relationship with a power disparity between participants can achieve a more productive focus by moving toward balance. The destructive attempts by lower-power parties to balance power are a move toward balance, but power must be balanced productively to lead to effective management. Power must be realigned in order for sharing to exist.

❧Approaches to Balancing Power

You can take steps to realign power; these techniques work for both high- and lower-power parties to bring power into balance.

Restraint

Higher-power parties can limit their power by refusing to use all the currencies they have at their disposal. A militarily powerful nation that refuses to invade a neighboring country and a physically powerful spouse who refuses to inflict damage on the other spouse are examples of a higher-power party limiting power usage. If the high-power person refuses to engage in "natural" responses, this restraint can alter the automatic nature of a destructive cycle. In this self-regulating approach, power is given to a higher partnership or unit, instead of being used as an individual right. Art, a college teacher, refuses to use punitive power when students present last-minute pleadings for more time to write final papers. Instead, Art simply says, "Why don't you set a deadline for the final paper that you can meet, and it will be fine with me. What day and time do you want to hand it in?" A married couple found a way to lower one member's economic power, thereby providing more balance in their relationship. They valued monetary equality and were used to having separate accounts and almost the same disposable income. The husband got an unexpected raise, however, and suddenly had more money to spend. They started arguing frequently because he would propose expensive weekends for recreation and his wife had difficulty paying for her half. In response to their increasingly destructive arguments, they decided to set up an automatic savings withdrawal from his monthly paycheck, to be put in a joint long-term savings plan. Then they would use this money occasionally for a "lost weekend." Even though he still earned more money than his partner, the negative effect on them as a couple was lessened, while he gained the long-term advantages of saving more money. He limited his immediate use of his higher monetary power, with positive effects on the couple's balance of power.

Focus on Interdependence: Power to the Unit

One way to balance the power in a relationship is for lower-power individuals to focus on ways the people involved in the conflict are dependent on each other instead of demanding attention to their own individual needs (Donohue and Kolt 1992). Higher-power individuals usually try to minimize interdependence; therefore, lower-power individuals need to point out how the conflict parties are more related than it might appear. (The strategy of searching for overlapping interests will be discussed in detail in chapter 8, "Negotiating for Mutual Gains.") When individuals are scared and feeling powerless, they often angrily demand that their own needs be met or begin to use threats. These are ineffective approaches, since the higher-power person has the ability to move away or lessen the interdependence.

A thorough understanding of interdependence clarifies power relationships. If John and Sarah are dating and decide to live together, they both increase their dependence on the other. Following Emerson's formula of **power-dependence relations,** as John becomes more dependent on Sarah, Sarah's power increases. Likewise, Sarah becomes more dependent on John, thereby increasing his power. When two people elevate their dependence on each other, both increase their sources of power. Each one expands his or her currencies that are valued by the other. Therefore, power in enduring relationships is not finite—it is an expandable commodity. The focus shouldn't be the singular amount of power each one has but the balance of power between them. John and Sarah may have little power with each other at the beginning of their relationship. Later, as each develops more power, the other's power rises approximately equally. The absolute amount of power may change, but the crucial issue is the comparative dependence that John and Sarah have on each other.

Application 4.11   Quick! It's an Emergency!

Conflict Parties: Tom, a midlevel manager in an office; Helen, the secretary for four people in the office.

Repetitive Conflict: Often when Helen is too busy to get all her work done immediately, she will set priorities and plan her schedule based on known deadlines. Tom's work makes up the largest share of Helen's work. Tom and the other three supervisors rank equally on the organizational scale. However, when Tom is busy and pressed, he rushes to Helen's desk with work that needs to be done immediately. Following is a typical exchange:

Tom: Helen, I have just this one little thing that has to go out today.

Helen [sighing]:   Yes, Tom, I know—just one little thing. But I have to get this out for Joe today, and it must be done first.

(continued)

Application 4.11   Quick! It's an Emergency!

Tom puts more pressure on Helen to do his job first by saying that it won't take long and that just this once she needs to respond to the emergency pressures. Helen gets angry and tries to persuade him that it can wait one more day. Then she pouts a bit.

Helen: I am only one person, you know. Just put it there and I'll try to get it done.

Tom: Helen, you're a sweetheart. When this madhouse calms down, I'll take you out to lunch. I knew I could count on you.

Helen then stays late to finish the work, but she asks her office manager to speak to Tom again about interfering with her ability to manage her work. Tom apologizes a few days later.

Tom: I didn't mean to make you mad. I didn't think that one report was going to tick you off so much.

Helen: It's OK; it's just that I can't please everybody.

In the "Quick! It's an Emergency!" case, the power may appear to be organized such that Tom has more because he is the boss and Helen has less because she occupies a lower position in the organization. A closer look reveals that the parties are fairly well balanced in power. The balancing act is, however, taking a toll on their relationship, and the work could be managed more creatively. Tom is dependent on Helen for getting his work out error free, quickly, and with the benefit of Helen's experience. He depends on Helen to respond to his needs before those of the others in the office, since he is carrying more of the work in the office than the other three at his level. He sees himself as a pleasant and noncontrolling person whose employees work because they want to. He depends on Helen to view him as a reasonable and professional person because this is how he views himself. Helen, meanwhile, depends on Tom for some of her self-esteem. She prizes her ability to skillfully organize her work so that it gets done on time. She wants to be treated as a valuable decision-making employee. She knows, too, that if Tom becomes dissatisfied with her work, he will complain to her immediate supervisor in the office, and she might be overlooked for promotions or might even lose her job. So Helen depends on Tom for positive ratings, a good work climate, and self-esteem. Restructuring their interactions could allow them to achieve more of their independent and interdependent goals. Helen could ask Tom to help her respond to disparate pressures; Tom could ask Helen how to set up a way to take care of emergencies. A problem-solving approach to conflict management would allow both to balance their power more collaboratively.

The Power of Calm Persistence

Lower-power people in a conflict often can gain more equal power by persisting in their requests. Substantive change, when power is unequal, seldom comes about through intense, angry confrontation. Rather, change results from careful thinking and from planning for small, manageable moves based on a solid understanding of the problem

(Lerner 1989, 15). When intensity is high, people react rather than observe and think. We overfocus on the other instead of an analysis of the problem, and we move toward polarization. Lower-power parties cannot afford to blow up. One source of power the lower-power person has, however, is careful, calm analysis that directs attention to the problem. If lower-power people have patience and avoid giving up out of frustration, they gain "nuisance value," and the higher-power person or group often listens and collaborates just to get them to go away. Persuasive skills become crucial. The low-power person must analyze the situation well, taking into account what will be judged appropriate, effective, credible, and practical.

Several examples of **calm persistence** illustrate this strategy for increasing one's power. Ellen is the head of a large, successful consulting organization. She travels a lot and has a tightly organized schedule. A few years ago her daughter, Linda, whined and pouted about not being able to go horseback riding alone with her mother. This was ineffective since Ellen hates whining. Finally, Linda, at age 8, hit upon a solution. She asked her mother for a "management meeting," in which she pointed out her complaints and asked for what she wanted. This approach so impressed her mother that, with affection and humor, they broke through an avoid-pursue spiral. Linda gained power, and Ellen felt much better about how the two of them were spending time.

Individuals in conflict with institutions often experience frustrating, demeaning powerlessness as they are shunted from one person to the next. Phone calls are not returned and frustration rises dramatically. Sometimes only calm, clear persistence increases an individual's power enough for him or her to be heard and dealt with. Some suggestions for dealing with large, impersonal institutions are as follows:

- Identify the individuals on the phone by name and ask for them when you call back.
- Stay pleasant and calm. State clearly what you want, and ask for help in solving the problem.
- Follow the rules even if you think they are ridiculous. If they want five copies of a form, typed and folded a certain way, give it to them. Then point out that you have followed the rules and expect results.
- Write simple, clear memos summarizing what you want, what you have done, and when you expect a response.
- Tell them all the steps you took to try to get a response from them.
- Avoid taking out your frustration on low-power individuals in the organization. They may respond with "I'm just following the rules," avoiding personal responsibility—and who could blame them? Instead, be courteous and ask for help. Humor always helps if it is not at someone else's expense.

Stay Actively Engaged

Remaining in a low-power position, assuming that one's weakness is a permanent instead of a temporary condition, and adopting low-power tactics set up a dangerously unbalanced situation that benefits no one, not even the high-power person. The higher-power person, who has the power to define the terms of the conflict in his or her own favor, often understands only one side of the conflict. Therefore, the higher-power person may not be able to find a constructive solution. People who perceive themselves as powerless usually do not talk effectively about their own needs and, after a while, may adopt a self-defeating, accommodating style that becomes fixed. When one person believes that the other person can go elsewhere for whatever is needed, the lower-power person tends to avoid conflict (Folger, Poole, and Stutman 1993). If the fixed power position becomes intolerable, the lower-power person may act out of desperation, doing something such as resigning, leaving a romantic relationship, blowing up and antagonizing the high-power person so that he or she ends the relationship, or threatening self-destructive behavior, such as by saying, "Just do what you want. Just tell me what to do. I'm tired of fighting. You win." This unstable situation invites escalation on the other person's part and may lead to the end of the relationship.

Rather than remaining in self-defeating spirals, Lerner (1989, 35) suggests that people in low-power positions adopt the following moves:

- *Speak up and present a balanced picture of strengths as well as weaknesses.* One might say, "It's true that I am afraid to ask my boss for a raise, even though you want me to. But I earn a steady paycheck and budget and plan well for our family. I want some credit for what I do already contribute."

- *Make clear what one's beliefs, values, and priorities are, and then keep one's behavior congruent with these.* An entry-level accountant in a large firm was asked by the comptroller to falsify taxable deductions, hiding some of the benefits given to employees. The accountant, just out of school and a single parent, said, "When you hired me I said I was committed to doing good work and being an honest accountant. What you are asking me to do is against the code of ethics and could result in my losing my license. I can't afford to take that risk. I'm sure you'll understand my position."

- *Stay emotionally connected to significant others even when things get intense.* It takes courage for a low-power person to let another person affect him or her. One teenage son was furious and hurt when his father decided to remarry, since the son did not like the wife-to-be at all and felt disloyal to his mother. After some tough thinking, he decided to tell his father honestly how he felt, what he did not like, and what he feared about the new marriage instead of taking another way out, such as angrily leaving his father's house to live with his mother in another state. This conversation balanced the power between father and son in an entirely new way.

- *State differences, and allow others to do the same.* The easiest, but often not the best, way for a low-power person to manage conflict is to avoid engagement. Again, courage is required to bring up differences when a power imbalance is in place. Brad, a college freshman, worked at a fast-food place during school. He was unhappy because the manager kept hiring unqualified people (without checking their references) and then expected Brad to train them and provide supervision, even though Brad was barely making more than minimum wage. Finally Brad told the manager, "I have a different way of looking at whom you should hire. I try to do a good job for you, but I have to try to work with people who have no experience and maybe don't have the personality to pitch in and work hard as part of the team. Would you consider letting me sit in on interviews and look over applications?" The manager was pleased with Brad's initiative and said yes.

Empowerment of Low-Power People by High-Power People

Sometimes it is clearly to the advantage of higher-power groups or individuals to purposely enhance the power of lower-power groups or individuals. Without this restructuring of power, working or intimate relationships may end or rigidify into bitter, silent, passive aggressive, and unsatisfactory entanglements. Currencies valued by higher-power people can be developed by lower-power people if they are allowed more training, more decision-making power, or more freedom. For instance, in one social service agency, Sharon was not doing well at directing a grant-funded program on finding housing for homeless people. Jan, the director of the agency, realized that Sharon was a good fundraiser but not a good program director. By switching Sharon's job description, the agency gained a good employee instead of continuing a series of negative job evaluations that would have resulted in Sharon's eventual termination.

Empowerment also occurs when third parties are invested with the power to intervene on the behalf of less powerful persons. For instance, children who have been abused by their parents or caretakers can be empowered if their plight is reported to the proper agency. The legal system will provide attorneys, caseworkers to monitor the situation, counselors to work with the parents, judges to arbitrate decisions involving the children, and free services to help the children recover from the effects of the abuse. Our society has decided, by passing certain laws, that extreme forms of power imbalance, such as abuse, will not be allowed to continue when they are discovered. Children are empowered by laws that give them rights and give responsibilities to others.

Metacommunication

Another way to balance power is to transcend the win/lose structure by jointly working to preserve the relationship during conflict. By metacommunicating during or before conflicts (talking about the relationship or about how the parties will handle their conflicts), the parties can agree about behaviors that will not be allowed (such as leaving during a fight).

Metacommunication focuses the parties on the process of their communication with each other. They talk about their communication, and if that fails, they can agree to bring in outside mediators or counselors. They can agree that whenever a serious imbalance occurs, the high-power party will work actively with the low-power party to alter the balance in a meaningful way. Usually romantic partners, friends, family members, and work partners can accomplish such joint moves if they agree that the maximization of individual power, left unrestrained, will destroy the relationship. They see that individual power is based relationally, that dependence begets power, and that successful relationships necessitate a balancing of dependencies and therefore of power. The lack of a balanced arrangement is a signal to reinvest in the relationship rather than a clue that the relationship is over. The person temporarily weaker in the relationship can draw on the relationship currencies, as if the relationship were a bank and the currencies were savings. The weaker party can claim extra time, space, money, training, empathy, or other special considerations until the power is brought back into an approximation of balance. The following case presents an example of an interpersonal peacemaking agreement.

Application 4.12   I'm Not Your Slave!

Cheryl and Melissa are two teenage girls who share a room in a foster home. Cheryl is more outgoing and friendly than Melissa, who is shy in groups but demanding of Cheryl's time and attention. Recently, Melissa increased small demands for Cheryl to shut the door, turn down the radio, bring her a drink of water, include her in phone gossip, and lend her clothes, records, and other items. Cheryl, after discussing the situation with several helpers, decided she did not want to continue to respond to Melissa in anger and disdain (e.g., "Get your own water—I'm not your slave!"). She then took the follow-ing steps to restore the balance of power:

1. She reminded Melissa that they had agreements about chores in the room, made at a family meeting, that Cheryl wanted to follow.

2. She voluntarily began to fill Melissa in on happenings at school that involved people whom Melissa admired.

3. She complied with Melissa's requests, such as getting her a drink of water, the first time they were made, but then said, "I'm glad to get it this once, but remember we agreed to be equal in who does what in the room. So you're on your own now."

4. She asked Melissa to go to basketball games with her and her friends. Melissa became sociable, made new friends of her own, and needed Cheryl's assistance less.

Granted, Cheryl was a remarkably compassionate teenager. But she reported that her life was better, too, since she got along so much better with her roommate.

Things to Say When You Are Low Power

We end this chapter with some specific low-power statements that can be used to bal-ance power. Since a power imbalance brings destructive behavior, these are offered in the spirit of helping bring a sense of balance into relationships. The assumption is that they will be used for productive ends to help work through relationship issues. When you are feeling low power, you might try

- Validating or acknowledging the other: "Noah, I appreciate how you . . ."
- Using "I" statements: "What I would like is . . ."
- Asking the higher-power person what he or she needs: "Sara, I'm wondering what would work for you in this situation?"

- Letting them know what they can gain from helping you: "Kathy, if I'm included in the discussions, I'll be able to support the decisions more fully."
- Announcing all intended escalation and looking for a way out: "Patricia, I really don't want to go to the union on this problem. I want to reach some understanding so we can put this to rest."
- Expressing optimism: "Juan, I know that if we just sit down together and talk we can resolve this pretty easily."

In power relationships, balance is the key to success.

Most of us are caught in a paradox of power. To be effective people, we need to maximize our abilities, take advantage of opportunities, and use resources at our disposal so we can lead the kind of lives we desire. Yet within the confines of an ongoing relationship, *maximization of individual power is counterproductive* for both the higher-power and lower-power parties. The unrestrained maximization of individual power leads to damaged relations, destructive moves, more destructive countermoves, and the eventual ending of the relationship. Since people are going to take steps to balance power—destructively if no other means are available—we can better manage conflict by working to balance power in productive and creative ways. Equity in power reduces violence and enables all participants to continue working for the good of all parties, even in conflict.

Summary

In this chapter we discuss what power is and note that people usually have negative connotations of power. We compare and contrast three different views of power—either/or power, both/and power, and designated power. Also, many times people deny power in various ways.

Power is presented as a relational concept rather than as an attribute of the individual. Our power currencies are described as "spendable" energy that can be used in conflictual relationships. Power imbalances often impede conflict management; the various ways to deal with too much or too little power are described, with specific suggestions on how to balance power in positive ways. Suggestions for people in low power end the chapter.

Key Terms

Use the text's Online Learning Center at **www.mhhe.com/wilmot7** to further your understanding of the following terminology.

∿Review Questions

Go to the self-quizzes on the Online Learning Center at **www.mhhe.com/wilmot7** to test your knowledge of the chapter concepts.

1. Define power.
2. Describe your own orientation to power.
3. How does power operate in a distressed system?
4. Clarify the difference between either/or power and both/and power.
5. What are the ways people deny their use of power?
6. Explain the relational theory of power.
7. What are power-dependence relations?
8. Define and give examples of power currencies.
9. What does the acronym RICE stand for?
10. What makes power difficult to assess?
11. What behaviors does feeling high power lead to?
12. What behaviors does feeling low power lead to?
13. List some approaches to balancing power.
14. What is metacommunication?
15. If you are low power, what can you do?

Chapter 5

Styles and Tactics

Style preferences develop over a person's lifetime based on a complicated blend of genetics, life experiences, family background, and personal philosophy. By the time you are an adult, your basic orientation to conflict is in place. Your preferences for either harmony and calm or high-energy engagement are apparent. For instance, if you traditionally go on a final, end-of-summer backpack trip involving 10 friends, and the main goal is a wonderful time, it would make no sense for you to stubbornly insist on going where you want to go. Instead, you cooperate to find a place to go that fits the goals of the group.

Developing a repertoire of diverse styles and tactics may require some stretching of your comfort zone. However, having a choice of styles you can use will enhance your chances for productive conflict. This chapter will introduce you to a variety of styles and tactics used in conflict situations and will show you the impact of each style or tactic.

❧The Nature of Styles and Tactics

Conflict **styles** are patterned responses, or clusters of behavior, that people use in conflict. **Tactics** are individual moves people make to carry out their general approach. Styles describe the big picture, whereas tactics describe the specific communicative pieces of the big picture. While "tactics" makes it sound like each move is planned, as in a war, most people do not plan their moves—they just act. Unfortunately, there is not an appropriate word to represent these "moves" or "behaviors" or "communication

Figure 5.1   Conflict Styles

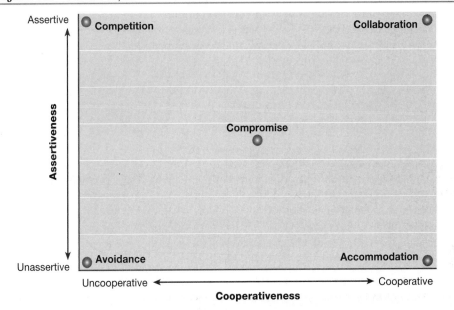

choices." When you use a tactic numerous times, it becomes a style—a patterned response. Because the topic of conflict styles has been researched more than any other in interpersonal conflict management, one can classify styles a number of ways. The classification schemes range from the two-style approach to the five-style approach and are as follows:

- Two styles: Cooperation and competition (Deutsch 1949; Tjosvold 1990).

- Three Styles: Nonconfrontation, solution orientation, and control (Putnam and Wilson 1982).

- Four Styles: Yielding, problem solving, inaction, and contending (Pruitt 1983b); accommodating/harmonizing, analyzing/preserving, achieving/directing, and affiliating/perfecting (Gilmore and Fraleigh 1992); aggressive/confrontive, assertive/persuasive, observant/introspective, and avoiding/reactive (Robert 1982); exit, voice, loyalty, neglect (Rusbult, Zembrodt, and Gunn 1982).

- Five styles: Integrating, obliging, dominating, avoiding, and compromising (Rahim 1983; Rahim and Magner 1995); collaboration, accommodation, competition, avoidance, and compromise (Thomas 1976; Kilmann and Thomas 1975).

Most trainers and researchers are currently using a five-style approach; therefore, this approach will be emphasized for the remainder of the chapter. Kilmann and Thomas (1975) most clearly defined the five styles when they located them on a graph according to two dimensions: (1) **assertiveness** and (2) **cooperativeness.** The five styles are presented in figure 5.1.

Because of the differences between various writers in labeling styles, this one set of labels is being used throughout this chapter. The original Kilmann and Thomas graph has been slightly modified, and Rahim and Magner's (1995) style questions and labeling have been modified for consistency in this presentation.

Notice that avoidance represents low assertiveness and low cooperativeness. Accommodation represents a low level of concern for yourself but a high level of concern for the other (you give them what they want). The opposite of accommodation is competition—you are highly concerned for yourself but have only a low level of concern for the other (you "go for it" regardless of the desires of the other). Collaboration factors in both your concerns and the other's concerns. Compromise is a middle ground, where there are moderate degrees of assertiveness and cooperativeness.

❧Measuring Your Styles

Before we proceed, take the style measure in the following box. This measure is adapted from Rahim and Magner (1995) and will give you scores on each of the five styles of avoidance, accommodation, competition, collaboration, and compromise.

As you will see later, our styles often vary according to different contexts or relationships. As a result, we would like you to fill out the style measure for two different situations, situation A and situation B. Make situation A describe a personal relationship—

| Application 5.1 | Measuring Your Conflict Style |

STYLES

Think of two different contexts (A and B) where you have a conflict, disagreement, argument, or disappointment with someone. An example might be someone you live with and a work associate. Then, according to the following scale, fill in your scores for situation A and situation B. *For each question, you will have two scores.* For example, on question 1 the scoring might look like this: 1. 2 | 4

Write the name of each person for the two contexts here:

Person A __Riley__   Person B __Claudia V.__

1 = never   2 = seldom   3 = sometimes   4 = often   5 = always

Person	Person
A	B

1. **2** |___ I avoid being "put on the spot"; I keep conflicts to myself.
2. **4** |___ I use my influence to get my ideas accepted.
3. **4** |___ I usually try to "split the difference" in order to resolve an issue.
4. **3** |___ I generally try to satisfy the other's needs.
5. **5** |___ I try to investigate an issue to find a solution acceptable to us.
6. **2** |___ I usually avoid open discussion of my differences with the other.
7. **2** |___ I use my authority to make a decision in my favor.

(continued)

Application 5.1 Measuring Your Conflict Style

8. **5**|___ I try to find a middle course to resolve an impasse.

9. **4**|___ I usually accommodate the other's wishes.

10. **4**|___ I try to integrate my ideas with the other's to come up with a decision jointly.

11. **3**|___ I try to stay away from disagreement with the other.

12. **3**|___ I use my expertise to make a decision that favors me.

13. **4**|___ I propose a middle ground for breaking deadlocks.

14. **3**|___ I give in to the other's wishes.

15. **4**|___ I try to work with the other to find solutions that satisfy both our expectations.

16. **2**|___ I try to keep my disagreement to myself in order to avoid hard feelings.

17. **3**|___ I generally pursue my side of an issue.

18. **4**|___ I negotiate with the other to reach a compromise.

19. **3**|___ I often go with the other's suggestions.

20. **5**|___ I exchange accurate information with the other so we can solve a problem together.

21. **4**|___ I try to avoid unpleasant exchanges with the other.

22. **3**|___ I sometimes use my power to win.

23. **4**|___ I use "give and take" so that a compromise can be made.

24. **4**|___ I try to satisfy the other's expectations.

25. **5**|___ I try to bring all our concerns out in the open so that the issues can be resolved.

Scoring: Add up your scores on the following questions:

A|B	A|B	A|B	A|B	A|B
1. __|__	2. __|__	3. __|__	4. __|__	5. __|__
6. __|__	7. __|__	8. __|__	9. __|__	10. __|__
11. __|__	12. __|__	13. __|__	14. __|__	15. __|__
16. __|__	17. __|__	18. __|__	19. __|__	20. __|__
21. __|__	22. __|__	23. __|__	24. __|__	25. __|__
__|__	__|__	__|__	__|__	__|__
A|B	A|B	A|B	A|B	A|B
Avoidance Totals	Competition Totals	Compromise Totals	Accommodation Totals	Collaboration Totals

Source: Adapted from M. A. Rahim and N. R. Magner (1995), "Confirmatory Factor Analysis of the Styles of Handling Interpersonal Conflict: First-Order Factor Model and Its Invariance across Groups," *Journal of Applied Psychology 80*, no. 1, 122–132.

with a friend, romantic partner, or close family member. Then, for situation B, pick a less personal relationship—someone you are doing a class project with, someone you don't know well at work, or some other less personal close relation. The key is to pick specific people for situation A and situation B. Do not fill out the scales "in general."

Now that you have scores for the five styles, across two different contexts, you can see what "styles" are. You may have different styles across the contexts (slightly more than 50 percent of people do), or you may be consistent across the relationships.

Application 5.2   Styles in Your Group

Compare your scores on the styles measure for situation A and situation B. In small groups, address these questions:

1. How many people of your group have relatively consistent styles in different contexts?
2. For those who have different answers, answer this question: "What is it about the two situations that prompts me to use different styles?"
3. As a group, discuss the advantages of using the same style across two different situations.
4. What are the advantages of using different styles across the two situations?
5. Do personal situations and less personal situations call for different styles?

Before we examine the five styles in depth, we look at our most fundamental orientation to conflict—**avoidance** or **engagement.**

❧Will You Avoid or Engage?

Recall a conflict in which you felt intense emotion. In such a situation you may not have been aware of making a specific choice about whether to engage or not, yet that choice defined all future interactions. Earlier we noted that destructive spirals occur when one person pursues and the other distances. This preference for engaging or avoiding the other can develop into a rigid style, and when this happens, constructive conflict becomes difficult. One needs to choose when to protect and disengage and when to engage and extend. Neither style is always the right choice. As Kaplan (1975) writes, one chooses "maintenance-by-*suppression*" or "maintenance-by-*expression*." For example, the following couple is struggling over how much engagement they will have:

Application 5.3   Avoid or Engage?

Brent: There is something bothering me.

Janette: I'm way too stressed out to talk about anything right now.

Brent: I'm upset about what you said about me at the party.

Janette: You're picking on me. Leave me alone! Another time!

(continued)

Application 5.3	Avoid or Engage?

Brent: When are we going to talk about things that bug me? You never want to talk if I'm upset.

Janette: You aren't respecting what I told you about my stress. I'm going for a walk. See you later.

Role-play the couple portrayed above. What could each have done to

- Assert his/her needs even more articulately, while
- Working with the stated needs of the other person?

Brent wants to engage in the conflict and Janette wants to protect herself by avoiding it. Each time an issue surfaces, they will have to reach agreement on avoidance/engagement, or this metaconflict will override any other emerging issues. Their fundamental issue is "How much conflict am I willing to risk to get what I want?" (Stuart 1980, 295). Of course, during the next conflict on a different topic, she may push for engagement and he may avoid, but usually members of couples specialize in one approach or the other. This overriding preference limits their ability to resolve their conflicts well.

Application 5.4	Thinking about Styles

Which is the best style for use in conflict? Read the four statements below and put a check mark by the one that you feel is the most accurate:

1. Avoidance of conflicts leads to unhappy marriages and work relationships—it just keeps important issues buried.

2. Avoidance of unnecessary conflict helps promote harmony and keeps people from getting involved in unnecessary upsets.

3. The only way to really manage conflict is to work through it by engaging the other ✓ person.

4. Engagement in conflict leads to escalatory spirals and hurt for all parties.

Both avoidance and engagement are workable options in different circumstances (Canary and Spitzberg 1987; Canary and Cupach 1988). Recall the example of the couple struggling over their level of engagement. The woman's avoidance may have prompted the man to examine his reaction, decide that he was too reactive in social situations, and back off to reduce the conflict. Or her avoidance may have signaled to him that she did not care for his feelings and that he should start exiting the relationship. Avoidance and lack of overt conflict may indicate that the participants are unable to reach accommodation, that they cannot work through problem areas, and that they will gradually drift apart.

Avoidance of conflict often leads to a cycle that is self-perpetuating. Here is a typical pattern that occurs when one avoids conflict:

- We think of conflict as bad.
- We get nervous about a conflict we are experiencing.
- We avoid the conflict as long as possible.
- The conflict gets out of control and must be confronted.
- We handle it badly (Lulofs 1994, 42).

Two cycles can be discerned in this one description, each with different dynamics. In both cases the avoidance is self-reinforcing, but there are two different trajectories. The **twin cycles of avoidance** are (1) avoidance leading to more avoidance and (2) avoidance leading to escalation and back to avoidance. Figure 5.2 illustrates the twin cycles.

In Cycle #1, you avoid issues, which leads to even more avoidance. After all, if you feel awkward discussing a topic, as you continue to avoid it, the prospect of bringing it up gets more and more scary. As you sit on things longer, the chances you will bring them up reduce. Since issues are not brought up, talked about, or resolved, the cycle just continues to breed even more avoidance.

An example of this kind of avoidance concerned a group of interns who banded together to support each other through their internship semester at a youth court agency. One of the interns missed breakfast meetings, came late, and talked excessively about herself rather than addressing the very difficult issues the other interns faced. The other four interns finally drifted away from the meetings. No one confronted the intern who violated their agreement they would support one another. Everyone lost a good opportunity to gain a much better experience.

Figure 5.2   The Twin Cycles of Avoidance

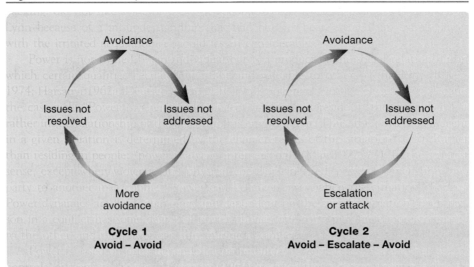

Twin Cycle #2 can be described as a dynamic that leads to the same result, more avoidance, but with a different path. In Cycle #2, you engage in typical avoidance behaviors such as not bringing up topics, joking when the other person is trying to be serious, or changing the subject. But in this cycle, the avoidance is followed by an explosion or escalation. For example, your friend Antonio lets you borrow $100 from him with the promise that you will repay by the end of the month. You forget to repay him, and neither you nor he brings it up when you are together. Four months pass and the issue is never broached. Then, one Tuesday night the two of you are at a local bar, and Antonio, after three beers, says in front of your friends, "Did you know that Sam lies to his friends and is cheap?" The escalatory attack, of course, backfires. You storm out of the bar and neither you nor Antonio bring up the issue again. You try to chalk up the attack to the effects of too much alcohol. You begin to spend less time together. The avoidance begets escalation, which begets even more intense avoidance. You both think, "I can't discuss this with him."

The same Cycle #2 pattern often describes the behavior of married couples—they will avoid issues for a long time, go through a period of verbal aggression, and then move back into avoidance (Martin 1990). As a child, you may have experienced this very pattern with your parents—they may have modeled both avoidance and escalation for you, but by example showed you that avoidance defines the beginning and the end of a conflict.

Both Cycle #1 and Cycle #2 are self-reinforcing patterns in which *one becomes more and more convinced* that it is impossible to work out issues. Both cycles of avoidance tend to recycle, preventing us from constructively dealing with the conflict. If you predict that your partner will just never talk with you (Cycle #1) or you are convinced that if you bring up a topic, your partner will attack you (Cycle #2), then you are more likely to avoid conflict in personal relationships. Predictions about a partner's potential aggression "chill" your expression of your feelings about the issue. Cloven and Roloff (1993a) call this the "chilling effect"—anticipating aggressive reactions leads to withholding grievances in personal relationships. Avoidance is designed to protect the self and other from discord, yet the avoidance may lead to lack of clarity, set the stage for later uncontrollable conflict, and, we argue, lead back to even more avoidance (Bullis 1983).

Many of us may have tried to change avoidance by using escalation, which makes us lapse back into avoidance (Cycle #2). Then, the chilling effect takes hold; we remember our partner's reaction and think about the unpleasant exchanges (he escalated and called you bad names), so we just move to Cycle #1—avoidance, chilling effect, and more avoidance. The result in both cycles is the same—not working through issues, not being able to move the relationship to a new level of agreement and understanding.

Also, with Cycle #1, the avoidance can lead to a stressful relationship with considerable unexpressed discord, which precludes a change in the relationship (Raush et al. 1974), leading to less understanding and agreement (Knudson, Sommers, and Golding 1980).

There are times when avoidance can also be productive for a relationship. Avoidance serves as a defense against engagement, or confrontation, with the partner (Raush et al. 1974, 65). Spouses who practice avoidance within a bond of mutual affection often describe their marriage as happy. On the other hand, if the relationship is not important to you, avoidance can conserve energy that would be expended needlessly. We cannot invest equally in all relationships. Similarly, when someone attempts to engage you in conflict over an issue that is of trivial importance to you, your best choice is avoidance (Thomas 1976).

The tension between avoiding and engaging can be seen in the following dialogue:

Application 5.5	Should I Bring Up the Problem or Let It Go?

Marjorie: Hi, Terry, what's going on?

Terry: Oh, not much. [He is thinking, "If I say how upset I am, we'll get into it, and I just want to cool out."]

Marjorie: You don't look very happy. [She's thinking, "I know you're upset about my mother's criticism of your job search plans. We might as well talk about it."]

Terry: No big deal. ["I hope she just lets it go."]

Marjorie: Are you mad at my mother? ["He must be more angry than I thought. This doesn't look good. Uh-oh."]

Terry: Why do you always have to blow everything out of proportion?

The conflict then escalates as they struggle tacitly over whether to engage or avoid. In Application 5.3 we asked you to role-play better options that preserved both individual needs and relational needs. In the case of Marjorie and Terry, discuss how more self-disclosure could help this couple keep from getting stuck in avoidance, or contain their escalation so the relationship is preserved.

In the following section, avoidance *as a style* with specific tactics will be presented.

❧Avoidance

We have discussed the basic choice of whether to avoid or to engage. In this section we will explore the dynamics of *avoidance as a style* characterized by denial of the conflict, changing and avoiding topics, being noncommittal, and joking rather than dealing with the conflict at hand. The avoider may sidestep an issue by changing the topic or simply withdrawing from dealing with the issue. Just as use of the competitive style does not mean that one will get what one wants (because of interdependence with the other party), the use of avoidance as a style does not mean that the avoider will be ineffective. For instance, if a person is having a conflict with a large organization, the organization can enhance its position by not responding to correspondence on the matter. By pretending that the conflict does not exist, the high-power party is freed from dealing with the low-power party.

Avoidance can serve similar functions in interpersonal conflicts. If two roommates are both dating the same woman, they may refuse to discuss the subject openly, even if both of them are aware of the problem. Furthermore, in intimate relationships the style of avoidance is often invoked during conflict over sensitive matters. If a couple is having some difficulty in dealing with each other's families, they may not feel free to discuss the problem. Avoiding a conflict, however, does not prevent it. Conflict occurs when parties have the perception of incompatible goals, regardless of the style they choose to use in responding to this perception. Avoidance is simply an alternative mode of conflict expression. Some of the advantages and disadvantages of avoidance are presented in the following box.

Avoidance

ADVANTAGES

Avoidance can supply time to think of some other response to the conflict, as some people cannot "think on their feet." It is useful if the issue is trivial or if other important issues demand one's attention. If the relationship itself is unimportant to one person or if others can manage the conflict without his or her involvement, avoidance is a wise choice. Avoidance can also keep one from harm if he or she is in a relationship in which anything other than avoidance will bring a negative response from the other party. If one's goal is to keep the other party from influencing him or her, then avoidance helps to accomplish that goal.

EXAMPLE:

Shirley is a 23-year-old graduate who has recently broken off a long relationship with a man her parents like very much. They ask her to tell them "what went wrong" and offer to pay for a trip to visit him. Shirley decides not to take them up on the trip offer and says, "Many things happened to make us want to break up. Thanks for caring about me." She avoided a discussion that she felt would end in conflict.

DISADVANTAGES

Avoidance tends to demonstrate to other people that one does not "care enough to confront" them and gives the impression that one cannot change. It allows conflict to simmer and heat up unnecessarily rather than providing an avenue for reducing it. It keeps one from working through a conflict and reinforces the notion that conflict is terrible and best avoided. It allows partners to each follow his or her own course and pretend there is no mutual influence when, in fact, each influences the other. It usually preserves the conflict and sets the stage for a later explosion or backlash.

EXAMPLE:

Professor Lane has recently made several sarcastic comments about low class attendance. Chuck has missed three classes. Upon receiving a midterm grade of C, Chuck decides to wait for a while before asking for the reasons for the low grade. Later he decides to forget trying to get a B and instead to concentrate on geology, in which he has a higher average.

In marriages, avoidance of conflict relates to lower satisfaction in general. Be aware that stonewalling and avoidance are different approaches—stonewalling is a hostile tactic (see chapter 1). In one study, partners who believed in their first year of marriage that conflicts should be avoided also reported lower levels of happiness in the first three years of marriage than those who believed that conflicts should not be avoided (Crohan 1992). In some traditional marriages, however, stability and predictability are emphasized and continual renegotiation of what the spouses expect of one another is not useful. As Pike and Sillars (1985) found, "Satisfied couples used conflict avoidance to a greater extent than dissatisfied couples" (319). Similarly, for couples who are not traditional and who lead somewhat independent lives, "Avoidance may be a satisfying style of communication" (321).

Avoidance also can cycle back and affect the one avoiding. Studies show that a lot of avoidance (1) tends to result in health problems and (2) affects well-being (Nicolotti, el-Sheikh, and Whitson 2003; Braman 1998).

Finally, older couples in our culture who avoid conflict can often be characterized as happy, although inexpressive (Zietlow and Sillars 1988). Avoidance can be useful and appropriate when (1) open communication is not an integral part of the system (family or organization); (2) one does not want to invest the energy to "work through" the conflict to reach accommodation with the other—he or she wants to stay at arm's length and not get close; (3) the costs of confrontation are too high (Van de Vliert 1985); or (4) one simply hasn't learned how to engage in collaborative conflict management.

Avoidance and Culture

Whether avoidance is productive or destructive generally depends on the cultural contexts. Cultures differ in their valuing of avoidance. The Japanese avoid conflict in order to preserve congeniality and consensus and out of sensitivity to others' feelings. When one avoids, the implicit social hierarchy is reinforced—so avoidance makes sure the social bonds are not disrupted. In one study, Japanese students avoided a potentially conflictual relationship 80 percent of the time (Barnlund 1989).

In such collectivistic cultures, if you avoid a conflict, others will talk to you about how to heal wounds, make amends, and solve the conflict in indirect ways. In individualistic cultures, like the United States, on the other hand, if you avoid someone as the result of a conflict, your friends might cheer you on, suggesting that you "don't have to take that junk" and making other escalatory suggestions. Depending on the culture, those around you push you either to reconciliation or into continual fighting. In collectivistic cultures, one is "more concerned with the group's needs, goals and interests than with individualistic-oriented interest" (Trubisky, Ting-Toomey, and Lin 1991, 67). Thus, avoidance serves different functions in collectivistic cultures than in individualistic ones. In collectivistic cultures, avoidance represents "indirect working through," but in individualistic cultures, avoidance represents "indirect escalation."

The Avoid/Criticize Loop

As noted earlier, one of the "cycles of avoidance" occurs when one avoids, continues to avoid, and then gets reinforcement that it is the only option. When Mira says, "I can't talk to him, he is just so uncaring," she is both avoiding and arguing that no other response is possible. There is one prominent pattern that goes with this type of avoidance—criticism.

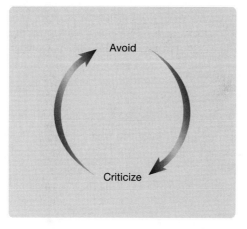

In the **avoid/criticize loop,** you avoid bringing up an issue to someone directly but spend a lot of time talking about them to others. Take the case of Viola, who owned a mountain cabin in Wyoming. It was in a group of cabins, where each of the cabin owners had horses and there was a general caretaker who took care of the horses. Each summer as Viola would return to live there for two months, she would stand on the front porch and say, "Can you believe that Mike, the caretaker, parks those horse trailers out there? They are in plain sight and really ugly—he should move them." When asked by her son, Bill, "Mom, have you ever asked Mike to move them?" she said, "No, I shouldn't have to ask him; he should know they are ugly and need moving." The son, wanting to see her get some relief from the negative energy of criticism, would say, "Well, Mom, he doesn't know what you are thinking, and I bet if you make a direct request, there's a good chance he will move them." Her response was, "If he were a *good* caretaker, he would know what I want." Thus, the avoid/criticize loop was kept in motion.

The avoid/criticize loop is quite common in professional circles and the business world. It allows one to spout off and actively talk about others, but not join with them face to face and solve the problem. Especially if you are good at your job, you can really get involved in criticizing others—"he doesn't understand the new initiative," "she hasn't the training to see this accurately," "he is just so negative I can't stand to be in meetings with him." All of these, and more, are used to keep us from directly asking for what we want, to make the other wrong, and to make us feel justified in not breaking out of avoidance. After all, if you can perfect criticism, you can gather friends and professional colleagues by spending your time talking negatively about others!

If you see conflict as about one-third your own fault, one-third the other's fault, and one-third caused by the interaction created between you, then the avoid/criticize loop can't possibly be viewed as productive. You are attending to only *one-third* of the dispute dynamics. It is like driving a car—if you have an engine but no tires or steering wheel, you can generate a lot of energy but not go anywhere.

The avoid/criticize loop is quite common for avoiders. If you spend all your energy criticizing, you expend negative energy, possibly gather people to be on your side, and still stay in avoidance. When you criticize others, it *looks like you are engaging in the conflict.* But you are not. Criticism to someone else is only another feature of avoidance—you aren't making a direct request to the only person who can help you. What you do is poison the well, ruin another's reputation (and maybe your own), or spread negative energy.

Avoidance Tactics

The lists of tactics presented in table 5.1 are from the work of Sillars et al. (1982), Sillars (1986), and Zietlow and Sillars (1988). This coding scheme is revised from earlier work and has been applied in various forms to conflict between college roommates and between marital couples. The codes have been rearranged for this presentation. Readers wishing to pursue the scheme in greater detail should consult Zietlow and Sillars (1988) and Sillars (1986).

Many times multiple forms of avoidance are used in combination. For example, a person in a low-power position may refuse to engage the other by using both topic management and noncommittal remarks. Often avoidance takes the form of what Brockriede (1972) termed "seduction," which Sillars would classify as a combination of joking, evasive remarks, and topic avoidance. The low-power person using seduction tries to charm or trick the other conflict party into going along with what he or she desires. Argument tactics vary from classical reasoning, such as "ignoring the question, begging the question, the red-herring appeal, and appeals to ignorance or to prejudice" (Brockriede 1972, 4). The clash between issues is not direct; the issues are circumvented in a sometimes deceptive, charming, or even "cutesy" way. It is not important to the seducer to appeal to the other party's sense of free choice. She or he wants what is wanted, no matter what, but is not willing (or perhaps able) to ask for it directly.

For instance, Liz asked friends of hers to help her find a job for the summer. She appeared weak, took little initiative, and became stuck in a low-energy period in her life. She frequently dropped in on her friends, politely asking for "any suggestions" they might have on finding a job, but was evasive and seemed confused when friends suggested that she needed help from an employment service. It appeared that she was trying to "seduce" her friends into taking responsibility for her but that she needed to preserve her own self-concept to avoid any direct clash with her friends. Finally, her choice of the avoidance strategy became a great disservice because her friends got tired of trying to help her and started avoiding her in return. All of the avoidance tactics in table 5.1 involve refusing to engage in the conflict. Note, however, that postponement of a conflict may not be avoidance per se but rather temporary avoidance with a promise to engage in the future. Bach and Wyden (1968) suggest that setting a time for a later conflict is a productive tactic. They suggest "fighting by

Table 5.1 Avoidance Tactics

Conflict Codes	Illustrations
A. Denial and equivocation	
1. *Direct denial.* Statements that deny that a conflict is present.	"That's not a problem."
2. *Implicit denial.* Statements that imply denial by providing a rationale for a denial statement, although the denial is not explicit.	"We've never had enough money to disagree over" (in response to a question about disagreements over money).
3. *Evasive remarks.* Failure to acknowledge or deny the presence of a conflict following a statement or inquiry about the conflict by the partner.	"That could be something that a person might resent but I don't know."
B. Topic management	
4. *Topic shifts.* Statements that terminate discussion of a conflict issue before each person has fully expressed an opinion or before the discussion has reached a sense of completion.	"Okay, the next issue is . . ." (the preceding statement occurs before each person has disclosed his or her opinion on the topic).
5. *Topic avoidance.* Statements that explicitly terminate discussion of a conflict issue before it has been fully discussed.	"I don't want to talk about that."
C. Noncommittal remarks	
6. *Noncommittal statements.* Statements that neither affirm nor deny the presence of conflict and are not evasive replies or topic shifts.	"The kids are growing up so fast I can't believe it."
7. *Noncommittal questions.* Unfocused and conflict-irrelevant questions.	"What do you think?"
8. *Abstract remarks.* Abstract principles, generalizations, or hypothetical statements that are not also evasive remarks.	"All people are irritable sometimes."
9. *Procedural remarks.* Procedural statements that supplant discussion of conflict.	"You aren't speaking loudly enough."
D. Irreverent remarks	
10. *Friendly joking.* Friendly joking or laughter.	"We need to either clean the house or torch it" (stated with friendly intonation).

Source: Reprinted, by permission of the publisher, from A. L. Sillars, "Procedures for Coding Interpersonal Conflict," rev. (Department of Communication Studies, University of Montana, 1986), 7–16.

appointment." Here are two examples of a conflict—the first using avoidance and the second using postponement:

Gloria is upset. She wants to talk to her husband, Sam, late at night. Sam, however, has an appointment at eight o'clock in the morning.

> Gloria: I am so upset that I can't sleep. Whatever possessed you to talk about our summer plans to the Carters at the party? You know we've been trying to get free of doing things with them. You said last week—
>
> Sam: Can't we talk about this in the morning?
>
> Gloria: It's fine for you to say that. You don't have to deal with Sandra when she calls tomorrow to decide where we'll take our families for a joint vacation. I have to talk to her and tell her we changed our minds.
>
> Sam: I'm sorry I brought it up. But I'm sleepy, and I don't want to talk about it.

At this point, the avoidance tactic Sam is using—"Maybe if I close my eyes all this hassle will go away"—is certainly not productive. His twin goals—to get some sleep and to avoid further antagonizing his wife—are not likely to be met. By this time Gloria is probably angry not only about his lack of discretion at the party but also about his refusal to talk to her about it. An example of a productive postponement tactic follows:

> Sam: Gloria, I know you're upset. I also feel foolish. But I am exhausted, and I really don't want to deal with all the issues now. When Sandra calls tomorrow, tell her we haven't had a chance to talk yet and you'll call her back. Then when I come home from work tomorrow, we'll discuss the whole thing.
>
> Gloria: You always say that, and it never gets talked about.
>
> Sam: This time it will. We'll sit down before dinner, banish the kids, and the two of us will talk. I know you're upset.
>
> Gloria: OK, if we really will. I know it's hard to know what to say in public like that. They presume so much . . .

Postponement as a tactic works best when several conditions are present. First of all, the emotional content of the conflict needs to be acknowledged while other issues are deferred to a later time. Sam said, "I know you're upset," acknowledging the depth of Gloria's feelings. She would not have been likely to go along with the postponement if he had said, "It's stupid for you to be upset. We'll work it out later." After the emotional content is acknowledged, all parties have to agree on a time that is soon and realistic. If Sam had said, "We'll talk about it sometime soon," that would not have been precise enough. The other party has to believe that the postponer really means to bring up the issue later. Postponement does not work well as a tactic if the other people involved think they are being put off, never to return to the issue. Vague statements such as "We'll have to work on that sometime" or "Let's all try harder to get along" are often giveaways that the person wants avoidance rather than genuine postponement.

As you study the avoidance tactics in table 5.1, note that although avoidance comes in many costumes, its function is always to deflect, avoid, or not engage in the conflict. Whether a professor who is confronted about a grade says, "That's an interesting point. It brings up an interesting question" (abstract remark), or a supervisor says, "That's enough complaining. Let's get back to the job" (topic shift), the basic dynamic is the same—to avoid the conflict.

Competition

A competitive, or "power over," style is characterized by aggressive and uncooperative behavior—pursuing your own concerns at the expense of another. People with competitive styles attempt to gain power by direct confrontation, by trying to "win" the argument without adjusting to the other's goals and desires. A person with a competitive style is one who usually thinks it necessary to engage the other participant in overt disagreement. The conflict is seen as a "battleground," where winning is the goal, and concern for the other is of little or no importance. Someone who adopts a competitive style in conflicts would probably agree with statements such as, "Once I get wound up in a heated discussion, I find it difficult to stop," and "I like the excitement of engaging in verbal fights."

Competitive tactics can be employed in an **assertive** rather than an aggressive manner. Usually, however, aggression creeps into a competitive style. Whereas nonassertive people deny themselves and inhibit their expression of feelings and open striving for goals, assertive people enhance the self, work toward achieving desired goals, and are expressive. The aggressive person, however, carries the desire for self-expression to the extreme. Goals are accomplished at the expense of others. The aggressive style results in a put-down of others while the aggressor actively works against their goals. The assertive person can be competitive without berating, ridiculing, or damaging the other. The aggressive person is competitive primarily by trying to destroy the opponent's options.

The competitive style of managing conflict is productive if one competes to accomplish individual goals without destroying the other person. Competition can be productively used in conflict, especially if the participants agree about the amount of aggressiveness that can legitimately be used in their conflict. The following box summarizes the advantages, as well as the disadvantages, of **competition.**

Competing

ADVANTAGES

Competition can be appropriate and useful when one has to make a quick, decisive action, such as in an emergency. Competition can generate creative ideas when others respond well to it or when one is in a situation in which the best performance or ideas are rewarded. It is useful if the external goal is more important than the relationship with the other person, such as in a short-term, nonrepeating relationship.

Competition also informs the other of one's degree of commitment to the issue and can be used to demonstrate to the other party the importance of the issue. Competition can be useful in situations in which everyone agrees that competitive behavior is a sign of strength and in which such behavior is treated as a natural response, such as in games and sports or in a court battle. In these cases, other styles may confuse the resolution of the conflict.

(continued)

Competing

EXAMPLE:

A human services agency competes with others for grant money from United Way. A limited amount is available, so the best proposal for solving a human services problem will be funded. The director of the agency competes with other directors for funding. The larger good of the community is served by the best program's gaining support.

DISADVANTAGES

Competition can harm the relationship between the parties because of the focus on external goals. Competition can be harmful if one party is unable or unwilling to deal with conflict in a head-on manner. Conflict waged competitively can encourage one party to go underground and use covert means to make the other pay. Competition tends to reduce all conflicts to two options—"either you are against me or with me," which limits one's roles to "winning" or "losing."

EXAMPLE:

Greg and Marcie, both young, competitive salespeople for the same company, live together. High sales, naturally, are rewarded by their manager. The couple keeps track of who's ahead of the other by placing a chart on the refrigerator. The week's loser has to do the laundry for the week. However, when Marcie's sales are low because she has been ill and has missed a lot of work, she angrily proclaims to Greg, "I'm not your slave! Do your own damn laundry!"

A competitive style is useful in showing the other party how important an issue is to you. Especially when both parties agree that a competitive style is the norm, the style can be useful. Competitiveness can be a sign of strength or commitment. For example, two attorneys who one-up each other during negotiation are each attempting to persuade the other to alter his or her position. On the other hand, as mentioned previously, competitive tactics can damage a relationship, lock the participants into round-robin sequences of attack on each other, and deprive the participants of cooperative solutions to their problems. In severe cases a competitive style can become self-encapsulating— the participants can't give up or stop because they get too caught up in winning at any cost. When people launch never-ending court challenges against one another or continue to verbally abuse their ex-spouses for many decades, such approaches indicate a frozen position of competitiveness. The ever competitive combatants lose all perspective on the original goal, and they dedicate their energies to triumphing over the other.

Competitive tactics involve "verbally competitive or individualistic behavior" (Sillars et al. 1982, 83). These tactics focus on a win/lose orientation and often reflect a belief that what one person gets, the other loses (Thomas 1976). As a result, the party using competitive tactics will try to one-up the other party to gain an advantage (Rogers and Farace 1975). Table 5.2 displays various competitive tactics (Sillars et al. 1982; Sillars 1986; Zietlow and Sillars 1988).

Table 5.2 Competitive Tactics

Communication Category	Illustrations
1. *Personal criticism*. Remarks that directly criticize the personal characteristics or behaviors of the partner.	"Sometimes you leave, and you don't say goodbye or anything. You just walk right out."
2. *Rejection*. Statements in response to the partner's previous statements that imply personal antagonism toward the partner as well as disagreement.	"Oh, come on." "You're exaggerating."
3. *Hostile imperatives*. Requests, demands, arguments, threats, or other prescriptive statements that implicitly blame the partner and seek change in the partner's behavior.	"If you're not willing to look for a new job, then don't complain to me about it."
4. *Hostile jokes*. Joking, teasing, or sarcasm that is at the expense of the partner and that is accompanied by hostile intonation.	"It's very easy to say, 'Gee, I *really* appreciate you' [said mockingly], but that doesn't mean anything." "Every time you send me flowers, two days later I get the bill."
5. *Hostile questions*. Directive or leading questions that fault the partner.	"Who does most of the cleaning around here?"
6. *Presumptive remarks*. Statements that attribute thoughts, feelings, motivations, or behaviors to the partner that the partner does not acknowledge.	"You're purposely making yourself miserable."
7. *Denial of responsibility*. Statements that minimize or deny personal responsibility for conflict.	"That's not my fault."

Source: Adapted, by permission of publisher, from A. L. Sillars, "Procedures for Coding Interpersonal Conflict," rev. (Department of Communication Studies, University of Montana, 1986), 7–16.

With these tactics the conflict participant pushes for self-interest, often at the expense of the other. These competitive tactics are so commonplace that many people see them as synonymous with conflict. If you saw two business partners calling each other names, finding fault with each other, and acting in forceful or controlling ways, you would conclude that a conflict was present. At their core, all competitive tactics involve pressuring the other person to change.

Confrontational remarks summarized in table 5.2 are the essence of competitive tactics. If someone personally criticizes you, rejects your statements, or acts in a verbally hostile manner (with threats, jokes, or questions), you become vividly aware of the competitive nature of the exchange. Confrontational remarks are at the heart of "I win–you lose" perspectives on conflict. Just as with avoidance tactics, competitive tactics are often used in combination. Denial of responsibility for the conflict ("I didn't cause it!") is usually linked with presumptive remarks ("It's your fault"). Whatever the specific tactical move, a competitive approach demands that the other give in, take responsibility for the conflict, and solve it.

When competitive tactics are extreme, they are characterized by the "rapist" style. In the rapist style (this metaphor is not meant to imply only sexual behavior but all kinds of dominating communicative behavior), participants "function through power, through an ability to apply psychic and physical sanctions, through rewards and especially punishments, and through commands and threats" (Brockriede 1972, 2). The conflict or argument is often escalated, since participants are interested in coercion instead of gaining assent through carefully reasoned argument. The intent of those using the rapist style is to manipulate and violate the personhood of the "victims," or other parties in the conflict. In some situations, such as the courtroom, legislative hearings, political debates, and forensic tournaments, the structure of the conflict encourages the coercion, or rapist, strategy.

Most of us know that alcohol makes conflict worse. We often hear stories about someone being drunk and "going after the other." Research on this is quite clear—there is a definite link between substance abuse and harmful competitive tactics. Alcohol especially makes conflict episodes much more damaging (MacDonald, Zanna, and Holmes 2000; Edelgard and Colsman, 2002; Huang et al. 2001). It is so common that in some classes we have given the admonition *never engage a conflict when you or the other has been drinking*. Of course, other drugs have even more dramatic effects. The recent surge in methamphetamine use is often correlated with violent interpersonal aggression. So, if you want your conflicts to be less damaging, avoid trying to work through difficult issues when you or the other is under the influence of a substance.

When one person has chosen, however tacitly, the rapist strategy, the other person functions as the victim, even though most people certainly do not want to be victimized. Often, the person who feels powerless and victimized escalates the conflict to a point, then gives up, thinking, "There's nothing I can do to win anyway." In effect, the participants cooperate in the escalation. A very angry person was once observed trying to take over the microphone and the floor at a convention. He shouted loudly, disrupted the proceedings, and was finally given five minutes to state his case. He did so, supporting with vehemence the pullout of his church group from a large national group, which he perceived as being too liberal. He chose the rapist style to escalate the conflict—soon he and the chairman were yelling back and forth at each other.

Threats

The most commonly used competitive tactic is the **threat.** We rush to use threats because we believe they are effective (Johnson and Ford 1996; Rubin, Pruitt, and Kim 1994). Many parents are quick to say, "If you don't eat your spinach, I'll spank you," or supervisors to say, "If you employees don't do what I say, someone will be gone tomorrow."

It is important to clearly understand what is and is not a threat, then to know the conditions under which they can be effective. Table 5.3 shows that a threat has to meet two criteria: the source of the threat must control the outcome and the threat must be seen as negative by the recipient. If you (the source) control the outcome ("If you don't go to bed, I'll spank you") and the sanction is seen as negative, then it is a threat. Similarly, if the professor says, "If you don't get your paper in on time, I will dock your grade," it is a threat. However, if the source does not control the outcome (a friend says, "If you don't get your paper in on time, it will hurt your grade"), it is not a threat—it

Table 5.3 The Nature of Threats

	Source controls the outcome	Source does not control the outcome
Negative sanction	Threat	Warning
Positive sanction	Promise	Recommendation

is a **warning.** Many parents get confused between warnings and threats. For example, "If you drink too much, you'll never graduate" seems like a threat, but it is not because the parent does not control the outcome. Or, if you say to a friend, "If you step out on your boyfriend, he will leave you," it is not a threat; it is a warning. If you say, "I wouldn't challenge her on that topic," you are recommending a course of action to your friend.

Small children understand the difference between a positive and a negative sanction. If the parent says, "If you don't do the dishes, you'll have to spend the evening in your room," and the child has a computer or TV so that going to the room is not negative, the child may well retort, "Is that a threat or a promise?" As you can see, if the source controls the outcome and the recipient sees the outcome as positive, the threat is, instead, a **promise.**

A threat is credible only if (1) the source is in a position to administer the punishment, (2) the source appears willing to invoke the punishment, and (3) the punishment is something to be avoided. If your friends say, "You had better quit trying to get your dad to buy you expensive gifts, or he will get mad and not give you anything," this is not a credible threat but rather a warning. Similarly, if your romantic partner says, "You better study harder or you will flunk out of school," it is not a threat. The threat is credible only if the person making the threat is capable of invoking the negative sanction.

Often the other party is able to administer a threat but not willing to follow through on the threat. A co-worker who threatens to tell the boss that someone's work is not up to par may not carry out the threat if the boss dislikes "whistle-blowers." Similarly, in an intimate relationship, one intimate might say, "If you want to make your summer plans alone, go ahead. But if you do, then don't expect to find me here when you come back." Such a threat (relational suicide) is effective only if the person who makes the threat is willing to lose the other person over this one issue. It is the perception that the other party is willing to carry out the threat that makes it effective. As a result, intimates often avoid testing the willingness of the other party to invoke the threat and instead live under the control of the other person for years. In poker, a "bluff" is the ability to convince the other party that you are willing to bet all your winnings on a single draw of cards. The only successful bluff is one that the other party believes is true.

Finally, threats are effective only if the sanction is something the threatened party wants to avoid. If you threaten to leave a relationship and your partner says, "So you think I'm going to cry over you?" your threat backfires. So before you issue your next threat to a close friend or family member, keep in mind that your threat is effective only if he or she does not want the "undesirable" end result. One faculty member was offered a job at a competing university; when he went to the department chair and threatened to leave unless his salary was raised, the chair replied, "I hope you enjoy the climate down south."

As you have seen, threats can be either constructive or destructive. They can be used constructively to highlight the importance of the conflict topic to you, to get the attention of the other party, and to clarify one's perceptions of the power balance. On the other hand, threats tend to elicit the same behavior from the other, starting escalatory conflict spirals. They also block collaborative agreements and undermine trust in the relationship. Worse, we can become enamored with them (Kellermann and Shea 1996). If two dormitory roommates have been getting along well except for the issue of sweeping the floor, then a threat of "If you don't sweep more often, I'll process a room change!" might damage the trust in an otherwise good relationship. The recipient of the threat is likely to respond with a feeling of "OK, then go ahead. Who needs you anyway?" Unless trust can be regained, forging agreements will be extremely difficult. Once a threat has damaged the trust in the relationship, it often leads to further destructive tactics.

In the case of nations that threaten one another with military intervention, "Threats are not bad merely because they do not work. They are also bad because they are dangerous" (Fisher 1986, 151). Threats are overused, used too quickly, destroy trust, and tend to promote retaliation.

Application 5.6   Threats in Personal
                              Relationships

Think of a time when you were threatened, or you used threats. What happened? Looking back, do you think the threats were effective in solving a problem and keeping the relationship intact? Were they harmful? What have you learned about your personal response to using threats or being threatened verbally?

Verbal Aggressiveness

Verbal aggressiveness is a broader category of communication than threats. Verbal aggressiveness is a form of communicative violence. Rather than just telling someone what might happen to them, when you use verbal aggression you "attack the self-concepts" of other people (Infante and Wigley 1986). Character attacks ("You are just a rotten wife"), insults ("Well, I suppose someone with your intelligence would see it that way"), rough teasing, ridicule, and profanity all are forms of verbal aggressiveness. Many conflict parties, when engaged in struggle, immediately begin attacking each other. Once one focuses on the other as the sole cause of the difficulties, it is easy to slip into disparaging personal remarks. Therefore, whether you label it as "personal criticism" or "verbal aggressiveness," this competitive tactic involves attacking the other person. The following are examples of verbal aggressiveness:

You're so stupid.

You're an imbecile.

You're ugly.

You're low class.

I wish you would die/get hit by a car/fall off the face of the earth.

No one else would have you.

In individualistic cultures, aggressive talk is common. It attacks the other's character, background, abilities, physical appearance, and the like (Carey and Mongeau 1996). The more important your relationship with someone, the more verbal aggression within the relationship hurts (Martin, Anderson, and Horvath 1996). In a collectivistic culture, on the other hand, the most damaging verbal abuse is directed toward a person's group, clan, tribe, village, or family, such as when you say, "He's a drunken Irishman" (Vissing and Baily 1996), or "You people are all animals."

One study examined the use of verbal aggression in college-age couples and found that based on 5,000 American couples, men and women engage in equal amounts of verbal aggression (Sabourin 1995). Yelsma (1995) found that 70 percent of partners in dating relationships reported some form of verbal abuse. If an occasional lapse into verbal aggression occurred, partners seemed able to absorb it, but in distressed relationships, verbal aggression was associated with ineffective conversation skills and was much more frequent than in satisfactory relationships.

The negative impact of verbal aggression is felt by most of us. When we hear someone in public verbally abusing another, we cringe. The person engaging in verbal aggression most often doesn't perceive their communication as aggressive. People who are **"high verbal aggressives"** claim that 46 percent of their verbally aggressive messages are humorous (Infante, Riddle, et al. 1992). But others view verbally aggressive people as less credible and as having fewer valid arguments than those who don't aggress (Infante, Hartley, et al. 1992). If a couple is verbally aggressive, they tend to infuriate each other and lack the skill to undo the relationship damage (Sabourin 1995). As shown in the following list of **abusive** versus **nonabusive talk,** verbally abusive couples differ from nonabusive couples in how they talk:

Abusive Talk		**Nonabusive Talk**
vague language	vs.	precise language
opposition	vs.	collaboration
relational talk	vs.	content talk
despair	vs.	optimism
interfering with interdependence	vs.	facilitating interdependence
complaints	vs.	compliments
ineffective change	vs.	effective change

Verbal aggression is closely associated with physical abuse. Verbal aggression is a precursor to and predictor of physical aggression in adolescents (White and Humphrey 1994). Similarly, verbal aggression in marriage is correlated with marital violence (Sabourin and Stamp 1995). Adding injury to insult, verbally aggressive couples sometimes do not see their aggression as a problem (Vivian and Langhinrichsen-Rohling 1994).

Sometimes, researchers label verbally aggressive tactics as **harassment.** A direct verbal attack on another can have serious consequences. In Sweden, for example, an estimated 100 to 300 people each year commit suicide as a result of harassment by work colleagues (Bjorkqvist, Osterman, and Lagerspetz 1994). One study found that in a Finnish university, women were more often harassed than men, and women holding administrative and service jobs were harassed more than female professors (Bjorkqvist, Osterman, and Hjelt-Back 1994). Making negative comments about appearance or clothing is considered harassment if the speaker is in a high-power relationship with the "target" person. Additionally, if a high-power person ridicules a low-power person's mode of speech or makes sexually explicit suggestions or observations, harassment is occurring. Finally, when a high-power person negatively labels a low-power person's personality, using words such as "brain-dead," "loser," "whiner," "bitch," or "wimp," the target person is being harassed. Such comments, whether labeled "harassment" or "verbal aggression," can occur at home, on the job, in public, or in any type of relationship. And sometimes, these destructive verbal tactics escalate to the next level—physical violence.

Bullying

Aggressive tactics that overlap with verbal aggressiveness and violence are acts of bullying. **Bullying** is "ongoing, persistent badgering, harassment and psychological terrorizing . . . that demoralizes, dehumanizes and isolates those targeted" (Tracy, Lutgen-Sandvik, and Alberts 2004, 3; Lutgen-Sandvik, Tracy, and Alberts 2005). Bullying can occur in any social setting, and, as we all know, it occurs in schools. Teachers and former victims of bullying in schools are now supplying insights into this destructive conflict behavior and making suggestions for how to deal with it.[1] Will was the smallest boy in his class. In his small town, all boys went out for sports and this young man received harassment on a daily basis in the locker room—being shoved, snapped with towels, and called demeaning names. Such persistent acts continued until he quit trying out for sports altogether.

Communication researchers have begun studying bullying in the workplace as well. The effects of workplace bullying everywhere are clear—the "target's psychological, occupational and family functioning decline" (Leymann 1990). Job performance slips and the organization's reputation is damaged (Tracy, Lutgen-Sandvik, and Alberts 2004). Bullying at work can take many forms—"supervisors abusing subordinates, same-level workers tormenting peers, and coworkers 'ganging up' on an individual" (Tracy, Lutgen-Sandvik, and Alberts 2004, 1; Einarsen 1999). When asked about his or her experience, the recipient of bullying feels vulnerable and tortured and that it is a "fixed fight" and has nightmares (Tracy, Lutgen-Sandvik, and Alberts 2004). Targets of bullying suffer long-term—sometimes permanent—damage (Einarsen 1999; Einarsen and Mikkelsen, 2003; Leymann 1990).

---

[1] For example, see http://www.education.unisa.edu.au/bullying, http://www.kidpower.org/, http://www.didax.com/, and http://www.ecsu.ctstateu.edu/depts/edu/textbooks/bullying.htm.

Bullying often starts as incivility. As Alberts, Lutgen-Sandvik, and Tracy (2005) write, "Workplace bullying does not arise out of a vacuum. Rather, it is often a consequence of **unmanaged incivility,** rudeness, and injustice that contaminates the workplace. Incivility, over time, can develop into bullying as repeated, long-term acts wear down, demoralize, stigmatize, and isolate those targeted" (7). Bullying, then, is one of a group of aggressive acts that have serious consequences for the recipient.

Incidence of Violence

The ultimate competitive tactic is physical **violence**—when conflictual interactions move beyond threats and verbal aggressiveness. We are faced with an epidemic of violence in the United States, with much of it occurring in the home and the workplace. Violence can occur in many forms. One scale measuring such physical aggression (Straus et al. 1996) lists these items:

- Threw something at my partner that could hurt.
- Twisted my partner's arm or hair.
- Pushed or shoved my partner.
- Grabbed my partner.
- Used a knife or gun on my partner.
- Punched or hit my partner with something that could hurt.
- Choked my partner.
- Slammed my partner against a wall.
- Beat up my partner.
- Burned or scalded my partner on purpose.
- Kicked my partner.

The more severe forms of violence occur less frequently (Deal and Wampler 1986). However, although we will never know the precise rates of violence, it is more common than we usually assume. Ponder for a moment these rates of incidence found in various surveys:

- Almost 20 percent of people reported experiencing a violent episode in the prior year of their romantic relationship (Marshall 1994).
- Premarital violence is a serious social problem that affects more than 30 percent of the young people in the United States who date (Sugarman and Hotaling 1989).
- In unhappy marriages, 71 percent of the couples reported physical aggression in the prior year (Vivian and Langhinrichsen-Rohling 1994).
- Men commit about 13 million violent crimes each year, with only half being simple assaults, while women commit about 2.1 million violent crimes a year, with three-quarters being simple assaults.

In another study of dating relationships, 23 percent of students reported being pushed, grabbed, or shoved by their dating partner (Deal and Wampler 1986). Studies of college students have indicated that rates of physical aggression against a current mate are between 20 and 35 percent, with all forms of physical assault decreasing dramatically with age. The most common forms of physical aggression practiced by both men and women were pushing, shoving, and slapping (O'Leary et al. 1989). Additionally, 16.3 out of 1,000 children were reported to have been abused and/or neglected, and in 16 percent of homes, some kind of violence between spouses had occurred in the year prior to the survey (Gelles and Cornell 1990).

In summary, most researchers conclude that "violence is indeed common in American families" (Gelles 1987). Further, "These incidents of violence are not isolated attacks nor are they just pushes and shoves. In many families, violence is patterned and regular and often results in broken bones and sutured cuts" (192). Violence spans all social and economic boundaries, though it is more prevalent in families with low income, low educational achievement, and low-status employment.

A working definition of violence is "an act carried out with the intention or perceived intention of causing physical pain or injury to another person" (Gelles and Cornell 1990, 22). In conflict terms, violent behavior is an attempt to force one's will on the other—to get him or her to stop doing something or to start doing something. Clearly, it is a one-sided tactic designed to force the other to do one's bidding.

Patterns of Violence

The following are some tenets of violence, based on research (adapted from Lloyd and Emery 1994):

Tenet 1: Physical Aggression Is Almost Always Preceded by Verbal Aggression Small, insignificant acts lead to verbal sparring, which then escalates into physical aggression or abuse. For instance, you burn the toast, your spouse screams at you, "Why can't you even do simple things right?" you shout back, "So what makes you think you are so high and mighty?" and the cycle continues unabated with the two of you shoving each other around the kitchen. The spiral of destruction continues until the physically stronger one, usually the man, gets an upper hand. The important feature here is that the physical abuse does not just arise out of nowhere—it follows hostile, competitive verbal acts (Evans 1992; Lloyd and Emery 1994). The partners engage in an "aggression ritual" that ends in violence (Harris, Gergen, and Lannamann 1986).

Tenet 2: Intimate Violence Is Usually Reciprocal—Both Participate Aggression and violence are reciprocal—once one partner engages in violence, the other is likely to respond in kind. In intimate male–female relationships, the woman is more likely than the man to engage in violent low-power tactics: the woman is 14 times more likely than the man to throw something and 15 times more likely than the man to slap (Stets and Henderson 1991). However, 40 percent of all women who are murdered are killed by someone close to them. Major differences in male and female violence are in the seriousness and the effects of violence. There is no question that women are seriously victimized much more often than are men. Both participants are likely to report being both victims and perpetrators of physical aggression; 85 percent of couples report that the aggression is bidirectional (Vivian and Langhinrichsen-Rohling 1994). These statistics suggest that there is an attack–counterattack sequence to the majority of violent episodes (Deal and Wampler 1986). Once violence begins, both people tend to participate—it is a dyadic, interactive event.

Tenet 3: Women and Children Suffer Many More Injuries Violence, regardless of the cycle of interaction leading up to it, damages women and children more than men. Advocates for battered women point to a "cohesive pattern of coercive controls that include verbal abuse, threats, psychological manipulation, sexual coercion, and control of economic resources" (Dobash and Dobash 1979). Additionally, many women learn not to confront, and remain unskilled in effective verbal defense. Many women try to placate rather than leave the scene. Socialization of women that teaches them to be forgiving also leads to women staying in abusive relationships.

All you have to do is volunteer at a battered women's shelter or read in the newspaper about child abuse to see who loses. As Gelles says, "When men hit women and women hit men, the real victims are almost certainly going to be the women" (1981, 128). Even when women use weapons as a way to gain the upper hand, they are still injured more often (Felson 1996). Throughout history, women have been the victims of violence.

Tenet 4: Victims of Abuse Are in a No-Win Situation Once the cycle of abuse begins, the victim of the abuse has few good options (Lloyd and Emery 1994). For example, it is fruitless to try to use aggression against a stronger and more violent person. Yet, on the other hand, it is extraordinarily difficult to leave because the perpetrator is trying to control all your actions. The complexity of abusive relationships is evidenced by the fact that nearly 40 percent of victims of dating violence continue their relationships and that most women who seek help from a battered women's shelter return to their spouses (Sugarman and Hotaling 1989). Many women go back to abusive situations because with children they cannot make a living. Many women feel guilty about the failure of the relationship and go back believing the abuser's promises to change. One study documented that 70 percent of fathers who sought custody of their children were successful, so many women, especially poor women, are afraid of losing their children if they stay away (Marano 1996). Tragically, abusers escalate their control tactics when victims try to leave. More domestic abuse victims are killed when they try to leave than at any other time. It is difficult for women with children to flee when they are so dependent on the very persons who are violent with them.

Tenet 5: Perpetrators and Victims Have Discrepant Narratives about Violence (Moffitt et al. 1997) One of the reasons that it is so difficult to decrease violence is that perpetrators of violent acts see their behavior as something "that could not be helped or as due to external, mitigating circumstances. Thus, they may cast themselves as unjustly persecuted for a minor, unavoidable, or nonexistent offense" (Baumeister, Stillwell, and Wotman 1990, 1003). One provocative study asked the participants to recall situations where they were perpetrators of violence and then write about the events. They also were asked to recall situations where they were victims and reflect on those events. What emerged was that "perpetrators apparently see the incident as a brief, uncharacteristic episode that has little or no relation to present circumstances whereas victims apparently continue to see harmful consequences and to feel lasting grievances" (1001).

The **discrepancies in accounts of violence** extend to the underreporting of violence. Husbands are more likely than wives to minimize and deny their violence (Browning and Dotton 1986). Furthermore, husbands are more likely than wives to count choking, punching, and beating someone up as self-defense rather than violence (Brygger and Edleson 1984), but what abusers often report as "self-defense" is in reality violent retaliation.

Even though violence from women to men occurs (Ridley and Feldman 2003), it is far less common. In any event, the accounts of the abuser and victim will be discrepant.

Explanations for Violence

Why does violence occur in personal relationships? One explanation is that violent responses to conflict are learned—those who experience violence have experienced it before, have witnessed it in their family of origin or in previous relationships (Yexley and Borowsky 2002). Studies find that perpetrators of violence were often victims of violence in their childhood and in their earlier relationships (Straus, Gelles, and Steinmetz 1980; Deal and Wampler 1986; Bernard and Bernard 1983). Yet, saying that "violence is passed on" is not a totally satisfying answer. We need to know much more about people who do not continue the patterns. Why do some people who are exposed to violence and aggression in childhood not continue these patterns into adulthood (Lenton 1995)? Patricia, for example, suffered both verbal and physical abuse at the hand of her father. He said and did terrible things to her when she was a child, and she ran away from home at age 17. Yet, in raising her children, she did not once verbally or physically abuse them. We need much more research on people like this who break the intergenerational transmission of aggression. Similarly, what about people in families and romantic relationships who stop escalating sequences of verbal aggression that might lead to violence? And, on the other hand, why do some people who were not previously exposed to violence and aggression develop violent and aggressive behaviors?

A second explanation for violence centers on the elements of a patriarchal culture that insists the man is always right. It has been found that the more discrepant the power between the husband and the wife, the greater the violence (Kim and Emery 2003). In "asymmetric power structures" (husband-dominant or wife-dominant marriages), there is "a much greater risk of violence than when conflict occurs among the equalitarian couples" (Coleman and Straus 1986, 152). When the power is "asymmetric," conflict episodes more often trigger violence. Similarly, one study demonstrated that the more dependent a wife is, the more tolerant she is of violence against her (Kalmuss and Straus 1982). Research shows multiple factors leading to abuse and that partriarchal explanations, while part of the picture, are too simplistic (Lenton 1995; Greene and Bogo 2002; Bell and Forde 1999).

A third explanation for violent tactics is that violence is the result of lack of communication skills in a situation of powerlessness. It has been found that physically aggressive wives and husbands display rigid communication patterns, automatically responding in kind to their partner rather than with an alternative response (Rosen 1996). If you can effectively argue (without being verbally aggressive), then you have a sense of power and impact. If you feel that you can have an impact on your spouse, there is no need to resort to physical aggression, even in the heat of conflict. Yet, there are also people who are both verbally skillful and physically violent.

Clearly, no one explanation can account for the complexity of violence. For example, why does a strong belief in pacifism correlate to fewer violent behaviors for Quaker women but not for Quaker men (Brutz and Allen 1986)? Why do surveys indicate that men are more often the recipients of violence than women? Is it because males are more likely to see any violence as a violation and report it? And why do people in marriages with a lot of physical aggression often not see it as a problem (Vivian and Langhinrichsen-Rohling 1994)?

Regardless of one's explanation of violence, it is time for us as a culture to take a firm stand on it. We desperately need to approach violence from a variety of platforms—in the home; in the schools; in the churches, synagogues, Zendos and gompas; and in the workplace. We are in need of programs to teach us how to stop violence in all contexts. We need to give assistance to both perpetrators and victims so the cycles of destruction can be stopped.[2]

Compromise

Compromise is an intermediate style resulting in some gains and some losses for each party. It is moderately assertive and cooperative. A compromising style is characterized by beliefs such as "You can be satisfied with part of the pie" and "Give a little and get a little." When compromising, parties give up some important goals to gain others. Compromise is dependent on shared power because if the other party is perceived as powerless, no compelling reason to compromise exists.

Compromise is frequently confused with collaboration, which requires creative solutions and flexibility. Compromise differs, however, in that it requires trade-offs and exchanges (Folger, Poole, and Stutman 1993). Many times people avoid using compromise because something valuable has to be given up. While North American norms, especially in public life, encourage compromising, the style is not often the first choice in personal relationships. When power is unequal, compromising is usually giving in or giving up. The following box summarizes the advantages and disadvantages of compromising.

Compromising

ADVANTAGES

Compromise sometimes lets conflict parties accomplish important goals with less time expenditure than collaboration requires. It also reinforces a power balance that can be used to achieve temporary or expedient settlements in time-pressured situations. It can be used as a backup method for decision making when other styles fail. Further, it has the advantage of having external moral force; therefore, it appears reasonable to most parties. Compromise works best when other styles have failed or are clearly unsuitable.

EXAMPLE:

Mark and Sheila, ages 10 and 8, both want to play with the new video game they received for Christmas. After a noisy argument, their parents tell them to work something out that is fair. They decide that if no one else is using the game, they can play without asking, but if they both want to play at the same time, they have to either play a game

(continued)

---

[2] If you or someone you know suffers from physical or sexual violence, help is available both locally and nationally. Contact local programs that help victims of violence and/or contact the National Domestic Violence Hotline at 1-800-799-7233 (1-800-799-SAFE) and the Web site www.ndvh.org.

Compromising

together or take turns by hours (every other hour). The compromise of taking turns works well as a conflict reduction device. The parents can intervene simply by asking, "Whose turn is it?"

DISADVANTAGES

Compromise can become an easy way out—a "formula" solution not based on the demands of a particular situation. For some people, compromise always seems to be a form of "loss" rather than a form of "win." It prevents creative new options because it is easy and handy to use. Flipping a coin or "splitting the difference" can be a sophisticated form of avoidance of issues that need to be discussed. These chance measures, such as drawing straws or picking a number, are not really compromise. They are arbitration, with the "arbiter" being chance. True compromise requires each side giving something in order to get an agreement; she is selling a bike and I pay more than I want to and she gets less than she wants for the bike.

EXAMPLE:

Two friends from home decide to room together at college. Sarah wants to live in Jesse dorm with some other friends she has met. Kate wants to live in Brantley, an all-female dorm, so she can have more privacy. They decide that it wouldn't be fair for either one to get her first choice, so they compromise on Craig, where neither knows anyone. At midyear, they want to change roommates since neither is happy with the choice. Sarah and Kate might have been able to come up with a better solution if they had worked at it.

Research has not clarified compromise tactics to the extent that it has avoidance and competition, but the tactics shown in table 5.4 have been compiled to exemplify compromise.

One's view of compromise is a good litmus test of how you view conflict in general. Think about the famous "the cup is half empty" versus "the cup is half full" aphorism that applies to compromise. Some see compromise as "both of us lose something" and others see it as "both of us win something." Clearly, compromise means a middle ground between you and the other and involves a moderate and balanced amount of concern for self and concern for other. "Compromises" can result from good-faith efforts, and may be very effective solutions. Compromise as a *style* sometimes shortchanges the conflict process, while at other times it effectively deals with the reality that not everyone can get everything they want.

❧Accommodation

One who practices **accommodation** does not assert individual needs and prefers a cooperative and harmonizing approach (Neff and Harter 2002). The individual sets aside his or her concerns in favor of pleasing the other people involved (this relational goal may be the most important goal for the accommodating person).

One may gladly yield to someone else or may do so grudgingly and bitterly. The accompanying emotion can be highly divergent for those using accommodation, from gentle pleasure at smoothing ruffled feelings to angry, hostile compliance because one

Table 5.4   Compromise Tactics

Communication Category	Illustrations
1. Appeal to fairness	"You got what you wanted last time." "It's not fair to ask me to do all the writing. We both are getting the grant support. Why don't you do your part and I'll do mine." "I don't make as much money as you do. It's not fair to make me pay half of all the expenses."
2. Suggest a trade-off	"How are we going to pay for all that summer help? Are you willing to wait to start the staff development program for half a year or so?" "I won't give on my expectations that you pay me back for the car accident, but I will consider your working off some of the money by doing jobs for me."
3. Maximize wins/minimize losses	"I'll give up the idea of going to my folks' for Christmas if you'll take a real vacation so we can spend some time together."
4. Offer a quick, short-term solution	"Since we don't have time to gather all the data, how about if we do it my way for a month and then reassess when the data comes in and you get a chance to see how you like it."

Source: Adapted, by permission of publisher, from A. L. Sillars, "Procedures for Coding Interpersonal Conflict," rev. (Department of Communication Studies, University of Montana, 1986), 7–16.

has too little power to protest what is being done. The accommodating person may think that he or she is serving the good of the group, family, or team by giving in, sacrificing, or stepping aside. Sometimes this is true; often, however, the accommodator could better serve the needs of the larger group by staying engaged longer and using a more assertive style. Sometimes people who habitually use this style play the role of the martyr, bitter complainer, whiner, or saboteur. They may yield in a passive way or concede when they have to (Folger, Poole, and Stutman 1993).

The following box summarizes the advantages and disadvantages of accommodation.

Accommodating

ADVANTAGES

When one finds that he or she is wrong, it can be best to accommodate the other to demonstrate reasonableness. If an issue is important to one person and not important to the other, the latter can give a little to gain a lot. In addition, accommodation can prevent

(continued)

Accommodating

one party from harming the other—one can minimize losses when he or she will probably lose anyway. If harmony or maintenance of the relationship is currently the most crucial goal, accommodation allows the relationship to continue without overt conflict. Accommodation to a senior or seasoned person can be a way of managing conflict by betting on the most experienced person's judgment.

EXAMPLE:

A forest service manager asks the newest staff member if he is interested in learning about land trades with other federal agencies. The new employee knows that the manager must assign someone from his office to help the person in charge of land trades. The employee says, "It's not something I know much about, but I wouldn't mind learning." The manager, who could have assigned the new employee anyway, thanks him for his positive attitude about new responsibilities. The new employee's goals would not have been well served by his saying, "I have no interest in getting into that area. There is too much red tape, and it moves too slowly."

DISADVANTAGES

Accommodation can foster an undertone of competitiveness if people develop a pattern of showing each other how nice they can be. People can one-up others by showing how eminently reasonable they are. Accommodation of this type tends to reduce creative options. Further, if partners overuse accommodation, their commitment to the relationship is never tested, since one or the other always gives in. This pattern can result in a pseudo-solution, especially if one or both parties resent the accommodation; it will almost surely boomerang later. Accommodation can further one person's lack of power. It may signal to that person that the other is not invested enough in the conflict to struggle through, thus encouraging the low-power party to withhold energy and caring. A female student wrote the following example of a learned pattern of avoidance and its resulting accommodation.

EXAMPLE:

"In our home, conflict was avoided or denied at all costs, so I grew up without seeing conflicts managed in a satisfactory way, and I felt that conflict was somehow 'bad' and would never be resolved. This experience fit well with the rewards of being a 'good' girl (accommodating to others), which combined to make a pattern for me in which I was not even sensitive to wishes and desires that might lead to conflict."

Table 5.5 presents tactics that accompany an accommodating style.

One of the interesting features of accommodation is that while it is one of the most common responses to differences between people, it is the least noticed or studied. One of the reasons is that when someone accommodates, you may not even be aware of it. If you say, "I want to go sledding" and your brother says, "whatever," accommodation has occurred. If it were more overt, like competitive moves, it would be easier to see and

Table 5.5 Accommodation Tactics

Communication Category	Illustrations
1. Giving up/giving in	"Have it your way."
	"I don't want to fight about this."
2. Disengagement	"I couldn't care less."
	"I won't be here anyway. It doesn't matter."
	"I don't need to be involved in this."
	"I don't have time to be working on this issue."
3. Denial of needs	"I'll be fine here. You go ahead."
	"It's OK. I can stay late and do it."
4. Expression of desire for harmony	"It's forgotten. Don't worry about it" (referring to a previous discount or hurt).
	"It's more important to me that we work together on this than that I do what I want."
	"I am miserable when we fight. Let's put all this behind us and start over. I don't even remember what we are hassling each other about."

Source: Adapted, by permission of publisher, from A. L. Sillars, "Procedures for Coding Interpersonal Conflict," rev. (Department of Communication Studies, University of Montana, 1986), 7–16.

classify. As a result, few communication studies look intensely at accommodation—they just don't see it.

Another reason that accommodation is not noticed is that it becomes such a patterned response that even the accommodator doesn't know he or she is making it. If you automatically agree with everything your romantic partner suggests, it is usually such a patterned response that you don't even realize you are making it. In a traditional marriage, if the husband comes home for dinner and says, "How about turkey tonight?" an accommodating wife will say, "OK, I bet I have some frozen we can thaw out, and I can make gravy." While she was planning on beef stroganoff, she automatically adjusts to his preferences and accommodates.

As you read back over Sillars's categories of accommodation in table 5.5, you can see why such responses are hard to identify and study. They are often seen as just being kind, as being responsive to the partner, or as moves that keep things from coming up. Certainly it is true that not every issue needs to be addressed, and accommodation can be a kind and helpful part of anyone's repertoire. The problem as we search for effective conflict management styles can be that accommodation can reflect a position of "I have no choice." That power imbalance, as we have discovered, harms ongoing relationships. As we become more sensitized to accommodation moves, we should be able to expand our understanding of them and their role in conflict events.

✒Collaboration

Collaborative processes unleash this catalytic power and mobilize joint action among the stakeholders.
—Barbara Gray, *Collaborating: Finding Common Ground for Multiparty Problems*

Collaboration demands the most constructive engagement of any of the conflict styles. Collaboration shows a high level of concern for one's own goals, the goals of others, the successful solution of the problem, and the enhancement of the relationship. Note that collaboration, unlike compromise, involves not a moderate level of concern for goals but a high level of concern for them. Collaboration is an "invitational rhetoric" that invites the other's perspective so the two of you can reach a resolution that honors you both (Foss and Griffin 1995).

A collaborative conflict does not conclude until both parties are reasonably satisfied and can support the solution that has been found. Relationships are better, not worse, than when the conflict began. No one person ends up feeling justified or right. The style is cooperative, effective, and focused on team effort, partnership, or shared personal goals. It is also sometimes called mutual problem solving. It is the style that calls on all your best communication skills.

Collaboration involves making descriptive and disclosing statements and soliciting disclosure and criticism from the other party. One makes concessions when necessary and accepts responsibility for one's own part in the conflict. Collaboration does not mean taking total responsibility, such as in saying, "It's all my fault. I shouldn't have gotten angry." Rather, collaboration is a struggle with the other to find mutually agreeable solutions. Parties engage at an exploratory, problem-solving level rather than avoiding or destroying each other.

Collaboration is characterized by statements such as "When I get in conflict with someone, I try to work creatively with them to find new options," or "I like to assert myself, and I also like to cooperate with others." Collaboration differs from compromise because in compromise, the parties look for an easy intermediate position that partially satisfies them both, whereas in collaboration, the parties work creatively to find new solutions that will maximize goals for them both.

Consider the use of collaboration in the following example: A married couple are experiencing conflict over their priorities. The wife thinks the husband works too much and does not spend enough time with her. The husband believes the wife is not interested enough in his work. One way to manage the conflict would be for him to shorten his work hours to spend more time with his wife and for her to increase her interest in his work. But if the two parties collaborated, they could work together to identify the concerns underlying the conflict. It may be, for example, that both of them want more warmth and affection in the relationship, and the conflict arose because neither one's way of seeking affection was working. Through collaborative effort, they explore the disagreement and learn from each other's insights. They may discover, for instance, that when they spend time together makes a big difference. They may be able to meet for lunch occasionally, or the husband may be able to work at home during the evening.

Research on the effect of integrative styles is quite consistent—when one learns how to use them, they are successful tools for conflict management (Kuhn and Poole

2000). Collaboration results in "high joint benefit for the bargainers" (Tutzauer and Roloff 1988) and provides a constructive response to the conflict (Rusbult, Johnson, and Morrow 1984). Collaborative styles in a variety of contexts result in better decisions and greater satisfaction with partners (Sillars 1980; Wall and Galanes 1986; Tutzauer and Roloff 1988; Pruitt 1981; Gayle-Hackett 1989a). Cooperative styles allow conflict parties to find mutually agreeable solutions, whether the conflict occurs in an intimate or work situation. Dating couples who survived the "First Big Fight" believe that a successful relationship requires joint problem solving (Siegert and Stamp 1994). When college students in collaborative, or win/win, relationships were asked to predict if the relationship would last, 85 percent said yes (Knox et al. 1995).

One of the downsides to collaboration is that one party sometimes tries to use it exclusively and denigrates the other conflict party for not using it. For example, if one party is trying to collaborate and the other party is avoiding or competing, the first party might say, "I tried to solve the conflict, but he wouldn't." Negative views of the other's chosen style can become a sophisticated form of "one up"—in other words, if what I did was fine, the other person must be the cause of the continued conflict.

The following box summarizes the advantages and disadvantages of collaboration.

Collaborating

ADVANTAGES

Collaboration works well when one wants to find an integrative solution that will satisfy both parties. It generates new ideas, shows respect for the other party, and gains commitment to the solution from both parties. Because collaboration incorporates the feelings of the concerned parties, they both feel that the solutions are reality based. Collaboration is a high-energy style that fits people in long-term, committed relationships, whether personal or professional. Collaboration actively affirms the importance of relationship and content goals and thus builds a team or partnership approach to conflict management. When collaboration works, it prevents one from using destructive means such as violence. It demonstrates to the parties that conflict can be productive.

EXAMPLE:

Anne, an intern at a hospital, has been given a "mission impossible" that requires that she diagnose and keep charts on patients under the supervision of four different doctors. Her fellow interns work collaboratively to relieve her of some of the work. They want to demonstrate the need for more reasonable assignments, support Anne as a friend, and avoid being assigned Anne's work if she gets sick or resigns.

DISADVANTAGES

As with any style, if collaboration is the only style used, one can become imprisoned in it. If investment in the relationship or issue is low, collaboration is not worth the time and energy consumed. Further, people who are more verbally skilled than others can use collaboration

(continued)

Collaborating

in very manipulative ways, which results in a continued power discrepancy between the parties. It can be used as a one-up move. For example, if one party uses collaboration, he or she may accuse the other of being "unreasonable" by choosing a different style. Often, high-power persons use pseudocollaboration to maintain the power imbalance. These latter cases are not really collaboration because at least two people are required to collaborate. However, one avoider can frustrate the intentions of four collaborators.

EXAMPLE:

Members of a small group in a communication class are under time pressure to finish their project, due in one week. They overuse collaborative techniques such as consensus building, brainstorming, paraphrasing, and bringing out silent members. Quickly breaking up into subgroups would better serve the individual and relational goals of the group, but the group clings to a time-consuming method of making decisions long after they should have adapted their style to meet the deadline.

The collaborative tactics presented in table 5.6 induce, or persuade, the other party to cooperate in finding a mutually favorable resolution to the conflict. They reflect a "mutual versus individual" orientation (Canary and Cupach 1988). Collaboration involves both parties working together for solutions that not only end the conflict but also maximize the gains for both parties. The term *integrative* can be used to describe collaborative tactics, since the tactics help people recognize their interdependence (Walton and McKersie 1965). Collaborative tactics also have been labeled prosocial (Roloff 1976; Sillars 1986). The goals of the individuals and the relationship as a whole are paramount.

Collaborative tactics involve a stance toward conflict management that is very different from that of competitive tactics. A competitive tactic assumes that the size of the pie is finite; therefore, one's tactics are designed to maximize gains for oneself and losses for the other. Collaborative tactics, however, assume that the size of the pie can be increased by working with the other party. Both can leave the conflict with something they value.

Some people experience only avoidant or competitive attitudes toward conflict and have a difficult time visualizing a collaborative approach. If each time you have conflict you immediately say to your conflict partner, "You are wrong," you are likely to receive a competitive response in return. Collaboration calls for a willingness to move with rather than against the other—a willingness to explore and struggle precisely when you may not feel like it. You do not give up your self-interest; you integrate it with the other's self-interest to reach agreement. Usually, a collaborative approach to conflict management involves the use of multiple tactics listed in table 5.6.

You need not like your co-collaborators. Collaboration, however, does require "we" language rather than "I" language. Because parties work together for mutually desirable outcomes and protect their own as well as each other's interests, many times respect and caring develop as by-products of the collaborative effort.

In table 5.6, the first major classification of collaborative tactics is "analytic remarks," which allow one to collaborate by making descriptive, disclosing, or other

Table 5.6 Collaborative Tactics	
Conflict Codes	**Illustrations**
A. Analytic remarks	
1. *Descriptive statements.* Nonevaluative statements about observable events related to conflict.	"I criticized you yesterday for getting angry with the kids."
2. *Disclosing statements.* Nonevaluative statements about events related to conflict that the partner cannot observe, such as thoughts, feelings, intentions, motivations, and past history.	"I swear I never had such a bad week as that week."
3. *Qualifying statements.* Statements that explicitly qualify the nature and extent of conflict.	"Communication is mainly a problem when we're tired."
4. *Solicitation of disclosure.* Nonhostile questions about events related to conflict that cannot be observed (thoughts, feelings, intentions, motives, or past history).	"What were you thinking when you said . . . ?"
5. *Solicitation of criticism.* Nonhostile questions soliciting criticism of oneself.	"Does it bother you when I stay up late?"
B. Conciliatory remarks	
1. *Supportive remarks.* Statements that refer to understanding, support, acceptance, positive regard for the partner, shared interests, and goals.	"I can see why you would be upset."
2. *Concessions.* Statements that express a willingness to change, show flexibility, make concessions, or consider mutually acceptable solutions to conflicts.	"I think I could work on that more."
3. *Acceptance of responsibility.* Statements that attribute responsibility for conflict to self or to both parties.	"I think we've both contributed to the problem."

Source: Adapted, by permission of publisher, from A. L. Sillars, "Procedures for Coding Interpersonal Conflict," rev. (Department of Communication Studies, University of Montana, 1986), 7–16.

types of statements. The following examples reflect descriptive statements, which are the first category of analytic remarks (Yarbrough 1977):

• Describe without interpretation. Describe what you feel, see, hear, touch, and smell instead of your guesses about the behavior.

> Example: "You're so quiet. Ever since I said I didn't want to go out tonight and would rather stay home and read, you haven't spoken to me," not "You never understand when I want to spend some time alone!"

- Focus on what is, instead of what should be.

    Example: "You look angry. Are you?" not "You shouldn't be angry just because I want to stay home."

- Describe your own experience instead of attributing things to the other person.

    Example: "I'm finding myself not wanting to bring up any ideas because I'm afraid you will ignore them," not "You are getting more critical all the time."

One makes disclosing statements by saying such things as "I am having trouble tracking this issue" or otherwise reporting one's feelings while in the conflict. The flip side of the coin is to solicit disclosure from the other party, such as by saying, "What makes you so upset when I bring up the summer plans?" As table 5.6 illustrates, one can also make qualifying statements and solicit criticism as ways to move the conflict toward collaboration.

The final three categories of collaborative tactics, classified as conciliatory remarks, are (1) supportive remarks ("I can see why that is difficult—we have all been ganging up on you"); (2) concessions ("OK, I agree I need to find new ways to deal with this problem"); and (3) acceptance of responsibility ("Yes, I have been acting aggressively lately"). All conciliatory remarks acknowledge one's own role in the conflict and offer an "olive branch" of hope and reconciliation to the other, paving the way to successful management of the conflict. All of the collaborative tactics move the conflict into a third dimension where partners neither avoid nor blame but grapple with the conflict as a joint problem to be solved.

Collaborative tactics are associated with successful conflict management. Although conflict participants use collaboration infrequently (Barnlund 1989), participants who do use collaboration report "relational intimacy" (Cupach 1980); "perceived communicator appropriateness, effectiveness and attractiveness" (Canary and Spitzberg 1987); "satisfaction with the partner and relationship" (Gottman 1982; Sillars 1980); and "satisfaction with the conflict outcomes" (Canary and Cupach 1988, 306; Wall and Galanes 1986). Similarly, popular prescriptions for conflict management specify that one should work with the partner to establish mutual gain and to preserve the relationship and should engage in neither avoidance nor verbal aggressiveness but try to find mutual solutions to the problems (Fisher and Ury 1981; Fisher and Brown 1988).

❧Cautions about Styles

Although considerable research has been done on individual conflict styles, there are limitations to the research. Especially when one decides to pursue partnership, collaborative, and mutual-influence approaches, purely individual styles do not exist. One is always influenced by others, and should be, when striving for cooperative goals. For instance, if you want to practice constructive partnership approaches, you will not automatically respond to a sarcastic threat (competition) with a counterthreat or by backing down (accommodation or avoidance). You will, instead, look for ways to reframe what has happened and for more constructive options, even if you feel justified in blasting back at what feels like a threatening opponent. You will find it useful to thoroughly understand the styles and their supporting tactics so you can make educated choices about moves that are available to you during conflict.

One limitation of the research on conflict styles is that most studies are based on participants' "perceptions" of their conflict styles. One's vantage point can significantly alter the given response. Various instruments measuring conflict style have been administered to hundreds of people experiencing conflict in the workplace. When participants fill out the conflict style scales on themselves and on others, two predominant findings emerge:

- People most often see themselves as trying to solve the problem (using integrative styles) (McCready et al. 1996).

- People most often see others as using controlling or aggressive styles.

These results indicate that one's perception of conflict style depends on *whether one is rating oneself or others*. People tend to see themselves as trying to solve the conflict and the other as blocking the resolution of the conflict. Although no large-scale studies have been completed on the differences between self and other perceptions of conflict styles, Thomas and Pondy (1977) asked 66 managers to recall a recent conflict and state which style was used by each party. Overwhelmingly, the managers saw themselves as cooperative, and the other party as primarily competitive, demanding, and refusing. Gayle (1991) found a similar social desirability bias (giving answers that "look good"). Unfortunately, your perception of what you did will probably not be corroborated by the other person. In conflict, we tend to see ourselves in a positive light and others in a negative light. Human beings tend to value their own individual approaches to life. All too often we assume that our choices about behavior, values, and goals are the right ones. Therefore, we are right if we are "aggressive," "cooperative," "polite," "fair-minded," or "realistic." Since we evaluate styles depending on whether they are ours or someone else's, our vantage point determines our perceptions.

A second limitation to styles research is that research demonstrates mixed results—some studies show differences between the genders and some show no differences (Gayle-Hackett 1989b). When style studies are done on high school and college students, women report themselves as being more collaborative than do men, who report themselves as being more competitive. However, when studies are done in the workplace with older adults, male–female differences disappear (Gayle-Hackett 1989a; Rahim 1986; Bell, Chafetz, and Horn 1982; Renwick 1977; Rossi and Todd-Mancillas 1987; Shockley-Zalabak 1981; Portello and Long 1994; Korabik, Baril, and Watson 1993; Gayle 1991). In real-life settings, conflict styles are more closely related to location in the structure (as supervisor, employee, or owner) than to gender.

A third reporting bias is the underreporting of the amount of avoidance people actually use (Gayle-Hackett 1989a; Gayle 1991). When a questionnaire asks you about an ongoing conflict, you answer about conflicts that are important to you. Those you have avoided and have no interest or investment in are most likely not even remembered; thus we underreport the amount of avoidance we actually use.

A fourth limitation of conflict style research is that *measures are not process oriented*. Some individuals develop preferred sequences of styles; for example, one may begin a conflict by avoiding, then move to competing, then finally collaborate with the other party. Most measuring instruments treat personal styles as if they are traits belonging to one person—something one always does or something that describes the person instead of the behavior. The accurate assessment of one's conflict style should presuppose some change over time to reflect the variability that most people enact in their lives. Baxter (1982), for example, demonstrated that conflict expressions of small-group participants differ depending on the phase of group decision making in which the group is engaged. The following chart illustrates predominate styles with fluctuations across time. Note the variability within the styles used by the two people, both of whom predominately avoid conflict.

	Time 1	Time 2	Time 3	Time 4	Time 5	Time 6	Time 7	Time 8	Time 9
Person A:	avoid	avoid	compete	avoid	avoid	avoid	compete	avoid	avoid
Person B:	avoid	avoid	accommodate	avoid	avoid	avoid	accommodate	avoid	avoid

Both would score as "avoiders" on a general style measure, yet over time, each one demonstrates a distinctly different pattern. Measuring general styles does not reflect over-time differences between people.

Not only do our styles change with the progress of the conflict, they also change as a result of our life experiences. A young man who is always competitive learns from his romantic partner how to collaborate—thus changing his style. Alternately, someone who avoids conflict learns through trial and error to engage in the conflict earlier, thus changing her predominant mode. One can change preferred conflict style, especially if the old style ceases to work well.

A fifth limitation of conflict style research is that measures give the impression of consistency across settings, relationships, and time. Most of the instruments, in fact, ask you to respond "in general." Of course, for many people, "in general" doesn't capture the changes they experience from relationship to relationship. When people respond to style measures "for a particular relationship" or conflict, about 50 percent of the people report disparate styles in different contexts. For example, many people compete at work but avoid conflict at home. Similarly, many avoid conflict at work but collaborate at home. Yet most instruments don't account for these differences. Recent work is finally beginning to assess conflict styles across contexts and is confirming that many people have disparate styles in different contexts (Marin, Sherblom, and Shipps 1994). For example, as Sun and Payne (2004) show, "situational characteristics play a strong role in determining police actions during conflict resolution" (516).

Even within one setting, such as work, we use different styles with different partners. Putnam and Wilson (1982) demonstrated that employees prefer nonconfrontation when in a peer-related conflict in an organization, but they choose forceful communication to manage conflict with subordinates. Eric, a college debater, uses different styles in different contexts when he is in public, he competes every chance he gets. He loves to match wits with others, push hard for what he wants, and win arguments. He is a good-humored and driven young man in public situations. Yet in private with his wife, he avoids conflict as though it were a dreaded disease. When Joan brings up conflictual issues, Eric either avoids or completely accommodates—he cannot stand conflict within an intimate relationship. Yet if Eric were to fill out a widely used style instrument, he would be asked to report how he acts in conflicts, without a specific context designated. It is easy to watch someone in conflict and assume that the chosen style reflects some underlying personality dimension. But since most people adapt to different situations, with a preferred choice in one context and another choice in a different context, to give them a single label, such as a "compromiser," is a gross oversimplification.

As you might expect, our styles change over time. One study showed, for instance, that married couples who were confrontational early in their marriage tended to "mellow" and become more collaborative across time (Mackey and O'Brien 1998).

A sixth limitation of conflict style research is that one's style of conflict is assumed to be a clear reflection of an underlying motivation—a stable personality trait. Competers, however, may not want to "run over you," and avoiders may actually care about their relationships. For example, in Ellen's first marriage, she developed the pattern of occasionally throwing dishes when she was intensely angry. Her first husband would then leave the house. A few years later, after she had married Mick, they got into a screaming argument. Ellen threw a dish at Mick, who promptly went to the kitchen, picked up most of the available dishes on the counter, smashed them on the floor, shouting that she would not throw dishes at him! As a result of this aggressive interaction, Ellen realized that what she wanted was someone who would stay and fight out the problem instead of leaving the scene. Neither has thrown a dish since. At first glance, one could say that Ellen's aggressive style was an attempt to get her own way, stifle all opposition, and dominate Mick. The "true" motivation emerged in the interaction—which was a desire for intimacy.

A seventh limitation of current research is that attempts to measure individual conflict styles ignore the interactive dynamics in a conflict situation. As noted previously, our choices are not just the results of some personality quirk—they are responses to many elements of a conflict. This issue is of such fundamental importance that the next section will examine it in detail.

Interaction Dynamics

Whether we are looking at an isolated tactical move or the overall conflict style of an individual, we cannot understand conflict dynamics by examining the individual in isolation. The interaction of two or more people determines the outcome of the conflict. No matter how hard one person tries to resolve a conflict, the outcome will not be constructive unless the other person is involved in working things out, too. Figure 5.3 shows two very different outcomes of conflict even though Curtis uses exactly the same tactics throughout. In one case the conflict escalates between the two participants. In the other, Pam's alternative tactics reduce the conflict. The outcome is the *joint product of both choices*, not the result of some inherent personality trait of either participant.

One chooses his or her conflict tactics and styles based on "attributions about the partner's intent to cooperate, the focus of responsibility for the conflict, and the stability of the conflict" (Sillars 1980, 182). Analysis must shift from the individual to the relationship level, viewing conflict preferences as resulting from a system of interlocking behaviors rather than as a function of personality (Knapp, Putnam, and Davis 1988). Relational variables (whom you interact with, how congruent your perceptions are with those of the other party, what intent you think the other party has, and the mirroring of each other's responses) explain conflict style choices better than does personality (Putnam and Poole 1987; Knapp, Putnam, and Davis 1988). When you are a party to a conflict, it is your perception of the other's choices that accounts for the choices you make (Rogers, Castleton, and Lloyd 1996).

Even though each conflictual interaction is unique, two patterns of interlocking behaviors are worthy of note. They are (1) complementary patterns and (2) symmetrical patterns.

Figure 5.3 Tactics in an Interaction Context

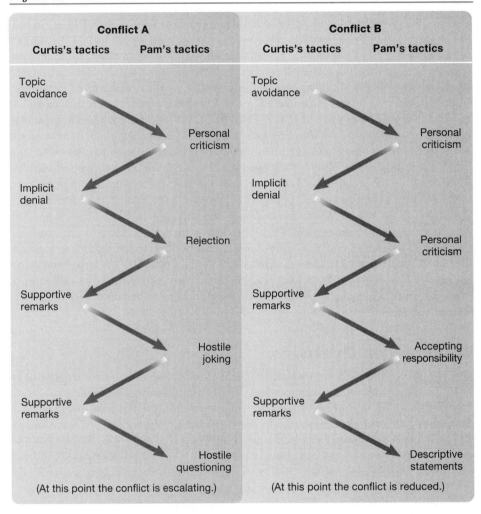

Complementary patterns are tactics or styles that are different from one another but mutually reinforcing. For example, if one person tries to engage and talk about the conflict and the other avoids, each one's moves reinforce those of the other. The engager begins to think, "If I don't force the issue, he will never talk to me," while the avoider thinks, "If she would just leave me alone, it would be all right." The more she engages, the more he avoids; the more he avoids, the more she engages; and they produce a "communication spiral" with each one magnifying his or her chosen response (Wilmot 1995).

Such complementary patterns occur in many contexts. In business settings, for example, supervisors and subordinates use different styles (Richmond et al. 1984), and in personal relationships, one person is often conciliatory and the other coercive. Raush et al. (1974) found that there was a "Jekyll-Hyde" quality to spouses in unsatisfactory marriages. In the first interaction, one person would be coercive and the other conciliatory, and then they would reverse roles. The individuals changed styles, but the overall interaction pattern was the same.

Two people can engage in complementary interactions that are not causing serious relationship difficulties. For example, nine-year-old Carina, when confronted by her father about being responsible, says, "Who cares?" (with a giggle). But, if the patterns persist for years, they can keep the two parties in recurring conflict.

Symmetrical sequences occur in conflicts when the participants' tactics mirror one another—both parties escalating, for example. One type of symmetrical pattern occurs when the parties both avoid a conflict, refuse to engage in the conflict overtly, and create a devitalized spiral. As a result, the relationship loses vitality and the partners become so independent of each other that the relationship withers away. Gottman (1982) noted that there is a "chaining" of identical tactics in distressed marriages. Distressed spouses get stuck in cycles of competitive tactics. For example, a sequence might occur as follows:

Husband: threat

Wife: counterthreat

Husband: intensified threat

Wife: intensified counterthreat

John: Don't even think of walking away from me when I'm talking.

Anita: I'll walk away, and I'll walk right out of the marriage if I do. You can't stop me.

John: Try it, and see how you get to work without a car. It's in my name, so you don't have a car!

Anita: And you don't have children. We're history!

People match their spouses' competitive tactics with an increase in their own. Such escalatory spirals lead the couple into irresolvable conflicts. In organizations, what starts as an "attack-defend" pattern evolves into symmetrical "attack-attack" patterns, with each party trying to one-up the other (Putnam and Jones 1982b). These patterns have been characterized in the following ways:

- attack-attack
- retaliatory chaining
- negative reciprocity
- cross-complaining
- threat-counterthreat
- round-robin attacks
- escalatory spirals

Other conflict tactics and styles, then, are best seen in the context of the relationship. Based on available research, the following conclusions are warranted:

1. If the conflict parties both want to avoid the conflict and, as a norm, do not generally work through conflicts, joint avoidance can be functional (Pike and Sillars 1985; Raush et al. 1974).

2. Once a conflict is engaged, dissatisfaction can be caused by either fight-flight or threat-threat patterns. Either the complementary pattern or the symmetrical pattern can be dysfunctional for the parties, especially when they get rigidly locked into habitual tactics and styles.

3. Once engagement has occurred, the conflict is best managed by moving to collaborative, integrative tactics (Pike and Sillars 1985; Raush et al. 1974). One useful sequence is (a) the agenda-building phase, (b) the arguing phase, and (c) the final, integrative negotiation phase (Gottman et al. 1976).

In summary, to preserve a good relationship while pursuing a goal that appears incompatible with that of the other person, collaborative tactics are needed. You may begin the conflict by avoiding, accommodating, compromising, or escalating, but at some point collaborative engagement is usually necessary. Competent communicators are those who use constructive, prosocial, collaborative tactics at some stage of the conflict (Cupach 1982). As Schuetz (1978) says, "In situations of conflict, as in other communicative events, the competent communicator engages in cooperative interaction that permits both persons (factions) involved to achieve their goals" (10). Sillars's work (1980) demonstrates that roommates who engaged in conflicts characterized by collaboration, rather than by avoidance or competition, were more satisfied with each other and more likely to successfully resolve conflict. Furthermore, various family researchers have clearly demonstrated the link between collaboration and relationship satisfaction (Gottman 1994; Noller et al. 1994). Collaborative tactical and stylistic choices depend on a certain level of cognitive complexity (Applegate 1982; Delia and Clark 1977). Collaborative tactics involve supporting a positive, autonomous identity for the other while working toward your own goals. Such multiple demands, although difficult to master, lead to productive results for both parties, for in the end you are working with rather than against the other for mutual collaborative gains.

Whatever communication moves you make, the basic question is whether those choices lead to the effective management of the conflict over time. No one set of moves at any point will guarantee productive conflict, but collaborative tactics at least set the stage for the containment and management of the conflict if both parties move toward a problem-solving perspective. When in doubt, collaborate.

❧Flexibility Creates Constructive Conflict

People often get "frozen" into a conflict style rather than developing style flexibility. Each time they are in a conflict, they make the same choices. The work associate who always avoids any conflict, smooths over everyone's feelings, and habitually refuses to talk about the difficulties between herself and others is frozen in a particular style. Individual lack of adaptation can occur in many forms. For example, a person might always avoid conflict until a situation heats up, at which point he or she engages in violent behavior. The pattern is self-sealing and difficult to alter. The person who competes on the job and is unable to relax off the job is just as stuck as the person who is unable to openly admit that conflict exists. People who are inflexible in their style selection are often unaware that their choice of style is an important contributor to the conflict.

People often get stuck in behaviors from their "golden age." The golden age is that period in which you felt best about yourself and from which you possibly still draw many positive feelings. The 45-year-old history teacher who fondly recalls participating in high school athletics might operate from the rule that "the way to handle conflict is to get out there and give it everything you've got, fight to win, and never let anything keep you from your goal." This rule probably worked beautifully in a football game, but it may cause real havoc if the principal does not want to work with aggressive teachers and recommends a teacher's transfer to another school.

Often people are stuck in a personal style because of early family experiences and gender identity (Neff and Harter 2002; Dumlao and Botta 2000). Young girls may have been taught to smooth others' feelings and not "make waves." If you were raised with such prescriptions and bring them to a conflictual situation, you will accommodate the other and fail to assert your own desires. In the following excerpt, a woman details some of the disadvantages of this particular lack of flexibility:

> As a child, I was forbidden to "talk back." As a result, I stifled all my replies until I was of sufficient age to walk out and did so. That was fifteen years ago—I have never been back . . . Thus, my strategy has been one of avoidance of a conflict to which I can see no resolution. Because I was raised by my father and stepmother, I scarcely knew my mother. When I was seventeen, I went to live with her. She wanted a mother-daughter relationship to which I could not respond. Legally bound to her, my attempts at confrontation ended in failure. Once again I walked out—this time into marriage. After seven years of marriage and abortive attempts at communication, I again walked out—this time with two children.

Likewise, many men are taught to compete regardless of the situation, learning that accommodation, compromise, and collaboration are all signs of weakness. Although the competitive style might be appropriate for certain business situations in which everyone understands the tacit rules making competition functional, carrying competition as one's only response into an intimate relationship can often result in the destruction of that relationship. Gender conditioning, whatever its particular form, is just one kind of learning that helps keep people stuck in conflict styles that may not work in certain situations.

Problems with Rigidity

How can you tell if you are *stuck in a conflict style?* Use the following diagnostic aid to determine if you are stuck in patterns that do not work well for you:

1. *Does your current conflict response feel like the only natural one?* For example, if your friends or family members suggest that you "might try talking it through" rather than repetitively escalating conflict, do such new options seem alien and almost impossible for you to enact?

2. *Does your conflict style remain constant across a number of conflicts that have similar characteristics?* For example, in every public conflict, do you accommodate others regardless of the issues at hand or your relationship with the others involved?

3. *Do you have a set of responses that follow a preset pattern?* For instance, do you "go for the jugular" then back off and accommodate the other because you fear you have made a "scene"? If you follow regular cycles of behavior, whatever the particulars, you may be in a process that could be altered.

4. *Do others seem to do the same thing with you?* If different people engage in similar behavior with you, you may be doing something that triggers their response. For

instance, has it been your experience that in public conflicts, others are always competitive? If so, their behavior may be a reaction to a competitive posture that you take toward public conflict. If you were more conciliatory, others might not feel the need to respond competitively to you.

5. *Do you carry a label that is affectionately or not so affectionately used to describe you?* If you grew up as "our little fireball," you may not have learned how to collaborate. If you are referred to as a "powerhouse," a "mover and a shaker," or "a bulldog," your conflict style might be overly inflexible. If you're known as "the judge" or "the dictator," you may need to take notice of an overly rigid style. Labels, although they often hurt and overgeneralize, may carry embedded grains of truth.

Application 5.7   Your Responses

Answer the above five questions, privately first, then with your small group. What did you learn? Is there anything you want to change about your style across various contexts? Maybe it's time for a change.

Individuals who can *change and adapt* are more likely to be effective conflict participants, accomplishing private and group goals better than people who avoid change. Hart and Burks (1972) discuss the concept of **rhetorical sensitivity,** the idea that people change their communication style based on the demands of different situations. The following five communication characteristics describe people who are rhetorically sensitive:

1. They are comfortable altering their roles in response to the behaviors of others.

2. They avoid stylizing their communication behavior, so they are able to adapt.

3. They develop skills to deal with different audiences and are able to withstand the pressure and ambiguity of constant adaptation.

4. They are able to monitor talk with others to make it purposive rather than expressive. They speak not so much to "spill their guts" as to solve problems.

5. They adapt and alter behaviors in a rational and orderly way.

In other words, effective interpersonal communicators expect change and adapt to change in their communication with others. They avoid getting "stuck" in certain conflict styles.

One reward for developing a repertoire of conflict styles is that we are then able to see the behavior of others in a different, more objective light. When we have a wide repertoire of conflict behaviors, we assume that other people do, too. We are far less likely to judge the behavior of others automatically as having evil intent, being childish, or being improper. After all, if we are reasonable and justified in our choices, we will probably be able to judge others as being reasonable when they choose different styles.

Another reason for actively working to widen one's repertoire of conflict styles is that many styles were developed from rules for children. Although it may be appropriate to "respect your elders" when you are eight years old, overgeneralizing that rule to include avoiding conflict with respected elders when you are an adult is much less appropriate. Learning to seek permission to speak might be fine behavior in the third grade, but waiting for permission to speak in a bargaining session, whether formal or informal, will assure that you will never be heard. As an adult, raising one's voice may not be as great a sin as stifling it.

Your choices of conflict styles are vitally important. By unfreezing your style options, you can adapt to conflictual situations depending on the goals you have for yourself and the relationship with the other person. Most of us learn retrospectively that our natural styles are dysfunctional. We examine our past conflicts and see that we have been stuck in a particular style or style sequence. Developing a repertoire of style choices opens the way to productive management of our conflicts.

❧Summary

Conflict participants face the basic choice of avoiding or engaging in a conflict. This choice leads to the five individual styles of conflict management: avoidance, competition, compromise, accommodation, and collaboration. An assessment instrument was included to measure conflict styles.

The specific styles were discussed as to their advantages and disadvantages. Competitive tactics include several subsets, such as threats, verbal aggressiveness, bullying, and violence.

One must be cautious about overinterpreting individual styles. Measures of styles depend on whether you are rating yourself or someone else,

are affected by gender, and suffer from "social desirability" biases. Further, style measures are not process oriented and give the impression of more consistency in behavior than there is across contexts. Finally, the measures give an impression of measuring an underlying trait (which they don't), and, finally, style measures ignore the interaction dynamics—one of the key determiners of what style someone will use.

We discussed the interaction dynamics in some detail and concluded by noting that flexibility in style choice enhances your chance for productive conflict.

❧Key Terms

 Use the text's Online Learning Center at **www.mhhe.com/wilmot7** to further your understanding of the following terminology.

style preferences 130
styles 130
tactics 130
assertiveness/cooperativeness graph 131
avoidance 134
engagement 134
twin cycles of avoidance 136
avoid/criticize loop 141
postponement 144

assertive competition 145
competition 145
threats 148
warnings 149
promises 149
verbal aggressiveness 150
high verbal aggressiveness 151
abusive talk 151
nonabusive talk 151
harassment 152

bullying 152
unmanaged incivility 153
violence 153
discrepancies in accounts of violence 155
compromise 157
accommodation 158
collaboration 162
rhetorical sensitivity 174

Review Questions

Go to the self-quizzes on the Online Learning Center at **www.mhhe.com/wilmot7**
to test your knowledge of the chapter concepts.

1. Define *styles*.
2. Distinguish styles from tactics.
3. Reproduce the graph showing styles varying in assertiveness and cooperativeness.
4. Define *avoidance*.
5. Give an example of the twin cycles of avoidance.
6. How does avoidance function differently in diverse cultures?
7. Give examples of avoidance tactics.
8. What are the advantages and disadvantages of competitive tactics?
9. Define *threats* and give examples of them.
10. Distinguish between threats, warnings, promises, and recommendations.
11. What is verbal aggressiveness?
12. Give examples of abusive talk.
13. What is bullying and what effects does it have?
14. Give examples of types of violence.
15. What different explanations are there for the incidence of violence?
16. Define *compromise*, listing its advantages and disadvantages.
17. How does accommodation differ from avoidance?
18. What are the advantages and disadvantages of accommodation?
19. Clarify collaboration and specify its advantages and disadvantages.
20. What are some cautions we should keep in mind when discussing styles?
21. Specify how styles are linked in interaction sequences.
22. What do you gain by having a flexible set of styles?
23. How can you tell if you are stuck in a style?
24. Describe rhetorically sensitive people.

Part Two

Intervention

~Chapter 6

Assessing Conflicts

~Introduction to Assessment

Have you ever been in a conflict in which you were so perplexed you asked, either silently or out loud, "What is going on here?" Conflicts often appear confusing, especially when you are a participant in them, and when feelings are running high. If you feel furious it's hard to feel curious (Gottman 1999). You may feel so discouraged that you don't think clearly. Conflict assessment guides can help you understand your own conflicts, as most of us are notoriously inaccurate at describing our own behavior in a conflict. We develop blind spots about our own behavior and fail to see certain aspects of the conflict. People repeatedly impose on others that which they later claim was imposed on them. The person who believes the world is a competitive, win/lose place often doesn't see that this view sets competitive processes in motion (Weick 1979). Self-fulfilling prophecies are enacted over and over as we provoke the very behavior we accuse the other in the conflict of perpetuating. Then we each make ourselves out to be the other's victim (Warner and Olson 1981). This chapter will help illuminate your conflicts, letting you see gaps in what you know. We will show you how to view the overall system dynamics in which you may feel trapped.

The assessment guides will also help you "get a handle" on conflicts when you are an outsider such as a parent, friend, or professional third-party facilitator. The techniques for assessment and intervention can be used in any role you play—as a manager, trainer, individual in conflict, teacher, parent, or organizational consultant. If you are asked to perform an in-depth analysis of a conflict or a system in trouble, either for a situation of your own or as a service to a group, you can choose several of the assessment devices in this chapter to help you describe the conflict with minimum bias.

Our inability to assimilate data often leaves all of us in the dark (Taylor 1979). The assessment approaches presented in this chapter can help with this kind of overload; they are "confusion-organizing tools" (480). As an assessor of conflicts, it is important that you identify some organizing scheme for reducing confusion before you begin the assessment. One such framework is *systems theory*, which offers a broadly based perspective on all social systems and is particularly useful when assessing an interpersonal conflict.

~Systems Theory: An Organizing Framework

Full assessment of a conflict can best be accomplished by (1) *assessing the workings* of the overall system, (2) *determining recurring patterns* inside the system that are associated with conflict, and (3) *identifying individual contributions* to the overall system. A combination of these methods, drawn from the different approaches discussed in this chapter, will provide you with data that can serve as background for constructing helpful interventions.

General **systems theory** tells us about the workings of entire systems and subsystems in organizations, small groups, and families. Many effective intervention techniques for productive conflict management derive from systems theorists who experiment with change. In this section, those systems concepts will be presented that have been the most helpful to our students, our clients, and us.

The genius of systems theory as a framework for assessment and intervention is that it provides a way to understand conflicts by giving information about patterns, interlocking sequences, functions of the parties, and methods of processing information. Systems theory helps us answer the question, "How does this work?" Conflicts are seldom managed productively by attention to blame or causality. If you tag someone with the "fault" label, you have not managed the conflict; you have only created an enemy. We call this blame process "putting the black hat on the villain."

Extensive discussions of systems theory applied to various contexts can be found in Gregory Bateson's two major works *Steps to an Ecology of Mind* (1972) and *Mind and Nature* (1980), cornerstones of systems theory writing and research. The systems approach to describing normal family processes is discussed thoroughly by Galvin and Brommel (1986) and Walsh (1984). Overviews of systems theory and the change process are provided by Minuchin (1974), Neill and Kniskern (1982), Hoffman (1981), Napier and Whitaker (1978), Weick (1979), Johnson (1977), and Papp, Silverstein, and Carter, (1973). These classic approaches provide a fresh perspective for viewing conflict from what we normally use. They give us a new "lens" from which to see what happens—that conflicts are interlocking sequences, like a play production in which everyone plays a part.

Key concepts of systems thinking follow:

- **Wholeness.** We must look at the entire system, not just a collection of individual behaviors.

- **Organization.** We are interested in how the parts of the system work together. Just as we could not understand a computer by looking only at the monitor or hard drive, but rather by looking at how they work as an integrated whole, so we must look at groupings of people as a unit. It is true that the unit is made up of individuals, but it nevertheless functions as a unit.

- **Patterning.** We are interested in what patterns seem connected. What patterns are predictable, and what function do these patterns serve? Many times people cling to patterns of behavior that seem to make no sense, but from the whole perspective, they do make sense. (Papp, Silverstein, and Carter, 1973)

Selected principles derived from systems theory will help you understand the holistic, or systemic, nature of any conflict. The following suggestions are adapted from a practical and helpful article by Papp, Silverstein, and Carter (1973):

1. Conflict in Systems Occurs in Chain Reactions. People Cannot Be Identified as Villains, Heroes, Good and Bad People, or Healthy and Unhealthy Members.

Rather than pinpointing one person as the cause of the conflict, look instead for predictable chain reactions, because what every person does affects every other person.

Study the chain reactions—see who picks up what cues and identify the part each plays in the runaway spiral. Satir (1972) uses an image of a family as a mobile in which members respond to changes in each other. If one member responds to a situation, the other members must consciously or unconsciously respond to the movement in the system. The same kind of interdependence exists in organizations and small groups. One cannot *not* affect other members of a system.

Systems operate with circular causality, a concept that suggests that assigning a beginning is less important than looking at the sequence of patterns in the conflict process. Almost always, conflict participants identify the other as the cause while portraying the self as innocent. The boy who runs home screaming, "Sasha hit me!" is clearly ignoring his part in the system (he threw dirt at her). All systems are characterized by circular causality—each one affects the other. We might take e-mail messages as an example. When people start sending negative e-mail messages, especially at work, they often feel justified and do not see the negative effect that inflammatory e-mails create. The person who "fires off" a nasty e-mail feels better, but the person who receives it (or hears about it) feels worse, fires off another message, and so forth. We suggest that negative information be communicated on the phone or in person, not by e-mail.

Descriptive language is the basic tool for assessing the system from a "no blame" perspective. Note the difference in the following vignettes:

> Wife: He's too needy. I don't know how he expects me to come home from a pressured day at work, wade through the three kids, all of whom want my attention, and ask him calmly, "How was your day?" while kissing him sweetly on the cheek. He should grow up. (Evaluative language.)

The same vignette using descriptive language.

> Wife: Scott wants to be greeted by me when I first get home. What happens, though, is that by the time I hit the front door, all three children clamor for my attention. Scott's usually in the back of the house, so by the time I physically get back to him, I'm involved with one of the children. Then he doesn't get my full attention. And frankly, I don't want to try to split myself in four pieces at that particular time.

In the second scenario, ideas for change already present themselves, whereas in the first scenario, Scott's wife labels Scott as the problem. The couple is not likely to find solutions to the conflict while the wife views Scott as the villain who is causing the problem.

2. Each Member Gets Labeled, or Programmed, into a Specific Role in the System.

Labeling serves an explanatory function for the entire group. Most labels keep people from changing; however, the labeling process itself can be changed. For instance, the "watchdog" in an organization may be carrying too much of the quality control. A person labeled as the watchdog may also be excluded, or seen as ready to pounce on any wrongdoing. Conflicts arise because if the watchdog stops performing the function reinforced by the group, others will try to pull her back into the role. The role may, however, limit her and others.

When certain individuals in the system specialize in specific functions, others may not develop those capabilities. For instance, in one sorority house, Jan was known as the "peacemaker" of the group. She could be counted on to help people solve their problems. In one ongoing conflict, however, Theresa and Pat disagreed vehemently with each other over how literally to enforce some house rules. They blew up at each other, knowing they could count on Jan to help patch things up. Theresa and Pat were not forced to make their own peace because Jan always rushed in.

3. Cooperation Is Necessary among System Members to Keep Conflicts Going.

One person cannot sustain an interaction. Therefore, the cycle can be changed by any one person changing his or her behavior. Healthy systems are characterized by morphogenesis, or "constructive system-enhancing behaviors that enable the system to grow, innovate and change" (Olson, Sprenkle, and Russell 1979). Conflict can be changed by one person initiating change or by members deciding together to initiate a change in their structure. A system that maintains conflicts by avoiding genuine change is called a *morphostatic system*, one characterized by moves designed to sustain the status quo, or no change.

If you are stuck in a system that does not change, one choice you always have is to change your own behavior, even if you cannot get others to change. In the Shepherd family, for instance, one of the five members usually felt left out. The family expectation was that four people together were enough but five people together were trouble, since each parent wanted to "take care of" one child. The family was able to change and make more room on the merry-go-round when Dad began sharing his time with all three children instead of paying attention to one child at a time.

4. Triangles Tend to Form in Systems When Relationships Are Close and Intense.

When one person feels a lower level of power, the tendency is to bring in another person to bolster the low-power position. Since the person brought in to build up the position of the low-power person maintains multiple relationships in the system, interlocking triangles begin functioning over and over in predictable ways. If these triangles lead to destructive behavior, they are termed toxic triangles (Satir 1972; Hoffman 1981; Minuchin 1974).

5. Systems Develop Rules for Conflict That Are Followed Even If They Work Poorly.

What may develop is a prescriptive rule about conflict that states, "If we are a happy family, we do not have conflict," or "We have polite conflict." At work there may be a rule that "if you have conflict with the boss, you will be fired." Some departments only enact conflict in writing. Others require conflicts to happen only in meetings, whereas some postpone or "table" most potential conflicts. System rules often block collaborative conflict. At one time they may have served the system well. Parents may have decided, for instance, never to fight in front of the children. When the children were infants, the rule protected them from angry faces and loud voices. But with children 12 and 16 years old, the rule makes little sense, as the children can always tell when Mom and Dad are in a conflict and are thus being taught to avoid overt conflict.

6. The Conflict Serves the System in Some Way.

The conflict may be substituting for other forms of intimacy and connection, or may serve as a launching pad for problem solving, or as an expression of dissatisfaction. Never assume that members of a system want the conflict to be resolved. They may fear a vacuum in their interaction if the conflict is no longer serving its particular function. Although almost everyone in a conflict will say, "Of course we want this over and done with," the fact that people keep conflicts going, sometimes for years at a time, indicates that some system function is served by the conflict. One church congregation carried on a repetitive conflict at board meetings about the propriety of using the church buildings for partisan and special interest group meetings. A third party helped them discover that the debate was a substitute for a subgroup's voicing dissatisfaction with the minister's involvement in social action projects. The board had been reluctant to confront the minister with their disapproval, so they always centered the discussion on "use of the building." The conflict allowed them to express their disapproval in an indirect way.

The following section presents techniques for identifying exactly how the conflicts occur inside the system.

Application 6.1   A Brief Systems Analysis

Write a brief paragraph about a group (system) you know inside and out. This may be a family, social group, work group, blended family, or any other group. Based on the principles just discussed, answer the following questions:

- What seems to "set off" conflicts? What are predictable trigger events?
- Does anyone have a label that people joke about? How does the label work for that person and the group?
- Who is the most likely person to change—to not do things the same old way?
- Are there any secret coalitions?
- Are there any expectations that now seem crazy, or nuts, to you, but that people more or less follow?
- What if there were no conflicts? Would anything be lost? What?

You can make use of this system analysis for a larger paper, or for understanding the principles by discussing them with others in your class.

Identifying Conflict Patterns

All conflicts follow patterns, predictable actions of communication and response. Often these **conflict patterns** seem circular—one can't quite tell where the pattern "starts." The conflict is composed of system regularities such as patterns of communication, rules for behavior, and characteristic dynamics of the system. Often the structure of the conflict is only expressed indirectly or implicitly so that assessment approaches cannot be constructed by asking the parties, "What is the structure of your conflict?" Rather, the structure has to be derived from inductive approaches such as (1) identifying specific system patterns, (2) using metaphoric/dramatic analysis, (3) drawing coalitions, (4) charting conflict triangles, (5) identifying system rules, (6) listing microevents, (7) making observations, and (8) conducting interviews.

System Patterns

Conflicts never occur in a vacuum. If Mary and Marty, just married, are having an ongoing dispute about finances, it is likely that Mary's sister and Marty's buddy, Samuel, are also involved in the conflict. We are all embedded within wider systems, so whether a conflict rages out of control or just simmers on the back burner, there are systemwide forces at work. Everyone affects everyone else.

Just as individuals develop characteristic styles, so do entire systems. Papp, Silverstein, and Carter (1973) note that in systems theory analyses, "attention is focused on connections and relationships rather than on individual characteristics. The central ideas of this theory are that the whole is considered to be greater than the sum of its parts; each part can only be understood in the context of the whole; a change in any one part will affect every other part" (197).

Each communication system has an identity that is more than the sum of the individual players. If Sally is aggressive, Tom is accommodating, and Linda avoids, simply combining their individual preferences for conflict does not tell us how they will manage conflict as a system. The following comments reflect systemwide observations:

> The research and development department ducks for cover whenever the bottom line is mentioned.
> They fight like cats and dogs, but they always make up.
> That whole group is plastic. They look so sweet, but I wouldn't trust them farther than I could throw them.

Unlike individual styles, systemwide styles have not been widely researched. Some of the most useful system descriptions will be presented, and hopefully, more research on the impact of various system styles will be forthcoming. Many system descriptions have emerged from researchers of family interaction (Fisher 1982). Lederer and Jackson's seminal book on the *Mirages of Marriage* (1968) focused attention on how marital partners act as a unit rather than as individuals. In that book, such phrases as the "gruesome twosome" and the "heavenly twins" were used to describe marriages rather than individuals. Cuber and Haroff (1955), often cited, described marriages as

1. *Conflict-habituated relationships*, in which conflict recurs constantly but has little productive effect; the fighters "don't get anywhere."

2. *Devitalized marriages*, in which the relationship is a hollow shell of what originally was vibrant and living.

3. *Passive-congenial relationships*, in which both partners accept a conventional, calm, ordered marriage that maintains little conflict.

4. *Vital relationships*, which involve intense mutual sharing of important life events.

5. *Total marriages*, characterized by the sharing of virtually every aspect of life, fulfilling each other almost completely (this may be more of an ideal than an observation of real marriages!).

The impact of conflict itself, as well as the way it is enacted, differs depending on the relational type. In a conflict-habituated couple, for example, conflict is so common that it may go almost unnoticed, but it slowly drains the energy that the couple needs for important growth or conflict. Devitalized partners might experience conflict as being so devastating that it tears apart the fragile fabric of their shared life. Conflict, after all, is energy producing and energy draining, and it therefore may destroy a devitalized couple. Likewise, avoidance in a total relationship would be a distress signal, whereas anything but avoidance in a passive-congenial relationship might break its implicit rules.

Another system-level description comes from Rands, Levinger, and Mellinger (1981), who provided an alternate view of conflict resolution types. They found that couples could be seen as belonging to one of four types:

Type I: Nonintimate-aggressive relationships foster escalation without corresponding intimacy. Couples are aggressive toward each other without enjoying the benefit of growing emotional closeness. Conflict for couples who maintain this pattern is usually not satisfying, since more energy is drained than is gained.

Type II: Nonintimate-nonaggressive couples lack vitality, intimacy, and escalation. Thus they are more satisfied than Type I people, since they do not have to contend with escalating conflict.

Type III: Intimate-aggressive couples combine intimate behavior with aggressive acts. Their conflict usually results in intimacy, even though they use aggressive, conflict modes. Their satisfaction depends on whether their conflicts lead to intimacy or someone derails the predictable outcome by aggression that is too vicious or comments that are "below the belt."

Type IV: Intimate-nonaggressive partners use small amounts of attacking or blaming behavior, retaining their intimacy in other ways. These couples are satisfied, whether they are "congenial" (i.e., they avoid full discussion of issues) or "expressive" (i.e., they confront important issues).

Multiple paths may be taken toward the goal of satisfied relationships. In an intimate relationship, for example, conflict avoidance reduces feelings of satisfaction for the couple, but in a nonintimate relationship, avoidance tends to increase satisfaction. The nature of the relationship, its definition, and its underlying patterns determine the existence and impact of conflict.

David Mace (1987), one of the originators of marital enrichment programs, has set forth a workable scheme for conflict patterns in marital systems. He finds that couples react to conflict in one of four ways. They may *avoid* it, *tolerate* it, *attempt to fight fairly*, or *process* it, which involves active listening and telling the emotional as well as factual truth.

How systems process conflict can also be put on a continuum, such as least processing to most processing. Guerin et al. (1987) have provided a four-stage model of marital conflict. Conflict within other systems, such as families or organizations, can also be classified according to the following **conflict stages:**

Stage I: Members experience a minimal amount of conflict, openly communicate, and share power. The level of conflict causes no distress for the system.

Stage II: Members experience significant conflict that they see as causing a problem. Criticism increases, but still there is little power polarization or overt struggle for control. Usually, one person is pursuing and the other is distancing, and as a system, they have some difficulty agreeing on how much separateness they should have.

Stage III: Members are in turbulence, experience high intensity, and are moving toward polarization. They are unable to exchange information accurately, and frequently criticize each other. Their power struggle is now serious and there is a life-or-death quality to much of their communication.

Stage IV: Members have *lost the ability to work through their conflicts and have engaged the services of a third party.* They see the relationship as adversarial and work to enhance their own individual bargaining positions. At this stage, a couple is headed toward disengagement and divorce (Guerin et al. 1987).

Just as with individual approaches to styles, a systemwide view has some limitations. First, conflict can be occurring in the system because the participants disagree about the type of system they want. One partner may want to be enmeshed, involving the other in all decisions, whereas the other may want more disengagement. In such cases, individual behaviors indicate a struggle with the definition of the system as a whole. Rather than being "nonintimate-aggressive," the system may reflect a struggle in process. When people work toward defining who they will be together, the rules that shape their interaction may be in flux. Some of the typologies discussed in the previous section may have given the impression that conflict patterns are fixed. However, they actually may change rapidly. Sharon and Don, for example, are the parents of three children who are entering their teens. In the past, the family could be described as "nonintimate-nonaggressive." Now that the children are growing up, the parents are rediscovering their intimacy with each other, which results in confusion in the family interactions, since the children are used to being the center of attention. No system description adequately reflects the complexity the family experiences during transition.

Second, just as with individual styles, various system patterns can be functional or not, depending on the needs of the situation. Not all groups are automatically better off with a highly processed, or "intimate-nonaggressive," style all the time. Relationships go through cycles of change on various dimensions. Mutual avoidance of conflict may be appropriate, for instance, if a remarried couple is determined to avoid the tense escalatory behavior of their first marriages. Avoidance may not continue to work for this couple for 10 years, but it may serve their goals well at first.

Application 6.2	My Family Patterns

Describe families you are part of, using some of the preceding system pattern descriptions.

- Identify the family itself (family of origin, step-family, current family, former family, extended family).
- Who are the members?
- What patterns best describe each family system?
- What are some advantages of each pattern? Disadvantages?
- Choose two or three constructive changes *you yourself* could put into motion.
- What is the emotional effect on you based on your role in each family system?

⚓Metaphoric/Dramatic Analysis

Metaphors, discussed in chapter 2, generated by conflict participants present an accurate description of their view of a conflict. Metaphors can be reflective of relational themes. Conflict parties can be asked to compare their conflict to a novel, film, or television program. One group of nurses said they were like characters in a detective novel, looking for "whodunit." A family saw themselves as a pioneer family in a Western movie, circling their wagons against possible attack, pulling together on the trail, but scattering once they were not in danger. Some people can write poems or draw pictures about their conflict. Others can visualize disconnected images then talk about what the images mean. One group generated the following images for the divorce process: "drowning," "having the road map taken away," "playing cards with no rules," and "being in surgery and waking up to find that you're on an artificial heart." One foster child, when asking her counselor for placement in a different family, said, "They speak, I don't know, Spanglish or something, and they won't teach me the language." Let your imagination be your guide in helping conflicting parties express the feel and structure of their conflicts, or in describing your own. The reason metaphors can be helpful in assessment is that by their nature they are *whole, visual, nonverbal,* and *symbolic.* This is a different form of data than you can get by observation of behavior, asking questions, using checklists (although these are helpful too), or studying documents. You will gain a fuller assessment if you include several different kinds of data.

During interviews and observation, people spontaneously speak of their conflicts in metaphoric ways. These expressions should be carefully noted and used in your overall analysis. You can ask people to explain how the metaphor works. For instance, a counseling center has a plaque reading "The Little Mental Health Center on the Prairie" hanging in the staff room. Values of neighborliness, assistance in times of trouble, and "pulling together" are evident in staff relationships. The following structured technique allows you to use metaphors to generate creative ideas for managing your conflicts. Use metaphoric analysis when you or others seem stuck in the "same old patterns." Think of metaphoric analysis as a creativity device.

| Application 6.3 | Playing with Your Conflict Metaphor |

1. Parties generate *a metaphor* for an important conflict, using one of the previous suggestions. Each party writes out their own metaphoric image. ("We are a . . .")

2. One person *shares the image* with the group of conflicting parties or the discussion group. The group then asks clarifying questions of the person sharing the metaphor, using the images developed in the original metaphor.

3. The group then *brainstorms*, still using the imaginary mode, about ways to resolve the conflict. (In brainstorming, you reserve "editing" until later.)

4. The facilitator or leader then asks the group to *translate* these imaginary resolutions into practical steps for conflict management.

(continued)

Application 6.3 — Playing with Your Conflict Metaphor

5. The primary party, or the group, then *chooses the options* that are most likely to lead to collaborative conflict management.

6. After all the conflict parties have repeated this procedure, a *contract* is made for selected change.

The following boxes present examples of the above metaphor exercise.

Application 6.4 — Beth and Ted

Beth and Ted are a couple who have been intimate for one year. Beth has considered leaving through the National Student Exchange program for one year at a school in Philadelphia, two thousand miles away. She wants to continue the relationship with Ted while at school but also wants freedom to date others. Ted wants a more intimate relationship and feels that can be achieved only if he and Beth can see each other often.

Beth and Ted agree that the following image describes their current attempts to solve their conflict:

We open a messy, heaping cupboard and upon seeing the disorganization and mess, we hurry to slam it shut before all the cans and bottles fall out, injuring one of us.

After following the discussion steps listed above, Beth and Ted agree that a new image will guide them to more productive conflict management:

We open a messy, heaping cupboard. We roll up our sleeves, take all the items off the shelves, clean up, throw out the spoiled goods, and put everything that is left back into a larger cupboard without doors—for easy reorganization.

Application 6.5 — The Dangerous Minefield

Margaret, a college student, writes:

My father and I are in a minefield. The sky is blue, the sun is shining, there is green grass and sudden death underneath. Each of us is responsible for some of the mines underfoot, and we have to avoid our own mines as well as those planted by the other person. There are scattered trees and bushes around the field, which is quite large. They provide limited cover. We are each trying to get in close enough to the other to get a good look without being seen.

My father throws rocks at me to try to flush me out into the open. I back around a bush and meet him. Boom! There's a big explosion—we both flee, wounded, only to begin the standoff over again.

Here are some metaphoric solutions for "The Dangerous Minefield" translated into practical steps for conflict management:

Metaphoric Solutions	Communication Possibilities
1. Dig up my mines, or tell him where they are	Disclose myself
2. Get a metal detector, locate his mines, and	Psych him out and
a. dig them up;	a. confront him;
b. throw heavy objects from a distance to set them off;	b. backstab him;
c. avoid them	c. avoid him or "be nice"
3. Wear explosion-proof armor	Decrease my dependence
4. Throw rocks at him	Attack or goad him
5. Abandon the field; leave	Don't communicate at all
6. Hold on to him during explosion so we can't run from each other	Increase closeness and interdependence
7. Cut down the foliage to get a better view	Describe our behaviors and feelings to each other
8. Use binoculars to see each other	Get information on him from other sources; focus carefully
9. Whistle as I go around the field	Let him know "where I'm coming from"
10. Stand in the open so he can see me	Give him a chance to get information about me; write him a letter

Options 1 and 7 through 10 seem to be moves that would help productively manage the conflict. Many more exist, but these are a good start.

Application 6.6   A Shady Deal

We're playing poker at a card table covered with green baize cloth, which is hanging down so no one can see under the table. Kevin is the dealer, and he also plays against me. He has the right to change the rules; sometimes I don't even know the game we're playing. The stakes are high; my tension mounts as the game progresses. Kevin smiles mysteriously; I hide my feelings, trying to bluff. An audience gathers, encouraging me to get out of such a lopsided game. I always stay for another hand, thinking that this time I'll understand the rules and have a fair chance. My tension continues to mount.

The shady deal mentioned in the previous box is an elaboration of a comment made by a student in a conflict class. Frustrated with a romantic relationship, she said that sometimes it seemed to her that Kevin "dealt all the cards." In class, her discussion group expanded this description of the shady deal and provided imaginary ways the game could be changed. People often use metaphoric language to communicate about the pattern of interaction they experience in a conflict. Many times, the person generating the metaphor is amazed at the precise insights strangers gain about the elements of the interpersonal conflict, based on the metaphor alone.

In addition to metaphoric analysis, two more approaches help you discover systemwide effects in conflicts. One rich device is *drawing coalition diagrams*, and the second involves *specifying conflict triangles*. We will begin with coalition diagrams, for they are simpler and easier to use; additionally, they show the entire system. Triangle analysis focuses more on subsystems. Used together, coalition diagrams and diagrams of triangles give a detailed description of a system.

❧Drawing Coalitions—Who Is In, Who Is Out?

Conflicts are created, reinforced, and best managed by focusing on the *communication patterns* within the system. The focus on coalition formation allows us to both examine destructive conflicts and provide a better conflict process. In all systems, whether family, in the dormitory, at work, or in a neighborhood, participants tend to cluster into "coalitions" in which some people are closer to each other than are others. For example, in a family, you may be the "outsider," the last to hear of important family events. Or, at work, there may be two groups, those who like the supervisor and those who do not. Or there may be departments that join together every time there is some decision, and exclude other departments. A **coalition** is formed by more communication with some people, compared to others. That communication is usually hidden in some way. Figure 6.1 is a simple diagram showing one possible set of coalitions.

When two people are "coalesced," they orient to one another, share more information, and feel closer than to others. When people feel excluded, they call the other people's coalitions "cliques." As you can see from the Williams family diagram, mom and son Seth are close, as are dad and daughter, Rachel. And son #2, Tom, is the "isolate"—the one who is more out of the loop than others.

Figure 6.1   Coalitions in the Williams Family

Figure 6.2   Coalitions With/Against the Boss

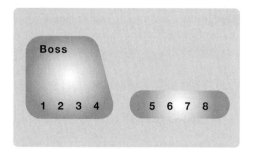

Coalitions also form in workplaces. Above are two examples to illustrate some of the diverse patterns that develop.

In figure 6.2, the executive director has a close relationship with four of her staff, and the other four form a coalition "against" the original group. Even without knowing any of the people involved, you can sense some of the system dynamics. In this case, the executive director shared a close bond with one person, and also with about one-half of the staff. The remainder of the professional staff, feeling excluded by the director, formed their own counter-coalition. Over time, the coalitions became so rigid that outside help was requested. Whatever one group wanted, the other resisted, and vice versa.

Drawing coalitions gives us an overall view of the system—who is in, who is out, who is closest to whom, what the power dynamics might be based on, who has the most power, and how coalitions might function to balance power. Coalitions follow a set of principles.

Principle #1: Coalitions Begin for Good Reasons

In all organizations and families with more than three members, coalitions exist. As the members go about their relating, they tend to "cluster" their communication. A parent talks more to a child than to the other parent; one group of teachers in an elementary school forms into two groups—"smokers" and "nonsmokers"; and half of a group of community college faculty give allegiance to the academic vice president while the other half ally themselves with the president. People form coalitions in order to (1) share content information, (2) have others who give support and understanding (3) have a sense of belonging, and (4) gain power. Thus, coalition formation is a natural process in all families and organizations—people tend to cluster together (and apart). In their initial stages such coalitions are positive. It is through them that we attain the positive feedback we need in the family and organization for support. Coalitions, then, serve positive functions for the participants—they provide a sense of place, give crucial interpersonal support, and allow for power and influence to be activated.

In all the workplaces and families where we have worked as change agents, there has yet to be one where the members were not in coalitions. Further, the members of the system know that the coalitions exist. When people are in conflict, they almost always disagree about everything—their "lenses" are so different. But, when asked to draw coalitions, they reproduce almost the same diagram. Coalitions are so powerful and ever present that all the members know about them and respond to them. We all know at each point in time, "who's in, who's out."

Principle #2: Coalitions and Counter-Coalitions Become Self-Justifying

Once we are in a coalition (or sometimes left out of one), we tend to feel justified in being "in the group" or "not in the group." If we are central, it is because we feel important. If we are isolated, we see ourselves as special and different from the others. One administrative assistant in an office of psychologists felt (and was) excluded by the other two assistants. She began to talk to the psychologists in the office about the assistants, saying polite but negative things about them. Soon, she was going to lunch with several of the psychologists. The two assistants then began to give her more of the tedious billing work, saying, "if she has so much time on her hands, she can help out more."

Once coalitions begin forming, they become self-justifying. In a family, as a parent and child form a close bond talking about the errant parent, for example, the bond becomes self-reinforcing. As we communicate with a coalition partner, we tend to justify the exclusion of others by stressing how similar we are to our coalition partners. It is a simple extension of the in-group/out-group phenomenon. As the coalition strengthens, the members (1) stress their similarities to one another, (2) highlight their dissimilarities to those not in the coalition, and (3) accelerate these differences throughout time. Each coalition forms its own reward structure, perceptually driving the members farther and farther from the "others."

Similarly, system isolates justify their exclusion. The teenage child or estranged parent isolated from the family and the lonely employee adopt the stance of, "I didn't want to be part of your group anyway." Isolates, after a certain point in time, resist joining and take pleasure in being "different." Whether the isolate is the loner who likes to work the night shift, the estranged teenager, or the only female employee, they provide for their own internal support system and decline offers to merge with the others. They may, of course, feel sad and disillusioned.

Principle #3: Coalitions Become the Problem

Coalitions become toxic when they become so tight that the groups get locked into destructive conflict with one another. In the eyes of coalition participants, they are "friends" whereas the people in the other group are forming cliques. The coalitions, because of their rigidity and heavy boundaries, begin causing problems for the system. The mother-daughter dyad excludes father so that he gives up on having influence in the family and acts out even more isolating behavior. The organization divides into voting blocks and power plays, with each group vying to outdo the other group on policy issues. Each iteration of communication rigidity reinforces the boundaries already existing and produces more and more perceptual distortion—accelerating the negative behavior and inaccurate metaperceptions of the other group. Rather than talking to others, each group spins off and takes action based on their guesses about the others' intentions— which they usually see as being negative.

Obviously, *communication patterns both reflect and create the difficulties.* People with-hold information, make overt power plays, act in competitive ways or avoid the others altogether. They stop solving problems. Communication exchanges become more toxic and damaging, with each discussion producing more distrust, hostility, and discord. In this sense, coalitions serve to scapegoat other individuals or coalitions. Inclusion and exclusion remain two of the most powerful human forces in social life.

Principle #4: Clarify Coalitions by Drawing Them

A good way to "get a picture of a conflict" is to draw the coalesced, partly private, pair-ings. In one romantic situation, Jane has separated from her husband, Tom. She has met a man at work and is flirting with him, considering a relationship with him. Jane and Noah talk about the problems Jane has with Tom. Tom, however, is isolated. He talks with Jane, but much of the truth of her emotional life is hidden from him. As Tom and Jane enter couples counseling, the counselor challenges Jane, in a private session, to stop telling Noah her complaints about Tom, and, instead, to tell Tom. If she does that, she will soften the coalition that further estranges her from Tom. If she does not, she will almost certainly lose her relationship with Tom. Jane still has the choice not to return to Tom; keeping the coalition with Noah assures that she will stay separated. Her closeness with Noah is self-reinforcing; her distance with Tom is self-reinforcing.

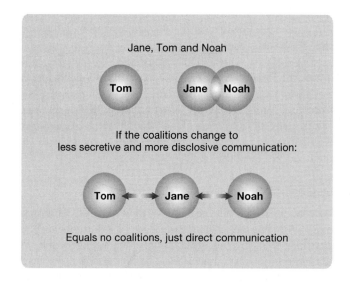

Principle #5: Coalitions Predict Future Conflict

When one locates each person in the system, the destructive patterns become clear *and* avenues to intervention are opened. For example, the **heavy communicators**—those who are central to passing and receiving messages from members—typically (1) resist being moved out of that central role and (2) at the same time complain about the "overwork," or effort, involved in keeping the system happy. In undergraduate classes, students diagram their family coalitions. In about 85 percent of the cases, the mother is a heavy communicator in the family and reflects these dynamics. Similarly, in an organization, if someone is in a central or mediating role, he or she will complain about others' apathy and lack of involvement—while maintaining their central role at all cost.

Organizational and family isolates also demonstrate predictable patterns. If there is an **isolate,** one member who is "out" compared to the others, the isolate (1) complains about the decisions or personalities of central people yet (2) resists coming closer to the center of communication flow. Both the isolate and the central members cooperate to keep him or her out.

1. Those close to the authority and power complain about the isolates, or less central people, "not doing their job."
2. Those who do not have the ear of the authority and are more peripheral will describe the "treatment" they get as negative and unwarranted.

System members specialize, with one group talking about *content* and the other group talking about *process and relationship*. Higher-power coalitions rely on "data" and facts, while lower-power coalitions talk about process and relationship issues.

One other macro communication pattern needs to be noted. Within each system the participants' main complaints are worsened by their own actions. In a community college, the academic vice president was accused by half of the faculty of being "weak." Meanwhile, every time this group disagreed with one of his decisions, they went "over his head" to the president, undercutting him and reinforcing his "weakness." Similarly, in a family, a grandparent might be concerned that his or her daughter or son is not a "good parent" to the grandchildren, yet the grandparent might make unkind comments in public about the parent and continue to undermine the parent's feelings of worth.

Principle #6: Change a System by Softening the Coalitions

In a healthy system, everyone can talk with everyone else. In a women's group formed to read fiction and discuss contemporary books, several members have begun attending erratically. Marcy and Tina talk with each other about how disgusted they are with the overly specialized and obscure fiction some of the natural leaders choose. Ruth and Maryanne talk with each other, and sometimes with Marcy and Tina, about how the group is becoming just a showcase for the most talkative leaders. By coalescing and isolating themselves, they are losing influence in the group, lessening their interdependence on the group, and creating uncertainty in the other members. The solution? For each woman to say to the whole group that her preferences aren't getting much regard, or for each woman to make suggestions about what she'd like to see the group read. One could offer to lead a book discussion. More involvement in the group and less involvement in the coalitions will probably solve the immediate problem. Right now, personality attributions are hardening and assumptions are being set in concrete. The group is in danger of dissolution.

The following exercise will give you practice in describing coalitions.

Application 6.7	Draw a System

For some system you know well (your family, your workplace, your social group), draw the coalitions, isolates, and lines of communication. Label the coalitions with a title, including the initials of each person in the coalition. Remember that some people may be in more than one coalition. Draw lines that indicate whether communication is interrupted or flows easily between the coalitions. Now, show your drawing to someone else, without telling him or her the specific content. See what that person can predict about (1) emotions, (2) tactics used, and (3) predictable communication problems.

Conflict Triangles

As we have seen in the discussion of coalitions, conflicts can be structurally analyzed using diagrams—**conflict triangles.** In this section, we will go into even more detail in subsystem analysis. You will probably want to practice these analytic techniques (coalitions and triangles) on simple systems, first. Then you can apply the techniques to more complicated, larger, and more "layered" systems. Several researchers note that the triangle is the basic unit of analysis for conflict communication (Satir 1972; Hoffman 1981; Minuchin 1974; Wilmot 1987). Why triangles? When people perceive that they are the low-power party in a two-person conflict, their typical response is to try to form a coalition with another person who can bolster their power. If another party joins the low-power party, that person then becomes part of the conflict, as you may have discovered if you have taken sides with a friend or co-worker who was in conflict with someone else. "Three's a crowd" is a cultural cliché based on sound reasoning. Three people find it difficult to maintain balance in a conflicted relationship. Usually they are structured as a "dyad plus one" (Wilmot 1987). However, three people may be able to interact with ease over a long period of time if they are not engaged in conflict. *Triadic analysis* can be used to study the relationships that make up an ongoing conflict of more than three people. The method is especially useful in conflicts involving five or more people. After interviewing and/or observing the conflict parties, follow these steps:

1. Ask about recurring experiences in the conflict system. Which are puzzling, painful, or frustrating, or trigger conflicts? Note these by drawing and labeling them.

2. Draw triangles demonstrating the different relationship combinations among the conflict parties. Mark conflicting dyads with ◄━┼━┼━┼━┼━┼━┼━►. In a conflict consisting of many people, choose the most problematic triangles to work with first.

    The following toxic triangles refer to Tom and Mary, a married couple who have both been married before. The word *toxic* (Satir 1972) was first applied to these kinds of relationships to describe the poisonous, dangerous, and potentially devastating nature of the relationships.

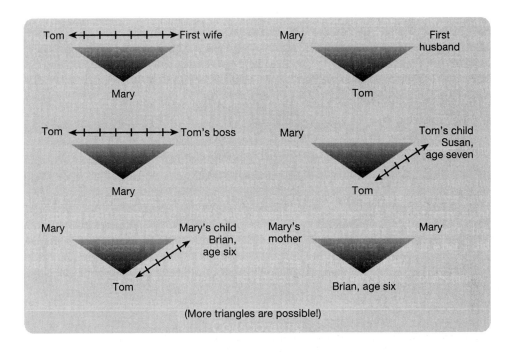

3. Code high-power persons with a + and low-power persons with a −. Whether a person is high-power or low-power may vary depending on the triangle he or she is in.

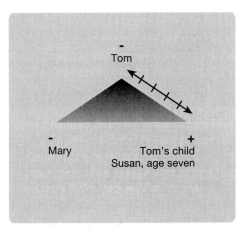

(Continue with all triangles.)

4. Identify alliances with a double arrow: ←→ Identify coalitions with an arrow in parentheses (←→), which denotes the hidden nature of the communication.

(Continue with all triangles.)

5. Identify isolates, or persons who are in few or no triangles. Can they be drawn in to productively restructure the conflict?

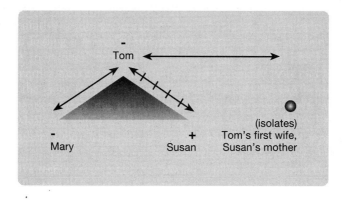

6. Identify persons involved in many or all of the triangles. Can they withdraw from some toxic triangles?

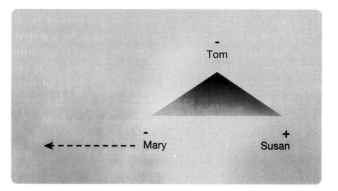

In this example, Mary could withdraw from active participation in Tom and Susan's conflict, giving them the opportunity to communicate directly with each other.

Tom ⟷ Susan

This might result in two collaborative dyadic interactions:

Tom ⟷ Susan
Tom ⟷ Tom's first wife

7. Discuss all toxic triangles (the ones that produce the most conflict), deciding how they might be productively restructured. (See chapter 4 for ideas on power balancing.)

8. Choose several options for beginning to process the conflict differently.

9. Have each person keep a list of agreements for change made during the session. These agreements are negotiated by the parties involved and the counselor or facilitator, and involve changes individuals are willing to make.

Diagrammatic techniques are not limited to use with intimate relationships; they also can be applied to conflict in small groups, work groups, or subunits of an organization. Although conflicts do change rapidly, the most confusing, often recurring, and damaging conflicts in systems present stable underlying dynamics. They occur over and over in different *content* guises, as discussed in chapter 3. Using a method such as identification of triangles makes the process understandable to members in a way that helps depersonalize the problems. In organizations, staff groups can participate in such an analysis, putting the triangles on a board and working cooperatively to understand what goes wrong and why. When members of a system understand that low-power people act in predictable ways, the members can more readily change the power balance in a productive way.

❧System Rules

You have undoubtedly experienced conflicts in which you wanted to say, "Here we go again. Same song, 14th verse." Sometimes no matter what content is being discussed, the outcome is the same. The same people collude together, the same people are left out, and the same indirect strategies are used (like "forgetting," avoiding the issue, and putting off a decision until something must be done). As we have seen, repetitive, unsatisfactory conflicts often operate on a set of unstated but very powerful rules that limit genuine change.

Rules used in this context means the underlying communication structure of the interaction. Underlying rules are like the structure of a language. Usually, no one person dictates the rules. Instead, the rules guide behavior in more subtle ways. They are "the way things are done" in a family, a business, a department, or a group of friends. A more precise definition of a rule is that it is "a followable prescription that indicates what behavior is obligated, preferred, or prohibited in certain contexts" (Shimanoff 1980, 57).

Usually the rules of communication remain implicit. However, analysis of conflict benefits from an explicit listing of the rules, which allows them to be understood, brought to the surface, and changed. The following are some examples of rules that conform to the above definition. Keep in mind that people can sometimes tell you the rules if you interview them, but the rules are never printed and posted. Those are different kinds of rules.

- *Rules are prescriptions for behavior stated in the following form*

    "When in context X, Y must/must not occur."

    "When Father shows sadness or anger, Mother must soothe him."

    "When the program director decides to assign a case to a counselor, the counselor must accept the case or convince the program director to reassign it."

- *Rules are stated in prescriptive, not evaluative, language.* They focus on communication behavior.

    "When brother and sister fight, Dad must intervene to stop it," not "Dad feels responsible for stopping brother and sister's fights even though they can handle them without interference" (this is interpretive and evaluative).

One of the characteristics of important rules in a system is that some implicit message *against knowing or stating the rule directly* is usually present. It's as if people must follow the rules but can't say what they are. For that reason, listing rules for the way a certain system of people engages in conflict may not be easy. You can elicit **system rules** from conflict parties by following these steps:

1. List explicit and implicit rules that prescribe your own and others' behavior in conflicts.

2. If you have trouble thinking of rules for your system, think of times when the rule was broken. How did you know the rule was broken? How was the violation communicated? Write about the prescription that became obvious upon breaking the rule.

3. Make sure you generate rules for both behavior that must and behavior that must not be performed.

4. Go back over your list. Make each rule simple and prescriptive. Write rules even for "obvious" communication patterns. They may prove to be important possibilities for change.
    Example: When new staff members attend the staff meeting they must not express opinions unless they have a sponsor who is an older staff member.

5. Code each rule as to the following:

    a. Whose rule is it?
    b. What keeps the rule going?
    c. Who enforces the rule?
    d. Who breaks the rule?
    e. What function does the rule serve?

6. Discuss how the rules help or harm the productive management of conflict. Make decisions for change.

    Example:

    Old rule—When Dad is angry at younger brother, older brother must protect younger brother from Dad's disapproval.

    Result—Older brother and Dad engage in conflict often, reducing effect of the protection (a toxic triangle).

    New rule—When Dad and younger brother get into a conflict, they must talk about their conflicts without older brother (a new affiliation).

Application 6.8   Discover Your System's Rules

Choose any of the above steps for your practice. Take 10 minutes or so, and see if you can follow the suggestions. Focus on one particular relationship, and begin to think about, and write, some of the rules that define that relationship. Check with others to see if you understand the way rules are written.

Many groups are amazed at the complexity of their conflict rules. A first step in collaboration can be to generate the list of rules together, brainstorming to add to the suggestions made by each member, then refining the rules for accuracy. Often groups and families can decide together which rules obstruct collaborative conflict processes.

Microevents

Microevents *are repetitive communication patterns that carry information about the underlying conflict structure.* The identification of such recurring episodes can lead to morphogenesis, or system change. Microevents are "repetitive loops of observable interpersonal behaviors . . . with a redundant outcome" (Metcoff and Whitaker 1982, 253). The microevent reinforces the structural patterns of relating to one another by supplying a repeatedly experienced interaction. In this way, microevents are similar to rules, but microevents are *descriptive*, not prescriptive, of behavior. They are clusters of behaviors organized into structurally repetitive episodes. In simpler, nontechnical terms, microevents are those small pictures that give a lot of clues about the bigger picture. An outsider could speculate about ongoing relationships based on what she or he sees in a 5- or 10-minute interaction.

Not every short interaction is a microevent; microevents are *interactions that give information about other interaction.* For instance, your new boyfriend/girlfriend might visit your parents' home with you. After one dinner, the new partner might ask you, "Does your dad always add to whatever you say, and try to kind of improve it? It seems like he's always teaching you. And your mom seems like she's the one who asks questions. Is that the way it usually is?"

Perhaps the clearest keys to the nature of an underlying structure are the "substitutable communication events that reveal the structure" (Metcoff and

Whitaker 1982, 258). Metcoff and Whitaker provide the following example of such repeatability:

$$\text{Every time the husband} \left\{ \begin{array}{l} \text{scratched his ear} \\ \text{rubbed his nose} \\ \text{tapped his right foot} \end{array} \right\} \text{during}$$

an argument with his wife, one of the children

$$\text{would} \left\{ \begin{array}{l} \text{ask to go to the bathroom} \\ \text{slap a sibling} \\ \text{begin to cry} \end{array} \right\} \text{so that the}$$

husband-wife dispute was never resolved. (258–259)

The implicit, unstated structure underlying these repetitive conflicts can be summarized as follows: "When the husband and wife initiate a conflict, one of the children makes a move to gain their attention, and the husband-wife conflict is not resolved" (259). Each system will, of course, have a different structure underlying the observable conflict. The microevent serves to define the conflict because it "embodies themes of stability and change within the family system" (263).

Once the underlying structure is decoded, one can begin to predict where, when, or how conflict will erupt. Emily and Gordon are a married couple in their 60s whose children are all grown and living elsewhere. Before each vacation, Gordon decides where they should go, then tries to persuade Emily of the wisdom of his choice. Emily won't agree to go, but neither will she say no. Then, the night before the trip, Gordon stays up most of the night packing, and the next day, Emily reluctantly goes with him. Their repetitive conflicts are structured in the following manner:

1.   He always initiates.

2.   She is always convinced to go (reluctantly).

3.   There is no discussion of their relationship; all issues are handled through content.

4.   Neither receives positive results from their respective stances.

5.   Neither one can solve or escape the conflict.

Their next conflict, over whether, when, and where to go for Christmas, will be based on a similar structure.

One can begin decoding the structure underlying a microevent by focusing on the following questions.

Application 6.9

Understanding Your Microevent

1.   Who initiates and in what way?

2.   Who responds and in what way?

3.   Who else is present but is not identified as a party to the conflict?

(continued)

Application 6.9
Understanding Your Microevent

4. Does anyone "speak for" someone else? If so, does this keep the participants embroiled in the conflict?
5. If there were no conflict, what would be missing?
   a. Who would not be connecting with whom?
   b. How would the parties structure their time?
   c. Would conflicts continue with new parties entering into the fray?
6. Is the conflict serving to fill emotional space so other parties cannot fight?

The communication patterns created in a conflict often cycle back and imprison the players. For example, Beverly went through a divorce two months ago, and her son Randy is having difficulty at school. At least twice a week, Beverly and Randy struggle over his poor work in the fifth grade. He has been labeled a "troublemaker" at school and has been sent home from school three times in the last month. This is embarrassing for Beverly; she also gets very angry at Randy for his "stupid behavior." The repetitive microevent that Beverly and Randy enact has the following features:

1. Beverly initiates each conflict by being distressed about Randy's school performance or disruptive behavior at school.
2. Randy responds by being sullen, pretending he is deaf and can't hear requests, and withdrawing.
3. The unemployed older brother is present in the house but serves as a bystander.
4. Randy and Beverly are both isolated parties—neither has anyone to come to his or her aid during the conflict.
5. Aside from the conflict, mother and son have few common interests. Beverly can't think of things that might be interesting for the two of them to do together. This recurring conflict both illustrates and crystallizes the family structure.

The following are some ways you can discover and describe microevents:

1. Act as a qualitative researcher who uses observation and interviewing to determine patterns.
2. Obtain a professional third-party (consultant, mediator, or therapist) description of common conflicts.
3. Keep a journal of conflict episodes that seem repetitive—those that have a "here we go again" theme.
4. Ask newcomers to a system, such as new employees, new family members, or new committee members, to describe what they have experienced so far.

Microevents can suggest ways to change the conflict structure just as rules can. In the following case, Melissa decided to give her schedule to her grandparents as soon as she arrived for a visit so her grandmother would not be left wondering about Melissa's schedule and Melissa could be open about her plans.

The Broken Plans

Every time there is a break from school and work, I go down to Medford to visit my relatives. I usually begin by staying at my grandparents' house, then spend a night or two at my brother's house, then visit my cousin or aunt. The following communication patterns are repeated the first morning of every visit with my grandparents:

When I get up, Grandma has already fixed my breakfast and has it set out on the kitchen table—cereal, toast, juice, fresh fruit, et cetera. Grandma always goes to great lengths to have everything perfect. "Would you like an egg, dear?" she asks.

"No thank you, Grandma; this is fine. You really don't have to fix me breakfast. I could do it fine."

"Well, we don't get to see our girl very often; you don't mind being spoiled a bit, do you?" She and Grandpa then bring their coffee into the kitchen and sit down and drink it while I eat my breakfast.

"What are your plans for this time?" asks Grandma. I have already told her that I only have three days, but I haven't mentioned what I am doing.

"Well, I'm not really sure. I hadn't really decided," I answer. At this point I am stalling a bit because I have actually already decided that I am going to leave later this evening and visit my brother. However, I don't want to hurt my grandparents' feelings.

"I hope you will be able to spend a little more time with us," says Grandma. Her hopeful look melts my strong will about sticking to my plans.

"Let her do what she wants," says Grandpa. "Must be pretty boring for a young girl like her hanging around with a pair of old fogies like us." He winks or pats me on the knee. "You know we love having you, dear, but there are other people who want to see you, too."

"She has plenty of time to see everyone else!" argues Grandma. "For once, I would like her and me to have a nice visit without worrying about her running off to visit some-one else."

"We will have a nice visit, Grandma," I say. By this time I am even more reluctant to mention my plans because I don't want to hurt her feelings. "Remember over Christmas I spent nearly a week with you, and the rest of the family only got a few days." I attempt to rationalize.

"Oh, that was months ago," she answers. "Can I get you something else for breakfast?"

"Grandma, I'm fine," I answer.

"I just want to make sure you're not hungry or anything. Whenever you are at our house, you just get whatever you need. You don't have to ask; you just get what you want," Grandma says. "Grandpa and I really enjoy having you, even though we don't get to see you that much."

I can sense her watching me while I concentrate on my dish of shredded wheat, which has gone soggy during our conversation. Breakfast usually ends with my deciding that it is better to spend an extra day with my grandparents instead of feeling guilty during the rest of my visit. The repetitive patterns of "We love you and will do nice things for you if you please stay with us" win out over my initial plans for the break.

Source: Courtesy of Melissa Price.

Application 6.10	One Microevent

Try writing a personal microevent. Think of the brief narrative as a defining moment, one that gives the outline of "This is the way it is in my (family, organization, small group)."

What do you notice as you read the microevent to others? Ask for their feedback in the form of "I notice that . . ." Ask that they give you descriptive, not prescriptive, feedback.

❧Observation and Interviews

Looking, listening, and asking structured questions can give the analyst of conflict a wealth of rich information. **Observation** and **interviewing** are essential tools for a third-party facilitator, such as a mediator, manager, or supervisor, or sometimes a parent or teacher. One recent graduate of a communication program was asked by the program director in the hospital in which she worked to provide a workshop on team building. Since Carol, the new program assistant, had worked in a similar program in the same hospital, she was aware that some conflicts had gone on for several months, primarily over what kind of advertising should be done for community service programs sponsored by the hospital on alcoholism, self-esteem for children, and caring for older parents. Carol realized that the director who had asked her to provide a two-hour workshop on team building had one perspective, and two other program assistants seemed to share a different perspective on how to advertise. Carol chose to interview several of the people involved, so she could specify how to build teamwork in this particular situation.

Interviews help participants think through their current conflict, enable the interviewer to coach people on how to present their ideas and search for common interests, build rapport with an outsider who might be able to help, and begin the process of helping people change (Yarbrough and Wilmot 1995). Questions can be drawn from the Wilmot-Hocker assessment guide presented later in this chapter.

As you try to understand complicated conflicts, remember to observe what happens—who says what, in what order, about what topics, and with what kind of nonverbal communication. Acting like a good anthropologist helps one become a good conflict analyst. And sometimes other people's conflicts seem as strange as a different culture. Understanding motivation is less important than clearly describing communication behavior.

In the case mentioned earlier, Carol observed, through interviewing and gathering written materials, that more advertising was done for certain courses. She noticed what people said about budget, teaching, personnel, and successful versus unsuccessful courses. Gradually she realized that the program director's agenda was for some courses to fill more quickly than others—the courses the program director thought were most important. Carol realized that clarifying goals had to be part of the team-building workshop. When you act as an interviewer, be aware that the interview process itself is part of the intervention, since people begin to think and feel differently as they answer your questions and try to explain the dynamics in question.

❧Comprehensive Assessment Guides

The two assessment guides presented here stress open-ended, participant-based data as the path to understanding conflict processes. They can form an outline for your interviews and observation. We often use them to help students organize data for a final paper. Such approaches are particularly useful for third parties such as intervention agents and students wishing to study a particular conflict. As a party to the conflict, you can use the guides to collect information about your own and the other party's views about the conflict. In either case, one needs to use primary information from the parties—for they are the ones who created and maintain the conflict.

The two assessment guides are (1) the *Wilmot-Hocker Conflict Assessment Guide* and (2) *The Difficult Conversations Guide*. Depending on the purpose of the assessment, the guides can be combined or altered to specifically address one's assessment goals. All conflicts change over time, and an assessment is limited to the time period in which the data were collected—one might obtain different information by making an assessment earlier or later in the conflict process.

Wilmot-Hocker Conflict Assessment Guide

The **Wilmot-Hocker Conflict Assessment Guide** is composed of a series of questions focusing on the components of conflict. It can be used to bring specific aspects of a conflict into focus and as a check on gaps in information about a conflict. The guide is best used in its complete form so that the interplay of conflict elements can be clearly highlighted. For important, recurring, long-term conflicts, you might want to use each question for your assessment. Another way of using the guide is to pick several questions from each section that appear to apply to your conflict. Even seemingly small interpersonal conflicts benefit from a careful, objective assessment. You might do this in writing, in guided discussion with others, or for your own reflection.

I. **Nature of the Conflict**
   A. What are the "triggering events" that brought this conflict into mutual awareness?
   B. What is the historical context of this conflict in terms of (1) the ongoing relationship between the parties and (2) other, external events within which this conflict is embedded?
   C. Do the parties have assumptions about conflict that are discernable by their choices of conflict metaphors, patterns of behavior, or clear expressions of their attitudes about conflict?
   D. Conflict elements:
      1. How is the struggle being expressed by each party?
      2. What are the perceived incompatible goals?
      3. What are the perceived scarce resources?
      4. In what ways are the parties interdependent? How are they interfering with one another? How are they cooperating to keep the conflict in motion?
   E. Has the conflict vacillated between productive and destructive phases? If so, which elements were transformed during the productive cycles? Which elements might be transformed by creative solutions to the conflict?

II. Orientation to the Conflict
    A. What attitudes toward conflict do participants seem to hold?
    B. Do they perceive conflict as positive, negative, or neutral? How can you tell?
    C. What metaphoric images do conflict participants use? What metaphors might you use to describe the conflict?
    D. What is the cultural background of the participants? What is the cultural context in which the conflict takes place?
    E. How might gender roles, limitations, and expectations be operating in this conflict?

III. Interests and Goals
    A. How do the parties clarify their goals? Do they phrase them in individualistic or systemic terms?
    B. What does each party think the other's goals are? Are they similar or dissimilar to the perceptions of self-goals?
    C. How have the goals been altered from the beginning of the conflict to the present? In what ways are the prospective, transactive, and retrospective goals similar or dissimilar?
    D. What are the content, relational, identity, and process goals?
    E. How do the TRIP goals overlap with one another?
    F. Which goals seem to be primary at different stages of the dispute?
    G. Are the conflict parties "specializing" in one type or the other?
    H. Are the identity and relational issues the "drivers" of this dispute?
    I. Are any of the goals emerging in different forms?
    J. How do the goals shift during the prospective, transactive, and retrospective phases?

IV. Power
    A. What attitudes about their own and the other's power does each party have? Do they talk openly about power, or is it not discussed?
    B. What do the parties see as their own and the other's dependencies on one another? As an external observer, can you classify some dependencies that they do not list?
    C. What power currencies do the parties see themselves and the other possessing?
    D. From an external perspective, what power currencies of which the participants are not aware seem to be operating?
    E. In what ways do the parties disagree on the balance of power between them? Do they underestimate their own or the other's influence?
    F. What impact does each party's assessment of power have on subsequent choices in the conflict?
    G. What evidence of destructive "power balancing" occurs?
    H. In what ways do observers of the conflict agree and disagree with the parties' assessments of their power?
    I. What are some unused sources of power that are present?

V. Styles
    A. What individual styles did each party use?
    B. How did the individual styles change during the course of the conflict?

  C. How did the parties perceive the other's style?

  D. In what way did a party's style reinforce the choices the other party made as the conflict progressed?

  E. Were the style choices primarily symmetrical or complementary?

  F. From an external perspective, what were the advantages and disadvantages of each style within this particular conflict?

  G. Can the overall system be characterized as having a predominant style? What do the participants say about the relationship as a whole?

  H. Do the participants appear to strategize about their conflict choices or remain spontaneous?

  I. How does each party view the other's strategizing?

  J. What are the tactical options used by both parties?

  K. Do the tactical options classify primarily into avoidance, competition, or collaboration?

  L. How are the participants' tactics mutually impacting on the other's choices? How are the tactics interlocking to push the conflict through phases of escalation, maintenance, and reduction?

VI. Assessment

  A. What rules of repetitive patterns characterize this conflict?

  B. What triangles and microevents best characterize the conflict?

  C. How destructive is the tone of this conflict?

  D. Are there coalitions that affect this conflict?

VII. Personal Intervention

  A. What options for change do the parties perceive?

  B. What philosophy of conflict characterizes the system?

  C. What techniques for self-regulation or system regulation have been used thus far? Which might be used productively by the system?

  D. How might anger be managed more productively?

VIII. Attempted Solutions

  A. What options have been explored for managing the conflict?

  B. Have attempted solutions become part of the problem?

  C. Have third parties been brought into the conflict? If so, what roles did they play and what was the impact of their involvement?

  D. Is this conflict a repetitive one, with attempted solutions providing temporary change but with the overall pattern remaining unchanged? If so, what is that overall pattern?

  E. Can you identify categories of solutions that have not been tried?

The *Conflict Assessment Guide* can be used in a variety of contexts. Students who are writing an analysis of a conflict can use the questions to explore the components of conflict. Constructing interviews or a questionnaire based on the guide enables one to discover the dynamics of a conflict.

A consultant to organizations or a counselor also can use the guide in an informal, conversational way, as an outline of relevant topics. In any case, care should be taken to modify the guide for the particular task, conflict parties, and intervention goals.

The guide also can be used as a form of self-intervention for conflict participants. You can use it to highlight what you and the other party perceive about your conflict. The questionnaire should be constructed for both parties to answer, and once the data are collected, the parties can discuss the similarities and differences in their perceptions of the conflict.

The *Difficult Conversations* Guide

Colleagues associated with the Harvard Negotiation Project (Stone, Patton, and Heen 1999) wrote an excellent book, *Difficult Conversations,* that explores what they call *"the three conversations."* These "conversations" help clarify the structure of a conflict by focusing on the stories people tell themselves and others, the difference between intention and impact, and the way one's identity needs to be restored after an important conflict. The authors of the book make it very clear that you should ask yourself important questions before undertaking a difficult conversation with another person. (See chapter 10 for further preparation suggestions.) Choose the most appropriate guide given the nature of the conflict you will analyze. Once you have decided to go ahead with a difficult conversation, you *prepare for the conversation* by assessing the following "stories." If you are assessing a conflict without the benefit of interviewing the other people involved, you must use compassionate imagination to answer some of the following questions.

I. **What Happened? What Is My Story?**
   A. What were my intentions?
   B. What do I think the other's intentions were?
   C. What did I contribute to the problem? (Specifically describe your behavior as well as your feelings and attributions.)

II. **What Happened? What Is the *Other*'s Story?**
   A. What was the impact on me?
   B. What impact did I have on the other?
   C. What did the other person contribute to the problem?

III. **The Feelings Conversation: My Story**
   A. What feelings underlie my attributions and judgments (e.g. angry, frustrated, disappointed, hurt, guilty, embarrassed, ashamed, grateful, sad)?
   B. What do I need or want in order to feel differently in the future?

IV. **The Feelings Conversations: The *Other*'s Story**
   A. What feelings underlie the other's attributions and judgments about me?
   B. What information can I get or do I have about this question?
   C. What does the other person need to feel differently in the future?

V. **The Identity Conversation**
   A. How has what happened affected my identity?
   B. How has what happened affected my sense of influence over the situation?
   C. What do I need to do to restore my sense of identity?
   D. How has what happened affected the other's identity?
   E. How has what happened affected the other's sense of influence over the situation?
   F. What does the other need to restore his/her sense of identity?

The ***Difficult Conversations* Guide** may be used very effectively by a counselor. If you seek the help of a counselor, many of these questions will help you "unpack" the levels of the conflict. You also may use these questions when you analyze a relationship that has very high value for you—one that is important, long-lasting, or very significant in your life. The key to gaining benefit from these questions is to ask yourself the questions and answer them honestly, and to ask someone else the questions and listen nondefensively to the answers. Sometimes people have done this in a "reconciling conversation" (again, see chapter 10).

Notice that the "what happened?" story is similar to the topic, relationship, and process approach explored in chapter 3. The "identity" conversation, of course, parallels the identity questions explored in chapter 3. By this time we are sure you are clear that all conflicts carry levels of meaning, and that no conflicts are simple and just about "one thing."

Whatever your preferred assessment technique, or combination of techniques, the assessment devices in this chapter enable you to see some order and regularity in conflicts that at first appear confusing and overwhelming. With careful assessment, the dynamics of conflict come into focus so you can fashion creative, productive options for management.

⚓Summary

Conflicts are often perplexing to both participants and outsiders. Usually, however, an interpersonal conflict is operating as a system of relations, complete with repetitive behavior, rules, and other identifiable dynamics. There are many possible ways to assess conflict patterns. Metaphoric/dramatic approaches search for the images of the process held by the participants and use those as stepping stones for creative management options. Drawing coalitions and charting triangular relations also provide useful information about system dynamics.

One also can focus on system rules, the prescriptions for what one ought to do in a given situation. Microevents are observable, recurring patterns of behavior that can be analyzed for underlying conflict structure. Finally, interviews and simple observation are essential tools of conflict analysis. The Wilmot-Hocker and the *Difficult Conversations* guides are two overall assessment guides used to generate information about the dynamics of specific conflicts; they can be used either by conflict participants or by outside observers.

⚓Key Terms

Use the text's Online Learning Center at **www.mhhe.com/wilmot7** to further your understanding of the following terminology.

systems theory 179	patterning 179	conflict stages 184
wholeness 179	descriptive language 180	coalitions 189
organization 179	conflict patterns 182	heavy communicator 192

❧Review Questions

OLC   Go to the self-quizzes on the Online Learning Center at **www.mhhe.com/wilmot 7** to test your knowledge of the chapter concepts.

1. Why would you want to assess a conflict?
2. Describe systems theory.
3. What are the principles of system theory?
4. What are the advantages of identifying conflict patterns?
5. What are five types of system patterns that occur in marriages?
6. What are the four stages of conflict?
7. How can conflict metaphors be used to give insight into creative approaches to a conflict?
8. Define coalitions, giving an example from your personal life and school.
9. What are the main principles of coalitions?
10. Why do people form coalitions?
11. How can you use a coalition diagram to predict future conflicts?
12. Describe the roles of the heavy communicator and the isolate.
13. What are the characteristics of a healthy system?
14. Explain how diagramming triangles in a larger system can clarify communication patterns.
15. Define system rules, including personal examples.
16. What are the questions to ask about system rules?
17. Define microevents and give a specific example of one from your life.
18. How can observations and interviews be used to understand conflict?
19. Compare and contrast the Wilmot-Hocker and *Difficult Conversations* assessment guides.

Chapter 7

Moderating Your Conflicts

What Is Wrong with This Picture?

A father in his early 20s was busy at the children's slide in the city park. He was keeping track of two young children plus his own two-year-old daughter. She kept heading for the ladder on the slide to go up by herself, and each time he said, "Cristy, if you don't wait for me, I'll spank you." Then, he would join her, and they would slide together. After one particular trip down the slide, she went to their small black puppy who was off to the side. When she picked him up by the neck, the father came running, spanked her four hard swats, and said in a loud voice, "Damn it, you shouldn't hurt animals smaller than you!"

This desperate father was inadvertently teaching his child to handle conflict by using force. In the half hour they were sliding, he hit the youngster on the rear end three times, each time saying something like, "Now, listen to your dad." This father clearly could profit from mastering techniques other than threats and physical force for dealing with his daughter.

❧Three Approaches to Change

Parties to conflicts, like the father in the previous example, have three basic options for altering the conflict:

1. *Try to change the other party.* This is a natural response, usually highly unsuccessful. Just as you choose your stance for what you believe are good reasons, the other party does the same. You will appear as unreasonable to the other as the other does to you—and your efforts to change the other will be met with his or her efforts to change you. You can influence the other party through constructive conflict techniques, but you have no power to directly change the other unless you have much more power, are willing to use power-over tactics, and are willing to ignore the subterranean resentment and desire to retaliate that may well emerge.

2. *Try to alter the conflict conditions.* If you can increase scarce resources, alter the nature of a problematic interdependence, change perceptions of incompatible goals, or make some other alteration in the conflict elements, you will be able to change a conflict. You have learned a lot so far about changing the structure of the conflict. Sometimes, however, that effort is not enough, so you must:

3. *Change your own communication and/or perceptions.* We call this "the humility option." This is usually the most difficult and, paradoxically, the most successful

way to alter a conflict. Changing what you do and what you think about the other will quickly and profoundly affect the conflict elements in the relationship. This is the option that challenges you to unilaterally change your own communication without a *quid pro quo* expectation. You change before the other person changes.

Deborah was a college student who spent her junior year abroad, then came home to finish her senior year. Her mother invited her to live at home while she finished school since Deborah had unavoidable debt from the junior year experience in New Zealand. Deborah's older brother was away at college, and her father lived in a nearby town. For a while, all went well. Then Mom began to complain about Deborah taking the house and all that went with it for granted. Deborah asked if Mom wanted her to pay some rent, and thought to herself that it would be better to pile up a little more debt rather than to have her mom so angry much of the time. Mom always said, "No, I don't want you deeper in debt; just remember that it costs money to run the household and I expect you to help." This vague complaint was not resolving the conflict. Finally, Deborah listed household tasks that she was willing to do, and asked her mother to put a dollar value on them. She said, "I am willing to do these things without being asked, on a weekly basis. Would you please tell me what they are worth to you?" Mom rather sheepishly did just that, and the conflict was resolved. Deborah took her responsibilities seriously, and Mom realized that Deborah was contributing greatly to the household. No amount of arguing on Deborah's part, or resentfully trying to do so much that Mom wouldn't be angry, would have been as successful.

Personal Changes and Choices

This chapter highlights the philosophy that *regulation of conflict "from the inside out," through personal communication change, is an effective technique for productive conflicts.* This kind of change is generated by you instead of by rules imposed by someone higher up— you can alter your own conflict behavior. Just as the Environmental Protection Agency regulates the amount of toxins in air and water, individuals may discipline themselves to monitor the intensity of conflict, use of destructive tactics, displays of unequal power, unfair goals, or demeaning and unproductive styles. The conflict parties themselves are responsible for the direction of their relationship. If you are in an unproductive or destructive conflict with another, you are responsible for making choices that will not feed into the destructive spiral. People create the systems of interaction that later encircle and entrap them into repetitive rounds of destructive conflict.

Change in one individual's communication or thoughts changes the entire system. Boulding (1989) calls this the **watershed principle,** based on where water flows along the Continental Divide. On one side, it flows toward the Atlantic, yet just a few feet over, it flows toward the Pacific. Very small changes can produce enormous effects. Similarly, in conflict interactions, small changes reverberate throughout the entire system and bring results that are much larger than you would ever imagine.

Two friends had been avoiding a budding conflict over doing the dishes. Instead of letting it build and then blasting the other, one of them decided to ask the other to lunch to discuss the conflict calmly in public. As a result, the spiral of avoidance and resentment was broken—which sent their relationship to a new level of problem solving and collaboration. Or maybe you and your romantic partner find that you continually escalate conflicts and complain to your friends about each other. If you agree, instead, that during a conflict neither of you will talk to others until you have resolved it with each other, you will develop a new type of interaction and save face for both of you.

Research on teacher–student interaction graphically illustrates the watershed principle. Marginal elementary students who often did not do their work, disrupted class, acted arrogantly, and engaged in other behavior considered unacceptable by teachers were given special training to modify the behavior of the *teachers* who were most hostile to these students. The students were taught to verbally reinforce the teachers for any positive attention and to point out to them in socially acceptable ways which teacher behaviors were harmful and which were helpful to the students. For instance, the children were taught to say things like, "I'd appreciate it if you would warn me about talking before sending me out of the room." The results, of course, were astonishing: many of the students experienced dramatic increases in their self-esteem and were socialized back into their classrooms, and teachers felt much more positively about the students (Gray, Graubard, and Rosenberg 1974).

Because self-change in a conflict is difficult, it usually requires prerequisites. If you are going to alter your own behavior rather than assert that your actions are "natural" or "only in response to what she did," you have to care about the relationship. If the relationship is of no consequence to you, then you feel little impetus to change. In addition, you have to be willing to accept that your own choices are influencing the conflict process—even if you cannot identify the effects. Finally, you have to be willing to give up whatever you are gaining from the conflict. Some possible "gains" in the midst of conflict are that (1) the relationship keeps going, though destructively; (2) you receive pleasure from proving to family or friends how wrong the other is (and how innocent and purely motivated you are); and (3) you are able to exert overt power. Each party to an ongoing conflict receives some gain from the conflict, even in the midst of the negative consequences. Choosing the option of regulating and changing your own communication will certainly affect the relationship. In fact, you will be making suggestions for what you do together, and you will be attempting to persuade the other person to cooperate with you. The essential point is that you are not waiting for the other to change first—someone has to "step up to the plate."

> *Out beyond the ideas of right doing and wrong doing,*
> *There is a field.*
> *I'll meet you there.*

Jelaluddin Rumi

- *What if the other person will not cooperate?* When we meet with work teams or couples to provide third-party assistance (explored in detail in chapter 9), usually a predictable response occurs. All the parties tell the potential third-party helpers that the other people absolutely will not change, cannot be trusted, have done terrible things in the past, are not worth working with, and have a personality problem. Does this sound familiar? Worse yet, sometimes this report turns out to be true, although usually the perception results from a destructive, escalated spiral. What if you are actually stuck with someone who is not interested in cooperation, and who is willing to use dominance power, manipulation, retaliation, and all the other dirty tricks we have described previously in this book? What can you do?

- *You can decide to disengage, if you have the option to do so.* Using the technique of decreasing your dependence on the other person, you can look for another job, tell the other person you won't discuss this problem in this way, move to a different living situation, change work shifts or tasks, or decide not to respond to destructive comments. You can firmly and forcefully disagree, then change the subject. Often it is difficult to disengage, because you have invested so much in the problem so far. But to save your own sanity and dignity, or keep the situation from escalating further, you may have to.

- *You can appeal to a higher authority.* If someone is continuing to act in a destructive and noncooperative manner, you can appeal to a higher authority for help. This is not weak behavior—it makes good sense, if you have tried everything you can think of. An English teacher in a junior high was paired with a history teacher to team teach a class. The history teacher, a senior teacher in the school, refused to meet with the younger teacher and continued to take as long as she wanted to for her lesson plans, ignoring the English teacher. She seemed to expect the English teacher to take more of a student-teacher, subservient role. A part of their dialogue follows:

Application 7.1   "I'd Like Us to Work
                                        Together, Please"

Lisa (the English teacher):   Karen, I want to plan the next six weeks. I am frustrated that you have not come to our last two scheduled conferences. I hope you will be there this Thursday for our planning period. I have laid out a potential calendar.

Karen (the history teacher):   You worry too much. It'll happen. We can wing it.

Lisa: I'm not at all comfortable winging it. I want to use the students' time well. I would like to meet with you.

Karen: I don't have time. I'm not the one who wanted to do this block approach. It's ridiculous and a waste of my time, anyway. So let's just make the best of it. You do your thing; I'll do mine.

Lisa: Let me be clear: You don't like the approach, and you won't plan with me?

Karen: You are obsessing about this.

Lisa: No. I'm attempting to plan responsibly. If I give you a schedule and topics, will you note in writing, on your own time, what changes you want?

Karen: I really can't be bothered.

Lisa: Your refusal to cooperate is not acceptable to me. I'm not going to let this go—my teaching is important, and I am not able to cover the material I need to cover. You must know that I am committed to the material, to the students, and to working with you. I am going to ask for help from Jane (the curriculum coordinator).

Karen: Jane can tell me anything she wants, but I'm not wasting my time on this garbage.

- *You can use constructive confrontation.* Many resources are available for giving you even more of the specifics of confrontation (Paul and Paul 1987; Young-Eisendrath 1993; Lerner 1985; Gottman 1999). *Confrontation* has a root meaning of "with strength." If you confront, you choose to escalate conflict for good reasons, not because you "lose it." Planning and self-awareness help you to confront effectively. (We will give further suggestions about confrontation later in this chapter in the section on escalation.)

❧The Midrange: Zone of Effectiveness

It is no accident that Aristotle wrote about the "Golden Mean" and Buddha preached about the "Middle Way." In our struggles with others, moderated conflicts have the greatest potential for productive management, whereas suppressed, ineffectively avoided conflict and unrestrained, runaway conflict spirals are equally unproductive. Figure 7.1 illustrates the potential for productive conflict depending on the degree of conflict.

Low productivity occurs when interpersonal conflicts are not identified or openly expressed to the other party. The unexpressed frustration prevents you from working through the conflict, gives you the entire burden of negative feelings, and precludes the other from joining you in creating solutions to the difficulty. You neither share the pain nor experience the productive release of pent-up feelings. Or the other party may be avoiding or stonewalling (Gottman 1999) when constructive engagement would better serve the relationship. Refer to the problems of thoughtless avoidance in chapter 5.

At the other extreme, with few restraints on conflict expression, a runaway destructive conflict spiral damages all. Two businessmen who have no restraints on their competition would logically end the conflict by burning down each other's businesses! Similarly, the lack of regulation in personal relationships is damaging. For instance, a

Figure 7.1   Continuum of Conflict Intensity

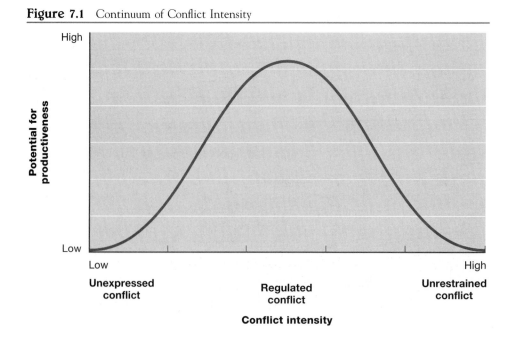

divorcing couple attempting to share the custody of their two children were close to agreement when the ex-wife exploded in the mediation session, saying, "He's selfish! He always was and he always will be!" Her unregulated outburst ruined the chance for collaboration on their problem. Regardless of the specific conflict, after an episode has passed, the other person will recall what you did during the conflict. This, in turn, sets the stage for the next enactment of conflict in your relationship. *People have long memories for poor treatment.* Keeping a conflict in the **midrange** through self-regulation will mitigate these negative long-term effects. *Venting* does nothing to help the conflict process. If you need to vent, do it with a safe friend, counselor, or third party, not the person you are having the struggle with. Venting can feel wonderful for a while—but the price is usually too high to warrant the "yes!" feeling of finally telling the other person off.

If people are successful at keeping their conflicts in the midrange or bringing them into midrange from avoidance or runaway escalation, they can expect some distinct advantages.

Advantages of Moderated Conflict

1. *Alters the escalatory conflict spiral and halts destructive behavior.*

2. *Allows for self-discovery;* when you use restraint, you have the time to explore sources of power you can use and to consider your own needs and goals for this particular conflict.

3. *Allows for more creative conflict management options* than either party could generate singly; each individual is induced into innovation.

4. *Prevents you from taking actions that you would later regret* or have to justify.

5. *Makes productive use of energy* that was previously being diverted into frustration.

6. *Allows trust to build when trust has broken down;* venting and hostile avoidance further reduce trust.

❧Choices about Avoidance

People choose avoidance for a lot of reasons. Patterns of avoidance (summarized in chapter 5) range from denial to shifting the topic to making irrelevant remarks. You do almost anything to keep from engaging the other in dispute. It is difficult to alter avoidance because (1) we are supported by others for not engaging (e.g., "I wouldn't tell him either, he is such a jerk") and (2) it is self-reinforcing—*avoidance begets more avoidance.* In destructive conflict, avoidance basically comes in two forms:

- Avoidance that leads to a downward spiral of avoidance.
- Avoidance that leads to escalation, then more avoidance, then more escalation, and so on.

In either form, what we call **unthinking avoidance** sets the stage for unproductive conflict. Failure to take action keeps you stuck. Regardless of which form of avoidance you use, you refrain from engaging the other conflict party because

- You feel that the other "wouldn't like it" or is so fragile he or she would fall apart if you brought up the issue.
- You feel that you don't have the "right" to bring up the issue or engage the other.
- You feel that you lack the skills to deal with the conflict.

A vice president and program director illustrated the first reason for avoidance. The vice president said to a third-party mediator, "I can't tell her that she is boring me to death. When she begins talking it goes on for an hour. But it would destroy her if I told her that." Meanwhile, the program director said, "I can't tell the vice president what I want—she is going through a divorce and is too fragile right now." When the two of them were brought together by the mediator, they very cautiously began to tell each other their concerns. When the vice president told the program director that "I need you to not take so much of my time—when we begin talking I feel like it will never end," the program director said, "Yeah, I kind of knew that; I hear that all the time. How about if we make an agenda for our meetings?" Then it was her turn. When she said, "I can't talk to you about the finances for my unit because I feel like you are too fragile, going through a divorce and all," the vice president gave a hearty laugh and said, "Well, gal, given what I've been going through personally, this sure isn't going to push me over the edge. What kind of financial support does your unit need?" They were both amazed that they had imagined totally different responses from each other.

Predictions of "They couldn't take it" or "It will blow things sky high" are almost always inaccurate. Actually, avoidance allows one to protect one's own identity without being corrected by the other. When you engage the other in productive conversation, you will find that (1) your behavior is being misinterpreted by the other and (2) your perception of the other is skewed. These misperceptions cannot be corrected if you continue to practice avoidance.

Lines from a poem by William Stafford challenge us to be clear and "wake up" with honest and direct communication:

> If you don't know the kind of person I am
> and I don't know the kind of person you are
> a pattern that others made may prevail in the world
> and following the wrong god home we may miss our star.
> . . . For it is important that awake people be awake,
> or a breaking line may discourage them back to sleep;
> the signals we give—yes or no, or maybe—
> should be clear: the darkness around us is deep.

William Stafford, from "A Ritual to Read to Each Other"

The second major reason for avoidance is that *people feel they don't have the "right" to engage the other.* This hesitation often comes from low levels of power in an organization or indoctrination in the family that prohibits straight talk about difficulties. As a result, people try not to feel and think as they do, but due to avoidance, they never receive correction from the other party. Students often think, "Professor X wouldn't have time for me," and convince themselves they are not important enough to have some of his or her time. Yet, if the issue is important, it will usually jump out at some inopportune time. If you have a relationship with someone, you have a right (perhaps even an obligation) to initiate dialogue to clear up misperceptions.

The third reason for avoidance is that *you may feel you don't have the skills to engage in the conflict.* Consultants, mediators, and therapists often "coach" others on what to say. After taking this course, you should have an entire repertoire of skills you may not have felt confident about before. Conflict parties may know that they want to engage but not know how to start. Take the case of Tara, a hard-driving director of an innovative program. She has two separate offices in different cities but is usually at the home office. She is an attorney by training and can fight on paper with the best of them. Yet when an employee needs correction, Tara can't figure out what to say. A new employee in the home office, Merrie, began parking in Tara's parking space. Rather than taking her aside and saying, "Merrie, I'm sorry, but the reserved parking space is for my use only—I come and go so much that I can't spend time finding parking spaces," Tara just steamed. She called her other office and ranted and raved for two days about how Merrie "is trying to get the upper hand" in the office. After she got some coaching on how to address the issue yet still be supportive so Merrie could save face, Tara easily handled the situation.

When you move out of avoidance you

1. Assert yourself as a legitimate party.

2. Verbalize the issues of which the other may be unaware.

3. Recognize the mutual dependence and importance of the relationship.

4. Allow solutions to emerge from both parties.

5. Use your own perspective to shape the conflict (you use your "voice").

6. Act with courage to change a situation that ought to change.

7. Slowly build your confidence in your own abilities, giving yourself more options in the future.

What can you do to break the spiral of avoidance? To assert yourself as a legitimate party, you can (1) stop making excuses and (2) recognize that witholding important information does no good for either you or the other. If you find yourself criticizing someone when he or she is not there, recognize it as *indirect anger* and a clue that you need to engage that person. When you begin to criticize, stop and ask yourself, "What is it that I need to tell him or her?"

When you find yourself *making excuses* for not acting rather than taking constructive action, you can choose to stop making excuses and start using your communication skills. The following box lists "favorite excuses" that we use. Do you recognize any of these? Could you add some of your own? (Adapted from Kottler 1994.)

Application 7.2	My Favorite Excuses
I didn't do it. S/he started it.	It was no big deal.
She asked for it.	I had no choice.
It wasn't my fault.	Nobody told me.
I couldn't help it.	She is impossible.
I didn't mean it.	No one could work with him.
There's nothing I can do.	He's an idiot.
It was just an unfortunate misunderstanding.	

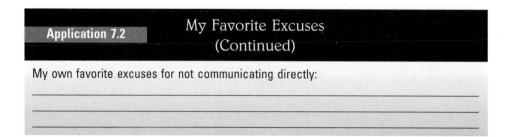

Application 7.2 — My Favorite Excuses (Continued)

My own favorite excuses for not communicating directly:

_____

_____

_____

The avoid/criticize, or demand/withdraw (Gottman 1999), pattern can keep one from ever engaging at all. Some people perfect the art of criticizing others, but never to their face. As the other does things to displease you, you talk to all your friends and family members but never to the other party. As a result, no corrective action takes place. You stay mad, the other doesn't get a direct request for change, and things stay stuck. The following skill-building technique, "moving from complaints to requests," can be very helpful in breaking this logjam.

Application 7.3 — Moving from Complaints to Requests

One effective management technique to help us break free from avoidance is to write down our complaints, *transpose* them into requests, and voice the requests to the other person. The object is to clarify for both you and the other what you need from the other, rather than staying stuck in the complaint cycle. Here are some examples:

Complaint	Request
You are too cold.	I need more warmth.
	I need you to look at me when you talk.
	I would like it if you would answer my questions.
You are unprofessional.	I want you to answer all my e-mail messages.
	It would work best for me if you would keep your appointments.
	When you don't give me information I request, I can't do my job well.

List Your Complaints	Transpose Them into Requests
_____	_____
_____	_____
_____	_____
_____	_____
_____	_____

This technique works well for work relationships as well as for personal relationships. Remember that the "four horsemen" are criticism, defensiveness, stonewalling, and contempt. Learning the formula of asking directly for what you want helps you stay away from negative communication. The person who has been avoiding bringing up an issue is able to lay it on the table in a form the other party can hear. If you say, "You are manipulative," chances are the other person will not respond positively. On the other hand, if you say, "I need you to discuss important items with me before you go public with them," the other will hear the request. The *request format* also helps the avoider clarify what he or she wants rather than blasting the other person. Thinking through specific requests keeps you responsible and increases the chances that the other will be responsive.

When you are altering avoidance spirals, it is helpful to practice on small conflicts before taking on big ones. Start small and gradually build up the confidence to talk to your boss, parent, teacher, overseer, or employee. Obtaining assertiveness training can be quite helpful—you gain a sense that you have the right to speak assertively, and you learn some specific phrases to use.

A final note about avoidance: Even though parties almost always overestimate the negative impacts of engaging in a conflict, sometimes your only reasonable choice is to avoid. If you are totally under the control of someone else, you may have to avoid or else pay serious consequences. People living in occupied countries, abused spouses, and others in dangerous circumstances usually find that avoidance is their only option. Most of us, however, usually continue avoidance because we convince ourselves that we have no power and that engaging the other "won't do any good anyway."

~Choices about Escalation

Recall that destructive spirals occur when the thoughts and actions of parties degenerate into worse and more damaging forms of communication. The interactions and perceptions feed one another and cycle out of control. It happens at work, in families of origin, and in friendships and romantic relationships. Beck (1988) aptly characterizes this process in the case of romantic couples:

> When a relationship goes downhill, the partners begin to see each other through a negative frame . . . ("He's mean and manipulative"; "She's irresponsible") that each attributes to the other . . . Even positive acts may be given a negative coloring . . . When you and your spouse clash, the less desirable aspects of your personality become accentuated, leading to a vicious cycle in which hitherto pleasing qualities come to be seen as unpleasant. (207–209)

Constructive escalation occurs when you decide to make a conflict bigger, more important, and more visible. You decide to confront for the sake of an important goal. The key idea in thinking about avoidance and escalation is just that—*to think about what you ought to do,* based on your hopes and your best skills. Emotions are not a good guide for when to escalate and when to avoid, unless your feelings are coupled with clear thinking.

Your Personal Conflict Philosophy

We cannot tell you what your personal philosophy is, or ought to be. You must decide these core values based on your background, culture, experiences, desire to change, and spiritual or religious beliefs. Nevertheless, certain ideas lead people to constructive conflict more than other ideas are likely to. We offer the following core values and ideas that we have found helpful, that we have taught for more than 35 years, and that seem to underlie creative conflict resolution. After you read this section, you might want to write or discuss your own ideas. What would you add? What would you question? What is your personal philosophy of interpersonal conflict?

Principles of nonviolence in relationships lay the groundwork for the kind of constructive, collaborative conflictual interaction taught in this book. Many people who do not come from a historic peace church or a particular religious background that espouses nonviolence nevertheless do attempt to ground their interactions in principles of mutual empowerment and restraint from coercion. Some of the principles of nonviolence will be explained in this section. *Nonviolent principles warn against the buildup of arms in the service of peace.* The Romans are well known for the credo *Si vis pacem, para bellum,* "If you want peace, prepare for war." Because of the precarious nature of threats, the difficulty of balancing power when harm is suspected, and the anxiety that accompanies another's higher power, deterrence does not work well to reduce conflict. *In interpersonal relationships, the equivalent of an arms buildup* might be such things as fostering private coalitions; keeping secrets to use against an opponent if needed; keeping a "paper trail" of warnings and complaints; telling only part of the truth in the hopes of not having to play all your cards; using the threat of blackmail, such as "If you don't make a C average or better, you can pay your own way to school next year"; gathering harmful gossip and spreading it against people who irritate you; and writing unsigned letters that disclose devastating information about someone you are in conflict with. Too many people focus on developing "first-strike capability" even in close relationships. Energy and personal resources are used up in stockpiling personal power rather than in the building of new problem-solving strategies. Rage, resentment, and hostility can be used as an "arms buildup." When one's fuse is short, an explosion is likely.

Nonviolent confrontation is a respectfully stubborn insistence that principles of right and fairness cannot be compromised. Former enemies or potential opponents working together can produce a better solution than presently exists through coercion. Gandhi's satyagraha movement in India resulted in the freeing of millions of Indians from British control without resorting to violence. Gandhi's approach and principles are not as well known as they were in the 1960s when Martin Luther King used many of the same principles in the civil rights movement in the United States. Gandhian principles were based on strong leadership and a continuous application of the brakes of nonviolence (Wehr 1979, 5). In interpersonal conflict situations, the same principles apply. They depend on a firmly grounded refusal to violate the boundaries of someone else and a belief that, working together, people can find an ethically just solution to even the most difficult conflict. Some of Gandhi's principles are summarized in the following box.

Another principle of nonviolence is that of self-control, or maintaining belief in an internal locus of control. One always has a choice about how to respond to provocation. Even

Gandhian Nonviolent Responses to Destructive Conflict

Destructive Conflict Forces	Gandhi's Strategy
1. Movement from specific to more general issues and from original to new issues	Tie each campaign to a single issue in a sharply limited arena.
2. Movement from disagreement to antagonism as the conflict develops	Reduce threat by stressing the maintenance of good personal relations with opponents while pressing the issue, simultaneously providing for confrontation and maximizing the potential for conciliation.
3. Distortion of information	Openly discuss tactics; eliminate secrecy and misinformation to reduce the perceived threat to opponents.
4. Mutual reinforcement of response (escalatory spiral)	Use positive reciprocal causation; nonviolent action promotes a nonhostile response.

Source: Adapted from Wehr 1979, 60–62.

if the choice (at an extreme) is to submit with grace to coercion and to feel pity for the person perpetrating the violence, a choice remains. One may experience a flash of anger but choose to take actions that reflect a different *feeling*. For instance, parents are often furious with their children. They report to counselors that they have fantasies about hurting their children, abandoning them, or wishing them dead. Yet most parents are able to restrain their occasional outbursts of destructive feeling. They exercise self-control in the interest of the larger, loving relationship. *We do not have to act the way we feel.*

Restraint includes the difficult task of holding back one's desire to act on vengeful feelings. **Revenge** is the attempt to inflict harm in return for harm and leads to an escalatory spiral. Revenge is considered for many reasons. One seeking revenge may wish to deter future unfair treatment, may have an exaggerated view of the other's power to harm, may long to revenge an injustice, or may have become locked into a spiral of feuding and vengeance in which the original conflict has been overshadowed by the vengeful acts (Kim and Smith 1993).

In classroom discussions in which students were asked to disclose an outrageous act they had contemplated but did not perform, the most common reasons for restraint were the following:

- Fear of reprisal.
- Wanting to save face and not look foolish.
- Believing that what goes around comes around.

- Moral principles.
- Fear of loss.
- Fear of breaking the law.
- Regaining common sense after a cooling-off period.
- Choosing to write out anger instead (some mailed these letters; some did not).
- Believing that getting even never solves anything.
- Not wanting to act the same way as the other ("sink to his/her level").

Even people who have not studied philosophies of nonviolence commonly realize that better ways have to exist. By itself, self-restraint doesn't solve the problem, but it doesn't exacerbate the problem either.

Commit to personal authenticity, reasonable self-disclosure, and truth telling. This way of being rests on a basic trust in your own reality and the underlying goodwill of others. We definitely are not suggesting that you take a naïve, unthinking approach, but that you find your own truth and try to tell it. Of course, we are coaching you to tell that truth in a way that others can hear. Remember, your truth is about yourself and your responses, not labeling the other person and his or her motives.

Use compassion. Joyce had a professor years ago in Texas who used to say, "Be kind. Everyone is fighting a hard battle." The more we extend compassion to others in their troubles, without giving up our own needs, the more fear is reduced and collaboration is increased. Compassion need not be weak and wishy-washy! It might sound like this:

> You are under an incredible amount of stress. But I have to tell you that your requests to me are not ones I want to honor. I feel taken advantage of. I think you must feel at the end of your rope to ask me to do all these favors. I can't comply.

Develop boundaries and let others know what they are. Kritek (1994) calls this "drawing a line in the sand without cruelty." One couple got themselves into a potentially negative pattern. When the woman was going to be late for work, she would let her husband know that she'd love to have him drive her to save time. Sometimes he was glad to do this, but other times it was a hassle. On one particularly tense morning, she said, "OK, I'm ready— let's hurry." The husband took her, but resented it. Later he said, "I've decided I don't want to be responsible for taking you to work. I will take you if your car won't start, but I find that I'm beginning to resent doing it so much. I wanted you to know so you would be able to plan ahead." The woman did not like the boundary, but she accepted it.

Stay involved in the dialogue as long as you can, and know when to end it. Often conflict is exhausting, frustrating, and no fun at all. Stay engaged, and when you can't stand it anymore, let the other person know you have to stop. You can come back to the discussion later. Sometimes, you simply have to leave, or end the discussion. Try never to leave with a "kick," which lays the groundwork for another fight later.

What do you think of these challenges? What would you add or change to create your personal philosophy of conflict resolution?

⮞Conflict and Emotion

Everyone is familiar with the overlap of strong feelings and the state of being in conflict. Contemporary scholars of conflict explain that to be in conflict is to be *emotionally aroused*—that one cannot be "in conflict" and not experience emotional upheaval

(Bodtker and Jameson 2001; Jones 2004). Human beings experience emotion in their verbal and nonverbal communication behavior, their physiological response to emotion, and their thinking (Gottman 1994). When we are attacked or perceive a threat to our identity or goals, we will feel some kind of strong emotion. Often people feel many different "layers" of emotion at the same time. Five principles of conflict and emotion, adapted from Jones (2004), follow:

- *Triggering events that result in conflict are emotional in nature.* We realize we are in conflict when we begin to *feel something uncomfortable.* Patricia, a junior, has just become engaged. She realizes that she is feeling resentful toward her fiance's family. Josh's family is large, gregarious, and warm. They often invite Josh and Patricia to join in on family events. Yet recently Patricia has noticed that she feels *resentful* and *hurt,* and is making up excuses to keep from seeing them. In a conflict with Josh, Patricia realizes that she feels left out or "blotted out" by the large, enthusiastic family. Her feelings alerted her to a problem.

- *Intensity of emotion varies through the conflict process.* You may feel very strongly at the beginning of a conflict, then less intensely as resolution or processing continues. For instance, you may begin feeling fury, move to irritation, then realize you are feeling relief. It is a mistake to make a prediction based on an emotion—to describe someone as "an angry person who can't be reasoned with" or not being able to move from resentment. Feelings change in intensity.

- *We experience emotion as good or bad, positive or negative, pleasant or unpleasant, and helpful or destructive.* While being able to use descriptive language is an essential conflict resolution skill, we humans *evaluate* our emotions. Not many people enjoy fury, resentment, anger, or fear.

- *We become emotional because something is at stake for us (our identity).* One person in a couple relationship will often say, "I can't discuss this while you are so emotional." Yet when important identity and relationship issues are at stake, emotion is simply part of the picture. We can regulate our expression of emotion, but should never require ourselves or others to "not feel."

- *Emotional communication helps define a relationship, and relationships are defined by the kind of emotion expressed.* Two acquaintances are working on a project in class. One person feels upset because the quality of work done by the other is disappointing and the due date is coming up soon. When she expresses disappointment, the project partner says, "If you don't like it, do it yourself. I am overwhelmed with work." The relationship has been defined as one in which even moderate emotion (disappointment) cannot be safely expressed. These two will not remain friends after the project is turned in—and they may not even be speaking at that point!

The most intense conflicts if overcome, leave behind a sense of security and calm that is not easily disturbed. It is just these intense conflicts and their conflagration which are needed to produce valuable and lasting results.
—C. G. Jung

Dynamics of Anger and Fear

While other emotions characterize conflict as well, anger is the feeling most closely associated with conflict. Angry emotion threatens most people; few healthy people enjoy

Figure 7.2   Anger-Fear Sequence

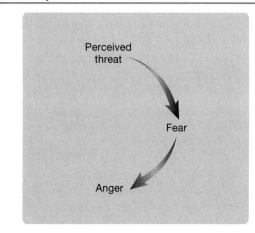

feeling angry or having others direct anger at them. Anger differs from aggression in that aggression is an attack, whereas "anger is the feeling connected to a perceived unfairness or injustice" (Young-Eisendrath 1993). When we believe that we are the victim of an injustice, our usual response is anger (Mikula, Scherer, and Athenstaedt 1998). Anger is a wake-up call, a motivator, and an energizer—a source of empowerment (usually) for the person who feels it. When anger is expressed directly, the person to whom it is directed is warned—change or face the consequences (Planalp 1999).

Anger is also the emotion connected to fear. Consider the diagram of the dynamics of anger (figure 7.2). Fear is one of the most important emotions associated with intense conflict. As we have noted earlier, fear and hurt underlie most angry communication. When we are deeply afraid, even if we are not fully aware of being so afraid, we are likely to escalate or run away. In so doing, we hope that the other person will stop making us afraid (and thus angry) or that at least we will get ourselves farther away from the source of fear. Combs (2004, xxv) makes a crucial point:

The key to staying in conflict is to stay out of fear.

Even though anger, when felt in the body, seems instinctive and unavoidable, it is actually a secondary emotion rather than a primary emotion. Anger has no direct bodily expression, only *indirect avenues for expression* such as heightened blood pressure, flushed face, sweating, muscle tightness, fast breathing, and a loud or high voice tone. Underneath every angry emotion, outburst, or withdrawal, one can find a *fearful emotion*. Fear makes human beings experience vulnerability that we transform into anger, which is more socially acceptable, especially for adults, than fear. Anger is also based on the frustration of unmet needs or thwarted desires. In the definition of conflict offered earlier, one's opponent is seen as interfering with desired goals. If another way to achieve the desired goal cannot easily be found, anger may well be the final result. Again, *anger is the secondary emotion* to frustration, which is a form of *fear* that one's needs will not be met. Anger is our response to a situation in which our sense of security is threatened, our self-esteem is damaged, and our feelings are hurt. In such a situation, the last thing we really want is to get into a fight. Our real need is to be understood, loved, and supported. As someone once said of teenagers, the time they need love most is the time they seem most unlovable (Mace 1987, 96–97).

Anger was termed **"the moral emotion"** by the ancients because it is based on a reflective judgment that we have been wronged or threatened. We feel anger when our core values are assaulted or threatened. Anger "is rooted in reason; it is equally of the heart and the head" (Young-Eisendrath 1993, 154). When an offense is real and important, the desire for revenge makes sense. The problem is that when we are angry, we may exaggerate an offense, seek revenge, and then lead ourselves and others into unproductive and wasteful conflict (Planalp 1999). We are well advised to talk with trusted people who share our value system or who can offer a different perspective before we act out our anger beyond clear verbal communication. Tavris's exhaustive reviews (1989) of research on anger concluded that *expressing anger in an unrestrained way simply makes people angrier* and does not discharge the emotion in a way that helps reduce the feeling. In conflictual situations, if one acts directly on the anger, feeling justified and self-righteous, the more primary issues are not likely to be discussed.

Application 7.4   The Anger-Fear Sequence

List some of your angry moments and see if you can "back up" through the anger-fear cycle to assess the threat. Once you have identified the underlying threat, clarify the original communication. The following are examples of fear, threats to self-esteem or well-being, or unjust treatment that might lead to feelings of anger:

1. A woman is angry at her friend for calling her a name in public. (She is fearful of not being accepted by others.)

2. A newly promoted employee is angry because his secretary didn't get the final report to him on time. (He is afraid that his own supervisor will think he is not working hard enough, and he really needs this job.)

3. A husband is furious that his wife has disclosed their private life to others in a hurtful way. (He is frightened that their bond is no longer strong and that their relationship is ending.)

4. A single parent overreacts to a child's misbehaving at a family reunion by raising his voice and ordering the child into a time-out. (He is afraid that other family members will criticize his parenting.)

5. An intimate partner casually indicates that she might change her plans and not visit when she had planned. Her partner says, "Well, if you have better things to do than honor your commitments, go ahead." (He has asked an old friend to visit to meet his significant other and fears looking foolish after speaking in glowing terms about the wonderful woman he wants his friend to meet. He is afraid he is unimportant to her.)

In each of the above examples of anger, analyze what the fear or hurt or point of vulnerability might be by drawing the anger-fear sequence and labeling the drawing.

Anger Moderation and Expression

A Poison Tree*

I was angry with my friend;
I told my wrath, my wrath did end.
I was angry with my foe;
I told it not, my wrath did grow.

William Blake

How we deal with both our own and others' anger often determines whether a conflict is productive or destructive. Anger can be a healthy emotion that energizes change. *Anger can be expressed in constructive ways.* We have witnessed many people becoming able to change their **destructive expression of anger** *to a constructive expression*. Attacks, venting, and demeaning tactics only make matters worse, no matter how justified you may feel. Most people view anger expression from one of two perspectives:

1. *At one extreme is the "never let it out" school* that believes in suppressing rather than expressing anger. Someone with this viewpoint might use the following phrases:

    *   It isn't nice to get angry.
    *   If you can't say something nice, don't say anything at all.
    *   Chill out.
    *   It's no big deal.
    *   Don't make a mountain out of a molehill.
    *   It'll all blow over.
    *   Don't sweat the small stuff.

2. *At the other extreme is the ventilation, or catharsis, view* suggesting one should release anger by venting it or expressing it fully. This viewpoint is reflected in the following phrases:

    *   Hot tempers run in my family.
    *   It's good to let off steam.
    *   The pressure will build until you explode.
    *   Let them have it.
    *   Go ahead, get it out of your system.

Each of these polar positions on anger presents some difficulties. The problem with suppressing anger and never expressing it is that such bottling up leads to resentment and physical ailments because the conflict "simmers" and cannot be engaged in or resolved (Tavris 1989; Rubin 1980; Planalp 1999).

One can learn to responsibly express anger in a way that does not hurt the relationship. Responsible anger expression, a specific form of regulated conflict, bridges

---

* From *Poetry and Prose of William Blake,* edited by Geoffrey Keynes (1967, 76).

the two nonproductive poles—unrestrained anger and unexpressed anger. Responsible expression allows one the "expression" supported by the catharsis school while maintaining the respect and responsibility supported by the suppression view of anger. On both the international and interpersonal levels, limited and regulated expressions will keep large-scale, uncontrollable explosions from occurring (Levy and Morgan 1984). Mace (1987) suggests the following guidelines for responsible expression of anger:

1. *Verbally state the anger.* Just as one says, "I am hungry," say, "I am angry."

2. *Distinguish between venting and acknowledging anger.*

3. *Agree that you will never attack each other in a state of anger.*

4. *Work to find the stimulus for the anger.* It won't go away just because it is expressed.

Mace summarizes his approach (for use with intimate partners) as follows: "I find myself getting angry with you. But you know I am pledged not to attack you, which would only make you angry, too, and alienate us. What I need is your help to get behind my anger to what is really causing it, so that we can do something about it together." The response to this is, "I don't like your being angry with me, but I don't blame you for it. And since I know you won't attack me, I needn't put up my defenses and get angry with you in turn. I appreciate your invitation to help you get through to the underlying cause of your anger, because I care about our relationship, and it should help both of us to find out what is really happening to us" (97).

Often, finding the right words to communicate anger is difficult. *The X-Y-Z formula* will help one express anger (Gottman et al. 1976). Using the X-Y-Z formula to responsibly express anger can have a profound impact on relationships. Here are its components:

• When you do X

• In situation Y

• I feel Z

An administrative assistant might say, "When you interrupt me (X) when I am on the phone (Y), I feel hassled and belittled (Z)." Her response, taking responsibility for feeling angry yet letting the other person know what produced the anger, is more likely to result in a constructive solution than if she had said, "I don't get any respect around here!" The X-Y-Z skill has the advantage of clarifying the issue of concern for the recipient of the anger and urging the sender to take responsibility for his or her emotional reaction. While X-Y-Z does not prescribe the desired change, the complaint is lodged in a specific, descriptive form so that the recipient might reduce defensiveness and respond appropriately.

Reception of Angry Communication

As a recipient of anger, you have a natural tendency to experience your own fear and respond defensively, as in, "I only interrupt you when it is important to me—get off my case." Remember, however, that when someone is angry at you, he or she needs to responsibly express that anger or the anger will build. You can't "argue" or "reason" someone out of his or her anger. When you say, "You shouldn't be angry," this injunction doesn't reduce the anger but adds frustration because you are devaluing the other's experience. Put another way, feelings are facts. When people feel intensely, their emotion provides important information about the conflict. The following are some useful steps to take when someone is angry with you:

1. *Acknowledge* the person's feelings.
2. *Clarify* the specific behaviors involved.
3. *Gauge the intensity* and importance of the issue.
4. *Invite* the other to join you in working toward solutions.
5. Make an *optimistic relational statement.*

The following dialogue illustrates both (1) responsible expression and (2) helpful reception of anger.

Application 7.5   **Roommate to Roommate**

Angry person: When you leave your clothes on the floor (X) and I have people in after my night class (Y), I feel disgusted (Z).

Recipient: So my clothes on the floor really get you mad? (#1). Does it make you mad all the time or just if people are coming over? (#2). Is this a big deal that bothers you a lot, or is it a minor irritation, or somewhere in between? (#3). Let's both come up with some ideas. I bet we'll figure something out (#4). It's important to me that we give and take because I like having you as a roommate (#5).

When another's expression of anger is out of control, you have a responsibility to protect yourself from verbal abuse. Listening to belittling; hostile blame; ridicule; demeaning, untrue accusations; sarcastic name-calling; contempt; or actual physical threats is not good conflict management. The other person should be told, firmly and consistently, "I won't listen to this kind of talk. I can't hear anything important you're trying to say when you're this out of control." Then you can leave or hang up the phone, giving the other person a chance to cool off. You can say, "Wait!" or "Stop!" in a firm voice. Never try to argue with a person who is engaged in verbal abuse (it's like arguing with an alcoholic—nothing healing can happen until the person is not drinking). But just as you would move to stop the abuse of a child, you have the responsibility to *stop verbal abuse* in a conflict. It leads to escalation or withdrawal, hinders conflict resolution, and lowers the dignity and self-esteem of all parties. Productive reception of someone's anger may not be possible until boundaries are reset and conversation takes a more constructive tone. You can raise your voice (without shouting) and speak in a firm, no-nonsense tone.

Conflict is not always polite, *but constructive conflict is never abusive or violent.* When you know you are overpowered, or cannot stop the verbal abuse from another, leave. You may need help from friends or professionals to do so. You are never responsible for someone else's verbal abuse, as long as you are using reasonably constructive communication. One woman reported that when she expressed feelings of sadness and disappointment, her boyfriend felt "attacked." He would then "give her a dose of her own medicine" just to let her know how it felt. This man was reacting irrationally to his girlfriend's feelings. Hurt and disappointment are not attacks. She had no option but to get out of the relationship, since she had tried persuasion, reason, examples, engaging when no one was upset, and everything else she could be coached to do.

One other helpful approach to managing our conflicts is, first and foremost, to reduce fear. As noted earlier, threat and counterthreat lead to damaged relationships. Similarly, ignoring the fear behind others' anger only intensifies their anger. They want to be heard, just as we do when we are angry. If you can reduce another's fear, that person can more successfully collaborate with you to work through the difficulties that naturally arise in all important relationships. When both parties can move past either suppressing or venting anger, they can process anger and utilize it for a more viable relationship, whether it be a marriage, a work association, a roommate situation, or any other type of relationship. Mace (1987) capsulizes the need for both parties in a marriage to learn to deal with anger productively:

> In observing marriages over the years, I have been interested in recognizing various combinations of types: venters married to venters are inveterate fighters; venters married to suppressors end up with a tyrant-slave relationship; suppressors married to suppressors achieve a peace-at-any-price relationship, which is drearily respectable but without warmth and tenderness. Processors, unfortunately, must exist in pairs, because this is an approach to anger that has to be cooperative. So a processor, unless married to another processor, must convert a venting or suppressing partner to become a processor too! (98–99)

You can manage anger. If you have been mistreated or abused, you may need help in learning to moderate your anger—to make it more or less heard. The following box presents a list of techniques that have been useful for many people in managing anger and that are worth your perusal and discussion. Read the list one strategy at a time, reflect on how you might use the strategy, and give one or more strategies a try.

Strategies for Managing and Transforming Anger

1. Reason with yourself
2. Stop hostile thoughts, feelings, and urges
3. Distract yourself
4. Meditate
5. Avoid overstimulation
6. Assert yourself
7. Care for a pet
8. Listen
9. Practice trusting others
10. Take on community service

(continued)

Strategies for Managing and Transforming Anger

11. Increase your empathy
12. Be tolerant
13. Forgive
14. Have a confidant
15. Laugh at yourself
16. Become more spiritual or religious
17. Pretend today is your last
18. Do what comes unnaturally to you—talk to conflict partners, move toward them
19. Ask for third-party help—mediate the dispute
20. Focus on your fear, not your anger

(The first 17 come from *Anger Kills* by Williams and Williams, 1994)

Sometimes in the middle of highly emotional conflict, six key questions will help you slow yourself and the other person down. We need enough space to breathe and think, rather than simply react. Whether you ask these questions of yourself or of the other, or about the situation, they will help you gain enough space to use your conflict resolution skills:

Questions for Reflection in the Midst of Emotionally Intense Conflict

How did we get here? What happened to get all of us to this point?

What do you wish I had done differently?

What do I wish I had done differently?

In the best of all possible worlds, what would you like in the future?

In the best of all possible worlds, what would I like in the future?

What should we do now?

Source: Adapted from Combs 2004.

Low Power and Emotions

Other emotions in addition to anger characterize the conflict cycle. Almost no one experiences exhilaration or creative energy surges when stuck in a low-power situation over time. People who are in positions of low power, such as entry-level workers in corporations, practical nurses in hospitals, children in abusive or neglectful families, night shift workers, medical and psychological interns, and support staff in organizations, find themselves spending time and energy "psyching out" the people with the power. This safety skill requires vigilance and often creates anxiety and a lack of spontaneity. Remember how you felt when you were visiting someone else's family or were in a new job, sports team, or living group. You undoubtedly watched and listened to others more closely than usual. Now imagine having that degree of watchfulness virtually all the time. When the low-power person realizes that his or her needs will not be met regardless of their reasonableness, then frustration, irritation, or anger is initially felt and expressed. If nothing changes, a depressing numbness takes over. *When people feel helpless to change their situation, they slowly give up, withdraw, and "numb out."* This state may not lead to actual clinical depression, but people begin performing at a lowered capacity, expecting little and feeling alienated, sad, or cynical.

If attempts to gain support from peers or to leave the situation do not work, the person may settle into resentment and repression. **Resentment** is *unexpressed anger that has nowhere to go.* Repression means the low-power person tries to block out the depressing situation by focusing on upcoming vacations, break times, or social activities. With constructive conflict skills, people in low-power situations might be able to employ constructive confrontation to break the downside cycle. The following box portrays what one woman experienced when she was stuck "on the downside."

| **Application 7.6** | "The Number Six Man" |

Shannon was a 40-year-old woman who had worked for years in a manufacturing plant, operating heavy machinery and working in an almost all-male environment. When a job opened up on the night shift at a larger manufacturing plant, she applied and was given a job operating a huge log splitter, a mechanical and technical operation that involved lifting. It also required coordinating timing with a work crew of five others and taking direction from a foreman. Shannon was "number six man" on the crew. Since the pay and benefits were so good, she wanted to make this job work because she was recently divorced and was supporting two children at home. Problems began almost immediately. When Shannon asked the foreman and the first and second men on the crew to tell her how she was doing, they made jokes, changed the subject, or taunted her with statements like "If you can't stand the heat go back to your own kitchen." Quickly, Shannon experienced frustration and anger and the growing realization that she was not going to receive cooperation from the crew. She talked with the few women on other shifts, who suggested she go to the foreman privately. She asked the foreman for a transfer, but no positions were open, and things became worse when the crew learned she had gone to the foreman. Her attempts to tease back, stay silent, or not show her feelings did not work. Finally, she left the job with physical disabilities exacerbated by stress and filed a lawsuit.

What could Shannon have done? Since none of her original attempts were helpful, she would have needed to continue up the hierarchy until she found help—in the human resources department, for example, which monitors sexual harassment. But Shannon did not know this and saw no choice but to resign. She was depressed, ill, physically injured, and deeply discouraged. Now the conflict remains in a stalemate until the trial.

Not all cases are so bleak. Remember, however, when you begin to feel cynical, depressed, numb, or resentful, or that you need to hide your feelings, you will need to invoke the low-power strategies reviewed in chapter 4, "Power: The Structure of Conflict," to break the cycle.

❧Constructive Communication Practices

We have been discussing ways that you might moderate your own communication, by making decisions about avoidance and escalation, deciding on your own conflict philosophy, recognizing the role of emotion in conflict, and developing your ability to analyze and moderate anger, both your own and that of others. Additionally, you can emphasize kinds of communication practices that will enhance constructive conflict.

The Dialogue Process

One's communication both indicates and creates the level of conflict intensity. Dialogue differs from usual conversation because although you may dislike what the other person advocates, you still listen and work to value the person. Although "you can't value all human behavior positively, . . . you can value each human positively" (Stewart 1978). Dialogue is possible only between two persons or two groups whose power relationship is more or less in balance (Tournier 1978). One constructively confronts the other so that "the answer to a conflict emerges 'between' the conflicting parties" (Arnett 1980a, 113). In this dialogic view of conflict, neither party alone possesses truth; truth emerges during the struggle with each other (Buber 1972; Stewart 1978). One of the most elegant descriptions of dialogue is explained by Zediker and Stewart (2002) as they describe dialogue as a practice of *maintaining tension*. In dialogue, we *"let the other happen to me while holding my own ground."* We are influenced by the other while working to clarify and maintain our own sense of self, our perspective, and what seems deeply right. We change in dialogue; we do not simply acquiesce. As you can well imagine, dialogue is not easy. As Keller says, "The true test of dialogue is in conflict, not in casual conversation" (Arnett 1980a, 124). Engaging in dialogue requires an "immense toughness of self," demanding that we confirm the opposing party while in conflict (Brown and Keller 1973). Engaging a person in dialogue is an act of commitment to the relationship and to one's own principles at the same time. If a person can find the courage to meet aggression with calm friendliness, this may have a powerful inhibiting effect (Frank 1978). *Dialogue leads to collaboration.*

One of the ways dialogue differs from normal conversation is that in dialogue, both people speak and listen to help each other clarify what is being said. One actively asks questions and probes what the other means to say, not for purposes of refutation but to help even an opposing viewpoint become crystallized and understood. This radical, active listening requires belief in the transformative power of hearing and being heard. Quality dialogue is slow, careful, full of feeling, respectful, and attentive. One "moves toward bad news" so that an opposing opinion can be fully heard. This movement toward an apparently opposing viewpoint must be learned; few develop this approach to others without a deep sense of the importance of each human being and a belief in collaboratively searching for new solutions that honor each person.

In summary, the following steps can lead highly interdependent parties such as close friends, work partners, couples, or family members toward conversational dialogue to deepen the level of collaboration:

1. *Explore different assumptions.* Listen with respect, without attacking the other's point of view.

2. *Develop an objective view and description of the conflict,* as if you were outside the conflict. Practice describing your opponent/partner's position.

3. *Give up persuasion in favor of exploration of different perspectives*. Treat each person as intelligent and worthy of attention.

4. *Look critically at all sides to the controversy*. All sides have strengths and weaknesses that can add to the analysis (adapted from Freeman, Littlejohn, and Pearce 1992).

5. *Express hope, belief in the goodwill of the other person, and your intention to work out your differences*.

Sometimes people in conflict tell us, when we are attempting to conciliate, "I don't have time for that kind of talk." But we say, "You don't have time not to use it, if what you are exploring is crucial."

Fractionation

The basic conflict reduction tactic known as fractionating was an idea developed by Follett (1940) and later called "fractionation" by Fisher (1971). They suggest that conflict can be reduced by focusing attention on the sizing of disputes. Conflicts can be broken down from one big mass into several smaller, more manageable conflicts. Fractionating conflict does not make it disappear, of course; it simply makes the components of large conflicts more approachable by parties who are trying to manage their disputes. Conflicts "do not have objective edges established by external events" (158). Rather, conflicts are like a seamless web, with indistinguishable beginnings and endings. Choices are almost always available as to how to size, and therefore manage, conflicts.

A group of 10 townspeople met at the instigation of one of the members to determine what should be done about the deteriorating quality of the town's air. Due to the poor quality of the air, residents suffered from respiratory problems, allergies, and asthma attacks, and several people had recently been hospitalized. In the group's opinion, the major culprit was the town's large paper mill, which had, they suspected, been violating air quality standards. One way to size the conflict would be to mount an all-out attack to try to close down the plant. One step down from that mode of attack would be to conceptualize the conflict as being between the citizens of the town and the management of the company. Defining the parties in this way suggests certain negotiation devices that might be used to resolve the conflict. An even smaller sizing might be to conceptualize the conflict as being between some concerned citizens and the county commissioners who enforced the air quality standards. If the conflict were conceptualized in this way, yet another plan of management would be appropriate. The smallest sizing of the conflict would be one between the committee of 10 and the engineers who monitored the air quality machinery at the plant. The group succeeded in reducing the conflict by defining the conflict carefully, assessing their resources, talking to the "other side," and carefully planning an incremental campaign to get more citizens involved in the issue. By fractionating the conflict for purposes of analysis, they were later able to successfully manage the conflict. After all, closing the plant would have had negative consequences for the town, too.

Fractionation not only involves defining conflict parties but also *involves making small conflicts out of larger ones*. This simple idea is one of the most useful conflict management tactics. Almost all conflicts can be made smaller without being trivialized. In a student-teacher conflict, for instance, the students might come into the classroom one day and ask for the abolition of all the grading in the course. The teacher could escalate the issue by becoming defensive or polarize the issue by resorting to rules or external authority. But the issue could be reduced in size if the teacher asked the students what they most objected to in the tests and then talked with the students about those features. By looking for subissues in the "Let's not have tests" statement, the teacher might find that the tests are misscheduled, unexpected, unclear, or too long. Then the parties could handle these small issues instead of expending their relational power over an issue that is too extreme and that probably cannot be resolved satisfactorily.

Some questions and statements that aid in the process of fractionation follow:

- What part of that problem is most important to your group right now?
- Who are the people most immediately involved?
- Whom could we go talk to about this? (This approach personalizes instead of stereotyping the other side.)
- Maybe we'll have to resort to that, but let's see what we might try first. (This statement acknowledges the possibility of escalation but expresses a preference for sizing the conflict.)
- I want to hear more about your objections. Please tell me what is not working for you. (This statement joins you with the other party, inviting dialogue rather than setting up a competitive stance.)
- You probably know I cannot accept what you are saying. That approach would violate what I hold most dear. I want to know what makes that decision your first choice. Then I can work with you to meet both our needs. (This statement reiterates that certain principles cannot be breached but that you are continuing the dialogue.)

Reframing

Reframing is *one of the basic communication skills of moderating conflicts.* When you reframe, you change the categories you use for the other person, yourself, or the conflict issues that keep you stuck. Reframing means looking for a constructive way to describe, or "frame," whatever is going on, with the goal of changing perceptions and positions from negative and fixed to more positive and flexible. For instance, you can reframe positions into interests, and independence into interdependence. When you reframe, you help move the resolution process along by giving an equally true, more positive view of what has been said. The following, from Yarbrough and Wilmot (1995), will give you some examples of reframing:

From: He is unprofessional.

   To: He tries to balance work and family demands.

From: She is not a team player.

   To: She is unusually clear about what she wants.

From: She is arrogant.

   To: She is self-assured.

From: He is uncooperative.

   To: The dispute between the two of you must have caused him to back off.

Reframing is much more than word play. The skill transforms perceptions, perceived options, and perceived interference by looking at the conflict through a different lens. For more detailed examples, see Yarbrough and Wilmot (1995).

❧Examples of Communication Formats That Help Regulate Conflict

Personal intervention in one's own conflicts involves moderation and the wisdom to be able to *choose a format* for conversation during conflict. Often, the security of a structure helps people move through stages of conflict, strong feelings, and seemingly impossible impasses. In chapter 9, forms of facilitated intervention will be presented. The rest of this chapter will present sample formats you might find useful when you, yourself, are part of the conflict. They can be adapted to meet your needs. Many come from couple and family interaction literature, since these long-term relationships make such intense focus on process worthwhile. Structured but informal formats also make sense in organizations. Too often organizations use the formal staff meeting or business meeting, in which reports are given, votes are taken, and announcements are made, but the constructive flow of conflicting opinions is not allowed. Then the conflict goes underground, only to surface in an inconvenient place. One of the reasons businesses use consultants to help resolve disputes is because consultants have the outside legitimacy to help the organization structure conversations. As a member of an organization, you can suggest that some form of the following structures be adapted to your organization's needs. Often, leadership can be shared, with one person taking charge of the content discussion and another facilitating the process. Creative use of conversations can help organizations as well as families and couples deal with their own conflicts earlier in the process, ideally in the preventive phase. You can make a positive contribution to conflict management by thinking about what format would help everyone be heard and would further problem solving.

Conflict Containment Model

Stuart's (1980) model provides an overall outline for conflict containment based on his work with married couples. He notes that issue expansion (Raush et al. 1974) and personal attacks accompany destructive conflicts; thus his model offers guidelines for containing and regulating the exchange. Stuart's model involves three approaches:

1. *Emphasizing a present orientation.* The focus is on the present, not the past. Rather than searching for the roots of conflict in the past, participants should search for solutions in the present. "Why" questions are replaced by "how" questions.

2. *Adopting a "conciliatory set."* This requires (1) labeling the behavior of the other in the most positive light and (2) planning moves to "resolve the issue equitably" rather than by winning. For instance, Margaret arrives home for dinner an hour late. Burt decides that she has no regard for his feelings, so he gets mad and labels her "selfish." He could have labeled Margaret's behavior differently, such as, "She has trouble managing time" or "She gets really involved in her work." Either of these attributions would have allowed him to respond differently to the trigger event (292–293). Labeling one person as the villain merely sets off counterattacks.

3. *Seeking solutions in small steps.* Address issues one at a time and sequentially. Sometimes writing is helpful in slowing the process down. One complaint is dealt with at a time, and each person takes a turn.

These basic techniques are adapted to the various stages of conflict outlined in the following box.

Stuart's Conflict Containment Stages

1. Trigger stage (you first recognize the conflict, often with an emotional reaction). Pause before responding and use that time to ask yourself these questions:

   a. Exactly what is the issue?
   b. Exactly what would satisfy me?
   c. Is the goal important?
   d. Have I tried to get what I want through problem solving?
   e. How much conflict am I willing to risk to get what I want?

2. Reflex stage (you respond to the other, often with the expression of anger). You can put your threatening messages into focus by asking yourself these four questions:

   a. Have I qualified my statement by accepting my anger?
   b. Have I expressed respect for the other person while communicating my displeasure with his or her actions?
   c. Have I made a threat that is modest and therefore credible?
   d. Have I asked for a specific and reasonable change?

3. Reflex fatigue stage (the reaction from having expressed one's anger). A useful two-step approach can move the interaction from conflict to problem solving:

   a. Express recognition of the other's anger.
   b. Refocus it by asking what he or she would like to do in the future.

4. Commitment stage (you and the other maneuver for relationship gain in the form of more power in future exchanges; you both harden into positions temporarily). You can assist the other by announcing your intentions before the fact, as in, "I am going to tell you how frustrating this has been for me so that you can understand my position." If you are the recipient, listening quietly and respecting the other's anger as legitimate will assist in its reduction.

5. Reconsolidation stage (you engage the problem mode). You can learn to signal the other when you are ready to problem solve, as in, "OK, I'm ready to begin working on how to stop this from happening again." People develop private signals that indicate their readiness to communicate, such as, "Let's work on it."

6. Reapproachment stage (you summarize what you have learned, acknowledge the lesson, and make agreements to change). Obviously, without this "learning" stage, the conflict will be left to simmer and erupt again. You need to take action to demonstrate to the other your willingness to alter elements of the conflict.

Source: From Stuart, *Helping Couples Change*, 1980, 295–300.

These stages may be useful to you in several ways. Use them as a guide to help you understand conflicts or to pinpoint the stage at which a conflict gets bogged down. Observers can help with Stuart's three recommended approaches (emphasizing the present, adopting a conciliatory set, and seeking solutions in small steps). Application of these three approaches, as well as others made throughout the book, will help parties move quickly through the stages of conflict containment. Finally, one person can employ self-limitation with an eye toward productive conflict even if the other person does not. The following box presents an example of such a situation.

Brenda and Gerry

(The following is a shortened version of a conflict in which Brenda tries self-limitation and Gerry does not.)

> Gerry: You never have understood how important my work is to me. Now you're trying to get me to stop working on my computer program for the new game. Somebody has to take work seriously.

CONCILIATORY SET

> Brenda: I want to work this out. It's not working for me to constantly ask for more time from you and for you to feel guilty and lock yourself in your study.

> Gerry: You didn't want me to go into programming from the beginning.

PRESENT SET

> Brenda: I don't want to change your profession at all. I want more time from you this year—I don't want to wait until vacation to spend time alone with you.

> Gerry: I guess I should quit doing creative work and just punch the old time clock. Would that make you happy?

SMALL STEPS CONCILIATORY SET

> Brenda: No, it wouldn't. I can't be happy if you're doing something you hate. We ought to be able to work out time together and some time for your new game. I miss you.

> Gerry: What is it you want so badly to do?

SMALL STEPS

> Brenda: I want to spend good time with you. We can work out how and what together.

Family Meetings

"Family meetings" can be used by families, work groups, roommates, or any intact system that is small enough for all the parties to convene. The meeting can be facilitated at first by a third party as an external check on the process as it unfolds; groups can also conduct such meetings without third-party assistance. The purpose of the meeting is to increase the number of positive behaviors and break out of dead-end destructive spirals through the use of (1) *gripe time*, (2) *agenda building*, and (3) *problem solving* (Gottman et al. 1976).

The family meeting outlined above is useful for making specific plans for change, especially if the family or group has tried to change before but has failed because the members tried to "have a better attitude" or "show more love" or make other kinds of nonspecific change attempts. Some feel the format of the negotiation meeting is too rigid, that it does not allow for expression of feeling. Yet for the group that needs help in learning that they can indeed change and that small steps need to be taken, the method works very well. This step-by-step procedure can be used with small children, who can follow pictured symbols on a chart to help them keep up with the steps. Some families use the meeting on a weekly basis, thus assuring that problems do not build up over a long period of time. Care needs to be taken to help more reticent members participate and to encourage more assertive members to take their turn fairly.

The Family Meeting

Stage	Your Job
Gripe time	1. State clearly the gripes you have about your spouse, parent, or child. 2. Follow the rules for constructive leveling. 3. Listen and accept others' gripes as legitimate feelings. 4. Work to understand gripes by summarizing and paraphrasing them. 5. Help to turn "negative nebulous" (fuzzy and nonspecific) gripes into specific negative gripes.
Agenda building	Decide on one or, at most, two gripes you feel are the most important to work on in the problem-solving stage. Other members do the same. Reach consensus about which gripes to solve.
Problem solving	1. Together with spouse or family member, turn the specific negative gripes (chosen during agenda building) into suggestions for increasing the frequency of a positive behavior that will answer the gripe. 2. Form a contract in which you agree to increase a positive behavior. Determine the reward you will get for increasing your behaviors.

In one family meeting, Mom stated a negative nebulous gripe to son Dan, a 14-year-old boy, by saying, "I wish you would show respect to your father and me." The family agreed to work on this gripe, which it was in Dan's interest to negotiate, since he had just been grounded by Mom for "not showing respect." The younger siblings were helpful in specifying exactly when Dan and Mom got into a negative spiral over respect. All made suggestions for how Mom and Dan could change their behavior. Not surprisingly, Dad and the younger brother and sisters had suggestions that involved them, too. They were able to agree on several suggestions made by the family, on a form like the one shown in the following box.

Negotiation Agreement

Dan	**Mom**
1. I will call home if I'm going to be more than 30 minutes late.	1. I will call around to see if our curfew is similar to that of Dan's friends.
2. I will tell Mom and Dad where I am going.	2. Dan may go see friends in the neighborhood before dinner without telling us where he is.
3. I will not use sarcasm when I'm asked about my plans.	3. I will ask Dan privately what his plans are instead of in front of his friends.

The reward I will receive for this behavior at the end of a week is ___Money for a movie___ (Dan)

Dan will help garden for 30 minutes _____ (Mom)

Signed _____ Date _____

Note that the agreements negotiated are noncontingent, that Dan and Mom do not wait to see whether the other will comply before they are obligated to follow their part of the agreement. Noncontingent contracts work well if there is a basic level of trust; if the group or family is seriously distrustful, a contingent agreement may have to be negotiated at first. When a negotiated agreement is contingent, it is usually a quid pro quo (Lederer and Jackson 1968). Quid pro quo means "getting something for something." Each party offers to alter some behavior if the other will also. For example, if two roommates are continually arguing over their apartment chores and each is angry at the other for "not doing her share," they can negotiate on a contingent basis. Susan might say, "OK, if you will take out the garbage during the week, I'll shovel the snow off the walk." This principle could be extended into other areas as well, with each person specifying what she will do in exchange for the other's efforts. The key to a successful quid pro quo is treating each other as equals in order to consummate the trade. Regardless of the specific agreements, if both parties are full participants, the agreement will be of like value to both of them.

Crisis Management

In a family (and other groups as well), the participants will often find themselves continually in crises, with tempers flaring and negative communicative behaviors rebounding with increased frequency. Gottman et al. (1976) suggest that in such crises, you should

1. *Stop action*. Halt the destructive exchanges.
2. *Be active*. Take action toward some solution. Imperfect solutions are better than none.
3. *Be agreeable*. Even if you feel hurt and wronged, both of you have to be agreeable to some solutions to reach accommodation.

In addition, the following six suggestions can be used to tip the balance of interaction in a positive direction. Usually, these are utilized after conflict participants are *out of crisis*.

1. *Set up ground rules*. For example, agree on "no more behavior X" (screaming, stomping out of the room, etc.).
2. *Define structure*. "Set rules for behaviors and interaction both inside and outside of the home" (129). Avoid actions that typically produce high levels of conflict.
3. *Engage in shaping*. Once you and the other begin to act more positively, give concrete praise, rewards, and attention to each other.
4. *Stop acting out*. As Gottman et al. say, "No acting out, just talking out" (10). Acting out is any desperate behavior—threatening to run away or leave, threatening to kill oneself or harm others, and so forth.
5. *Use ABCD analysis*. Describe the conflict process in sequence, making suggestions for change, as follows:

- Antecedents: What led up to the crisis? What were the precipitating events?
- Behaviors: How did each person act in response to the crisis?
- Consequences: What were the consequences of these behaviors?
- Do differently: What can be done differently now?

6. *Negotiate a temporary agreement*. After the problematic behaviors are identified, specify the changes each person can make. List these in a written contract.

The analysis, recording, and alteration of specific behaviors on the part of the participants leads to more productive patterns of communicating. Parents, especially, can teach these self-limiting steps to themselves and to their children.

A Postscript on Further Education

The techniques in the preceding section are oriented toward individual use in conflicts, although many require some level of cooperation from conflict partners. Further education about effective communication can allow for lifelong training in effective conflict management. Destructive conflict sometimes results from ignorance of or lack of practice in growth-producing communication. When we know only destructive tactics, those are the tactics we use. If you are interested in further study in conflict management techniques specifically adapted for individuals, families, and groups, many opportunities for such study exist. Human relations and management workshops and short courses are offered around the country every month. You might want to pursue training as a mediator, taking graduate courses in mediation and other third-party skills. Some communication studies, counseling education, social work, and psychology programs offer applied studies. Talk with your instructor if you are interested in pursuing advanced education in some of these approaches.

❧Summary

The theme of this chapter is personal change in your own conflicts. Three approaches to change are presented: (1) change the other person, (2) change the situation, and (3) change yourself. Conflict is most productive when it is moderated in the middle range between avoidance and escalation. The importance of change that is initiated by individuals is stressed, such as in student-teacher interactions and when the other party is resistant to change. Options for creating change when you have less power than the other party are explored. Advantages for moderated conflict, rather than conflict that is avoided or escalated, are discussed. Personal reasons for choosing avoidance are presented, then excuses for avoiding are explored. A technique for changing complaints into requests is presented. Then we discuss constructive escalation as a thoughtful choice rather than an automatic reaction to conflict.

One's personal philosophy of conflict is explored using principles of nonviolence, restraint and the reasons for restraint, and reasons for setting boundaries. Then we present a theory of emotion and conflict, giving five principles of conflict and emotion. Since anger and fear are key emotions, the dynamics of both are presented in the context of conflict. Anger and fear dynamics are explored. The regulation of anger and its expression are discussed, along with suggestions for communicating anger constructively. When people experience low power, they experience emotions common to that low-power state. Suggestions for constructive communication in low power and questions for reflection on emotionally intense conflict are given. At the end of the chapter, we present dialogue as a refined kind of communication that leads to discovery and transformation of conflict. Key skills of fractionation and reframing are explained. Finally, specific organized formats that help regulate conflict are presented. The Stuart conflict containment model for couples is explained, then a technique for holding family meetings is suggested. Finally, some practical suggestions for crisis management are presented, along with suggestions for further education in the skills of professional conflict management.

❧Key Terms

Use the text's Online Learning Center at **www.mhhe.com/wilmot7**
to further your understanding of the following terminology.

watershed principle 211
midrange of conflict 215
unthinking avoidance 215
constructive escalation 219
restraint 221

revenge 221
"the moral emotion" 225
destructive expressions of anger 226
resentment 231

fractionation 233
reframing 234

~Review Questions

Go to the self-quizzes on the Online Learning Center at **www.mhhe.com/wilmot7** to test your knowledge of the chapter concepts.

1. What are three usual approaches to change?

2. What does it mean to regulate conflict "from the inside out"?

3. Summarize research on how students were able to change their teachers' behavior.

4. How can you approach barriers to change in other people?

5. Summarize advantages of moderated conflict.

6. What is your personal philosophy of interpersonal conflict? How do you agree and differ from the ideas in the book so far?

7. Explain two approaches for breaking the spiral of avoidance.

8. What are interpersonal communication equivalents of "an arms buildup"?

9. Explain the theory of emotion and conflict.

10. Explain the relationship between anger and fear.

11. Explain the "suppression" and the "expression" views of anger.

12. What are some ways to stop verbal abuse?

13. Explain key ideas in the process of dialogue.

14. Give examples of fractionating and reframing.

15. Describe the important ideas in the conflict containment model, family meetings, and crisis management.

Chapter 8

Negotiating for Mutual Gains

~Negotiation in Everyday Life

Do you think of yourself as a "negotiator"? The word *negotiation* usually brings to mind labor and management representatives negotiating a work contract. In fact, until recently most of the literature on negotiation has referred to a formal work-related context. Yet negotiation occurs every day in both private and public contexts. The following situations might call for **everyday negotiation:**

- Your friend wants to have you over for dinner at 8:00 p.m., and you want to come earlier.

- You have a computer problem and want to persuade your professor to give you more time for completion of a paper.

- Your elderly mother, who has lived alone for decades, has fallen and broken her hip, and you and the other siblings need to talk about possible nursing home care.

- Your father has agreed to pay for four years of college for you, but you now need one extra semester beyond four years to complete school.

- You and your roommate, who was your best friend, bought many household items together. Recently, because you now are dating her ex-boyfriend, you have had a serious falling out with each other. You agree to stop rooming together but now have to decide who gets what items in the apartment.

- You are in charge of scheduling co-workers, and there is disagreement over who has to take over holiday and late-night shifts.

- You are an hourly employee, and your boss says, "I don't care what hours you guys work just so the store is covered, so the four of you decide what hours you want to work."

- You buy carpet from a store and clearly tell the salesperson that you want the old carpet saved so that you can give it to your friend. You come home at the end of the day, and the new carpet looks nice, but the old carpet is gone. A quick phone call reveals that it was taken to the landfill and cannot be retrieved.

In both our personal and work lives, we negotiate to make decisions that are acceptable to everyone concerned. One survey found that human services administrators spend 26 percent of their time negotiating (Files 1981). Further, with the advent of "self-directed work teams," the ability to negotiate both within the team and from the team to the wider organization takes on added importance.

Application 8.1   Negotiation Opportunities

List as many situations as you can think of that involve negotiation possibilities:

- Situations when you could have negotiated, but did not.
- Situations when you did not negotiate well.
- Situations when you were overpowered and could not negotiate at all.
- Situations when you used power as "power over" rather than taking time to negotiate.
- Situations you are involved in that might benefit from negotiating.

Negotiation Is Part of Conflict Resolution

Negotiation occurs in conflict resolution when the parties recognize their interdependence, have been able to establish their concerns, are willing to work on both incompatible and overlapping goals (Bartos 1974), have been able to establish enough power balance so people can "come to the table," and when procedures are in place so people can talk to each other in a problem-solving way. Thus, we think of negotiation as *the active phase of conflict resolution when people generate many options, brainstorm ideas, give and take, and attempt to get their mutual goals met.* Negotiation can be either competitive ("I want my goals met and I don't care about yours") or collaborative ("We have to reach a mutually satisfying conclusion"). Negotiating involves active engagement, not **avoidance.**

When people bargain, or negotiate, they *"attempt to settle what each shall give and take, or perform and receive"* (Rubin and Brown 1975, 2). Negotiation allows conflict parties to state their preferences, discuss their relationship, restrain themselves from certain actions, and increase predictability about each other (Wall 1985). It covers a wide range and falls midway between avoidance and domination, as shown in figure 8.1.

Although some writers distinguish between *bargaining* and *negotiation* (Keltner 1994), most people treat them as virtually synonymous terms. The definitions in most dictionaries send you into a loop between bargaining ("to negotiate") and **negotiation** ("to bargain"). For the remainder of this chapter, the two terms will be used equally to represent the same activity. Negotiation presumes the following:

Figure 8.1   The Location of Negotiation in a Conflict Spectrum

Avoidance ——— { Negotiation } ——— Domination

- Participants engage in the conflict rather than avoiding.
- Parties resist using domination, or power-over tactics.
- Parties use persuasive communication tactics in a variety of styles.
- Parties have reached an active, problem-solving phase in which specific proposals are traded.

In the active negotiation process, all the parties depend on their assessment of the power and the structure of the situation, regulate their own behavior to maximize their own gains, and search for acceptable proposals so resolution can be achieved. Parties must be able to provide resources and to influence goal achievement, and they must be willing to do so through cooperation (Donohue and Kolt 1992). No purpose is served by negotiating with someone who has nothing to offer you. You need to be induced to struggle together to achieve common and individual goals. Parties in conflict agree tacitly to a framework of ground rules to manage conflict (Putnam and Poole 1987).

❧Negotiation and Culture

In contemporary Western cultures, we receive contradictory messages about negotiation. On the one hand, you are supposed to "get a good deal," but on the other, you are expected to walk into commercial establishments and pay the listed prices. No wonder some of us are confused about negotiation and its role in the management of potential disputes. Examine the following situations and decide in which ones you would go along with others and in which ones you would negotiate:

Negotiable?

- The price of a new house
- The part(s) of the apartment/house/dorm room you and your roommates will use
- The price of a used car
- The price of an item on sale at a chain store (CD, book, portable radio, etc.)
- The price of pens and paper at the college bookstore
- The salary offered at McDonald's or Burger King for you to "flip burgers"
- The amount of time you work at your job
- The final paper assignment in your class
- The final grade you receive in your conflict class
- The price of a used toaster at a garage sale
- The person(s) who will care for your aging parents

As you can see, some items are negotiable and others are not. How do we know? Each **culture** designates areas that are off-limits to negotiation and areas in which negotiation is acceptable. If you have traveled in different cultures, you may have experienced cultural differences relating to negotiating over prices.

The "case of the cheap statue" illustrates a clash of cultures.

Application 8.2	The Cheap Statue

Wallace, a U.S. citizen, was new to Kathmandu. He had been told by his friend Liz to "be a hard bargainer" when in this culture, where sellers thrive on negotiation. His first day on the streets, many vendors approached him and Liz as they strolled about. One young man, in particular, would not go away. He was selling "good, high-quality statues" for, as he said, a "rock price" (rock-bottom price). When the statue vendor first approached, Wallace stopped and looked intently at the statue. The vendor then stayed close to him for almost an hour, with Wallace saying, "I don't want to buy," but knowing that his looking at the statue made this protest sound rather hollow.

The vendor started at 500 rupees (about $10). After the first hour, Wallace gave in and started bargaining. His final offer was 300 rupees, which the vendor would not accept. Wallace and Liz left and returned to the market square some six hours later. The vendor spied them and started tagging along. Wallace bargained for a few minutes, then said, "OK, I now will give you only 250 rupees for the statue." The vendor, after giving a speech about his family starving, and wringing his hands in agony, completed the sale and handed over the statue. Just as Wallace was beginning to feel smug about his fine bargaining ability, the vendor turned to Liz and said, "I'll sell you one for 175 rupees."

Negotiation itself is viewed differently in different cultures. For instance, one would not negotiate over price in most establishments in Switzerland, but would in Greece and Turkey. Many cultures see North Americans as rude and aggressive in our insistence on trying to get what we want. Others see North Americans as naïve for not bargaining.

We differ considerably from one another in our comfort with negotiating and our willingness to negotiate in different situations. For some of us negotiation in private relationships is fine, whereas for others of us it is off-limits. Similarly, many people take along a friend to negotiate for them when they buy a large item like a car because they are not comfortable "haggling over price."

Equalizing Power

In negotiations, the most basic task is to actively attempt to structure an **"even playing field,"** a **"level table,"** *or somewhat equal power.* Since this difficult task of **equalizing power** is not always possible, sometimes you must decide whether to "leave the table." For example, if you know that you do not have the skills, the support, the power, and the opportunity to negotiate equally, you may decide to disengage, avoid, or get help from someone who can balance the power. That help might come from an attorney, mediator, supervisor, parent, friend, or co-worker. Sometimes, you can't stay at the table and keep your sanity and dignity.

Destructive Ways to Equalize Power

If we are in a high-power situation and feel justified in exercising **dominance,** we may become insensitive to the effects of that dominance on others. After all, we are right and feel justified! When we have the power, we all too often use it to take shortcuts to get what we want. We exercise such control not only to help or protect others, or out of genuine need, but out of "fear, insecurity, vengeance, vanity, habit, self-will, boredom, and laziness" (Kritek 1994, 90). Dominance from one party promotes manipulation and avoidance tactics from those lower in power. The cycle becomes an escalating cycle; seldom do people exercising dominance see that they caused the cycle in the first place. Then low-power people feel victimized and begin to act like victims. We have discussed low-power tactics previously. Some of the most common manipulative tactics are insincere praise, lying and deception, tricks and secret deals, attacks and threats, deliberate stupidity or resistance, flirtatiousness and cuteness, harping on things, withholding something important, and deference (Kritek 1994, 108).

Persons using dominance often escalate the cycle by not listening to the needs of others, numbing themselves to injustice, focusing only on their own needs and tasks, making light of others' needs, trivializing and minimizing the needs of others, and blaming the victim.

People who use the classic destructive low-power tactics such as deceit and manipulation and cannot ask for what they want contribute to an unhealthy dynamic. One way out of these cycles is for both parties to engage in constructive argument.

Constructive Argument

What comes to mind when someone says, "Oh, he is just arguing again"? For many people it implies that someone is disagreeing on content and using a disagreeable tone. The following quotation from a student paper exemplifies this common stance:

> When I get into an argument with a person over something I really stand for, then I really like to get involved and have a good battle. If my competitor has a good stand on his issues, then I like to "rip" at him until he breaks or if things go wrong, I break. The excitement of confrontation when I'm battling it out with another person has a tremendous thrill for me if I come out as the victor. I love it when we are at each other's throats.

Topic and relationship issues, as discussed in chapter 3, can be separated. For example, you can disagree on content and be pleasant (maintaining the relationship component) at the same time. Or you can offer forcible opinions about an issue yet protect the face/identity of the other and follow the procedural rules (one talking at a time, for example). In negotiation situations the following phrases allow participants to disagree on content without being "disagreeable":

- I'm sorry, but I don't agree with your position about the election.
- I'm pretty firm about not agreeing with you, but tell me more.
- We still disagree about the role of government in our private lives.
- John, that sure isn't my memory about what I agreed to about the deposit.
- We agreed to negotiate on vacation benefits. Our benefits package was circulated without any input from the paralegal staff. As their supervisor, I'm asking you as the human resources director to intervene with the managers and set up a meeting so we can negotiate, as they said they would.

As you can see from these examples, one doesn't have to destroy the relational dimension in order to carry a strong content argument. In fact, the whole tradition of debate (such as college debates and the presidential debates during campaign years) rests on *agreeing on process rules to protect identity, procedural, and relationship dimensions so that the arguments can focus on the topic.* One of the losses in our society is the ability to follow a process while arguing content and avoiding personal attacks. In professional debate circles, it is considered a logical fallacy to attack the other debater personally. It is called *argumentum ad hominen,* which means "argument against the man." If you are a professional advocate in a courtroom, there are strict rules about not attacking the other side personally, and the rules are interpreted and enforced by the judge—ensuring that argument will occur on the content level. The judge won't let you, for example, make the following statement: "The other attorney is just a jerk, and I can't believe the defendant is wasting his money employing him."

Argument is "reason giving" (Benoit 1992; Rowland and Barge 1991), trying to convince others of your side of the issue. One makes claims and backs them up (Keough 1992). The arguer tries to get others to "recognize the rightness" of his or her beliefs or actions (Benoit 1983, 550). Interpersonal argumentation, then, has a place in our everyday conflicts and negotiations (Trapp 1981, 1989). One of the positive features of interpersonal arguments (in the sense defined here) is that they are comprised of exchanges between two people who feel powerful enough to set forth reasons for their beliefs. If two people are arguing, it is because they are balanced enough in power (or in their desire to reestablish a power balance) to proceed. Lack of argument, in fact, may show that one of the parties feels so powerless that he or she avoids engaging directly with the other (Cloven and Roloff 1993b).

Interpersonal argument, done properly, may in fact be the heart and soul of modern-day interpersonal problem solving and conflict management. We trade positions, set forth evidence, and let the free exchange of ideas reign. But we do not destroy our relationships with others, personally attack them, destroy their face, or violate standards of procedure. When one person says something sarcastic such as, "I wouldn't expect you to understand. You're sitting on a trust fund and couldn't be expected to know the value of money to ordinary people," the relationship and identity levels become the field of argument, with destructive effects.

Some recent research about face threat and negotiation shows that threatening face of the other derails the negotiations (White et al. 2004). Furthermore, we respond differently in negotiating (1) a public issue or (2) a personal issue in a relationship. When arguing about public issues, parties tend to enjoy it more and not be so ego-involved as when arguing about their personal relationship (Johnson 2002).

In constructive conflicts, arguments focus on levels of discourse that will move the conflict toward resolution. When argument focuses on relationship or identity issues, the conflict may generate much heat but little light. As in classical debate, the honorable approach is to engage on those issues that are real and will help the dialogue. Anything else blocks progress. In ancient Rome, Quintilian, one of the earliest rhetoricians, wrote of the characteristics of an effective orator: intelligence, character, and goodwill. These attributes describe the effective negotiator as well.

The renewed call to "civility" in public discourse comes from experiences of personal attacks and unproductive negotiation tactics. In civil argumentation and negotiation, cordial, firm, and passionate communication takes place, but attacks on the personhood of the other do not.

Application 8.3	Watching an Argument

Watch a televised or live exchange, debate, or argument. You might watch an interview with at least two people and an interviewer. What kinds of argumentation can you identify? Does the conflict seem to be fairly argued? Assess the power among the participants. Is anyone using manipulative or dominance power? Now take what you saw one step farther. Imagine these participants are actually sitting down to negotiate one of the problems they argued about. What might they do to set up an equal negotiating situation? If a moderator were to take part, what could he or she do to help?

Approaches to Negotiation

Most views of negotiation present a limited perspective. Since negotiation is such a pervasive conflict management process, it is little wonder that scores of books have been written about it. Unfortunately, some of the popular advice reinforces a win/lose perspective. For instance, one book offers "examples to guide you in getting the upper hand every time!" or "33 ways to use the power in you to get your way in any situation" (Ilich 1981). Likewise, much of the research on negotiation focuses exclusively on aggressive maneuvers of negotiators and views negotiation as a debate (Putnam and Jones 1982a). Further, many popular authors see bargaining as a "game of managing impressions and manipulating information. Bargaining is a struggle for advantage, for with the advantage comes beneficial outcomes" (Walker 1988, 219). It is not surprising, then, that amateur negotiators often adopt a win/lose view of negotiation (Bazerman and Neale 1983).

Another limited view of negotiation is seeing it as a "series of compromises" (Haynes 1983, 79). From this perspective, negotiation is simply a trade-off in which each gives up something to reach a middle ground; the development of creative options is ignored. One final limitation of most literature on negotiation is that it centers on (1) formal negotiations, between (2) negotiating representatives, where (3) the beginnings and endings of the negotiations are clearly delineated. International negotiators, labor management representatives, and lawyers negotiating for their clients all engage in explicit negotiations. We will discuss many aspects of such negotiations; however, most of us will never be professional negotiators. Therefore, this chapter will emphasize the process and outcomes of negotiations that can be used in everyday situations, ranging from explicit interpersonal negotiations, such as speaking out for your child at school, to tacitly bargaining with your spouse or roommate.

In implicit negotiations, the communication is often indirect, in the form of hints, signs, and obscure intimations (Wall 1985). Still, the conflict parties are choosing to settle their differences without resorting to force or avoidance. They use commonly understood ground rules and advance offers and suggestions without losing face (Holloway and Brager 1985).

Everything you have learned about conflict so far will be useful in the negotiation situations you face. The key items to consider are the TRIP—topic, relationship, identity, and process—goals of you and the other party, as these are what you will negotiate about. There are two main approaches to negotiation, competitive and collaborative, and they differ in the way they deal with TRIP goals.

Competitive Approaches

Assumptions

Competitive, or "distributive," **negotiations** are what most people think of when discussing negotiation. For example, you and your sister both want to use your dad's car. Competitive negotiators assume that the conflict is *win/lose* (or **"zero-sum"** in game theory terms). What you win, she loses, and vice versa. The rewards in such a conflict are seen as a "fixed pie" to be distributed between the parties—thus the name "distributive" bargaining (Walton and McKersie 1965). In competitive, or distributive, negotiations, each party usually has a "resistance point" or a "bargaining range" beyond which he or she will not go (Popple 1984). For example, from a competitive approach, the relevant information for buying a house is this:

Buyer's range: $165,000–$190,000
Seller's range: $175,000–$200,000

Each person's range determines his or her offers and counteroffers. The seller lists the house for $200,000. The buyer makes a first offer of $165,000. After negotiations, the buyer offers $178,000. The seller says that she will not part with the house for less than $190,000. But, in her heart of hearts, she knows that she can buy a new place she wants with $176,500. Buyer and seller slowly move toward their "settlement range" (between $176,500 and $178,000). In this example, the settlement range is already discovered, and when the buyer says, "$178,000 is my final offer," the seller takes the offer.

Typically, the **distributive bargainer** is not concerned about a future relationship with the other party and is trying to maximize gain and minimize loss. The basic assumptions of distributive, or competitive, negotiation are as follows:

- The negotiating world is controlled by egocentric self-interest.
- The underlying motivation is competitive/antagonistic.
- Limited resources prevail.
- One can make independent choices: tomorrow's decision remains unaffected materially by today's.
- The resource distribution system is distributive in nature (either/or).
- The goal is to win as much as you can—and especially more than the other side. (Murray 1986)

Communication Patterns

Since competitive bargaining assumes that the goals of the parties are in direct conflict and that what you gain the other loses (Walker 1988), you gain a competitive advantage by starting with a high or extreme offer (Fisher 1985). For instance, if you sue someone, you will ask for large amounts of money—for what the other loses you gain. Similarly, if you are a competitive negotiator negotiating for a new job and employers ask you, "What salary do you want?" you will say "$41,000," knowing you would be happy with $35,000. Competitive bargainers withhold data from each other and try to throw off each other's ability to predict responses, meanwhile learning as much as possible about each other's position (Putnam and Poole 1987). The competitive bargainer

- Makes high opening demands and concedes slowly.
- Tries to maximize tangible resource gains, within the limits of the current dispute.
- Exaggerates the value of concessions that are offered.
- Uses threats, confrontations, argumentation, and forceful speaking.
- Conceals information.
- Manipulates people and the process by distorting intentions, resources, and goals.
- Tries to resist persuasion on issues.
- Is oriented to quantitative and competitive goals rather than relational goals (adapted from Murray 1986; Lax and Sebenius 1986).

The competitive bargainer times concessions (giving in and moving toward the other's position) carefully and moves in a stepwise fashion—giving a little bit at a time until a settlement range can be reached with the other. Since both people are probably in a competitive mode, each is trying to get the other to make concessions. However, one is more likely to receive concessions from someone else when one can convince the other that one cannot make a concession (Schelling 1960). Thus, each negotiator is trying to convince the other that he or she cannot "give" any more and that the only way the negotiations can reach settlement is if the other gives in (Edwards and White 1977). Former president Jimmy Carter spoke about his role as mediator in the Camp David accords, in which Anwar Sadat of Egypt and Menachem Begin of Israel spent 13 days in isolation negotiating peace in their region. To convince Sadat of his seriousness, Begin had taken a religious oath that he would strike off his right hand if he gave up land in the Sinai desert. Carter came up with the idea that the Israeli parliament, not Begin personally, could enact the moves that would give land back to Egypt. Begin saved face and was able to go ahead with a plan he personally endorsed, after days of negotiating.

Many well-known competitive strategies can be used to advance one's own goals. You only behave cooperatively if it helps you attain a larger share of the pie. You see the "game" of negotiation as one of picking the right maneuvers, much like a military strategy, and you must present a strong defense and try to stay on the offensive. If you show elements of "weakness"—showing your hand or offering concessions too large or too early (Wall 1985)—these weaknesses will work against you. If you are a competitive negotiator you will go to great lengths to convince the opponent that you will not be swayed. When you say, "This is my bottom line!" you are trying to convince the other that you will not make concessions, so the other party had better make some.

Disadvantages to a competitive approach to negotiations abound. As Follett (1940) observed many years ago, working out a position without first consulting others "blocks conflict management." The following list summarizes the most prominent negative features of a competitive approach to negotiations:

- *Has a strong bias toward confrontation,* encouraging the use of coercion and emotional pressure as persuasive means; is hard on relationships, breeding mistrust, feelings of separateness, frustration, and anger, resulting in more frequent breakdowns in negotiations; and distorts communication, producing misinformation and misjudgment.

- *Works against responsiveness and openness to opponent,* thereby restricting access to joint gains.

- *Encourages brinkmanship* by creating many opportunities for impasse.

- *Increases difficulty in predicting responses of opponent* because reliance is on manipulation and confrontation to control process.

- *Contributes to an overestimation of the payoffs of competitive actions* such as litigation because the focus is not on a relatively objective analysis of substantive merits (Murray 1986, 184).

The situations most appropriate for a competitive approach to negotiations are those that are truly win/lose, where one party stands to lose and the other stands to gain. For example, most lawsuits for malpractice can be seen as win/lose. When no ongoing relationship with the person is predicted, a competitive approach can make sense—take what you can get and leave. Such an approach, obviously, is only acceptable in a culture in which individual gain is valued and relationships are given secondary consideration. If someone is truly Machiavellian, planning each move in life strategically to obtain a payoff, competitiveness is at the center of his or her worldview. Someone with an extreme "dog-eat-dog" worldview may say such things as "I have to treat him well because someday I'll need him." A truly competitive person keeps his or her eyes on the prize at all times!

Collaborative Approaches

Negotiation requires ongoing back-and-forth use of reflective listening and assertion skills by one or both parties. Management of conflict through effective negotiation requires listening to the other party; indicating that you understand his or her concerns; expressing your feelings; stating your points in a firm but friendly manner; linking your points to points expressed by the other party; and working toward a joint resolution that builds on the ideas of both parties and addresses all concerns.

—Umbreit, *Mediating Interpersonal Conflicts*

Competitive, or distributive, negotiations assume that what one person wins the other loses. Integrative, or collaborative, bargaining, on the other hand, assumes that the parties have both (1) diverse interests and (2) common interests and that the negotiation process can result in both parties' gaining something. There are mixed motives—separate needs and interdependent needs. Whereas the competitive model assumes that someone loses and someone wins, **collaborative negotiation** assumes that creativity can transcend the win/lose aspect of competitive negotiations.

One classic example, often repeated in a variety of forms, comes from Mary Parker Follett (1940), who coined the term *integrative*. She illustrates an integrative solution to a conflict that at first appears to be competitive.

> In the Harvard Library one day, in one of the smaller rooms, someone wanted the window open, I wanted it shut. We opened the window in the next room, where no one was sitting. This was not a compromise because there was no curtailing of desire; we both got what we really wanted. For I did not want a closed room, I simply did not want the north wind to blow directly on me; likewise the other occupant did not want that particular window open, he merely wanted more air in the room. (32)

Although she doesn't detail her bargaining process, the result was clearly integrative—it integrated the needs of both parties. Integrative, or collaborative, negotiations emphasize maximizing joint benefits for both parties, often in creative ways (Bazerman, Magliozzi, and Neale 1985). Such bargaining places value on the relationship between the conflict parties, requires trust, and relies on full disclosure of relevant information (Walker 1988).

One of the assumptions of collaborative, or integrative, negotiation is that polar opposites are not necessarily in conflict. For example, if two people are negotiating, sometimes they can reach a satisfactory solution precisely because they want different things. Fisher, Ury, and Patton (1991, 74) list some of the polar opposites that can be reconciled in integrative negotiation:

One party cares more about	Other party cares more about
form, appearance	substance
economic considerations	political considerations
internal considerations	external considerations
symbolic considerations	practical considerations
immediate future	more distant future
ad hoc results	the relationship
hardware	ideology
progress	respect for tradition
precedent	this case
prestige, reputation	results
political points	group welfare

Do you recall that in chapter 3, "Interests and Goals," we suggested that conflict parties often specialize in certain goals? If you are most concerned about "getting things done" (results) and your work associate is more concerned about "looking good" (prestige, reputation), your needs are not necessarily incompatible. For instance, you may want to make sure the work is done for your campus committee and the other may want to make sure there is newspaper coverage of the event you are sponsoring. He can help you get the job done, and you can put him in touch with a reporter you know. Collaborative approaches treat assumed opposites as connected and not incompatible.

Follett (1940) relates yet another story that provides insight into collaborative, or integrative, negotiations. Two sisters were fighting over an orange and, after much acrimony, agreed to split the orange in half—a compromise. One sister used her half of the orange for juice and the other sister used the peel of her half of the orange for a cake. They overlooked the integrative, or collaborative, elements of negotiation. They each could have had a full orange since they wanted different parts! Unlike the sisters, collaborative negotiators engage in joint problem solving, jointly devising solutions that maximize benefits for both parties.

Assumptions

Just as the competitive model of negotiation has basic assumptions, so does the integrative, or collaborative, model of negotiation. The process presumes the following:

- The negotiating world is controlled by enlightened self-interest.
- Common interests are valued and sought.
- Interdependence is recognized and enhanced.
- Limited resources do exist, but they can usually be expanded through cooperation.
- The resource distribution system is integrative (joint) in nature.
- The goal is a mutually agreeable solution that is fair to all parties and efficient for the community (Murray 1986).

As you can see, the collaborative approach has very different assumptions about the world than does the competitive approach. Rather than taking a dog-eat-dog view, it presumes that we can, even in the midst of a conflict, work from "enlightened self-interest." We get what we need from others but do it in a way that also helps them achieve some of their goals. The collaborative bargainer is interested in preserving the relationship with the other. Therefore, driving a hard bargain at the expense of the other is not seen as a victory. Collaborative bargainers must maintain some interest in the other while holding out for their own goals. Unlike a win/lose situation, a collaborative agreement allows both of you to come away from the negotiation with an intact relationship, willing to trust and work with each other in the next bargaining situation.

Communication Patterns

The obvious next question is, "How does one *do* collaborative negotiations?" Unless we can specify communicative behaviors that can activate a collaborative negotiation set, the basic principles won't take us very far. All of the collaborative tactics we discussed in chapter 5, "Styles and Tactics," can be put to use by the collaborative negotiator. You might want to review that section on collaborative tactics as a basis for collaborative negotiation. Also worthy of note are some specific techniques that lead to collaborative outcomes. If you want more lengthy treatment of these techniques, consult Rubin, Pruitt, and Kim (1994) and Lewicki and Litterer (1985).

Expanding the pie encourages collaborative outcomes because most conflicts are based on the perception of scarce resources; expanding the resources alters the structure of the conflict. For example, if Jane wants to go to the mountains and Sandy wants to go to the seashore, they might collaborate to find mountainous seashore. Although it won't be the perfect mountain and the shore may have some limitations, they will get to spend their vacation together—they have expanded the pie. Often, children squabble with one another because of the perception that there is not enough parental care and consideration to go around. They fight, say mean things to one another, and struggle over the available love. As the parent, if you refuse to "parcel out" the love and attention, giving each child attention without leaving out the other, you have expanded the pie. Whether the "pie" is actual or metaphoric, its expansion alters the conflict.

Application 8.4	You've Got to Do It!

Caitlin, an entry-level employee who had just received her BA, worked for a veterans' program. The program was underfunded, with many demands being placed on the staff members. The program director of the family services division asked Caitlin to design and teach a family communication program to families with preschool children. Caitlin felt unprepared, pushed too far and too fast, and unsupported for this high-visibility program (it would be filmed and put on public-access TV). Although Caitlin was newly hired, she had been given a lot of responsibility and did have legitimate power in the organization. She also wanted to work for the organization so didn't want to resign under the pressure of three times too much work. Two possible scenarios follow:

Competitive Mode

Boss: Caitlin, you've got to do this program, and it has got to be good. Our grant funding for next year depends on delivering this service, which we said we'd provide.

Caitlin: I'd need a master's degree, at least, to be able to design and teach this course. I can't do it and keep track of the after-school program, too. I have too little secretarial support and too many projects that are needing my attention right now. I'm so stressed out I don't know whether I can keep on.

Boss: I hired you to run this entire program. If you didn't think you could do it, you shouldn't have applied. Drop something less important and do this.

Collaborative Mode

Boss: Caitlin, I really need to get this program on family communication done. Our grant funding for next year depends on delivering this service, which we said we'd provide. Could you take it on?

(continued)

Application 8.4	**You've Got to Do It!**

Caitlin: I don't see how. I have to keep track of the after-school program, and there are a lot of other things that are half-done, too. And I'm stressed out and have almost no secretarial support. Besides, I don't have the training to put this course together. I'd need a master's degree, at least.

Boss: What if I get you some staff help from social work? There's a graduate student over there who said he'd like to do an internship with us. Maybe he could do the program development with you.

Caitlin: That sounds great, but I still need some secretarial help. Could you loan my program someone from your office?

Boss: I can't do that permanently, but you can bring work over and I'll delegate it.

Caitlin: OK. I'll see what I can do. (She continues planning with the boss.)

In the example of the overworked employee, **nonspecific compensation,** a process in which one of the parties is "paid off" with some creative form of compensation, could also help break a competitive spiral and begin a collaborative set. For instance, the boss could have offered extra time off after the project was finished or offered to move up Caitlin's evaluation, which would result in the possibility of an early promotion. If two roommates are bargaining over use of a car, one may say, "OK, you can have my car, but I get to have the apartment for an all-night party after graduation." Another example is looking to purchase a house and discovering that the owner is more interested in moving rapidly than in getting the stated purchase price. Your cousin owns a moving company, so you arrange to have the house owner moved at no cost. Your cousin charges you less than the going rate, and you get the house for less money than was originally asked. If the deal is sealed, you have created a form of nonspecific compensation. You have found some dimension that is valued by the other and have made an offer to offset your gains in the negotiation.

Logrolling is similar to creating nonspecific compensation, only one offers to "trade off" issues that are the top priority for the other. The parties have to find multiple issues in the conflict (for example, time is of the essence to you, money to him). Then, you arrange agreements so that each of you gets the top-priority item while giving on the lower-priority item. You "roll the logs" and shuffle the issues until the top-priority issues come to the top of the pile. In one organization the supervisor wanted more work from a particular employee. The employee wanted a fairer evaluation at the end of the year. With the help of an outsider, they negotiated so that (1) the evaluation process would involve discussion before memos were sent and (2) the employee would take on some extra work. Each received acknowledgment of his main concern and gave on the item that was vitally important to the other.

Cost cutting minimizes the other's costs for going along with you. For example, you want to go skiing with your friend. She is overloaded with work, so you offer to ski only half a day and not let her incur the "cost" of missing all her work time. Alternatively, you are negotiating with your romantic partner about going on vacation. He is tied up and feels he can't take off so many days, yet you both want to vacation together. So you offer to drive your car to the resort you wish to visit, giving you the "decompression time" that you value, and suggest he fly to join you two days later. You shorten his total vacation time yet make it possible for the two of you to vacation together at the resort you want to visit.

Bridging invents new options to meet the other side's needs. You want to rent an apartment, but it is too expensive. You discover that the landlord is concerned about the appearance of the property. So you offer her a rent somewhat below what she wants but agree to do 15 hours of "fix-it work" each month. She receives property improvements, and you receive reduced rent. Everyone gains!

In collaborative negotiations, parties brainstorm to invent new and creative options to meet everyone's needs. For example, Sally is negotiating with her work partner. She is frustrated about the job not being done, and Chuck is feeling that the work intrudes too much on his personal time. So, she offers to do more of the work on the spreadsheet if he will bring her coffee and sandwiches. Chuck gains more free time, Sally sees the project moving ahead, and both of them contribute to the task while maintaining their working relationship.

Bargainers who employ collaborative approaches view negotiation as being complex; thus, they find creative ways to "package" agreements and invent new options (Raiffa 1982). The collaborator moves from "fighting" to "conferring" (Follett 1940), assuming that working with the other will bring joint benefit. Information serves as fact-finding material for the bargainers rather than as a wedge that drives between the two parties. With information, one problem solves, explores causes, and generates alternative solutions (Lewicki and Litterer 1985).

Disadvantages

As with competitive tactics, collaborative approaches have some disadvantages. Probably the biggest overall difficulty is that they require "a high order of intelligence, keen perception and discrimination, and, more than all, a brilliant inventiveness" (Follett 1940, 45). If it hasn't been modeled in the home or on the job, collaboration may require specific training. Unless the beginning bargainer (whether an attorney, spouse, friend, or co-worker) has some level of training, the usual approach is to equate "good" bargaining with competitive tactics.

Murray (1986) has provided a comprehensive list of the disadvantages of collaborative, problem-solving, integrative bargaining approaches. According to Murray, collaborative negotiation

- Is strongly biased toward cooperation, creating internal pressures to compromise and accommodate that may not be in one's best interests.

- Avoids strategies that are confrontational because they carry the risk of impasse, which is viewed as failure.

- Focuses on being sensitive to others' perceived interests; increases vulnerability to deception and manipulation by a competitive opponent; and increases the possibility that the settlement may be more favorable to the other side than fairness would warrant.

- Increases the difficulty of establishing definite aspiration levels and bottom lines because of the reliance on qualitative (value-laden) goals.

- Requires substantial skill and knowledge of the process to do well.

- Requires strong confidence in one's own assessment powers (perception) regarding the interests and needs of the other side and the other's payoff schedule (184).

Collaborative negotiations, then, are not easily used in every conflict. They require considerable skill on the part of the negotiator, who strives to keep the negotiations from disintegrating into a win/lose approach.

Principled Negotiation

Fisher and Ury (1981) present a practical approach to collaborative negotiation that has become very popular, for good reason. They present four principles: *people, interests, options,* and *criteria.* Fisher and Ury term the process *"negotiation on merits"* or **"principled negotiation."** The four principles are worth memorizing. Many times, you will be able to get destructive negotiation back into a cooperative mode if you remember these basic approaches. They are not so much skills as procedures that should be used throughout constructive conflict resolution.

1. People: Separate the People from the Problem.

The participants should come to see themselves as working side by side on a problem, attacking the problem instead of each other. The overarching process goal is "We, working together, can solve this problem that is confronting us." It is in the self-interest of both conflict parties to preserve a workable relationship; focusing on the problem instead of the other person assists in relational maintenance. The problem is faced as one would face an enemy, working cooperatively with one's conflict partner to solve the problem. For example, a divorcing couple, rather than asking, "Why are you causing me difficulties?" might ask, "What can we, working together, create that will be in the best interests of the children?"

In collaborative negotiations, relational preservation becomes a superordinate goal (Sherif and Sherif 1956). In the classic description of superordinate goals, groups of boys at camp were placed in situations that created conflicts of interest between the two groups. The researchers then introduced a common enemy, thus stimulating the two groups to work together, which reduced their intergroup hostility. For partners in interpersonal conflicts, long-term relational or content goals can become superordinate goals that reduce conflict over short-term goals, but only if partners can separate "the people" from "the problem."

2. Interests: Focus on Interests, Not Positions.

In the Harvard Negotiation Project, researchers found that when people stated their goals in terms of **positions** that had to be defended, they were less able to produce wise agreements. The more you clarify your position and defend yourself, the more committed you become to the position. Arguing over positions endangers ongoing relationships, since the conflict often becomes a contest of wills. Researchers found that "whether a negotiation concerns a contract, a family quarrel, or a peace settlement among nations, people routinely engage in positional bargaining. Each side takes a position, argues for it, and makes concessions to reach a compromise" (Fisher and Ury 1981, 3). The parties in the library, earlier in this chapter, focused on **interests**. Rather than starting with "Do you want the window closed or open?" (a position), each party searched for their own underlying interest. Interests always underlie positions, and many possible positions can be derived from one's interests. But a position is a specific solution to an interest; if you start with the position, you will overlook many creative options for meeting the interests. Interests are more diffuse than positions and sometimes are difficult to identify, but you keep the process of collaboration in motion when you focus on them.

Finding Interests

The following questions are useful in finding interests. Use them to find the other person's TRIP interests and goals.

What if? If she or he would apologize, what would that do for you?

What will it take? What gets in your way so you can't cooperate?

What would be the perfect situation? How would you like to be treated?

What process could be used to keep you involved and on board?

What problems are we trying to solve? What could the other do or say that would impact you? What concerns you the most?

When are you the most irritated? Most satisfied?

Describe when things went well. What do you want? What would it mean if you got it?

What are two other ways you can get what you want?

Can you tell me why you feel so strongly about this?

Before this conflict started, what did you want?

What would help you feel good?

How do you want to be treated by him or her?

If you could have anything you wanted, what would it be?

Source: Adapted from Yarbrough and Wilmot 1995.

Understanding the difference between positions and interests is the central aspect of the principled negotiation approach. In our work with interests, we have discovered the following principles.

Principle #1: Parties Have Multiple Interests. When someone takes a firm position, it is usually because there are **multiple interests** underlying it. Look at the many possible interests that might underlie a parent saying, "you have to be in by 10:00 p.m." to a teenage child.

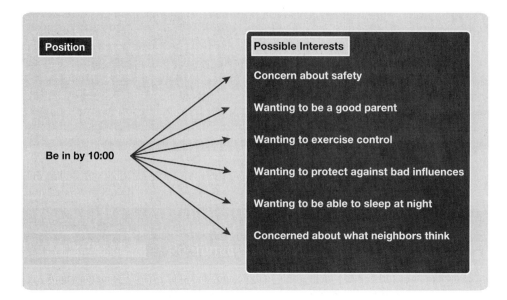

Principle #2: In Conflict Situations, We Usually Misread the Other's Interests.
Recall that we said earlier that when we are in a dispute, we usually feel we know what
the other wants. But this guess is usually inaccurate. When we don't ask the other about
his or her interests, we simply project ours onto him or her. In the case of the teenager
above, if you ask him what his parent's interests are, he is likely to say (with great
confidence), "Oh, he is just a control freak," and not see any of the legitimate interests
as even possible.

Take the case of Joan, who puts her house on the market for $225,000. If you are
negotiating with her on the price of the house and someone asks you, "why is she asking so much?" you may well answer, "because she wants to maximize her money." You
conclude that based on what your interests would be in her situation. In fact, she asks
$225,000 as proof of the value of the improvements she has added to the house during
the 10 years she owned it. So, unless the other tells you what he or she wants, you are
playing a guessing game.

***Principle #3: In Disputes, Relational and Identity Interests Are Always Pres-
ent, Often under the Surface.*** Go back to Joan for a moment. She was raised in a small
town; how people treat one another is very important to her. She puts her house on the
market for $225,000. You, as a prospective buyer, try to bargain hard. The Realtor you are
sending the offers through tends to be rather tough in negotiations—pushing hard, making "low ball" offers, and using competitive tactics to try and reduce the price. In making
your first offer to Joan, the Realtor says, in a nasty tone of voice, "Well, my client will only
come up to $118,000 because he feels you have overpriced the house." After many back-
and-forth offers and counteroffers, you and Joan agree to $222,500. Then, just before sign-
ing the buy-sell agreement, Joan takes the house off the market. A month later, she puts
it back on the market and sells it for $150,000 to another buyer going through a Realtor
who is a friend of Joan. What are your guesses about what interests are primary for Joan?

Application 8.5   Multiple Interests

In small groups of four or five people, take the following *"position"* statements and brainstorm possible *interests* that might underlie them. You should have a minimum of five possible interests for each position, all different from one another.

> "I have to take 19 credits next term."
>
> "I want $250 for those skis."
>
> "You have to do the dishes every other night."
>
> "I want the kids to take my name, not their biological father's."
>
> "Quit throwing your clothes on the floor of our apartment."
>
> "Pick me up at 8:00 sharp on Mondays to go to school."
>
> "You have to type the first draft of our project."

3. Options: Generate a Variety of Possibilities before Deciding What to Do.

Trying to resolve a conflict in the face of an adversary narrows one's vision. Pressure reduces creative thinking at the very time when creativity is most needed. Searching for the one right solution may be futile. You can get around this problem by setting up time to focus on new solutions instead of defending your prospective goals endlessly. Goal setting continues throughout the period of active conflict management, and afterward as well. A good decision is one that springs from many options generated by concerned conflict parties.

4. Criteria: Insist That the Result Be Based on Some Objective Standard.

One person's will is not enough to justify a conflict solution. Some principle of fairness or objective judgment should be used. One can develop objective criteria by using fair procedures (equalizing power in the process) and by seeking fair standards. Menzel (1991) suggests six external standards for fairness: simple success at reaching an agreement, compliance with the agreement, cost of the agreement, efficiency through which the agreement is reached, access to justice presented to disputants, and stability of the agreement over time. These standards might be important to a court, to a branch of the government such as the department of family services, to family members, or to managers overseeing an agreement in their department. Other fair standards can be based on the following:

market value	moral standards
costs	professional standards
precedent	equal treatment
what a court would decide	efficiency
scientific judgment	reciprocity
	(Fisher and Ury 1981, 89)

An individual may effectively use the four principles of collaboration by informally adopting and using them in one-on-one conflicts that arise. The following are some statements that you might use when you are in conflict over perceptions of incompatible goals.

Collaborative Principle	Sample Statement
People	"This is a problem you and I haven't had to face before. I'm sure we can work it out."
Interests	"What is it that you are most hoping for?"
	or
	"Let's figure out where we agree, and that will give us a base to work from."
Options	"I'd like to postpone making a decision about filing a grievance until our next meeting. Today I want to explore all the options that are available to us in addition to filing a grievance. Is that all right with you?"
Criteria	"I can't be satisfied with getting my way if you're disgruntled. Let's get an example of market value from an objective source."

From the standpoint of a competitive approach, one can be assumed to be "weak" if one "gives in" to the superior strength and force of one's opponent. Interestingly, the collaborative bargainer can be just as "tough" as the competitive bargainer. However, you get tough about different aspects. You remain firm about your goals but flexible regarding how to accomplish them—what Pruitt (1983a) calls *firm flexibility*. You work with the other party, but you don't capitulate; your goals are always firm in your mind, but the means you use are flexible and adapted to the other person's needs as well. As Follett (1940) noted, "Mushy people are no more good at this than stubborn people" (40).

The Language of Collaboration

As has been true of other processes throughout this book, no specific set of techniques will assure collaboration. Collaboration is both a mind-set and a set of techniques. If one does not believe that energetic cooperation will provide better solutions than competitive techniques, all the **language of collaboration** that could be memorized will not ultimately produce collaboration. Sometimes, however, you may get stuck looking for the right phrase to help a negotiation move toward collaboration. If so, consider some of the following phrases.

- I know this is difficult, but we can work it out.
- I can understand why you want to "split the difference," but let's try for some creative alternatives.
- I certainly appreciate your stance. Let's also talk about what I need to be satisfied.
- Your threat tells me how important this issue is to you, but it will work better with me not to threaten. Can we back this up and come at it another way?

- I don't see any conflict in both of us getting more of what we want, but we have been acting as if what we each get the other loses.

- I really do want a fair and durable settlement for both of us. That requires, of course, more direct information about what we each want. Let's explore that awhile.

- I will discuss with you as long as it takes to reach a settlement that will work for both of us.

- Yes, I see that you think that is the best solution. Remember, however, that there are two of us here. Let's see if both of us can be satisfied with an outcome.

Most people approach negotiations from a competitive frame of mind—assuming both sides have to lose part of the pie. The competitive or collaborative approaches are more a function of the bargainers than of any other factors. In fact, you can be in a negotiation in which one person takes a cooperative and the other a competitive stance (Walker 1988). If you take a competitive approach, whether you are negotiating about how to spend the evening with a friend or how much to offer on a house, the negotiation process will probably be a competitive, win/lose experience. On the other hand, if you stick firmly to a collaborative approach, you will find creative options that someone with a competitive approach simply would not find. Creative options are often available (Fogg 1985), but unless the negotiators believe them possible and work to jointly produce those options, the negotiations will begin and end on a win/lose footing. Having had experience negotiating and serving as third-party interveners, we are always gratified by how many creative, jointly satisfying options are available and constantly are reminded of how difficult they are for the parties to initially see.

Work by Kolb and Putnam (1997) and Putnam (1996) suggest that collaborative "moves" are not analyzed as genuinely collaborative if the intent is still, as in a competitive system, to promote self-interest at the expense of the other. Kolb and Putnam rightly point out the difference between a relational approach used for personal gain, which is manipulative, and true collaboration. As long as predetermined goals benefiting the self are pursued, the underlying assumptions of both competitive and collaborative modes are

- Self-interest
- Competitiveness
- Rationality
- An individualistic focus
- The exchange model

These underlying assumptions limit the transformative potential of negotiation. Transformation creates something new from what existed before. New ways to cooperate emerge, new feelings arise, and new solutions become possible. The transformative approach to negotiation rests on

- Community concerns
- Cooperativeness
- Subjectivity

- Intuition
- Emotion (Putnam 1996)

A negotiator following such a set of assumptions would focus on relationships, using connectedness, transformation, dialogue, and storytelling (Kolb and Putnam 1997). Such approaches reflect a relational unit of analysis (Wilmot 1995), which transcends the individualistic "I have to have mine," or seeing the self as separate from the other. The unit of analysis would not be the individual but rather the ongoing exchange produced from the joint actions of the participants. The Kolb and Putnam approach highlights many aspects of negotiation taken for granted even in collaborative approaches and is worthy of serious consideration, argumentation, and examination. For an extensive treatment of some common assumptions, ranging from individualistic to spiritual levels of communication, see chapter 2, "Self and Other in Relation," in Wilmot (1995).

You may be thinking, "Why negotiate from a shared perspective?" When relationships are ongoing and the current dispute is just one of a series to be solved over time, no one gains from a narrowly focused, self-interested perspective. A common phrase from the ecology movement is "we are all downstream from each other," referring to the fact that there is no safe place for toxic wastes or pollutants to be dumped—someone will be adversely affected. Many conflicts are like this: downstream of the current conflict, another will surface, and if the relationship becomes polluted, the entire future will be poisoned.

Application 8.6   The Rainbow Development Water Problem

A group of summer home owners in the high mountains of Colorado faces an ongoing problem with their water well, which keeps testing as polluted, thus making it necessary for the residents to boil or buy their water. Recently some of the elected officials of the volunteer board authorized a road to be built so heavy equipment could reach the wellhead and the well could be dug out and rebuilt. The road was built through wetlands, which raised some federal legal problems, and through a pristine meadow cherished by some of the residents as a quiet, beautiful spot at the end of the property. The road goes through commonly owned property, skirting the edge of privately owned lots. Three factions have formed, and full-scale conflict has erupted, with letters, private conversations, procedural challenges, content arguments, relationship destruction, and face-saving struggles going on at a high level of intensity. Thirty-five or so families are involved. It is a long-standing group of friends and acquaintances who have considerable monetary and emotional investment in the property and dramatically different ecological, political, financial, and community values.

1. The "water first" group: This group consists primarily of engineers, scientists, builders, and practical people who are sick and tired of dealing with a half-solution to the water problem year after year. They want to get a new well, install purification systems if they are needed, and assess the membership for what is required.

(continued)

The Rainbow Development
Water Problem

They rely on scientific studies of the water quality as a database. In their view, the road was simply a means to an important end. They are convinced that their mandate was clear: to provide potable water for the group. They can't understand the outrage of the second group. Many of this group have volunteered countless hours through the years for the practical maintenance of the roads, water system, fences, and governing system. This group is concerned with content goals and face saving. They argue that the content goals are the most important and that they did what they had to do (face saving).

2. The "road has to go" group: This group consists of a few older home owners and their adult children. The view of this group is that environmental concerns are primary. They will not tolerate compromise about the sensitive wetlands along the stream and feel outraged at the destruction of the most beautiful area of common property. They think the board acted without proper authorization by the membership and feel strongly that not only should the road never have been built but that it must be taken out and the area reclaimed. They prefer any solution, including boiling water for drinking, to the degradation of the environment. Many of this group will be second-generation home owners when they inherit the property from their parents. However, these group members have no vote in the association, since only property owners can vote. This group as a whole is concerned about appropriate process and has strongly held content goals.

3. The "we simply have to live with it" group: This group sees itself as the middle group between two extremes. Many of these people feel disappointed or angry about the gravel road and the fact that the water problem still is not solved. They want to support the elected board but don't like all the conflict and alienation in what used to be a very close and friendly group, which had potlucks, birthday celebrations, and outings together. Now that the road is in, they think it should be accepted and used to solve the water problem. This group is concerned with relationships and face saving for the board. They keep their private opinions, whatever they might be, to themselves. They look to the future.

Now that you have read "The Rainbow Development Water Problem," answer these questions:

- Specify (1) competitive, (2) collaborative, and (3) transformative approaches to defining this problem.

- How can concerns be addressed, relationships be enhanced, and solutions be found?

- What communicative moves from each of the three groups would enhance rather than destroy the ongoing relationships?

- If you were a negotiator for one of the groups, how might you approach the problem?

∾Competitive and Collaborative Phases

Negotiations are characteristically complex. Early in negotiations, it is common for the participants to have a fixed-sum assumption (Bazerman, Magliozzi, and Neale 1995). Bargainers can, regardless of their initial positions and approaches, move to integrative, or collaborative, outcomes (Tutzauer and Roloff 1988; Gulliver 1979; Lewicki and Litterer 1985). Many negotiations travel between cooperative and competitive phases, often returning to collaborative phases when someone stresses the gains to be had by both sides (Popple 1984; Holmes 1992). Sometimes dyads will reach an impasse, return to earlier phases of negotiations, and seem to regress (Holmes 1992). An example of "impasse dyads" is often found when couples are negotiating details of their divorce. Often, the couple will get stuck on one issue, such as how to work out holiday access to the children, then get so angry they will try to redo all the earlier negotiation, even agreements that had been problem free, such as division of furniture or where each partner would live. Skillful third-party help can often enable the couple to move out of the impasse.

The central finding from phase research is that successful negotiations eventually move toward collaborative, or integrative, processes (Holmes 1992; Gulliver 1979). Further, collaborative and competitive processes can be seen as intertwined—as the participants utilize more competitive approaches, a natural tension builds to move toward collaboration (Putnam 1986, 1988b). Usually the bargainers begin with a competitive orientation and, through the process of bargaining, move toward a collaborative stance (Jones 1988). The bargainers can be seen as moving from differentiation—stressing their differences with each other, attacking each other's positions, and venting emotions—to integration, or collaboration, in which the negotiators adopt a problem-solving orientation. These processes would look, sequentially, like this:

1. Extreme statements of positions.
2. Clashes about positions.
3. De-emphasis of differences and decreased use of antagonistic tactics (Jones 1988, 472).

An almost identical set of stages also has been specified:

1. Lengthy public orations characterized by a high degree of "spirited" conflict.
2. Tactical maneuvers and arguments for and against proposals.
3. Reducing alternatives to formal agreements (Putnam and Jones 1982a).

Note that these phases have been used in negotiations that resulted in agreements. Also, they are more characteristic of explicit bargaining situations, such as negotiations over contracts. There simply has not been enough research on implicit, informal bargaining processes to specify the phases they involve. Clearly, however, successful negotiations typically arrive at workable agreements by going through collaborative phases.

As noted previously, *most inexperienced bargainers automatically assume a competitive stance regarding negotiations* since they believe that "toughness" can only be achieved through competitive tactics. Since collaborative tactics generally have to be learned, people often have difficulty understanding them. Yet, for negotiations to come to fruition, collaborative tactics have to be called on, or there is a strong possibility of negotiations breaking down and the relationship between the parties being damaged. One's choice of negotiation strategies sets forces in motion that may be difficult to alter. For example, using pressure tactics increases competitiveness (Tutzauer and Roloff 1988); spirals of competitiveness tend to bring impasse (Putnam 1988b); competitive strategies lessen satisfaction with the process (Putnam and Folger 1988); and a competitive orientation coupled with time pressure secures poorer agreements (Carnevale and Lawler 1986). Basically, cooperative and competitive climates are self-reinforcing—competition encourages more competition and collaboration brings collaboration in return (Folger and Poole 1984; Carnevale and Lawler 1986; Pace 1988).

How, then, can one move toward collaboration during the negotiation process? Surely, the mental set you have about negotiations is important and determines whether you see bargaining as essentially competitive or collaborative (Gulliver 1979). In most cases it is your orientation toward negotiating rather than facts about a particular conflict that determines your style of negotiating during that conflict. Practiced collaborative negotiators are able to work with the other even when a conflict "objectively" seems to be zero-sum or win/lose.

The mental set you have toward collaboration, however, only works in a conflictual situation if you can communicate collaboratively. Although there are limits to learning about collaboration by reading about it, some collaborative communicative moves can be learned in this manner. These specific communicative moves can lead one toward a collaborative stance in negotiations.

☙Collaboration Checklist

The following list of collaborative principles—the **collaboration checklist**—may be helpful in leading you toward a collaborative approach to negotiations.

1. *Join "with" the other:*
    Use "we" language.
    Seek common interests.
    Consult before acting.
    Move closer nonverbally.

2. *Control the process, not the person:*
    Use setting, timing, and other factors creatively.
    Either limit or increase the number of people involved.
    Encourage the other to expound fully—listen actively even when you disagree.

3. *Use principles of productive communication:*
    Be unconditionally constructive.
    Refuse to sabotage the process.
    Separate the people from the problem.
    Persuade rather than coerce.
    Refuse to hate the other.

4. *Be firm in your goals and flexible in your means:*
    Be provisional—seek alternate means to your goals.

Separate content and relationship issues.
Focus on interests, not positions.

5. *Assume there is a solution:*
Invent options for mutual gain.
Approach issues one at a time.
First tackle issues that you can easily agree upon.
Refuse to be pessimistic.

These principles help in adopting a collaborative approach to negotiations, in particular, and conflict, in general. These guidelines serve as a reminder that in all conflict situations, parties using a collaborative approach can find solutions that will benefit both parties.

Summary

Negotiation is one mechanism for solving ongoing conflicts with others. Negotiation allows us to resolve conflicts peacefully by recognizing the stake that all parties have in the successful resolution of conflict.

Negotiation occurs in everyday life, as well as in structured public arenas such as labor-management bargaining. At the heart of all negotiations are considerations of power. We can equalize power through destructive means or by learning to be effective at argumentation.

The two major types of negotiations are (1) competitive and (2) collaborative. There are assumptions, communication patterns, and downsides associated with each type of negotiation. Negotiations also pass between phases, often beginning with a competitive tone and concluding with a collaborative tone. Successful negotiators are eventually able to collaborate with the other party, even if the initial stances involved extreme positions, lack of concession, and hostility. In addition to the two major types of negotiation, a third perspective has recently emerged that presumes a relational orientation.

Principled negotiation is a collaborative approach that stresses (1) separating the people from the problem, (2) focusing on parties' interests not their positions, (3) generating multiple options, and (4) using objective criteria. We supplied guidelines that help you find interests that underlie positions.

The following are specific communicative moves that induce a collaborative atmosphere: (1) join with the other; (2) control the process, not the people; (3) use productive communication; (4) be firm in your goals and flexible in your means; and (5) remain optimistic about finding solutions to your conflict.

Key Terms

Use the text's Online Learning Center at **www.mhhe.com/wilmot7**
to further your understanding of the following terminology.

everyday negotiation 243
avoidance 244
negotiation, definition 244
culture (and negotiation) 245

even playing field/level
table 246
equalizing power 246
dominance 246

argument 248
competitive negotiation 250
zero-sum game 250
distributive bargaining 250

～Review Questions

Go to the self-quizzes on the Online Learning Center at **www.mhhe.com/wilmot7** to test your knowledge of the chapter concepts.

1. What is the place of negotiation in everyday life?
2. Explain how negotiation is part of conflict resolution.
3. Define negotiation.
4. How does negotiation fit between avoidance and domination?
5. What impacts do our cultures have on negotiation?
6. List destructive ways to equalize power.
7. How are arguments part of constructive negotiation?
8. List the assumptions and communication elements of competitive negotiation.
9. Describe the assumptions of collaborative negotiation.

10. List some collaborative communication moves.
11. What are the four key elements to principled negotiation?
12. Why are interests so important?
13. What is the difference between positions and interests?
14. List some questions you can use to find interests.
15. What might be some multiple interests you have in a current conflict?
16. Give some examples of collaborative language.
17. How do conflicts move through competitive and collaborative phases?
18. Reproduce from memory the collaborative checklist.

Chapter 9

Third-Party Intervention

❧The Need for Third Parties

Conflicts often are so difficult that we turn to others for help. When you and the other party are not talking, or you are yelling at one another and destroying trust, outside help is needed. If your roommate and you have been arguing about rent payments for weeks on end, it may be time for outside help. If you have a family dispute that drags on for years, that is certainly a clear sign of the need for help. If you have a situation at work where you continually fight with your supervisor over your job assignments, it is time to ask for help. When talk typically is sarcastic, indirect, or defensive, special help may be needed. When you and your partner love each other but keep getting caught in the same destructive spirals, you should consider third-party help. Asking for help from the right people usually stops the destructive spiral and enables people to use their best skills.

At times of such conflict trouble, we turn to friends, advisors, pastors, parents, co-workers, human resources department personnel, counselors, mediators, lawyers—anyone we think can help. Third-party help may be appropriate in situations such as these:

- A roommate stops paying her share of the rent.
- A friend keeps using your clothes without permission.
- Your sister hangs up on every phone call and refuses to talk, after making bitter comments.
- You and your romantic partner are separating *but neither of you wants to.*
- Young students are fighting during recess.
- An entire workgroup is no longer meeting or cooperating with one another.
- An employee is injured on the job and wants health benefits.
- Violence is beginning to erupt between two young men (Funk et al. 2003).
- Students are being harassed (Newman 2004).
- Two ranchers have a dispute over water rights that involves the entire community.
- A customer tries to return a defective product, but the retailer refuses to accept it.
- Only one worker, a relative of the supervisor, gets a raise. The rest of the employees protest by filing a grievance.
- An employee is fired and seeks redress (Bingham 2004).

These situations call for a variety of third-party interventions, ranging from informal intervention to formal intervention. You might become involved by (1) serving as a third-party yourself, (2) assisting others in finding appropriate third parties, or (3) asking for third-party assistance for your own conflicts.

Third-party activity is a normal part of everyday life. You may have a friend like Angela, for example, who is often in the role of getting two other friends to "talk it out" when there is a dispute. Many professional roles require third-party skills. Teachers separate students on the playground, ministers help families through crises, dormitory head residents help residents, and mediators help married couples separate and divorce. Lawyers, judges, probation officers, hearings officers, union representatives, and professional meeting facilitators all help people work through their conflicts. Counselors use third-party skills with couples and families.

In this chapter, we will provide an overview of (1) **informal** and (2) **formal intervention** into disputes. For informal interventions (like helping two friends or family members), we will supply cautions about entering others' disputes and some guidelines for success. For formal interventions (using mediators, counselors, arbitrators, and the courts, for example), we will acquaint you with the various approaches so you can be an informed consumer of such services. Whether you are seeking third-party help for your own disputes or helping others connect with appropriate services, you can be most helpful if you know the differences in the third-party services. Counselors are not lawyers, mediators are not psychologists, and best friends should not arbitrate.

You might become intrigued with the role of third parties and work in some of these roles yourself. In that case, volunteering for a mediation program, serving as an intern in a student government ombudsman office, and getting trained as a meeting facilitator are just some of the possibilities.

∿Advantages of Using Competent Third Parties

Many conflicts require the use of a competent third party who *does not have a vested interest in a specific outcome*. Whether informal or formal, the goal of all intervention is to assist in a *transformation of the conflict elements*. The transformation may take many forms. It may

- *Change the expression of conflict.*
- *Alter the degree of interdependence between the parties.*
- *Change their perceptions or their goals* so they are not seen as incompatible.
- *Balance the power.*
- *Modify the actual or perceived scarcity of resources.*
- *Adjust the actual or perceived interference* by the opposing parties.

Competent intervention transforms the conflict so that issues can be put to rest and people can move on.

After third-party intervention, co-workers may be able to speak to the boss directly instead of forming coalitions, and the boss may agree to give feedback in person instead of in writing. Parents may agree to help their 18-year-old daughter go to college in a different state, or a conflict over scarce parking space may be redefined so that co-workers can talk about their relational conflicts instead of the content conflict. A judgment may be rendered that alters a company's hiring practices.

⮴Informal Intervention

Most everyday conflicts are settled out of court or without the aid of a professional helper through the assistance of friends, neighbors, and other natural helpers (McGillis 1981). These interveners serve the same objective as more defined agents, that is, "to interrupt a self-maintaining or escalating-malevolent cycle in one way or another and to initiate a de-escalating-benevolent cycle" (Walton 1969). In some circumstances, third parties pass messages back and forth. You may have informed a friend when her angry boyfriend was ready to talk over a conflict or told your brother that your younger sister was upset and needed to talk.

Informal third parties enter conflicts through diverse routes. Parties may ask for help indirectly. A friend may call to discuss a potential romantic breakup. You may guess that he wants you to carry a message or come over to talk with the unhappy couple. A staff person may say, "What would you think about coming to the meeting Tuesday with Julie and Chris? I think we could use your level head." Children, for instance, sense that parents will step into the role of a third party when they get beaten up on the playground, when "Jill won't give me back my teddy bear," or when big brother picks on them behind their parents' backs. The complaint, accompanied by anger or tears, serves as a request for help.

The following are indirect cues indicating that your help may be needed:

Indirectly Asking for Help

1. A person spends more time with you than usual, sharing feelings.
2. A person shares private information with you.
3. A person indicates that a crucial decision is impending.
4. A person makes you understand that his or her life is not smooth, that distress is present, or that things seem out of control.
5. A person makes dramatic, noticeable changes.

A teacher may notice that a student, usually happy and in love with life, talks more and more of negative feelings and events. Accounts of events may focus on blaming. A student who says, "They won't hire me. They don't think I have any useful experience," may be indirectly asking for the teacher's intervention in the form of a phone call or letter of recommendation.

Personal Intervention

If you want to help people resolve their conflict, you must now choose when to intervene, what your role will be, what your intervention style will be, and what skills you will bring to the conflict. Before you make a commitment to help, answer the following questions:

1. Are they ready for a third party? What evidence do you have to indicate such readiness?

2. How do you know that they want *you* to help?

3. What skills prepare you to help them? Can you best help by referring them to someone else?

4. Are you biased, committed to one of the parties, grinding your own ax, or unable to help because of time, position, or other matters?

5. Can you say no? If not, then you are probably too involved in the conflict to be an effective helper.

If you are satisfied with the answers to these questions, take the time to think about the consequences of your intervention. Remember, someone else's problem is not necessarily your problem—you have a choice. If you think you have no choice, you cannot be useful as an informal intervener. Many people get involved in conflicts between their parents only to discover the futility of trying to solve marital problems not of their making. If you do not want to get involved in a conflict but think that you should, your lack of enthusiasm for the role will result in lessened energy and creativity, a lack of sensitivity, and ineffective intervention. If you don't want to help, don't.

If you do choose to take a role in a conflict, however informal or nonspecific that role may be, take special care to retain your neutrality. Informal third parties often take sides (Van de Vliert 1981, 1985). If one of the parties succeeds in allying with you, the resulting alliance lessens the other side's power in the conflict and creates a new issue in the conflict—that of *unfair bonding*. Consultants to organizations are trained to avoid such biased behavior, but friends and relatives may slip into taking sides only to find that their "help" has made the conflict worse. **Siding** with one party has these effects:

- Siding implies that the outsider adopts the win/lose thinking of the principal parties, which reinforces the destructive effects of such thinking.

- Siding creates a winner (the chosen party) and a loser (the rejected party), precipitating escalation by the rejected party.

- Siding increases the number of conflict participants.

- By adding views, siding complicates the conflict issues.

- The siding outsider invests energy, increasing the stake of the parties in the conflict outcome. (Adapted from Van de Vliert 1981, 497–498)

Siding with one conflict party, although not wise for an intervener, does have its place. If, for example, your close friend is breaking off a relationship with her fiancé, you may choose to side with her to give her support. Anything else would be unrealistic. However, you should be aware that siding with one of the conflict parties *precludes you from being an effective neutral helper*; you will become an additional party to the conflict.

Refusing to take sides can result in your readiness to be an effective change agent. A new employee of a hospital was approached by persons on opposite sides of a conflict over whether the assignment of nursing shifts should be based on seniority only or on seniority and experience. The new nurse found himself being pushed toward the middle—both sides wanted him to persuade the other side of the rightness of their position. He wisely told all parties, "I am too new to have an informed opinion. Besides, I value my relationships with all of you. I prefer not to be involved with this problem."

On a university campus, a faculty member's neutrality set the stage for an effective intervention. The faculty member heard from a student who wanted to graduate early that another faculty member refused to consider a petition to waive or substitute a required course. The neutral faculty member offered to intervene by privately asking the resistant faculty member to discuss the issue in a meeting. The intervening professor did not take sides; she provided a forum for handling the matter creatively.

If you are going to intervene, clarify any change in your role from your usual role with the conflict parties. If you have been a buddy, boss, romantic partner, co-worker, or casual acquaintance, any change in that role needs to be negotiated. For example, a 14-year-old girl, Toni, lived with a couple in their mid-50s who cared for her as foster parents. The state children's service worker, Anne, had functioned in the past as a person who found placements for Toni, certified potential foster homes for her, and provided her with ongoing counseling. Mr. and Mrs. Black began to quarrel about whether to continue providing care for Toni, since their own children were out of the home and they were beginning to want time without children. Mrs. Black wanted to wait until Toni graduated from high school to request another placement, whereas Mr. Black wanted Toni to be moved during the summer. Anne was able to act as a third party to their conflict, after making clear that her first loyalty was to Toni's best interests. Since all three people agreed on the interests, they were able, with Anne's help, to find a solution to the conflict. If Anne had not clarified her role, which involved not taking sides with either parent and keeping Toni's interests prominent, both parents would have tried to elicit Anne's support for their side.

Several cautions are in order for the helper who is a friend or co-worker:

1. Be certain the parties want help in managing their conflict. Any time a third party enters into an existing relationship, the relationship is changed.

2. Be careful that the successful conflict management of the original parties is not built at the expense of the third party—they may cast you as the enemy, thus temporarily bonding with each other and excluding you. Remember, you are entering an already existing system, whether it be two friends, two employees, or any greater number of interdependent persons. Your focus, even if you are taking an informal role, is the relationship. If you become a common enemy by pushing the parties too hard, they will not solve their problem and you will lose two relationships.

3. You must constantly remain aware of coalitions. Once you coalesce with one person, you lose your helpful role and weaken the relationship between the two parties. Because you cannot predict ahead of time exactly what will happen when you involve yourself, you do need to monitor the interactions to watch for shifts in coalitions or destruction of the original bond. If you begin thinking, "No wonder he is struggling with her; she is completely unreasonable," you have formed a coalition and lost your effectiveness.

4. Intervene only when people want your help and not for your own purposes. You may at some point need to request the help of an outside helper for your organization, family, or personal relationship. You can be helpful to the third party by asking for what you want and clarifying what you do not want. Once the work is completed, the third party exits from the system. In both formal and informal intervention, the goal is to train the parties to manage their own relations. A conciliator who does not work himself or herself out of a job is not doing the job properly; the parties must become independent of the third party.

In one mediated conflict, the leaders of two departments agreed to set up weekly meetings to discuss ongoing or potential conflicts. A three-month follow-up meeting with the original conflict parties was scheduled to assess how the weekly meetings were working—and to make sure the meetings were occurring. An effective third party trains people in the process of conflict management so that the clients will not need ongoing services. In either formal or informal roles, a helper who improves the parties' relations over time contributes what is actually needed.

Application 9.1   My Informal Role

1. List the skills you have that help you serve as a third party to others. What skills do you lack at this point?

2. Discuss some times you have effectively helped others.

3. List the times you have tried to help others and your efforts backfired.

    a.   How did the parties ask, directly or indirectly, for help?
    b.   What role did you negotiate ahead of time?
    c.   To whom were you closest? Whom did you know the best?
    d.   What process did they agree to before you intervened?
    e.   How could you tell that your "help" was actually making things worse?

4. What did you learn from those experiences about serving as an informal third party?

Counseling as Informal Intervention

Individuals, couples, and families often seek the services of a professional counselor to help them resolve disputes. Counseling is halfway between informal and formal intervention. The setting is usually defined, payment is required, and the counselor must have certain, usually licensed, credentials to serve as a counselor. Conversation, however, may be informal. The counselor focuses on emotional, relational, and feeling issues rather than only on the topics that might have brought people into counseling. Reconciliation is sometimes desired, but not always. Many counselors are interested not so much in diagnosis of what is wrong, psychologically, with the individual but what might be transformed about relationships. Certainly people enter counseling because of psychological issues such as depression, bipolar disorders, anxiety issues, personality disorders, or substance abuse. Very often people also want help with relationship issues. A professional counselor usually does not control the conversation process in the same way that an arbitrator or mediator might. Yet constructive counselors always balance the needs of the triggering issues in the clients' minds with their identity, their feelings, and what a constructive dialogue might entail.

You might consider asking for help from a professional counselor when your own feelings are so highly engaged that you cannot use the conflict skills you know about, or when others have put you in a low-power position or your own lack of confidence has landed you in a low-power position. You might ask for help when you have been deeply hurt or have hurt others. When a psychological disorder, chronic or temporary, claims so much attention for both yourself and others, and when you are suffering emotionally or relationally, you will benefit from professional counseling. Remember that you do not have the power to coerce others to enter counseling with you. You can only invite them, and continue to seek help for yourself.

❧The Formal Intervention Continuum

When someone has been trained in a specific third-party role, and when that person is specifically requested to perform conflict resolution or reduction procedures, we refer to the process as *formal intervention*. Usually, in Western culture, the formal third party is paid, such as in counseling, mediation, legal interventions, or organizational consultation. However, in some cultures and subcultures of the United States, formal intervention is traditional and is as binding as, for instance, legal intervention may be, but is not paid. Some Native American, Cambodian, Malaysian, and many other cultures use formal intervention to restore peace and justice in the culture. Some religious organizations use a form of unpaid but formalized peacemaking efforts, whether performed by one person or a council of designated persons. One of the costs of our Western, mobile culture is that we no longer have as much access to such traditional councils. Thus, we turn more and more to paid, formal intervention.

These intervention modes differ according to the degree to which *conflict parties determine the final outcome*. In some forms of third-party intervention, the conciliator serves as a facilitator to parties who make their own decisions, whereas other forms impose a resolution to the conflict upon the parties (see the following).

Representative modes of intervention

High ↑

Degree to which the conflicting parties determine the solutions to their conflicts

- Facilitation
- Mediation
- Counseling and therapy
- Organizational development
- Conciliation
- Quasi-judicial bodies
- Informal tribunals
- Arbitration of all types

Low ↓
- Criminal and civil justice system

In many interventions, combinations of these approaches are used. For instance, both mediation and arbitration can be used by the third party who is assisting the parties in reaching agreement (Buzzard and Eck 1982). Similarly, contracts between labor and management often specify a sequence of steps such as (1) negotiation, (2) mediation, and, if necessary, (3) arbitration. Divorce mediators often specify that if the mediation breaks down on a specific issue, that particular issue will be taken to an arbitrator; then the parties return to mediation to finish their work (Coogler 1978; Moore 1986). ADR, or **alternative dispute resolution, procedures** are alternatives to litigation in which a third party other than a judge or jury is asked to resolve a dispute. Given the breadth of the procedures, it might be better if ADR stood for *appropriate dispute resolution*. The term lumps together very different processes—arbitration, mediation, and conciliation. When someone says, "use ADR," they may be calling for arbitration, which follows the structure outlined in figure 9.1, or mediation, which is an entirely different process. Or they may be ordered by a judge into conciliation, in which the third-party reports to the judge about what process should be tried next. ADR, then, is sometimes not the best term to use because, conceptually, it may refer to very different dispute resolution structures. In this chapter, the more precise terms *arbitration* and *mediation* are used rather than *ADR*.

When an Outsider Decides

Adjudication: Judge or Jury Decides

Adjudication is a process in which parties present their case before a judge or jury. Adjudication assumes that parties are unable to solve their own conflicts, and a decision must be imported from outside (Wissler 2004). It is similar to arbitration in that a third party decides, but adjudication can be put into motion without mutual consent. In adjudication, you can sue the other party, forcing a decision whether the other wants to participate or not. Additionally, the officials of the criminal justice system can initiate charges, for instance, in cases of bodily assault, robbery, and related offenses. Adjudication assumes that a full argument of each side of a conflict will allow a judge or jury to make a just decision. Figure 9.1 illustrates the *communication structure* that is common to both adjudication and arbitration.

As figure 9.1 illustrates, once a suit has been filed with the court (or a petition filed for arbitration), lawyers or other advocates negotiate with each other, often instructing the conflict parties (the litigants) to not talk to each other. In this structure, the litigants

Figure 9.1   Lines of Communication with Professional Advocates. (Solid lines indicate heavy communication; broken lines signify that the judge or jury is used as a reference point for the attorneys, often without direct communication; absence of lines signifies no direct communication.)

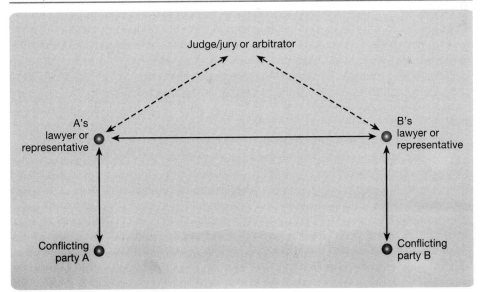

set into motion a struggle that the lawyers act out. The original conflict metamorphoses into a conflict between the two lawyers (Irving and Bohm 1978). The attorneys become the prime players, who negotiate with each other, trying to estimate what the judge (or jury) will do with the case. Each lawyer's estimate of the judge's, jury's, or arbitrator's probable response becomes the basis of his or her negotiation strategy. The lawyers then try to persuade each other that their views are correct.

Court processes are fairly well known. One party files charges in court and the other must appear to respond. Between the time of the filing and the court date, the lawyers usually negotiate with each other regarding the case. For example, a landlord charges a tenant with violation of a lease agreement because the tenant signed a one-year lease and moved after four months. The landlord files suit to recover the rent for the eight months the renter was not living there. The two lawyers typically begin negotiations, calling and writing back and forth. If they are not able to reach settlement, the case goes to court; a judge or jury, after hearing testimony and evidence from both sides, may decide that the tenant must pay the eight months' rent, plus attorney fees. If no appeal is filed, the resolution process will end with the enforcement of the action. In a case like this, a justice of the peace may decide the case.

Litigating a dispute is both an alternative to negotiating and at the same time a way to force negotiation. Since most lawsuits are settled before trial, it is useful to view litigation not only as a way to "go to court" but also as a highly structured negotiation game, a "refined and constrained version of competitive bargaining" (Goodpaster 1992, 221). Filing a lawsuit forces a nonresponding party to attend to the complaint—avoidance is not possible once a suit is filed. The law enables lawyers to translate the dispute into a form that can be adjudicated. About 90 percent of the time, parties negotiate an out-of-court settlement because of high court costs, time delays, and the financial and emotional toll a court battle takes. Because of the form of litigation, these negotiations are competitive in nature (Goodpaster 1992, 234).

Advantages of Adjudication

Adjudication as a form of conflict management has a number of positive features. "Equal protection of the law" allows everyone access to a resolution process and does not require the agreement of the other party. Therefore, adjudication serves as a power-balancing mechanism. For example, individuals can sue large corporations. In the case of abused or neglected children, a state agency can bring the parents before a court to determine their suitability for continued parenting. The children's representative, a **guardian ad litem,** acts as their agent. As Wehr (1979) notes, "Asymmetrical conflict is best resolved through intervention that empowers the weaker party" (37).

A second positive feature of adjudication is that it provides rules for fairness, such as the admission of evidence. In some interpersonal conflicts, one party monopolizes the process, with few restraints. Process restraints are, however, built into the legal system. Each party has equal right to speak. The process rules allow both parties to fully explicate their positions.

Third, the use of professionals to speak for the conflict parties is an advantage for parties who need assistance in preparation or presentation of their case. The trained legal expert can develop the best case for the client, ensure fair procedures, and set forth the case with vigor.

Finally, *adjudication serves as a backup for other conflict management procedures*. When arbitration, mediation, conciliation, and negotiation fail to produce agreement, the disputants can go to court. The appeal process allows people to present their case in a higher court if they dislike an earlier judgment. The moral as well as physical power present in our judicial and criminal justice systems provides a last-resort option when necessary.

Limitations of Adjudication

The judicial system also has some limitations in dealing with conflict. First, it has been overused and, as a consequence, is overburdened and misused. Former chief justice Warren Burger, referring to the legal profession, said, "The obligation of our profession is to serve as healers of human conflicts" (Ray 1982), but "suing has become an American parlor game" (Marks 1981). As a result, there is an "unprecedented demand upon the judicial system, leading to considerable frustration and delay . . ." (Sander 1977, 2). Guarantees of speedy justice are difficult to receive; delays of as much as two years between filing and first court appearances are common. Because the judicial system has been used and talked about so much, many individuals automatically think of it as the way to "get even" for some wrong. They often do not realize they have chosen a mode of conflict resolution until "they find themselves caught up in it with apparently no way out" (Coogler 1978, 6). One legal scholar concludes, "It seems clear that it is simply too cumbersome and expensive for most (minor) disputes" (Sander 1977, 24). A continuing round of court battles in order to "win" can deplete almost anyone's finances.

A second disadvantage of using the legal system for conflict resolution is that *conflict parties no longer make their own decisions*. For example, in a dispute involving a community (such as one over an environmental issue), "Litigation takes the decision out of the hands of the communities who must live with its consequences" (Wehr 1979, 123). Similarly, if two people are involved in a protracted domestic dispute such as a contested divorce, the parties stop dealing directly with each other and the attorneys take over the negotiation process.

Sometimes the conflict parties, after seeing the communication structure inherent in adjudication, decide to go a different route. For example, Sharon and her ex-husband, Ted, had been divorced for three years and were having difficulties agreeing on child visitation arrangements. They lived in different towns, and each had consulted an attorney about visitation options. One day in April, Sharon flew to Ted's city and called him, only to discover that his attorney had told him, "Don't talk to her, and hold out for all you can get." Sharon told Ted that she had received the same advice from her attorney. They realized that if they both followed their lawyers' advice, they would be in for a long court battle. The two of them wisely decided to empower themselves. They met the next day and worked out an agreement—though the process was difficult for them. They were the original parties to the dispute and were the ones who would have to live with the long-term results of a decision. Therefore, turning over the decision to their representatives wasn't desirable.

A final disadvantage of adjudication is that the *adversarial system operates on a win/lose set of conflict assumptions that encourages escalation tactics* (Menkel-Meadow 1986; Hartje 1984). Often the lawyer is seen as each client's only champion in a hostile world. This belief promotes escalation when, in fact, it might not be necessary. In order to file an action, one has to blow up the magnitude of the conflict to a "You owe us" or "We'll get you" frame of mind; one tries to win at the other's expense. Filing an action is a signal of serious conflict, and unfortunately, filing sets an escalating process in motion. Because attorneys are charged with solely representing the interests of their client, "The client's interest is always perceived as being in opposition to the interests of the other party. The lawyer cannot and does not regard the parties as having a common problem which he or she will help resolve" (Coogler 1978, 7). The gathering of evidence for one side of the conflict disregards the relational and face-saving interests of both parties. Parties cooperate in following procedure, but this level of commonality does not open up many potentially creative outcomes. The escalating, win/lose atmosphere is often difficult to disengage from once it has been set into motion. Suits and countersuits reflect continual escalation, with each "loser" trying again on some other basis until resources or options are exhausted.

Arbitration: An Expert Decides

The structure of arbitration is identical to adjudication. In arbitration, as in adjudication, a third party is empowered to decide the outcome of a conflict. Parties who cannot resolve their conflict unassisted mutually empower an arbitrator to solve their conflict, are ordered to do so by a judge or manager, or are compelled by contract to seek arbitration.

The arbitration process varies according to the type of dispute and the needs of the parties. For example, a grievance procedure initiated by a worker who feels unfairly treated may be long and require numerous others to testify. Contract disputes are a common form of "rights" arbitration; many managers and line workers routinely sign contracts with a clause calling for arbitration in the case of disagreement. If you buy a car, have to make numerous repairs, and cannot get compensation from the dealer, you can ask for arbitration. The arbitrator listens to both sides of the dispute, questions you and the car dealer (or your representatives), and renders a judgment. When the parties contractually agree to arbitration, the arbitrated judgment is enforceable in court. This process is called **binding arbitration;** the judgment is final. Voluntary, or **nonbinding, arbitration** is sometimes used when the parties will not agree to binding arbitration. It allows for further arbitration or the initiation of a court case if parties do not accept the judgment.

Arbitration has some distinct features that make it useful as a form of third-party intervention. First, unlike adjudication, both parties enter into arbitration voluntarily. Second, it keeps one party from using passive aggressive or impasse tactics on the other—sooner or later the issue *will* be resolved (Coogler 1978). Third, in many cases the arbitrator has special training in the content area of the dispute, such as in contract arbitration. When the arbitrator has special expertise in the content of the arbitration, he or she can often offer creative content solutions. Fourth, arbitration is readily available for use in situations in which the participants experience a communication breakdown and are no longer able to solve their own problems. Finally, arbitration is a process that can be used for a wide variety of content areas, ranging from contract disputes, medical malpractice, or landlord-tenant conflicts to domestic relations (Alper and Nichols 1981; Tyler 1987; Keltner 1994).

Arbitration does have some limitations. It tends to resolve conflicts solely on a content basis. Arbitration typically does not address the relational or face-saving aspects of the dispute, which is unfortunate because if parties can reach some accord in their relationship, the content issues can often be worked out. Arbitration reinforces the assumption that the parties cannot learn to manage their own difficulties—that only a third party can find a solution. Arbitration reinforces escalation as a legitimate tactic because intransigence will automatically bring in an outsider. Despite these disadvantages, arbitration is still a widely used alternative in conflict management because it binds parties procedurally to seek resolution. The prerequisite that parties agree to arbitrate (either contractually before the dispute begins or voluntarily once they are in conflict) enhances the chances for productive conflict management.

When the Parties Decide
Mediation

The mediator has no power to render a decision or impose a solution. Instead, the mediator helps the parties themselves to work out their differences and to construct a mutually acceptable solution.
—Gray, *Collaborating: Finding Common Ground for Multiparty Problems*

Mediation offers a completely different approach from adjudication and arbitration. In mediation, rather than having an "authority" decide the issues, *mediators help the parties negotiate so they can reach agreement.* Mediation is the "art of changing people's positions with the explicit aim of acceptance of a package put together by both sides, with the mediator as listener, suggestion-giver, the formulator of final agreements to which both sides have contributed" (Alper and Nichols 1981, 31). As Keltner (1983) says, "Your job is to facilitate the parties to the dispute to reach an agreement themselves."

As shown in figure 9.2, the structure of communication differs profoundly between the mediation model and the adjudication/arbitration model. Note that the mediator is there to facilitate communication between the parties. The mediator is the convener, the facilitator, but not the one who makes the decision. In true mediation, the mediator is a neutral party who does not try to push the parties to a specific decision. In some cases, as when mediation is required by the court, the parties have less freedom than when they themselves decide to use mediation.

Figure 9.2   Mediation (the solid lines indicate flow of communication)

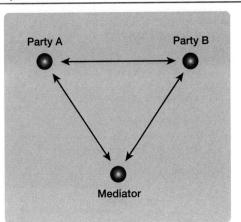

The communication in the initial stages might consist of the parties talking mostly to the mediator, but as mediation progresses, the parties talk more and more to each other with the mediator guiding the process. The mediator is there to *control the process*—not letting the participants interrupt, call names, or engage in other destructive moves. But the mediator does not *control the outcome*—the solutions to the dispute come from the parties themselves. Sometimes mediators engage in "shuttle diplomacy," in which they keep the parties separate and bring messages back and forth. Separation of the parties is common in intense disputes such as war, court-ordered divorce mediation, or other situations in which the parties are unable to be in the same room with each other. However, the bulk of mediation is performed with the parties in the same room, with the mediator controlling the communication process for mutual benefit.

The process of mediation assumes that conflict is inevitable and resolvable. It further assumes that people in a conflicted relationship have enough common interest to bring about an agreement and that the parties will ultimately be responsible for settling their own conflict. It assumes that the parties' solutions will be more responsive to their needs than a settlement imposed by a third party (Moore 1996).

Advantages

Mediation brings distinct advantages to the management of conflict. First, because it relies on the parties' active negotiation and involvement, it *promotes a mutual stake in the resolution;* solutions derived through the process are more likely to be carried out by the parties. The agreement is theirs, not imposed, and as a result there is no "loser" who feels compelled to strike back. The parties created the conflict, and they work for its solution. Their active involvement is a source of mutual empowerment; they take ownership of the conflict and, with the mediator's assistance, impose some limits on the process. Mediation recognizes that the parties "have had some sort of prior relationship that will continue long after the dispute has been resolved" (Alper and Nichols 1981, 13; Kelly 2004).

Second, since mediated agreements represent the work of the parties, the *solutions are more likely to be integrative and creative.* The parties know better than any outsider what will work for them, and with the assistance of the mediator, they can craft unique solutions that work for them. An example of this is two businessmen in a mediation. When they first entered, Nick demanded that Paul pay him $60,000 for his part of their business that Paul developed in Hawaii without Nick's input. Had they gone to court or arbitration, they would have "settled" for some amount between $0 and $60,000 (probably $25,000 to $35,000). They would have ruptured their business relationship and friendship. During mediation it was discovered that Nick really wanted (1) to be included and involved and (2) to be valued by his partner for his selling skills. They agreed to have Paul send Nick and Nick's wife twice a year to Hawaii, where Nick would train Paul's salespeople free of charge. This integrative and creative solution never would have happened in adjudication or arbitration.

Third, as this example also illustrates, mediation *helps the parties meet their underlying interests* rather than fight over positions. Nick's real needs were for involvement and being valued, not money. Fighting over the position of $60,000 would not have kept the business partnership together, and would have obscured the underlying interests. Often, someone wants an apology rather than money.

Fourth, mediation is usually *cheaper than adjudication or arbitration*. For instance, in one study of 449 cases, mediation settled 78 percent of them with an average cost of $2,750 compared to $11,800 for arbitration (Brett, Barsness and Goldberg 1996). The settlement rates for different types of mediation vary but are generally high (Kelly 2004).

Fifth, *mediated parties are more satisfied with the process* than are participants in adjudication or arbitration. All you have to do is talk to someone who has gone to court and ask, "how was that process for you?" You will hear frustration, blame and anger. In contrast is a couple whose divorce was successfully mediated some years ago. They remain satisfied as their children have grown and their circumstances changed. They had two young girls and were committed to some form of co-parenting. Since the father planned a move to the West Coast, they had to work out living arrangements, child support, and how to make travel and holiday agreements. Ten years later, the couple came back to the original mediators for help with a problem that developed when the girls went to college. As they called for an appointment, the wife said, "We didn't dare fight. We've told everyone how great this process is, so everybody is looking to us to see how we will do. We *have* to work it out."

The mediation process is becoming much more widely available. For example, more than 10,000 schools now have peer mediation programs (Kowalski 1998). Many communities provide nonprofit agencies or groups who train people to be volunteer mediators, or who assist in court-mandated mediation of child living arrangements (Hedeen 2004). Community disputes often are mediated by a neutral party. Neighborhood associations use volunteer mediators to resolve local disputes, centered on such things as zoning violations, rental problems, pet problems, and traffic concerns, as well as more serious issues such as theft and safety.

Limitations

Limitations to the use of mediation as a settlement option do exist. First, not all conflict parties will agree to work through their conflict with the "enemy." They may either not want to talk openly about their difficulties with the other or not want to be in the presence of the other person. Many conflicts escalate to the point where conjoint constructive work is not possible. The conflict may be so protracted that the only solution is a win/lose structure in which an outside party decides. In addition, if someone thinks he or she can win by going to court, that person is less likely to want mediation. For example, in one study of couples who either did or did not choose mediation during their divorce, the man's perceived chances of winning in the adversarial system affected his willingness to try mediation (Pearson, Thonnes, and Vanderkooi 1982). Furthermore, attorneys who do not favor mediation will not refer clients to mediation. Attorneys who have not been exposed to nonadversarial methods of conflict resolution are less likely to refer clients to mediation.

Mediation may not be appropriate for certain types of relationships. Mediation involves considerable commitment to working on the conflict. However, many parties are not prepared to reinvest in a relationship that has been problematic for them; they would rather try other routes to settlement or just continue the conflict. For example, Kressel et al. (1980) discovered that enmeshed couples were so intertwined in their dynamics that mediation was not successful for them. Similarly, couples with weak relationship bonds are often not good candidates for mediation. Both too much involvement and too little involvement with the other work against mediation.

Another limitation of mediation is that when one person, usually the woman, has been abused physically or emotionally, she may not be able to speak up with enough authority in mediation to generate options, argue for her perspective, and avoid being manipulated. Even when no overt abuse has occurred, many women are not able to negotiate with the person they once loved (and may still love) even if the relationship is breaking up. Some women try to work on the relationship as it is breaking up, sometimes out of concern for the children, but sometimes because of cultural conditioning.

A final limitation of mediation is that for some disputes, involvement in mediation is not worth the effort. Many small disputes may be more efficiently handled by third-party adjudication, such as by small-claims court or a justice of the peace, than by the disputants trying to work with each other. The conflict may not be serious enough to warrant "working through" by the conflict parties.

Mediation Settings

Mediation may be applied to a wide variety of settings and disputes. It has been used successfully in such diverse arenas as

- *Domestic disputes*
    separation and divorce
    estate distribution after a death
    parental conflicts
    parent-child concerns
    disputes between romantic partners who are splitting up
    grandparental visitation of children
- *Business disputes*
    partnership concerns
    contract disagreements
    management team disputes
    entire work groups split into coalitions
    employee grievances
    sexual harassment
    employee disputes
- *Educational settings*
    disputes over grades or treatment in class
    relationships between students and campus groups
    student-faculty relationships
    faculty-administration disputes
- *Community/neighborhood disputes*
    barking dogs
    property line disputes

> small claims
>
> landlord-tenant disputes

- *The criminal justice system*

  > juvenile court situations
  >
  > VOR (victim-offender restitution)
  >
  > treatment in detention facilities

- *Labor-management conflicts*

  > contract disputes
  >
  > work rules
  >
  > fringe benefits packages

- *International conflicts*

  > border disputes
  >
  > rights of citizens traveling
  >
  > shared resources such as bodies of water
  >
  > land ownership
  >
  > wars

A few examples will indicate the usefulness of mediation across settings ranging from community disputes to business disputes.

Community mediation programs continue to expand across much of the United States with high rates of success in settling a variety of disputes. In Massachusetts, New York, North Carolina, and other states, the success rates for mediating community disputes range from 75 to 95 percent (Umbreit 1995, 59). Community centers typically rely on volunteers who are trained by the local dispute resolution center. Community mediation programs offer excellent training, supervision, and guidance, as well as opportunities to help others resolve disputes. Complaints range from noisy neighbors to "He took my parking space"—almost any issue one can imagine that arises in a neighborhood. You can contact your local mediation center where you might volunteer and receive training.

In schools and universities, considerable mediation is occurring (Association for Conflict Resolution 2004). For instance, many grade schools, middle schools, and high schools have instituted programs of **peer mediation.** These programs train students, teachers, and administrators in constructive conflict resolution, teach mediation skills to peer mediators, and provide mediators for disputes ranging from playground difficulties to teacher-student problems. As an example of peer mediation, here are some tasks for fourth- and fifth-grade mediators when they see a conflict beginning:

1. When you see a conflict brewing during recess or lunch, introduce yourself and ask both parties if they want to solve their problem.

2. If they do, go to the area designated for solving problems. Explain and get agreement to the four basic rules: (a) agree to solve the problem, (b) don't call each other names, (c) do not interrupt, and (d) tell the truth.

3. Decide who will talk first. Ask that person what happened and how he or she feels, using active listening skills to repeat back what is said. Do the same with the other person.

4. Ask the first party and then the second party for alternative solutions.

5. Work with the students toward a solution that they both think is good.

6. After the agreement is reached, congratulate the parties and fill out the Conflict Manager Report Form. (Umbreit 1995, 78)

School mediation programs have had considerable success (Kowalski 1998). Of 137 disputes between students in Honolulu, 92 percent resulted in complete agreement, and after the institution of peer mediation in New York schools, suspensions decreased by more than half. Clearly, school mediation is a viable form of third-party intervention for a variety of disputes (Umbreit 1995; Burrell and Cahn 1994). In the university and college setting, campus mediation centers deal with disputes over grades and behavior in classrooms and in dorms and married-student housing. Some of the centers provide family mediation services to students as well.

Family mediation takes many forms, the most common application being separation and divorce. With almost half of all marriages ending in divorce and the pain of going through the court system all too evident, mediation of separation and divorce is becoming increasingly common. It is not a replacement for the legal process but an adjunct to it. By law, the judge retains all the authority to decide the details of a divorce, but a cooperative couple that comes to a judge with a fair agreement will find the process much easier than trying to "prove the other one wrong." The couple, with the mediator's help, fashions (within the constraints of the law) an agreement that will work best for their unique situation. The acrimony, lingering conflict, and repeated trips to court by couples who take the legal adversarial approach have fueled the mediation movement. One study concluded the following after examining mediation in divorces:

> Despite the high levels of stress, anxiety, and fear associated with the breakup of a marriage, the vast majority of the parties in mediation believed that their needs and interests had been considered by the mediator and that the agreements reached in mediation were substantively fair to both parties, and they recommended the mediation process to others. Long-term satisfaction with the agreements was demonstrated by the continued compliance with the original agreements and changes by mutual consent, modifications that were reached through constructive private discussion or by a return to mediation. (Meierding 1993, 169)

In the family context, family business and estate mediation are becoming more popular. When a family owns a small business, for example, and the time comes for Mom or Dad to retire, mediation involves all family members in the decision making so options can be charted that work best for all. Whether it is the family pharmacy, ranch, or Subway franchise, (1) topic, (2) relationship, (3) identity, and (4) process issues need to be carefully addressed. Mediation provides a framework for discussing important family issues, in addition to the usual issues of taxes, estate planning, and control of decisions. With mediation, all the issues can be brought to the surface and dealt with, which brings the participants to a mediated agreement that serves the entire family. The following article demonstrates the advantages of using mediation in estate planning.

The Family Estate

Reader: My mother, in her late 70s, is worried about her fairly sizable estate. It includes real estate, stock and our long-time family cabin in the mountains. She wants to do the "right" thing for her three grown children and their grown families so we won't fight or bicker after she's gone. She vividly remembers a nephew who, after her father's death, broke into the family house and took one of his guns. After 25 years, the family still talks about it! Should Mom think about using mediation?

Mediators: Absolutely. The two biggest mistakes people make about their estates, as well as in other types of mediation, are (1) not preplanning and (2) not dealing with relationship issues.

One cannot, should not, and must not try to pass on a sizable estate without specialized legal help. Estate and tax laws are complex and impose severe consequences for the unprepared (read "$$$"). Issues abound, such as whether to create a trust, if so, what kind, and how to handle the $10,000 annual gift exemption. These "content" issues need careful thought and expert advice. Equally, however, your mother dares not neglect the relational issues in her family—how she and the three children react to the content issues. Before, during and after consulting with attorneys, she should listen to and address the concerns of each person affected. Current research starkly paints the picture: If one tries to plan an estate using only legal and financial advisors, the children left out of the discussion will react negatively regardless of the elegance of the plan. Just ask families who've tried to craft even the most thorough estate plan without involving all the impacted players—smoldering resentments and "what ifs" remain.

In the safe environment of mediation, both the content and relational issues can be put on the table and examined. Assumptions about people's needs and feelings can be checked out, before they're locked into the text of a will. Creative problem solving can be used to derive solutions that work for the whole family. We have seen cases of people (1) retaining the family business intact in the face of children reluctant to participate and (2) passing on financial assets in ways that work for everyone.

Find a competent, experienced mediator to work with the family and with your estate lawyer, and your chances of somebody stealing the guns will diminish.

Source: Reprinted from *The Missoulian*, September 23, 1996, by Bill Wilmot and Roy Andes.

Mediation can be used in conjunction with counseling to resolve adolescent-parent conflicts—those natural calamities that arise in most families. Whereas for some, adolescence is a minor inconvenience, for others it is "a painful exhausting journey that cuts into the bond between parent and child" (Umbreit 1995, 116). A trained mediator can help both the adolescent and the parent(s) develop workable agreements to get them through this often contentious stage of family life. Whatever the need for family mediation, mediators who are members of the Association for Conflict Resolution follow specific standards for practice (see appendix for Web address).

VOR (Victim-Offender Restitution) is a specialized form of mediation designed for cases in which someone is guilty of a crime (Umbreit, Coates, and Vos 2004). Rather than resolving the issue by involving the defendant and the court system, VOR brings the victim into the process. Both the victim and the perpetrator tell their story and review options for compensation of the victim. Such an approach allows the victim participation, brings the reality of the crime home to the offender, and sets the conditions under which the offender can compensate the victim for what was done. It recognizes the victim's rights, allows the offender to take responsibility for what he or she has done, and provides avenues for restoration. Good reviews of VOR can be found in Umbreit (1995) and in a special issue of *Mediation Quarterly* (vol. 12, no. 3, 1995). A poignant example of a creative use of mediation for a minor crime is presented in the following box.

"I Stole Your TV"

An example illustrates the constructive use of mediation to achieve both symbolic and actual restitution. An elderly woman returned to her home one afternoon to find her television set gone. The youth who had stolen it was apprehended and admitted that he had sold the set to a fence. Rather than face a fine or continuance under probation, the defendant, in the presence of the mediation board and of the victim, sat down to work out a nonpunitive resolution to submit to the judge for his approval. The woman broke down in the course of telling the boy, "I watch television all day. This is all I do. I watch 16 hours a day. You have taken the heart of my life away." Confronted with personal implications of his act, the youth agreed to accept a job in order to buy the widow a new set. In addition, he agreed that he would accompany her to the bank to cash her weekly check and escort her to the market to do her shopping. A postscript to the case reports that after inviting the boy to have coffee with her, the woman learned from him that his mother had died and that he lived in an uncongenial relationship with his father and brother. Thereafter these Saturday morning coffee hours became a weekly feature. The closing entry reports that the boy had volunteered to paint the woman's kitchen.

Source: Alper and Nichols 1981, 146–147.

Mediation is beginning to be used in the business setting as well. When a dispute arises between two co-workers, between a supervisor and an employee, or within a self-directed work team, mediation allows the parties to address the issue in a confidential way. Advantages to using mediation in the workplace include the following:

- Mediation reduces the cost of protracted disputes.
- Mediation increases everyone's satisfaction with the outcomes of the dispute.
- Mediation enhances relationships among people.
- Mediation reduces the recurrence of conflict. (Yarbrough and Wilmot 1995, 3)

Some examples of the use of mediation in business settings are as follows: A man and wife were co-owners of a business, and he took out loans against the business without consulting her. With the ongoing help of the mediator, they restored their working rela-tionship, got their employees out of the middle of their struggles, and began cooperat-ing fully with each other. A male supervisor in a large institution was investigated by the personnel office for sexual harassment. After he was found not guilty of harassment, something had to be done to reestablish the working relationship between him and his female administrative aide. The mediator worked with the two of them to (1) set clear boundaries on appropriate behavior on both their parts, (2) stop "end runs" to higher authorities, and (3) establish clear protocols for how to run the office. These are sam-ples of the kinds of disputes that can be successfully handled via mediation. Yarbrough and Wilmot (1995) provide numerous examples of the mediation of diverse organiza-tional disputes ranging from employee-employee disputes to disputes within management teams.

✎Mediation: Agreement or Transformation?

Mediators' views of the mediation process differ on two primary points: (1) what issues are tackled in sessions and (2) what the goals are for the mediation. Some mediators (usually those with technical and/or legal training) will only mediate on the topic or content issues. For example, many legal jurisdictions have a "settlement week" when they convene groups of attorneys to mediate cases that are backlogged on the court calendars. This type of mediation is usually quite different from, for example, family mediation that deals with topic, relationship, identity, and process issues. Both types of mediation have their place, but as a user of the services you should be aware that the mediators' views of mediation result in vastly different processes. A local attorney who was going to mediate between two different factions (an insurance company with an attorney and a tribal elder with a representative) called for advice. In the phone call, it became apparent that his only considerations were content (topic) issues. The case did settle the topic issues exclusively, primarily because of the natural empathy of the attorney, whom everyone saw as a warm and friendly person.

Disputants who have an ongoing relationship are more satisfied and more willing to adhere to agreements when mediators expand the issues being considered. The results of research on family mediation are quite clear—when mediators bypass the rela-tional issues and focus only on "facts," they have trouble obtaining agreement from the parties (Donohue 1991; Donohue, Allen, and Burrell 1988; Donohue, Drake, and Roberto 1994). Sustainable agreements take relationship and identity issues into account.

Mediators also have different goals for mediation. Bush and Folger (1994) have detailed goals that range from getting agreement (problem solving) to transformation. Many mediators just want agreement—to settle the conflict. Others want to see clients undergo transformation—a change in how they see themselves and the other.

Transformation occurs when clients experience empowerment and give recognition. Clients are empowered when they more clearly realize their goals (empowerment of goals), become aware of a wider range of options (empowerment of options), increase their skills (empowerment of skills), gain new awareness of resources (empowerment of resources), and make conscious decisions about what they want to do (empowerment of decision making). As Bush and Folger note, "When these kinds of things occur within relationships, the party experiences a greater sense of self-worth, security, self-determination, and autonomy" (87). In a similar vein, one gives recognition by (a) having the desire to recognize the other, (b) thinking about giving recognition, (c) giving recognition in words, and (d) giving recognition in actions. When these things occur, "The party realizes and enacts his capacity to acknowledge, consider and be concerned about others" (91).

The problem-solving approach to mediation, Bush and Folger argue, is more aligned with an individualistic world view, in which we see ourselves as separate, concrete entities. On the other hand, the transformative view has as its underpinnings a relational view—that we are all interconnected and part of an organic whole. For an overview of these two world views and how they might affect one's mediation, see Bush and Folger (1994) and Wilmot (1995).

Mediation Process and Skills

Depending on the type of mediation being used, different skill sets are needed. The mediator needs to have an expansive set of skills to control the process of communication, affirm both parties, and move the parties toward creative content and relational solutions, all the while staying within legal and cultural parameters. Yarbrough and Wilmot (1995) specify the primary skills that are necessary at each stage of the mediation process. The mediator needs to have both "reflective" skills and "directive" skills.

The stages of mediation are as follows:

- Entry
- Diagnosis
- Negotiation
- Agreements
- Follow-up

When one follows these steps in mediation, key tasks are accomplished at each step. The mediator wants to do the following things at each stage:

Entry

1. Explain the process.
2. Clarify your role and establish your credibility.
3. Explore consequences of not proceeding.

Diagnosis

1. Gather data with interviews and observations.
2. Look at the conflict elements:
    - topic
    - relational
    - identity/face-saving
    - procedure
3. *Not* rush to solutions.

Negotiation

1. Create a safe setting.
2. Establish common ground.
3. Set an agenda.
4. Balance power/enforce equal talk time.

Agreements

1. Generate different ways to meet interests.
2. Specify who, what, when, where, and how.
3. Agree on the form of the agreement—oral, written, legal.

Follow-up

1. Decide on exact follow-up procedure.
2. Notify other stakeholders of actions.
3. Reach agreement for how to deal with future disputes.
4. Embed the agreement within the system. (Yarbrough and Wilmot 1995)

The key to effective mediation is the level of competence of the mediator. It is imperative, if you are to be a mediator or other type of third-party intervener, that you (1) receive extensive training in the necessary skills, (2) have the opportunity to try those skills with co-mediators or mentors, (3) be supervised by experienced mediators, and (4) continue your skill training and exposure to the literature on mediation.

One cannot learn mediation skills solely from a book—they have to be practiced and critiqued. You should continually question all of your assumptions about what mediation is and what it can accomplish. The following section on cultural assumptions about mediation illustrates some of the ideas being gathered from other cultures.

A study of how other cultures use third parties to manage disputes highlights the automatic assumptions derived from one's own culture. Much can be learned from forms used in other cultures. For instance, look at the steps for resolving conflict in a Hawaiian context, based on ancient Polynesian culture (Miura 1999). *Ho'oponopono* consists of

1. Gathering of the disputants by a high-status family or community member who knows the parties.
2. Opening prayer to the gods (or God).
3. A statement of the problem to be solved or prevented from growing worse.
4. Questioning of involved participants by the leader.
5. Replies to the leader and a discussion channeled through the leader.
6. Periods of silence.
7. Honest confession to the gods (or God) and to each of the disputants.
8. Immediate restitution or arrangements to make restitution as soon as possible.
9. "Setting to right" of each successive problem that becomes apparent as Ho'oponopono proceeds (repeating the preceding steps if necessary).

10. Mutual forgiveness of the other and releasing him or her from guilt, grudges, and tensions for the wrongdoing.

11. Closing prayer.

12. A meal or snack. (Wall and Callister 1995)

In different cultures, the forms of intervention, the selection of the third party, and the methods used by the third party to move the parties to resolution vary dramatically. In most Asian approaches to third-party involvement, for example, face saving and relationship building play a more predominant role than in Western approaches. Social harmony is paramount, rather than the disputants' "getting what they want" (Wall 1993). The disputants might not initiate the intervention; rather, a family or community member might ask the third party to intervene (Ma 1992).

Ury (1995) studied the Kalahari Bushmen, who follow a sequence for solving conflicts that taps the "third force"—the power of the community. The disputants actually meet in front of others and work the conflict through with the participation of others.

In every serious dispute between two individuals or groups, then, there is a third party at work. The third party is usually not a single individual but a collective of third parties: a third force of concerned relatives, friends, and elders. These third parties are typically "insider third parties" with strong ties to either one or both sides. There can be no private disputes of any seriousness because a dispute affects everyone.

The role of spirit or religion in resolving disputes is also recognized in other societies. In Malay society, for example, the spiritual elements play a prominent role, and the mediator spends informal time with the disputants in all kinds of contexts—attending family gatherings and weddings, for example. Native American cultures that keep their spiritual traditions alive continue to use spiritual force to resolve conflicts. Umbreit (1995) provides a comprehensive overview of some of these approaches and says this about Native American traditions of dispute resolution:

> A model of mediation that is culturally sensitive to Native Americans and aboriginal people in Canada would be quite different from the dominant Western models. Such a model is likely to include consensus decision making; preference for co-mediation; separate premediation sessions with each person; involvement of elders in the mediation; presence of chosen family members; circular seating; silence as comfortable; interruptions as inappropriate; nonlinear agenda; and the use of cultural metaphors and symbols. From this culture perspective, mediation occurs within a large cultural context. (37)

Just as we cannot import other cultural forms into mainstream Western culture without modification, neither can we export Western modes directly into other cultural situations. Similarly, when there are subcultures within Western society, one needs to adapt dispute resolution mechanisms to address their special situations. As Buitrago (1997) says, "with Hispanics the issue of trust is as essential for a positive outcome as for any conflictive party, but can be harder to obtain due to variables like discrimination and powerlessness" (16). Many community mediation centers solicit volunteers who are from unique groups as a way to bridge the gap between traditional mediation techniques and the special needs of subcultures.

Umbreit (1995) provides a step-by-step look at some of the central differences between mediation in modern cultures and mediation in traditional cultures. For example, in a modern culture, mediation might end with a written and signed agreement, whereas in a traditional culture, mediation often ends with participants giving their personal word.

Dispute Systems Design

The pioneering work of Ury, Brett, and Goldberg (1988) revealed the need to analyze the entire system to decide how best to match dispute resolution to the specific needs of the involved parties. For example, third-party involvement is best used after the parties have had a chance to work out their problem themselves. For example, a typical sequence of a dispute between two employees would be

- Direct discussion with each other.
- Involvement of their immediate supervisor.
- Involvement of a neutral third party, such as human resource personnel.
- Filing a grievance.
- Going to court (possibly).

Such a sequence allows the participants to solve their conflict themselves, and, if they are unsuccessful at an early step, to move the dispute slowly to where they have less control over the outcome—grievance and then court. Furthermore, these steps can be expanded (for an excellent example in health care, see Slaikeu 1989, 399).

Ury and others suggest these principles for designing dispute systems:

1. *Focus on interests.* Examine the driving interests behind disputes rather than letting the parties rush into positional statements. As was noted in the goals and interests, and negotiation chapters, once the driving interests are uncovered, the management of the dispute proceeds rapidly.

2. *Build in "loop-back" procedures that encourage disputants to return to negotiation.* Provide cooling-off periods when participants get locked into power or rights struggles. Or make sure the parties meet with each other before strong tactics, such as strikes, are used.

3. *Provide low-cost rights and power backup procedures.* This means that when people are stuck in an unbalanced power situation, they have somewhere to go. Not everyone who mediates is at an even table, as we have seen. Provide arbitration or other mechanisms to settle issues rather than having parties go to adjudication.

   Use combinations of mediation and arbitration (med-arb), or use "final offer arbitration" in which you "threaten" to choose between the parties' positions, which usually results in the parties' moving closer together so that they won't "lose" the decision.

4. *Build in consultation before, feedback after.* Work to notify parties, keep parties in communication with each other, and provide post-dispute analysis and feedback. For example, company employees and union members might establish common interest forums after a dispute to refocus on what they have in common with each other.

5. *Arrange procedures in a low-to-high-cost sequence.* Work to establish settlement at the lowest possible cost. For example, try to catch the dispute early by resolving

it through negotiation, bring in upper-level executives in labor-management disputes, if necessary; and move on to more extensive mechanisms later.

6. *Provide the motivation, skills, and resources necessary to make the procedures work.* Provide training for participants so that the mechanisms of intervention can be successful. The entire system must support proactive conflict resolution so that when disputes arise, parties are supportive of settlement efforts (Ury, Brett, and Goldberg 1988).

One can adapt these same principles to all types of interpersonal conflicts in dormitories, families, and the workplace. The key is to think ahead about what type of dispute design will best serve the participants and manage the conflict with a minimum of time, expense, and public posturing.

Application 9.2   Friends' Dispute Mechanism

Four friends (two couples) bought land together where they were going to live in two separate houses on the land. When they began discussing the purchase, they realized that some disputes might arise. They decided up front how to split costs, how to use the land, and agreements on visitors. To further protect their relationship and investment, they reached an agreement that

- When a dispute arises, they will sit down and talk directly with the other couple and try to resolve it.

- If they are unable to work it out, they will call in a mediator agreeable to all to work the dispute through.

- If mediation is not successful, then they will seek an outside arbitrator.

- If arbitration does not work, and only as a last resort, will anyone be allowed to file a lawsuit.

They all signed the agreement, making it legally binding. They put into motion a legally binding set of mechanisms to both resolve disputes and preserve their good relationship. Because they had been proactive, over the next two years they only had two situations that arose—and they informally resolved both. If something were to "blow up," they are ready with a productive dispute mechanism.

The design of dispute systems should be appropriate to the parties, their relationship, and their goals. Some research is now emerging that will guide this process more closely. For example, Harrison and Morrill (2004) focused on the role of the ombudsman in campus disputes. They found that ombudsmen would sometimes settle cases without having a specific student in the room, as when there were issues with the professor's syllabus. Designing a dispute mechanism for such one-time relationships that many students have with professors would bypass reconciliation as a goal and focus more heavily on topic or content features. As Harrison and Morrill (2004) note, community-style mediation that factors in reconciliation is much more appropriate in a close-knit community than for typical academic disputes.

Dispute resolution mechanisms are like a menu, with the customer selecting the right item given the circumstances (Ertel 1991). Dispute processes for the same type of behavior, for example, would be different in diverse contexts. Bullying behavior on an elementary school ground would demand a different process than bullying in the board-room (Ballard 2004). Each setting demands a type of dispute design appropriate for the parties (Lande 2004).

Education in conflict is beginning to take hold nationwide (Jones 2004). The hope is that as our citizenry becomes more informed, we will work to engage processes such as the third-party interventions discussed here, for the benefit of disputing parties and people connected to them.

❧Summary

This chapter gives an overview of resolution for-mats that may be helpful in resolving conflict, ranging from informal to formal modes.

The purpose of intervening in conflict is to transform the conflict elements, thereby allowing for effective management. You can intervene infor-mally especially when you are aware of the pitfalls. Formal intervention modes differ according to how much the original conflict parties determine the outcome. In both adjudication and arbitration, an outsider (judge, jury, or arbitrator) decides the out-come of the dispute. Mediation, on the other hand, involves the participants in the management of their own struggle. The mediator facilitates communication and helps the parties reach an agreement that will work for both of them. Vari-ous settings for mediation exist, ranging from fam-ily disputes to business concerns all the way to international conflicts. For instance, school medi-ation programs are useful throughout all levels of schools.

Although some mediators want only agree-ment, others strive for transformation of the con-flict parties. Regardless of the desired outcome, however, mediation processes and skills vary depending on the particular stage of mediation, beginning with softer skills such as listening and ending with setting rules so the parties can keep their agreements. There are profound differences in third-party intervention across cultures; Eastern cultures, for example, often use extended networks of people to help parties keep agreements, whereas Western cultures generally do not. Helpers can focus attention on the proactive design of dispute systems to handle conflicts as they arise.

❧Key Terms

Use the text's Online Learning Center at **www.mhhe.com/wilmot7** to further your understanding of the following terminology.

informal intervention 271

formal intervention 271

siding 273

alternative dispute resolution procedures 276

adjudication 277

guardian ad litem 278

binding arbitration 280

nonbinding arbitration 280

peer mediation 285

family mediation 286

victim-offender restitution (VOR) 288

Review Questions

Go to the self-quizzes on the Online Learning Center at **www.mhhe.com/wilmot7**
to test your knowledge of the chapter concepts.

1. Explain the statement, "The goal of all intervention is to transform the conflict elements." Choose an example to illustrate the idea.

2. What are the effects of siding with one of the conflict parties?

3. What are cautions to remember when you are considering being a third-party helper?

4. What is the role of counseling as informal intervention?

5. What are the interpersonal advantages and disadvantages of adjudication?

6. What are the interpersonal advantages and disadvantages of arbitration?

7. Explain how negotiation functions in all the forms of third-party intervention discussed in chapter 9.

8. Explain how the mediator controls the process but not the outcome of a conflict.

9. What are the advantages and limitations of mediation?

10. What are the basic tasks of mediation according to "stages of mediation"?

11. What are some differences between Western and traditional cultural expectations and procedures of mediation?

12. What are some principles of dispute system design?

Chapter 10

Mending the Broken Branch: Forgiveness and Reconciliation

by Gary W. Hawk, University of Montana

He has ruined my past. I'm beginning to toy with the idea of forgiveness so that I don't allow him to destroy my future as well.
—Lynn Shriner (Zehr 2001)

❧Forgiveness and Reconciliation in the Context of Interpersonal Conflict

Sometimes our best efforts to prevent conflict or engage in it constructively fail and we are left feeling betrayed, deceived, embittered, or isolated. Despite efforts to learn rather than defend, to tell and hear the truth about a situation, to refrain from retaliation or move empathically toward another person, the bonds of relationship suffer injury or break apart. A marriage once warmed by romance and shared history grows cold or shatters into pieces. An employee's legitimate needs or contributions do not receive the respect they deserve in the workplace. People who live next to each other may become caught up in cycles of increasingly destructive conflict. Rather than reverse the spiral, they begin to avoid one another, accuse one another of failing to honor agreements, or resort to courts of law in an attempt to solve a common problem. Bonds of friendship may weaken from neglect or indifference. A person's addictive behavior can cause emotional distress and financial loss for friends and family members to such an extent that they become lost to one another.

In an effort to find comfort or make sense of things, we sometimes tell ourselves stories about another person. One story can link up with another until a trajectory takes shape that seems impossible to bend in a more positive direction. Sometimes we do things to other people that seem to violate all that we value and believe. In the process we become incomprehensible to ourselves. Sometimes people do things to us that leave us feeling victimized. An assault or theft, for example, may forever change our view of the world and our place in it. In the aftermath of the things that people do to us, then we may wonder about forgiveness.

While forgiveness is not necessarily the last thing we try in a relationship, it often *follows* an effort, more or less determined, to alter the terms of a relationship that has become the source of disappointment, hurt, frustration, or harm (Stone, Patton, and Heen 1999, 140). All the preceding chapters of this book have been devoted to conflict *before* this stage. We have sought to define conflict and help you understand different attitudes toward and metaphors for conflict. We have explored in depth the patterns of communication that contribute to destructive conflict or reverse the spiral and direct it toward mutual understanding and collaboration. We have offered tools for assessing conflict, negotiating our way through it, or seeking third-party assistance in processing it. In this chapter we seek to cross the threshold of all our best efforts to understand, process, or resolve conflict. Here we will define forgiveness and reconciliation, recognizing the growing body of literature on this topic. We will note common conceptions and misconceptions about forgiveness. We will explore both the internal process of forgiveness and the way forgiveness can be aided by communication interaction with the other person. We will describe various forms of communication, explicit and implicit, that aid the process. We'll explore the complex role of apology in the movement toward forgiveness, adding necessary words of caution. We also will offer words of hope, calling attention to both some exceptional individuals and key principles that inform and enhance the process of repairing relational wounds. Along the way we'll offer insights from the counselor's office, human history, film, and literature where the story of human conflict and efforts to repair the hurt we cause one another find creative means of expression. Some of these insights, perspectives, and examples flow from the writer's teaching of forgiveness and reconciliation at The Davidson Honors College, University of Montana, and a practice in pastoral counseling.

☙Some Definitions

What is forgiveness? Because of its complexity, forgiveness is defined many ways. These definitions represent some of the possibilities. In a conversation with Robert J. Lifton, journalist Bill Moyers quoted William Faulkner as saying that *Forgiveness is giving up the idea of a better past.*" In a volume that reveals how much attention has been given in recent years to the study of forgiveness, Thoresen, Harris, and Luskin say, "Interpersonal forgiveness can be seen as the decision to reduce negative thoughts, affect, and behavior, such as blame and anger, toward an offender or hurtful situation, and to begin to gain better understanding of the offense and the offender" (McCullough, Pargament, and Thoresen 2000). Emphasizing the emotional dimension of forgiveness, Kornfield (2001) says, "Forgiveness is the heart's capacity to release its grasp on the pains of the past and free itself to go on" (236). Sensing how the emotional, cognitive, and behavioral dimensions overlap, Morton Deutsch defines forgiveness as "giving up rage, the desire for vengeance, and a grudge toward those who have inflicted grievous harm on you, your loved ones, or groups with whom you identify. It also implies willingness to accept the other into one's moral community so that he or she is entitled to care and justice" (Deutsch and Coleman 2000, 58).

After studying clinicians who favored forgiveness as a therapeutic strategy, Martin and Denton (1998) concluded that forgiveness is "an inner process, central to psychotherapy, where the injured person without request of the other releases those negative feelings and no longer seeks to hurt, and this process has psychological and emotional benefits" (285).

☙What's to Forgive?

People harm one another not just by what they do to each other but also by what they say and don't say. Relational harm occurs across a wide spectrum from regrettable and hurtful messages to psychological and physical violence. While this array is an entire field of study in itself,[1] a brief review of the elements within it helps us to see very quickly some of the relational transgressions that pose the question of forgiveness.

In a study of "messages that hurt," Vangelisiti (1994) describes a variety of "speech acts" that may cause harm. These messages include such things as

- *Accusations:* "You're a liar."
- *Evaluations or judgments:* "I knew you weren't up to the task."
- *Orders or commands:* "Get that done now!"
- *Advice:* "I strongly suggest that you get a job before the Christmas break."
- A *statement of preference:* "I wish you were more like your brother."
- A *disclosure of information:* "We've decided your job is not needed with the company."
- A *question disguised as a statement:* "When are you going to quit feeling sorry for yourself?"
- A *threat:* "If I ever see you with her again . . ."
- A *lie:* "I told you I'd quit drinking."

Metts (1994) adds to this list such things as

- *Blunders:* "How's your wife?" (not knowing that the person is divorced)
- *Direct attacks:* "Get out of my face, you mfer."
- *Group reference:* "Well, what did you expect from a <u>white guy</u>?"

These various hurtful and regrettable messages may offend cherished values, contaminate the relational climate, make it difficult to maintain closeness, and, in some cases, become grounds for ending the relationship altogether.

Going beyond an analysis of specific hurtful messages, Stewart, Zediker, and Logan (2002, 415ff) describe the damaging effects of deception, betrayal, and aggression. When someone deceives or betrays us, these relational transgressions can erode and jeopardize our sense of identity or well-being, not to mention the relationship. In addition, Cissna and Sieburg (Stewart 2002, 431ff) contend that "that disconfirmation" is a particularly damaging form of interpersonal behavior. A person is being disconfirmed when she feels invisible to another, unrecognized, unacknowledged, or without endorsement. When we are being disconfirmed it seems as though we do not exist in the eyes of someone else. Disconfirmation is a form of psychological abuse with potentially long-term consequences that may actually be more harmful than direct criticism or verbal attack.

Sitting at the far end of the spectrum, but *not* necessarily more damaging than these communicative ways of harming each other, is physical violence that we discussed earlier. It seems important, at the very least, to acknowledge that physical violence includes the neglect, and abuse, of children. In the relationship between

---

[1] For a more complete treatment of different types of transgressions, see Metts 1994; Roloff and Cloven 1994; and Wilmot 1995.

adult men and women, we must recognize the prevalence of domestic violence. This expression of the harm we cause one another often follows verbal aggression. While the abuse of men does occur, men are more likely than women to engage in physical violence when faced with noncompliant behavior, challenges to their behavior, or questions about their authority. As the tragedy of domestic violence becomes less concealed, we learn that 40 percent of the women killed each year will be killed by a spouse or lover. For an excellent summary of these and related findings, see Lulofs and Cahn (2000, 324–325).

Whether harm comes to a relationship as the result of something as seemingly minor as a slight or blunder or as major as exclusion on the basis of race, sexual harassment, or an outright assault, all of the ways that people mistreat each other become the backdrop for a discussion of forgiveness. In the classroom and the therapist's office we have learned not to rank or judge these relational transgressions but to recognize their impact. The things that people say and do to one another inevitably cause us to ask, "Does this person know who I am?" "Does this person know the harm s/he caused?" "How am I ever going to forgive this person?"

Application 10.1   Case: An Unplanned Pregnancy

After a relatively short-term but intense relationship, you and your partner become sexually active. Much to your surprise, despite various precautions on your part and assurances on his, you discover that you are pregnant. After feeling shock and disbelief, you immerse yourself in an intense period of reflection about your choices. You consider the impact of this pregnancy on your relationship, on your family, and on your plans for further education and a career. You reflect on your own values with respect to human life. Eventually you decide that your best option is to seek an abortion at the local family planning clinic. You contact your partner and discuss your decision with him. He recognizes that the decision is yours to make. At the time he seems extremely concerned and supportive. He offers to go with you to the clinic. You feel very grateful for his willingness to accompany you. You hope that he will be the only other person to know about this pregnancy and the decision to terminate it. It is hard to believe that your family would handle this situation with the compassion, support, and understanding you need. You call the clinic for an appointment and then call your partner to let him know when to meet you. He promises to see you at the appointed time. During the next few days you reflect on your decision, review your values, plans, and hopes. It is a very stressful time in your life. On the day of the procedure, you work your way through traffic to the clinic. In the parking lot you look for your partner's car but do not find it. You look for him at the entrance, but he is not there. You look around the waiting room for his familiar face, but he is not in the room. You wait until your name is called, hoping that your partner, though delayed, will appear. As you hear the nurse call

(continued)

Application 10.1   Case: An Unplanned
                                              Pregnancy

---

your name, you look around the room one more time and realize that your partner is not coming. When you return home after the abortion, you check your answering machine and see that no one has called while you were away.

- *After the abortion what do you do?* Do you contact your partner to let him know how you feel and about the impact of his absence? How will you respond if you hear a string of excuses and explanations? How will you respond if you hear an explanation that sounds legitimate (a car accident, a medical emergency, etc.)?

- *What would lead you to forgive him for his absence, his failure to communicate, and his failure to keep an agreement? What would cause you to withhold your forgiveness?*

- *Do you want to talk with him before deciding,* or have you decided that the failure to keep his promise in this situation is grounds for breaking off the relationship?

Some Misconceptions About Forgiveness

In their formative work at the University of Wisconsin, Enright and others help us to understand what forgiveness is by reminding us of what it is *not* (Enright, Gassin, and Wu 1992, 102):

- *Forgiveness does not dismiss or minimize an event or situation.* It acknowledges the truth about what happened and the consequences that followed. Forgiveness does not excuse or condone the behavior or actions of another. It does not say, "Oh well, he just couldn't help it."

- *Forgiveness is not indifferent about justice.* It might very well hold someone to account, seek restitution or a form of reparation while releasing the resentment that often accompanies a protracted conflict or violation.

In a collection of first-person essays from crime victims, Zehr (2001, 192) recognizes that pursuit of vindication or redress may actually be a relief from the humiliation and shame of having been victimized. Pursuing justice does not necessarily deny the possibility of forgiveness. Drawing a distinction between punitive or retributive justice and "restorative justice," Shriver (1995, 30–32) and others point out that retribution may exacerbate conflict, but "restorative justice" may help people through their victimization and make it possible for the offender to remain in or return to the community. In addition, forgiveness is not the same as a pardon, which refers to a legal transaction that releases someone from a penalty.

Forgiveness is *not* a sign of weakness. Choosing to forgive another person may plunge one into the deepest reflection about who one is and how that identity is sustained.

It requires us to consider who we are independent of what has been done to us. *Forgiveness requires an act of imagination* because it invites us to consider a future that is not merely a reaction to the past. Forgiveness requires movement, as in a long journey, and cannot possibly be for the faint of heart.

A misuse of forgiveness further obscures the process we hope to clarify. After a crime, a shooting at a school, for example, people other than the victim sometimes presume to offer forgiveness on behalf of the one who was harmed. This gift is often motivated by the best of intentions and may be an attempt to spare an individual, family, or community the suffering it cannot avoid. We take the view, however, that whatever the intentions behind offering forgiveness on behalf of someone else, this form of forgiveness may actually compound the original injury. It violates the moral agency of the person who has been harmed, and it minimizes or may even circum-vent the victim's struggle, choice, and freedom. This problem is at the heart of Simon Wiesenthal's book *The Sunflower*. Wiesenthal, a death camp prisoner during World War II, is summoned to the side of a dying S.S. soldier who confesses to heinous crimes against Jews. After listening to the soldier, Wiesenthal leaves him without the reassurance and absolution he craves. Later, Wiesenthal wonders if he has done the right thing by withholding forgiveness on behalf of his Jewish brothers and sisters. The consensus among the renowned people whom Wiesenthal summons to reflect on this problem is that forgiveness, for all its value, cannot be offered by one person on behalf of another (Wiesenthal 1998). Ellis Cose (2004, 49) also reflects on this prob-lem. While he upholds the consensus in *The Sunflower*, he adds that we may choose to offer forgiveness for the harm that the person caused *us*. In other words, we might say something like, "On my child's behalf I cannot forgive you for what you did to her; but I can forgive you for the pain you have caused me." The distinction he makes may seem small; but *we uphold the right of people to make a decision about forgiveness on their own behalf*.

Another distinction seems important. Although the two words are often used together, as in the subtitle of this chapter, or in a course name, forgiveness and rec-onciliation are *not* the same thing. In the context of interpersonal conflict, *forgive-ness* is a process undertaken by one person in relation to another, with or without interaction with that person. On the other hand, *reconciliation* is a process of reestab-lishing relationship, renewing trust, settling differences so that cooperation and a sense of harmony are restored. Reconciliation brings two parties together in a way that forgiveness may not. For this reason, in speaking of forgiveness and reconcilia-tion, we believe it is essential to emphasize that forgiveness does not necessarily reestablish relationship. Forgiveness neither obligates one to reconciliation nor necessitates it. As countless students have told us, "If I have to reconcile, I won't even consider forgiveness." Forgiveness, then, may benefit the one who violates the terms of a relationship, but first and foremost it is for the benefit of the person who has been harmed. Reconciliation, on the other hand, reflects the mutual interests of two parties and embodies a willingness to reengage in the relationship in the belief that further injury is less likely to occur and that the benefits of a new association outweigh the risks. Because it is difficult to buck the tide of popular usage in which the two words are linked in a casual fashion, we will continue to speak of "forgiveness and reconciliation," but only with the awareness that the two words do not mean the same thing.

❧When There Is an Imbalance of Power

This distinction between forgiveness and reconciliation is particularly crucial when there is a serious imbalance in power between two parties or between an individual and an institution. The authors of this book analyze the subject of power in Chapter 4 and pay particular attention to power imbalances in conflict situations. Conscience requires that we return briefly to the matter here. Given the frequency with which women are victimized and that they often fall under pressure to forgive, we want to acknowledge that some authors argue against forgiveness. In an article that stirred up considerable controversy in ecclesiastical circles, Lord (1991) described a situation in which a woman came to him asking if she should forgive the man who shot and killed her sons and nearly killed her as well. Later, and while in prison, the man made an appeal to this woman on the basis of his religious conversion and asked her to forgive him. After a period of study, Lord concluded that the woman was not obligated to forgive in this situation. Other authors reflecting on this kind of problem come to similar conclusions. Placing greater emphasis on righteous anger and remembrance—over forgiveness—may represent a steadfast commitment to the truth, hold people to moral account appropriately, and serve as a necessary protest against things that should not have occurred. McFall (1991, 156) says that bitterness can serve "as a necessary reminder that something hoped for and greatly valued has been lost."

In a similar vein Keene (1995) tells a story about a woman who was sexually abused as an adolescent by her Episcopal priest, a man who was clearly in a position of superior power. He describes the pressure to forgive that can be brought to bear on women in this situation. The church's teachings on forgiveness can be used against someone in the form of added pressure, as though a woman resisting forgiveness is guilty of moral failure. This pressure may be compounded when combined with the assertion that forgiveness is good for one's mental health and spiritual well-being.

Keene warns that pressure to forgive, especially when it is applied by those with more power, may serve to protect the hierarchical structures that made the abuse possible in the first place. Sometimes people in positions of greater authority or power expect those with less power to forgive because this release of another in the form of forgiveness *preserves* the imbalance of power. Necessary accountability and potential consequences for the actions of those in power can be evaded if the less powerful are pressured to forgive. Furthermore, pressure to forgive a person who retains a position of power may, in effect, ask an injured person to bear the additional suffering of remaining in contact with the abuser. The additional burden, on top of the original injury, may become unbearable. At the very least, it is an affront to justice. In such situations, proximity threatens the person who has already suffered harm. While we continue to hold the view that forgiveness is a choice and not an obligation, situations like those cited above make it extremely clear why forgiveness and reconciliation must not be easily blended. In situations like these, forgiveness, if chosen, should never obligate a person to reconcile. We will say much more about reconciliation later in the chapter.

Application 10.2

As a junior at a university where you major in Biology you take an elective class in Philosophy. You know this class will be a stretch but you need a break from "hard science" classes. With some anxiety you turn in your first paper on Plato. A week later your professor returns your paper. After looking through his critical comments, you see that he has given you a "D" for the paper. Because your scholarship depends on maintaining a certain grade point, and a "D" would hurt that average, you make arrangements to meet your professor during his office hour.

During your meeting he explains his critical remarks. Suddenly, though, you sense that the conversation has changed directions. He begins to ask more personal questions that leave you feeling uncomfortable. Eventually he seems to hint that he is willing to discuss your grade over a meal or movie together.

- Do you trust your instincts about the shift in the conversation?
- Do you pretend that you haven't heard what you think you heard?
- Do you ask him to clarify his expectations?
- Do you discuss this situation with friends or even the chair of the department?
- Or, are you clear enough about his boundary violation that you confront your professor on the spot and point out the transgression?
- What are your reasons for your decision?

The Matter of Memory

Just as the words forgiveness and reconciliation are often joined, people often say, "Forgive and forget." This is a particularly unfortunate conjunction. The relationship between memory and forgiveness is extremely complex and important. We will give an overview of the problem.

Memory is absolutely essential to the forgiveness process. People say "Forgive and forget" with the best of intentions, hoping to reduce a person's pain. But "Forgive and forget" seems like dangerous counsel to an abused woman who believed she was safe, only to discover upon returning to a relationship, that she has again been physically harmed. It is unwise advise to an employee who trusted his employer to communicate expectations in person only to find that the employer consistently exposes the employee in front of a group. To ask a child abused by a priest or other religious figure to forget what happened, for example, creates a **secondary wound** because it asks the child not to trust his own perceptions. If no one remembers what happened, if no one receives a person's story about a transgression, the person who was harmed may come to feel that his or her identity is in jeopardy. While it is true that we are not what happened to us, we almost certainly are what we make of what happened to us. People who have suffered some form of sexual abuse or violence, for example, often feel as though the recovery of memory after a period of suppression or repression seems like the first step in the recovery of self. There can be no deep healing without it. The denial of memory comes to feel like the denial of being and is a genuine threat to personhood. Memory denied or ignored is like an untreated infection. It festers and threatens the whole body. Using exactly this metaphor, Isabel Amaral-Gueterres, truth commissioner for East Timor says in relation to conflict within his country, "For some people, it may seem better to leave the past untouched. But the past does not go away and, if untreated, may eat away at those people and maybe even destroy them. Remembering is not easy, but forgetting may be impossible" (Cose, 2004, 182).

Archbishop Desmond Tutu makes much the same point throughout his book on South Africa's Truth and Reconciliation Commission (Tutu, 1999). In the case of South Africa, the commissioners felt so strongly about the value of historical memory that they were willing to trade criminal prosecution of apartheid's torturers and executioners in exchange for the truth about what happened. While it may have seemed a "devil's bargain" to offer partial amnesty in exchange for truth, Tutu asserted that "To be able to forgive one needs to know whom one is forgiving and why. That is why the truth is so central to this whole exercise" (Cose, 2004, 182).

Yet, the matter of memory in relation to forgiveness is complex. While forgiveness does not require the denial of memory, the recollection of past injuries can be used as the basis for perpetuating injury to others. All this becomes especially clear when one looks on the international stage. In the 1990s the battle of Kosovo in 1389 was used by Bosnian Serbs to justify the murder of Muslim Croats. The memory of European favoritism toward Tutsis in Rwanda provided the pretext for their murder by Hutus. The memory of the destruction of the World Trade Towers may have seemed to justify the mistreatment of prisoners at the Abu Ghraib prison in Iraq or at Guantanamo Bay, which became the basis for beheading U.S. citizens and allies by Islamists. As one can see, memories misused can become the basis for inflicting more harm. The challenge, then, is to learn to remember in what one author calls "a living way"—in a way that serves individuals, families, and societies in the future (Anonymous 1993, p. 24). To get over something in the hope of creating something new in our lives requires that we remember the harm we experienced without letting that memory create momentum that leads to revenge. **Memory is absolutely essential to the forgiveness process** because it is central to the identity of individuals, peoples, and nations and may reduce the susceptibility to repeated injury in the future.

Application 10.3	Bad Memories

Imagine that you are a junior at the university. In the fall of the year, you begin to suffer from insomnia. You lose your appetite. Your interest in sports, basketball in particular, seems to have waned. You begin to withdraw from friends and make excuses when they invite you to participate in social events.

After several weeks of deepening depression, you consult a doctor at the health center. In the course of the interview, you tell the doctor about persistent memories of an incident when you were about eight years old. As you recall, you were at home one day after school. Your mom was still at work. Three teenage boys, living in the neighborhood, came to your house. Initially, they expressed interest in seeing your remote-controlled car. After a while, however, they began to engage in coercive sexual play and forced you to participate. As you give an account of this violation, you realize that, as horrible as the original incident had been, in the present you are even more troubled by the way your

(continued)

Application 10.3   Bad Memories

mother reacted when you tried to tell her the story on the telephone. She expressed skepticism about your account and eventually denied that the incident happened.

You tell the doctor that you feel doubly betrayed, first by your mother's failure to protect you, and second, by her refusal to believe you. You attribute much of your current depression to the lasting trauma of this incident and to your mother's refusal to take your story seriously.

Planning to return home for Thanksgiving, you feel a lot of internal pressure to work through your anger and sense of betrayal. In the two weeks leading up to Thanksgiving, what do you do to try to help yourself? What do you do with the anger? How do you think you'll approach your mother? If you decide to approach your mother, hoping for a conversation, how will you begin?

Now that we have presented a few definitions for forgiveness and have discussed some misconceptions about it, we are ready to look more carefully at how it works.

❧Decision or Process?

Is forgiveness a decision or a process? In this chapter we hope to give you an appreciation for both sides of the question, knowing that it cannot be given a simple answer. In fact, the answer may be yes.

In cases involving marital infidelity, but influenced by the forgiveness that takes place by the bedside of dying patients, DiBlasio (2000) argues for a decision to let go of resentment and bitterness rather than waiting for a more or less lengthy process to unfold. He contends that "emotional readiness" is not necessarily a factor in the decision to forgive; forgiveness is more "an act of will," temporarily separating reason and feeling. Not wanting to bog clients down in a protracted emotional process, he says, "When clients discover that they need not be victims of their feelings but can decide to move forward despite the hurt, they become empowered" (151). DiBlasio then goes on to describe an intense and ambitious therapeutic session that may last two to three hours. It includes such things as

1. The therapist explains decision-based forgiveness to the client(s).
2. The therapist gives the client(s) an opportunity to establish the wrongful action that needs to be forgiven.
3. The "forgiveness treatment" is explained.
4. The offense(s) is stated.
5. The offender is given an opportunity to provide an explanation.
6. A question and answer period about the infidelity takes place.
7. The offended person responds, expressing feelings and explaining the impact.
8. The offender extends empathy for the hurt he or she caused.
9. The offender develops a plan to stop or prevent similar future behavior, giving the partner an opportunity to check up on commitment to this plan.

10. The offended party recognizes the offender's shame and/or regret.

11. Emphasis is placed on choice and commitment to letting go.

12. The offender makes a formal request for forgiveness.

13. A ceremonial act follows in which both parties recognize that a decision to forgive has taken place.

In a meta-analysis of this question about decision and process, Baskin and Enright (2004) explains that DiBlasio's proposal is one among several that emphasizes the centrality of a **decision to forgive.** In the context of psychotherapy a decision-based model may save time and serve to empower the client(s) trying to move toward forgiveness. Helping people *decide* to forgive gives them something to *do* at a time when they may feel helpless to change their situation.

Interestingly, outside of the therapy setting, people sometimes commit themselves to forgiving another person by a certain date. So, someone in the Christian tradition may decide to forgive someone in the weeks between Ash Wednesday and Easter or before receiving the sacrament of Holy Communion. Or someone in the Jewish tradition may decide to forgive by Yom Kippur. There may be analogous dates in other religious traditions that provide the impetus for a decision to forgive. Stories we hear about people deciding to forgive by a specific date, especially one sanctioned by a religious institution or spiritual tradition, require us to take this approach seriously.

❧Forgiveness as a Process

Other researchers in the field emphasize that forgiveness is part of a complex internal process, one that may not necessarily end in a decision to forgive. Perhaps Enright and the Human Development Study Group (1991) provide the most notable example of this model. They delineate 20 separate steps in four major categories: an *"Uncovering Phase,"* a *"Decision Phase,"* a *"Work Phase,"* and an *"Outcome Phase."*

Summarizing this process, in the "Uncovering Phase" we ask such things as, "What am I *feeling* about what happened and how am I defending myself against these feelings?" Here one may also explore feelings of shame, as though we were "stained" by the transgression.

In the "Decision Phase" we acknowledge how much emotional *energy* is tied up by the injury we suffered and how we seem to repeat its images and consequences endlessly. In this phase we begin to acknowledge the extent to which our lives and worldview have been changed or threatened by what happened.

In the "Work Phase" we explore our *choices* for the future and may consider forgiveness as an option, especially if we begin to feel some empathy for the person who caused the harm, considering the circumstances of the offender's life.

In the "Outcome Phase" we reflect on the *impact* of what happened and how we must reformulate a meaning for our lives in light of the harm we suffered. In this phase we are no longer quite so defended and begin to consider ways that we, too, may have caused harm to others. At the end of this process we embrace the possibility of joy and hope. For a list of the 20 steps in this process, translated into questions, please consult the Instructor's Manual.

Before comparing these two models, one that emphasizes a *decision* and the other that emphasizes a *process*, another description of **forgiveness as a process** follows. On the surface at least, it seems strikingly simple. Layton (1999) describes a **three-step model of forgiveness** that is particularly helpful because it is memorable. She uses her own divorce to explain how she entered a stage of

> *Injured innocence.* In this stage it feels as though everything we believe about life is suddenly in question, especially the idea that if we are good we will never have to suffer. A deep personal injury; an escalating, costly, and dangerous spiral of conflict; or a gross violation of trust threatens what we believe about the world and how to function in it. This is especially true for victims of crime. In the stage of injured innocence, we feel as if the ground on which we stand is unreliable and that we cannot move across its surface. In this stage we are likely to ask, "Am I no longer safe in the world?"
>
> *Obsession.* In this stage we replay things that were done to us, words that were spoken, all the details of our suffering. It is common in this stage to feel fully victimized. It feels as though our lives are defined by what we have suffered. In this stage we are likely to ask, "Will he/she ever be held accountable? Am I stuck picturing this situation forever?" While "obsession" may have a negative connotation for us, this stage of the process takes seriously the impact of what happened. In this stage one reality is trying to catch up with another—what we believe we deserved and what actually happened. The work of this stage cannot be rushed.
>
> *Transcendence.* No longer contending with the shock of realizing that the world is not as fair as we first believed, and no longer replaying every scene in the death of a marriage, or some other relationship, we come to believe, despite everything, that life will continue and that it may still be a "prize" worth having. In Layton's case, it was at this stage of her adjustment to the loss of her marriage that she began to give up her hatred, the desire for revenge, and her sense of being at the center of the world's unjust treatment of the innocent. She began to realize that the distinctions we make between perpetrator and victim are often drawn too sharply, that the hardness around each identity can soften in the balm of forgiveness, and that both sides need compassion. She began to realize that through our own suffering we become more deeply acquainted with the suffering of others. In time she learned to transcend what had happened to her and to join the rest of the human family. It was this movement from injured innocence and through the self-absorbed cycles of obsession that helped her get to the point where she could transcend her own pain. In this stage we are likely to wonder, "What will this experience mean to me in the future? How will I be able to integrate it into the whole picture of my life?"

This section began with the question, "Is forgiveness a decision or a process?" The two models, *decision* and *process,* help us to see that in every case a person is faced with a decision: will I forgive or not? The element of decision is actually present in both of the models. The variation is in the amount of emotional distress that is explored and experienced *before* making the decision. The models also may differ with respect to the amount of time devoted to this exploration. As with any attempt to delineate stages of change, as Kubler-Ross (1970) has done with the grieving process, these models can be misconstrued. People in the process of grieving need to be reassured that there is no right order to the sequence and that it is often necessary to cycle back through earlier stages. In much the same way, before a person reaches a decision to forgive, he may need to review an offense repeatedly, search a long time for reasons to be empathic toward the offender, or dismantle and reconstruct his view of the world numerous times. He may need to reject the notion that he is anything like the person who did him harm before coming back to the realization that we have things in common with those who hurt us. The struggle to forgive may be arrested at almost any point, be completed only partially, or come so easily that some stages seem unnecessary. Whether we decide to forgive and *then* have to work through the emotions later, or work through the emotions *before* deciding to forgive, forgiveness can be both a decision *and* a process.

Getting Stuck: Eddies in the River

We live in a valley where powerful rivers descend and converge on a long journey to the ocean. The landscape affects how we view things. One of our rivers drops through a gorge with major rapids with names like "Fang," "Tumbleweed," and "Cliffside." Wherever the river bends sharply or pushes up against a boulder, the current creates an eddy. People who descend this river often catch their breath in the **eddies.** This feature of our watershed has given us an image that has proven helpful in explaining forgiveness. If you live in an urban area, you might think instead of traffic jams. Listening to students, clients, and other people, we find that people sometimes get stuck in an *eddy of long-term, low-grade, simmering resentment* (see figure 10.1). In this eddy a person may circle round and round looking for an opportunity to get even. Here we may concentrate on the other person's offense, how that person has fared since doing us harm, and how they are in our debt, a debt they will never be able to pay. The impulse to get even may or may not be contained.

If we do not get caught in this eddy of *resentment and revenge,* we may get caught in an eddy of *depression and withdrawal.* In this eddy the hurt we have suffered seems so great that it seems better to withdraw from life because it poses too many challenges. In this eddy a person attempts to create a small and safe world out of the current. As a collective example of this phenomenon, Enright discovered that nearly half of a group of over 200 seven-year-olds in Northern Ireland were clinically depressed as a result of "the troubles."

Figure 10.1   Eddies in the River

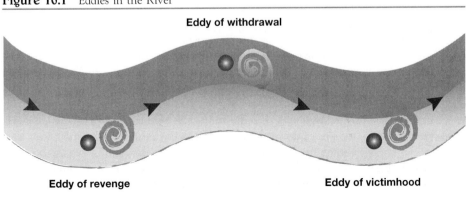

Eddy of withdrawal

Eddy of revenge   Eddy of victimhood

Around the next bend someone may become caught in the eddy of *being a victim*. In this whirlpool a person may ascribe special status to having been victimized. In this eddy people become what happened to them, and may use their story to elicit sympathy from others, demand extra attention, induce guilt in others, or excuse their own passivity (Exline and Baumeister 2000).

When we see a friend or family member in an eddy, we may grow impatient and be tempted to *push* that person back out into the current. Having observed this process carefully in many situations, we believe that it is best to be patient, to see the eddies as resting places, to have a keen sense of timing, and to watch for a person's own motivation to return to the flow of life. This observation may be helpful to you as a friend, family member, or third-party agent. A friend who has expertise in the world of river-running tells us that in certain rapids, it may be necessary to take off one's life-jacket, temporarily at least, so as to descend deeper into the current and be carried back into the river. This image seems particularly helpful when we encounter people who seem to take a very long time to forgive. Even the first step in the process (recognizing one's defenses against the pain of what happened) can seem like an overwhelming task. Sometimes people need to use dissociation, denial, or anger, for example, to protect themselves for a while before reengaging with life after a major violation or betrayal.

The Personal and Interpersonal Dimensions of Forgiveness

Reflecting on the models developed by Enright, applied by Palmer, or distilled by Layton, the reader might conclude that forgiveness is something we work toward by ourselves and without interaction with the person who caused us harm. In some cases, after a violent incident, for example, or because of a person's extreme defensiveness, unwillingness, or inability to accept responsibility, interaction with such a person can seem unsafe, unwise, or undesirable, but this does not foreclose the possibility of forgiveness; it means that forgiveness takes place internally. In a closely argued article from a philosophical point of view, Holmgren (1993) describes the value of this approach. Internal or "intrapersonal" forgiveness is not dependent upon the responsiveness, contrition, attitudes, or apologies of the person who caused the harm. This kind of forgiveness is "unilateral" in that it focuses strictly on the beliefs, feelings, attitudes, decisions, and behavior of the victim (345). The value of this approach is that it recognizes that our autonomy may be compromised by any of the things people do and say to each other that cause harm. Seeing forgiveness as an internal process helps a person recover that lost sense of autonomy. We may proceed without waiting on subsequent action, communication, or acknowledgment from the person who caused the injury. We cease to be the prisoner of someone else's actions. We reclaim ourselves as the active center of our own choices.

At the same time we must recognize that all of us belong to networks of relationships from which we are not easily removed. We often encounter, work across from, eat, or share children or parents with people who have caused us harm or whom we have harmed. The fact of our interrelatedness requires that we pay attention to the *interpersonal* dimension of forgiveness.

❧Laying the Groundwork for Forgiveness or Reconciliation

In a comprehensive article that explores the role of communication between aggrieved parties, and that corroborates the research of others, Kelley (1998) points out that people who have been harmed by others are more willing to renegotiate a relationship when they know the following three things: (1) that there is *essential agreement as to the nature of the violation,* (2) *that the other person acknowledges the hurt and pain that the violation caused,* and (3) *that the offending person will make an apology for the hurt and pain that the violation caused.* These three elements sound something like "I am so sorry that I failed to return your car in the condition it was in when you loaned it to me. I did not realize how important this is to you and I see now that my carelessness really upset you. I am willing to do everything necessary to set things right."

Confirming the work of McCullough, Worthington, and Rachal (1997), Kelley also found a correlation between a person's apology and the extension of empathy toward the offending partner. This empathic response to a sincere apology sounds something like, "Now that I understand how badly you feel about hurting me, I am willing to forgive you." When an offender makes a direct explanation of the offense, acknowledges responsibility, requests forgiveness, shows remorse, and apologizes, this form of communication is likely in 76 percent of the cases studied to influence the decision to forgive. The influence of this strategy is so significant that Kelley (1998) concludes that we need "to conceptualize forgiveness as a dynamic interpersonal process" (267). Reflecting on this same process, Exline and Baumeister (2000) say that these actions "may intercept a downward spiral started by the transgression . . ." (136).

People renegotiate a relationship after an offense and work toward forgiveness in both implicit and explicit forms of communication (Worthington and Drinkard 2000). Sharing this perspective, Exline and Baumeister (2000) say, "In implicit forgiveness, one's statements or behaviors communicate either that no transgression was committed . . . or that the transgression was so minor as to be of no consequence" (136). In effect a person is able to interact with the person who caused the harm without reference to the injury, transcending it indirectly.

Just because an apology is rendered doesn't mean one is able to receive it, as in the following case.

Application 10.4   Not Ready for an Apology

You work with one other member of a team that does graphic design for an advertising firm. You and your partner have agreed to come up with a proposal for an ad campaign on behalf of a company that makes sunglasses. Though your partner seems as excited as you about working on this project, every time you propose time to work on it you hear excuses that cause delay. The Sunday before you are due to present your proposal you work all day and into the night, having turned down invitations from friends to do something outside the office.

(continued)

Application 10.4   Not Ready for an Apology

Monday morning you go into the meeting feeling tired and only half-prepared. Your partner shows up silent and chagrined. Without exposing your partner's lack of help, and making no apologies for a proposal you did your best to complete, you show your ideas to the boss. She seems particularly unimpressed. At the end of the process she comes down pretty hard on you as though this proposal was your responsibility alone. When the meeting is over you get outside the door and your partner catches your eye and says, "Hey, I'm really sorry about not contributing to the presentation." You are in no mood to hear this.

- Do you accept this apology quickly, passing over your feelings, so that you can move on to something else?

- Do you let your partner catch the full force of your frustration, never mind the consequences for your future relationship?

- Or, do you say something like, "Thanks for the apology, but you've got to know that I'm really frustrated that I caught all the criticism and you didn't even help me with the proposal. I've got to cool off. I can't talk about this right now. After I work through some of my feelings we will talk. I don't ever want to be in this situation again."

❧Gestures

We are particularly intrigued by communicative *gestures*, not necessarily verbal, that indicate that the process of forgiveness is underway or may have been completed in an implicit way. For example, one person in a romantic relationship may kiss another as a sign that an earlier conflict or disappointment has been transcended. We may visit someone who caused us harm, attend their musical performance, graduation, wedding, or thesis defense. In these instances the willingness to be physically present becomes a sign that a wound is beginning to mend. A willingness to collaborate in a work setting after a time of estrangement may be a sign of forgiveness. Two colleagues may agree to work again on a joint project without first verbally processing an old conflict. One neighbor might bring a meal to another as a sign that a boundary line dispute has been resolved satisfactorily, the offer of food being an ancient gesture that helps to mend a relationship. Very often a touch signals the shift away from resentment, putting a hand on someone's shoulder, for example. Historically speaking, a handshake is such a gesture. It signals that the open hand does not contain a weapon. A small gift is a highly communicative act—presenting a vase of flowers, offering a glass of water, sending a humorous cartoon or sketch, offering a ticket to a concert or sporting event—any of these gestures may communicate at least as effectively as words that something has been released and that the door is open. Also, it may be the case that one gesture begets another, setting in motion a positive, even "generative spiral" that replaces longstanding resentment.

To summarize this section, we believe that forgiveness may come about as a result of an intensely private process or it may come about in interpersonal communication. Forgiveness may be influenced by verbal communication, such as an expression of remorse. Or a wide range of communicative and creative gestures may be the means by which people request or convey forgiveness. In one relationship, the process may start in the solitude of one's memories. In another relationship, the decision to forgive may be facilitated by an apology. Both the private and interactive dimensions of this process influence each other. The internal work of forgiveness may eventually make someone more receptive to an apology if it is offered, accelerating the process of repair. Likewise, the internal process that helps a person forgive may change the conditions in a relationship so that it is more likely that an apology is offered, again accelerating the repair and mending the broken branch.

In this review of the "intrapersonal" and "interpersonal" forms and expressions of forgiveness, we came close to talking about reconciliation, especially when describing gestures. Before exploring reconciliation more completely, however, it seems wise to say more about apology and express some words of caution.

The Value and Limits of Apology

Application 10.5   A Case of a Medical Tragedy

In January you get a call from your brother-in-law. He says that your sister has a Stage Four cancer in her brain and lungs. You immediately make arrangements to spend time with her. Over the next several weeks, you help her in every way possible. You take her to medical appointments, arrange for neighbors and friends to bring meals, help her evaluate her treatment options, simplify her closet and kitchen, take her for a drive through the countryside. Given the assurances of her oncologist, your sister and her husband decide that chemotherapy is the best option for extending her life. Your sister is rushed through the ordeal of this treatment on a Friday afternoon. Within days of receiving the chemotherapy, your sister is semi-conscious and confined to bed. This response to treatment is drastically different than what you were led to expect. Ten days later your sister is dead. During the final stages of your sister's dying process, a supportive friend of the family, who also happens to be a nurse, spends time with you. After your sister's death she says, "You know, I think the chemo killed her." Her words correspond exactly to what you have been telling yourself. You decide to learn more about what happened. In the course of your investigation, you and your brother-in-law discover that some of the records related to your sister's treatment seem not quite right. Strangely, the *amount* of medicine administered on the day of treatment has been obscured. Using your copy of these records, you decide to confront the oncologist.

With other students, develop a role-play in which two people play the surviving sister and brother-in-law and another person plays the oncologist. If you are the sister and brother-in-law, how do you approach the doctor? How do you respond to what you hear? What do you need or want from her? If you are the oncologist, how do you prepare for this conversation? Develop both a defensive, self-protective strategy and one in which you may be willing to acknowledge some contribution to this outcome and issue an apology.

In the previous section of this chapter, we saw evidence that apology is a very effective tool in softening the position of someone who has been harmed. When apology is accompanied by acknowledgment of responsibility, awareness of the harm that has resulted from our actions, and expressed feelings of regret, remorse, or penitence, its effectiveness increases. Nevertheless, we live in an age when it has become common, if not fashionable, to apologize. In France the Catholic Church apologizes for complicity with the Nazis in the extermination of the Jews. In America and Canada, apologies have been offered for the treatment of native children held in boarding schools. New Zealanders apologize to indigenous populations for introducing disease, as in the case of Western Samoa. In 1980, the United States apologized to Japanese-American citizens forced into prison camps during World War II. Former President Bill Clinton apologized for "the Tuskegee Study of Untreated Syphilis in the Negro Male." Secretary of Defense Donald Rumsfeld seemed to take responsibility for the treatment of Iraqi prisoners at Abu Ghraib.

The problem is that not all apologies are created equal. Apologies can create the illusion that something profound has happened or will soon be set right. Apologies can be another form of manipulation, put an aggrieved person under extraordinary pressure to respond graciously, or serve as a means of self-protection. There are three forms of apology that cause us particular concern:

- *Compelled or insincere apology.* A compelled apology is empty because it is offered without an adequate understanding of the full effect of one's actions. A compelled apology may be as commonplace as a parent saying to a child, "Say you're sorry." Or a compelled apology may seem as necessary as the one called for in the aftermath of former President Reagan's visit to the Kolmeshohe cemetery in Bitburg, Germany, where 49 S.S. soldiers were buried (Shriver 1995, 93–100). Compelled apologies only seem to cover a wound that remains highly infected. They do little to open the door on forgiveness or incline people to reconciliation.

- *Expedient apology.* An expedient apology, often arranged in private, merely benefits the one who offers the apology and provides little or no benefit for the person who was harmed. A person offering an expedient apology says something like, "To avoid more controversy over this, let's issue an apology so we can move on." Clearly, the goal is to avoid rather than engage, to escape the consequences of one's actions rather than learn more about the actual harm caused by one's actions. Recently, physicians in Michigan have been encouraged to apologize for medical mistakes. Insurance companies have discovered that malpractice suits have dropped significantly in situations where physicians offer a sincere apology (Merriam 2004). Reporting on similar stories, a Chicago Public Radio program on apology also indicated that patients and families are extremely astute at discerning whether an apology is genuine or designed merely to placate (Glass 2004).

- *Delayed apology.* In a delayed apology, someone far removed from the wrongdoing accepts responsibility for the harm and offers an apology on behalf of people no longer present. Someone issues a delayed apology when they say something like, "I know that a lot of water has gone under the bridge and the person who did this harm is long gone, but . . ." Sometimes a delayed apology may be helpful, as when Australians proclaim "Sorry Day" and apologize to aboriginal peoples for removing their children from their families. But the value of this kind of apology must be determined by the person or people who suffered the harm, not by the person offering the apology.

Our concerns about the potential harm that an apology can cause, especially when it is *compelled*, *expedient*, or *delayed*, led us to develop a set of questions that we invite people to ask when receiving or offering an apology.

When Receiving an Apology, Ask:

1. Who is served by this apology?
2. Can I trust that change in behavior will follow this apology?
3. Does the apology seem sincere, genuine, or authentic? Is it accompanied by acceptance of responsibility for the wrongdoing?
4. Was the apology followed by a justification or excuse for the action that harmed me?
5. What is the purpose of this apology? (repair of the relationship, preparation for another harmful act, an attempt to disarm or equalize power?)
6. Is the apology accompanied by pressure to forgive the person who caused the harm, thus transforming a choice into an obligation?
7. Does the apology precede confrontation or follow it? In other words, how well does the person understand the harm he/she caused?

When Offering an Apology, Ask:

1. Do I really understand what hurt or offended the other person?
2. Am I conscious of what I did?
3. Do I intend to change so that the injury or transgression won't be repeated? Am I prepared to make some kind of restitution if that is requested?
4. Do I mean what I say?
5. Is the apology for me, the other person, or the relationship?
6. Can I apologize without also adding justification for my actions?

It may be that no apology is purely without the alloy of some kind of self-interest. But these questions may help a person receiving an apology be appropriately skeptical. The bar for a good apology should be set high. In addition, these questions may help a person making an apology issue one that is more genuine and worthy of the trust he or she seeks to restore.

Atonement: Going beyond Apology

In Ian McEwan's novel *Atonement,* he tells a story about a particularly destructive lie. Briony, the younger of two sisters, sees her older sister, Cecilia, making love with her boyfriend Robbie. Later, when another woman at a party is raped, Briony blames Robbie. Tried, imprisoned, and later forced into the British army during WWII, Robbie is severely injured and nearly dies. Toward the end of the novel, Briony decides to visit her sister, confess her lie, acknowledge its effects, and make amends. Upon arriving she discovers that Robbie, on leave from the army, is present in the apartment. An extremely tense drama unfolds. In the course of the conversation, Robbie and Cecilia refuse to forgive Briony but require of her an exacting set of conditions and amends. This novel presents a gripping account of the cost of a lie, the demands of an interactive repair process, the need for apology, and the way we sometimes need to go far beyond apology to restitution and reparation. For a rich analysis of this problem in national and international affairs, see the final chapters of Cose's *Bone to Pick* (2004).

❧Switching the Point of View: Receiving Forgiveness and Forgiving Oneself

Thus far in this chapter, we have approached the subject of forgiveness from the stand-point of the person who is in a position to forgive someone else. This discussion would be incomplete, however, without looking at the process from another angle: what is it like to *receive* forgiveness? While it can be extremely difficult to offer forgiveness to someone who has hurt us, it also can be very hard to receive it after *we* have done the harm. Accepting forgiveness requires that we shift our attention from the fear of retri-bution or guilt over something we have done wrong to the possibility of freedom from this fear. Such freedom can seem more terrifying than the repercussions we anticipate. Once we receive someone's offer of forgiveness, we can no longer focus exclusively on the harm we caused. Suddenly the vista is broad. We can look beyond what we did and how our actions affected another person. But such a view can sometimes seem daunt-ing because the basis for defining ourselves suddenly becomes more complex. Instead of seeing ourselves only in relation to something we did in the past, we are confronted now with responsibility for new choices.

Receiving forgiveness can be difficult for another reason. In his formative article where he outlines the relationship between forgiveness, receiving forgiveness, and self-forgiveness, Enright (1996) asserts that a person hoping to receive forgiveness must *wait* for the *gift* of forgiveness to come from the person who has been harmed. It is as if there is an interval between the action that hurt another person and the forgiveness that releases that person from resentment and anger. In this interval, a person's choice about whether or not to for-give must be upheld. As we have said, a person is not obligated to forgive. In this pro-foundly important interval, the person who caused harm has an opportunity to *reflect rather than deflect* awareness about the actual harm that was caused. Waiting in that interval can be extremely difficult because it requires that a person stay close to awareness of the harm he or she caused. Yet, this interval also may be the birthplace for self-forgiveness.

As with receiving forgiveness, self-forgiveness presents some major challenges. Students sometimes report that they may be willing to receive forgiveness from someone they have harmed but find that they will not grant themselves this same gift. To use another image from the novel *Atonement*, the inability to forgive oneself can seem like being held in a locked and doorless room. Inside this room it seems impossible to live past the shame asso-ciated with some wrongdoing. Meanwhile, on the *outside* of the room, people talk, eat, dance, or stroll through a marketplace, wonder at the stars, and wait to be joined by the presence of the one who locked himself inside this doorless room. Some people stay in this room for a very long time, sometimes because it seems safe. In fact the refusal or inability to forgive oneself may be another version of the eddies described earlier in the chapter.

Forgiving oneself can be particularly difficult because it first requires that we recon-cile *two different images of ourselves*: the person we think we are and the person who caused someone harm. The person we think we are (and would like to be) may resist the truth about the self who told the lie, stole some money, or betrayed a friend. It may seem that as long as we withhold forgiveness from ourselves, then we can't possibly be the per-son who did this deed. To accept forgiveness, whether from someone else or from one-self, is a form of admission that, yes, we are both these people—the one who finds such actions abhorrent and the one who did them. Self-forgiveness requires that we see these two selves clearly and help them recognize and accept each other, extending compassion to each until the self becomes less divided. Undertaking this work requires us to reckon with the complexity of our identity, seeing the "both/and" quality of who we are.

In this chapter we described the internal process of forgiveness, using Enright's four phases and Layton's movement from injured innocence and obsession to transcendence. It is quite possible for people to apply these same steps to themselves. As in the effort to forgive someone else, we must take steps to *uncover* what happened and face that truth courageously. We must *work* at facing our self-protective defenses and begin to let them down. We must be willing to extend empathy and compassion to ourselves in the same way that we might readily offer it to someone else. We must be willing to move toward a *decision* to release ourselves from self-punishing tendencies, without denying accountability. And finally, we must be willing to move toward an *outcome* phase where the truth has been integrated and the story of our life becomes more rich and complicated than we first thought it would be. The end result can be the same sense of freedom as when we forgive someone else, in this case making what we did to someone else less the center of our lives.

Application 10.6   Looking for an Oasis

Imagine that you are a young female enlisted soldier serving in Iraq. Two days ago, three soldiers from your unit, two men and a woman, were ambushed on a night patrol as they tried to protect an oil facility against sabotage. All three of them were good friends. You feel devastated by the loss, aware, too, that you could have been on that same patrol. After the losses, your commanding officer warns all of you in the unit to be extra vigilant in the days leading up to the Muslim holiday of Ramadan.

On patrol yourself a few days after this incident, you see a white van traveling toward an Army checkpoint. Estimating speed and distance, you conclude that the van will not be able to stop at the checkpoint and may even be a danger to the soldiers monitoring all vehicles passing through the area. You fire a warning shot in front of the van. It does not stop. Fearing that the van will ram the checkpoint and may even be loaded with explosives, you fire a rapid volley of shots through the side windows of the van. Moments later the van veers into a roadside ditch and stops. You and several soldiers from the checkpoint run toward the van, weapons ready. Encountering no further threat, you open the van and try to determine what has happened. In the front seat are two adults, a man and a woman, both dead. In the back of the van you find a crying child. She has been wounded not by your bullets but by a land mine explosion. Through a translator who communicates with the child, you learn that her parents were rushing her to the hospital after the explosion. Suddenly you realize that you have killed the child's parents as they tried to help their daughter.

Immediately other soldiers come to your aid. They reassure you that you did exactly what the situation required even if these people were not an actual threat to your unit. Despite their support and time off to recover, you have nightly dreams that haunt you. In one you are in the van being shot at. In another you shoot at the van and, as you approach, see your parents in the front seat.

(continued)

Application 10.6   Looking for an Oasis

In the days ahead, the post-traumatic stress associated with this event and the death of your comrades makes it increasingly difficult for you to serve effectively. You ask permission to see the chaplain assigned to your unit. As the time for the first appointment approaches,

- What do you want to tell this person?
- What do you want to hear from this person?
- What would make it easier to begin the process of self-forgiveness?
- What would make the process much harder?

Reconciliation: A Late Stage in the Journey

Trying to be clear about forgiveness, we have kept reconciliation waiting for a long time, almost like a friend in a nearby room. Our friend has been patient while waiting in the room next door, but now she wants to claim her rightful place. If forgiveness is a process or decision involving the whole person that releases feelings such as anger, resentment, and the desire to retaliate, **reconciliation** is *the process of repairing a relationship so that reengagement, trust, and cooperation become possible after a transgression or violation.* The things we say and do to each other create chasms that divide us. When we forgive someone, or when someone else forgives us, the chasm may remain in place. It is not necessarily filled in or spanned by a bridge. For reasons we've explained, it may be good to forgive but not safe to reconcile. When it is safe, reconciliation is about the spanning of the chasms between people. It is about the bridges that people build, one stone at a time, sometimes from one side, occasionally from both.

What are the cables in this bridge? We are already familiar with some of them. A genuine and trustworthy apology may be a central cable in the span. Explicit and implicit actions, as well as gestures, help signal that forgiveness has taken place and open the way for reconciliation. What are some of the other ways we cross over toward each other?

Insights from History, Politics, and Literature

Living in the land of rivers, we remember a time when a winter flood wiped out a key bridge linking a community to a major east-west highway. A resourceful man in the community offered to shoot an arrow across the swollen river. He tied to the arrow a strand of monofilament. This fishing line allowed people on the other side to haul a heavier line across the river, and then a rope, and finally a cable strong enough to allow for passage across the river. The cable prepared the way for rebuilding the bridge.

In his remarkably comprehensive book *An Ethic for Enemies, Forgiveness in Politics,* Donald Shriver (1995, 9) develops the same metaphor to help us understand *four key aspects of reconciliation.* He invites the reader to imagine a cable spanning the chasm of conflict and alienation that divides individuals, groups, and nations. Based on his knowledge of history, politics, and world literature, Shriver asserts that this cable is woven of four strands—*truth, forbearance, empathy,* and *a commitment to remain in a relationship because of our essential interdependence.* Let's examine each of these strands that together form the cable spanning the chasm.

The Strand of Truth

Nothing obstructs the effort to repair a relationship as much as the experience of having your own sense of truth denied. When a friend denies having taken a possession you know he borrowed, when an employer denies having made an agreement that you were counting on, or when a person refuses to hear your point of view, movement toward each other seems impossible. For this reason the ability to acknowledge, honor, and communicate about what happened and its effects is the first bundle of wire woven into the cable. When people trust their memory of what happened, when they feel free and safe as they share their memory, conditions are established that make possible every succeeding step.

The film *Dead Man Walking* provides a particularly powerful example of the role truth plays in the process of reconciliation. In the film, Sister Helen Prejean, portrayed by Susan Sarandon, agrees to serve as the spiritual advisor for Matthew Poncelet, portrayed by Sean Penn. Poncelet sits on death row for his part in the rape and murder of two teenagers. Through the course of the movie, Sister Helen goes from being a naïve person of goodwill who has never seen the inside of a prison to being a mature, brave, and loyal advisor to a criminal in search of his soul. Likewise, Poncelet changes from a truth-denying shell of a man to a human being who finds his liberation, if not his redemption, in an acknowledgment of the truth and genuine expression of sorrow for his crime. This change takes place because Prejean offers Poncelet a carefully distilled combination of kindness that makes the telling of truth seem possible and tough insistence on truth apart from attempts to place blame on others. Without Prejean's steadfast commitment to Poncelet, no truth would emerge. Without her unswerving demand that Poncelet tell the truth and assume moral responsibility for his crime, Poncelet would never move toward the penitence that makes forgiveness seem thinkable. Change in Poncelet's relationship with himself, with his family, with the parents of his victims, and with his God is predicated on the telling of truth.

Application 10.7   Discovering an Affair

For a few weeks, your partner's behavior has seemed suspicious. Several times he has arrived home later than he promised. While on a business trip, he called to say that the meetings had been extended for a couple of days and that his return would be delayed. When you called the hotel where you thought he was staying, you were informed that "No one by that name is in the hotel." You feel shaken by your suspicions. After his return you feel irritation as he works on his e-mail late into the night, protecting the screen when you approach. The next day you do something you swore you'd never do. You enter his e-mail records. Torn between a sense of guilt about compromising his privacy and a desperate need to know, you read the record of his affair. Armed with this information, you set a time to confront him.

(continued)

Application 10.7   Discovering an Affair

In a role-play with others, enact the first part of this conversation. Remember and apply the communication approaches we describe and recommend. Speak your truth with as much strength as you are able. Imagine your partner acknowledging responsibility for the affair in one version and vehemently denying the affair in another. What is your reaction if he accepts responsibility and seems forthcoming? What is your reaction if he denies responsibility and demeans your perception of the situation? What is the impact on the relationship of "truth" or its denial? Do you think that your *approach* affects the outcome? In other words, does one approach facilitate the telling of truth and another make it more likely that the other person will respond with denial?

The Strand of Forbearance

The second strand in the cable that crosses the canyon of alienation is what Shriver calls *forbearance*. To forbear means to refrain from revenge or punishment after someone has hurt us or transgressed against us. Forbearance is essential to the forgiveness process and to reconciliation because its opposite in revenge sets in motion an uncontrollable chain of consequences that often eliminates the possibility of reconciliation. Revenge, especially in the form of violence, seems to settle the score in the short run, but almost always provides justification for counter-revenge. Revenge has no foresight. It is incapable of looking beyond the action it intends to consider the wider consequences of meeting one terrible act with another. *Resentment enacted in revenge, then, is self-defeating.* It guarantees that the retribution that seems like justice will double back in some form and strike the ones who imposed it. As Anne Lamott says in *Traveling Mercies* (1999, 134), it is like taking rat poison and hoping that the rat will die. Putting the matter more elegantly, Sobonfu Some (2003, 37) says, "Resentment is like making a cup of tea with poison in it for the other person. Somewhere along the line you always forget and drink it yourself." Or, as Gandhi reminded us, if everyone were to follow the principle of "an eye for an eye," then the whole world would go blind.

In his short story "Pray Without Ceasing," Wendell Berry (1992) provides a particularly clear example of forbearance. In the story we learn that Thad Coulter has spent his life transforming a west Kentucky hillside into a productive farm. Not long after clawing his way out of the hole of debt, Thad mortgages his hard-won farm in order to help his profligate son, who uses his father's money to buy a business in a larger neighboring town. Predictably, the son squanders his father's money and fails at business. Faced with foreclosure, Thad goes to visit his trusted friend Ben Feltner, hoping for a loan sufficient to save the farm. Ashamed of his own foolishness in trying to float his son's grandiose and ungrounded ideas, Thad gets drunk. When Ben finds it impossible to talk sense with him, he shows Thad the door. Later that same day, incensed by this rejection and ruined by his own sense of shame, Thad shoots and kills Ben, his last best friend. Word of his father's murder eventually reaches Ben's son Mat. After kneeling beside his limp father, Mat rises up, strengthened by the idea of revenge. As Berry says, Mat feels "new created by rage" (34). But as Mat turns from his dead father toward what seems like the sacred duty of revenge, his uncle, Jack Beecham, instantly sees that no good will come from trying to balance one murder with another. At great physical and emotional cost to himself, Jack, an older man, takes hold of Mat. He clamps Mat's arms to his side and holds him through the "concentrated fury" of grief and the desire to get even. The men heave and stagger and kick up the dust. But eventually something flows out of Mat and is replaced by something that flows into him from Jack. In the end, Jack can let Mat go because the younger man has become a new man free of the violence that only *seems* to make things right. Later in the story, a group of men, vigilantes really, come to the house where Mat sits with the body of his father. When they ask Mat's permission to hunt down Thad, Mat turns down their request, having already seen that one bad deed cannot be made right by another. In the end, Mat invites the men into the house to eat, a reconciling gesture in itself.

The beauty of fiction is that it allows us to see in concentrated form something that remains obscure or dilute in life. It distills the problem for us until it becomes clear. In this case, when Mat learns to contain the desire for revenge, Jack can let him go. In this way, Mat is spared the consequences of his own potential violence and the community is spared the effects of the spreading contagion of one killing for another. While few of us live in small towns and agrarian settings, we are not unfamiliar with the need for forbearance. Hardly a day goes by that someone does not cut in front of us at the grocery store or bank, make a bad move in heavy traffic, justify one sexual infidelity with another, demean with words or postures a person worthy of respect and care. Forbearance is essential because its opposite in revenge sets in motion a tide that cannot be predicted and that guarantees that people will have an even harder time coming back together in a renewed state of trust.

The Strand of Empathy

If forgiveness and its sometimes appropriate aim of reconciliation are predicated on truth, and made possible by forbearance rather than revenge, then developing and expressing empathy for the offending person form the third essential strand in the cable stretching across the chasm. Empathy is rooted in the realization that the one who hurt us is at least human and needs our kindness. The expression of empathy communicates that we have some understanding of the other person's motives and needs, however confused they may be. Empathy recognizes that at some point in time we may have done to someone else the very thing we are now trying to transcend or, at the very least, we have felt our own capacity for such an action.

Mr. Ives' Christmas, a novel by Oscar Hijuelos (1995), provides a particularly powerful narrative about the effects of a crime and the long, difficult journey toward compassion for the person who committed it. Set in New York City, *Mr. Ives' Christmas* tells the story of an advertising executive whose gentle and gifted son is murdered by a teenage thug. Like a sustained rain, the grief and anger that Ives feels over the loss of his son erode the ground on which he stands. The death of Robert affects Ives' concentration at work, his friendships, his marriage, his interest in sex, the once vital quality of his spiritual life, his social commitments and interests, his sleep, his appetite, and his beliefs about the nature of the world. In short, this loss affects everything. Through the course of the novel, a priest makes concerted efforts to bring Ives and Robert's murderer together. Toward the end of his life, Ives consents to meet Daniel Gomez, the man who killed his son. In the tense moments around this event, two images meet, clash, and influence each other—Ives' mental image of the man who shot his son with a handgun and the man who actually appears before him. Ives meets Gomez in the man's run-down apartment, where the furniture is covered in plastic, photographs are placed in cheap Woolworth's frames, a crucifix and plaster Virgin Mary sit on the table, and a back door leads to a porch where garbage and bicycles are indiscriminately piled. Extremely anxious, Gomez has spent the morning throwing up in anticipation of this meeting. As Gomez comes down the stairs, Ives sees a man who has grown to 300 pounds. His scuffed black shoes have been made over with enamel paint. Ives encounters not a vicious murderer, not a hard-shelled teenage boy with contempt for the world around him, but a fairly pathetic figure lost in regret and fear. Not surprisingly, the actual man, rather than the murderer fixed in the mind of Ives by a newspaper photo, awakens in Ives a compassionate response that finally is communicated by an embrace.

While hugging a murderer as sign of reconciliation may not be appropriate, this novel helps us to see that both victim and victimizer can suffer as a result of a crime. In starting across the bridge that spans the chasm of human suffering, we may discover our shared vulnerability and that we are human together. We may come to see how all of us can be exposed on the far limb of fate waiting for a kind word or deed. By means of empathy, we begin to cross over toward each other.

Commitment to the Relationship out of Awareness of Our Interdependence

In some ways this fourth strand in Shriver's cable across the chasm is the hardest to understand, yet it is the most crucial. Perhaps we can best approach this concept indirectly. In his song "Earthtown Square," singer/songwriter Peter Mayer reminds us of our global and economic interdependence. After describing advances in our technological capabilities, he sings,

> . . . Now it's feeling like a small town
> With six billion people downtown.
> At a little sidewalk fair
> In Earth Town Square.
> There are Germans selling Audis
> Filled with gasoline from Saudis
> To Australians sipping Kenyan coffee in their Chinese shoes
> Argentines are meeting Mongols
> Over French fries at McDonald's
> And the place looks strangely tiny when you see it from the moon.

Peter Mayer 2002

What is true on the economic level is often true on the psychological or relational level as well. If global economics binds us together, so does our web of relationships, whether in our families or our communities. A sense of how what happens to one affects the rest places responsibility on us to work things out with one another. "Because this place looks strangely tiny from the moon," we are charged to work together in the household to which we all belong. People like Martin Luther King Jr. and Archbishop

Desmond Tutu have a particularly firm grasp of this fourth strand. In King's case, he knew that the goal was not just a seat on the bus in Montgomery, Alabama, where his activism began, but the creation of a "beloved community" among all the races and classes (Lampman 2005). Deeply steeped in the African tradition of "Ubuntu," which recognizes that no one person can be a human being without belonging in some sense to another human being, Desmond Tutu (1999) has a clear understanding of the same point. He knows that "we experience fleetingly that we are made for togetherness, for friendship, for community, for family, that we are created to live in a delicate network of interdependence" (265). It is because of this interdependence that we are called upon to use all our interpersonal skills and ability to communicate with one another for the sake of some small version of our place in the "beloved community."

For a way of pulling all these strands together—courage to speak and hear the truth, forbearance, empathy, and commitment to one another—an extended guide to a "reconciling conversation" has been placed in the Instructor's Manual.

⌁Conclusion

In 1973 Marietta Jaeger and her family were camping in Montana near the town of Three Forks. During the night, someone slit the tent in which her seven-year-old daughter Susie was sleeping and removed her. A well-coordinated search was set in motion, but Susie was not found. About a week later, a phone call from the killer, a man later identified as David Meinhofer, was the first break in the case. In this call, he revealed a detail about one of Susie's fingernails that linked him to the crime. Initially Marietta was filled with rage about what had happened to her daughter. But in time and with the help of her own particular faith, she was able to transcend this initial impulse to kill the man who had taken her daughter. She knew that she had to overcome her hatred, for her own sake and for Susie's, if her daughter were to be found alive. If she hung on to the hate, she would be enslaved to what had happened. Asking for a change of heart, Marietta found a more compassionate way of being. Exactly a year after Susie's abduction, the kidnapper called again. Marietta reached deep inside herself for the implausible kindness she knew was needed. She asked David, "How can I help you?" Her genuine concern for the man kept him on the phone about an hour until he revealed enough information so that police were able to track him down and arrest him. Marietta later met the man face to face. He confessed to kidnapping, molesting, and killing Susie and three other young people. After returning to his jail cell he hung himself. Despite the doubly tragic outcome, Marietta knew in her own heart that she had forgiven her daughter's murderer.

Realizing that she and Meinhofer's mother had something in common in the loss of their children, Marietta eventually reached out to Meinhofer's mother. Years later, Marietta returned to Montana for the 25th anniversary of Susie's death. In touch with Meinhofer's mother since the murder, Marietta and this woman both visited the graves where their children were buried. Years later Marietta moved from her home state of Michigan to the community where Susie and the family had vacationed. Here, she married a local rancher. Marietta is now a tireless and determined advocate for eliminating the death penalty in Montana. She is firmly convinced that carrying out justice as revenge in the form of the death penalty would not have been an appropriate way to honor the memory of her daughter.

~Summary

Marietta's case, while dramatic, is not unique. In less dramatic ways people work through the apparently ironclad logic of revenge and make their way to forgiveness and, in some cases, reconciliation. They make this journey as a result of a complex internal process that may involve numerous steps or sometimes a relatively swift decision. In this chapter, we define forgiveness, discuss misconceptions about forgiveness, and address the problem of power imbalance. We discuss the matter of memory and assert that forgiveness is more a choice than an obligation. We present forgiveness as a process and as a decision. We discuss ways that people get stuck in the process, and the need for patience in the journey of forgiveness. Forgiveness is both intrapersonal and interpersonal in nature. Nonverbal gestures may lay the groundwork for forgiveness. An approach to apology is presented with extensive notes on how to receive and give authentic apologies. Reconciliation is defined and explained, acknowledging that it may not always be appropriate. Shriver's four strands of reconciliation are presented in their historical, fictional, and personal applications. In short, people can be aided in their journey toward forgiveness when someone believes the story they are telling; if they remember that revenge, taken to recover a lost sense of honor, may in turn be perceived by others as a new injury to avenge; that empathy can soften the hardest heart; and, finally, by the awareness that we are bound together and all the suffering we cause one another does not remove this fact. At the end of this journey, people say things like, "I found that the stones I wanted to throw simply slipped out of my fingers." "The gate to a future I could not have imagined simply swung open when I let go of what they did to me. Resentment no longer holds me hostage." "Like a scarred tree, I've begun to heal." "The journey is not over, but I have started out on the road."

Using examples from the lives of our students, from film, fiction, and international relations, we have illustrated some of the challenges inherent in this process. We now see that forgiveness and reconciliation, its close cousin in the next room, are the byproduct of a complex interaction of several factors. Forgiveness that restores us to ourselves and reconciliation that restores us to one another are the result of time; the human desire to transcend injury; the courage to place a violation, betrayal, deception, or some other wound in the larger context of additional experience; and perhaps the mysterious effect of what some call "grace." When we forgive someone else or ourselves, or when we are forgiven, we affirm the world is much larger than the injury that dominates our thoughts and feelings. An invisible door opens and we step out onto a stage where it is possible to associate with one another in ways less constricted by old memories. In this light we subjugate the memory of past harm to the hope of a new future. In the face of conflict or injury, we see our mutual vulnerability, our inevitable interdependence, and the need for compassion so all of us may transcend the injuries of the past.

~Key Terms

Use the text's Online Learning Center at **www.mhhe.com/wilmot7** to further your understanding of the following terminology.

secondary wound 304

forgiveness as a decision 307

forgiveness as a process 307

Layton's three-step model of forgiveness 308

eddies 309

reconciliation 318

Review Questions

 Go to the self-quizzes on the Online Learning Center at **www.mhhe.com/wilmot7** to test your knowledge of the chapter concepts.

1. Discuss some definitions of forgiveness. What are key components of forgiveness?
2. What are differences between forgiveness and reconciliation?
3. What is the problem with the phrase "forgive and forget"?
4. Compare and contrast the ideas of "forgiveness as decision" and "forgiveness as process," giving your own opinions based on the ideas presented.
5. Explain the "eddies" in which a person may be caught.
6. In what way is forgiveness both intrapersonal and interpersonal?
7. How do gestures function to lay the groundwork for further change?
8. What makes apologies ineffective or inappropriate?
9. What makes self-forgiveness so difficult?
10. Explain Shriver's four strands of reconciliation.
11. What are some of the guidelines for a reconciling conversation?

Chapter 11

Preventing Destructive Conflict

❧Prevention Defined

At this point in the book and your conflict class, our fervent hope is that you have learned a great deal about resolving, managing, mitigating, and working with conflict. One final task remains—to be an excellent interpersonal conflict practitioner, you need to know how to *prevent destructive conflict*. Everything you have learned thus far will help you to prevent those conflicts that do not enhance the relationship, solve problems, or enable people to work and live constructively together. In this chapter we will highlight some of the most important prevention practices; we will help you think creatively about preventing destructive conflict; and we will synthesize the "Best Practices in Prevention" from the book. As an interpersonal conflict artist, you can learn to prevent many destructive conflicts. That set of skills will be a genuine contribution to your personal and work relationships.

Prevention of conflict presents a paradoxical task. On the one hand, we now know that conflict is one of the normal states of human communication; on the other hand, we would like to do what we can to prevent destructive, time-wasting, relationship-harming conflict. You learned in the first two chapters of this book that conflict presents both a danger and an opportunity for creative change. We'd like to enhance the possibility of creative change and decrease the probability of destructive conflict. To prevent means *"to anticipate, to forestall, to come before, to be in readiness for an occasion, to deprive something of power, to hold or keep back, and to deal with beforehand."* Prevention implies taking advance measures against something, to forestall something from its course. Prevention implies taking effective measures to ward off something destructive. We've all used the saying, "An ounce of prevention is worth a pound of cure." How might we prevent destructive conflict?

❧The Importance of Prevention

The Rescue Crew: A Fable

Once upon a time, in a beautiful meadow close to town, a group of friends was having a picnic on a sunny spring day. They'd brought along a kayak and a canoe for playing in the river, some softball equipment, great food, and some music. They had several

(continued)

The Rescue Crew: A Fable

backpack tents and sleeping bags in case they decided to stay overnight. It was spring break and all the friends were elated to be out of classes and just hanging out. Jack and Stacey jumped in their canoe and began to explore the other side of the river. Suddenly Stacey saw what looked like a person floating downstream. Sure enough, it was a woman who had been battered by the river rocks and was almost dead. The group sprang into action: someone knew CPR and revived her, someone else made temporary bandages for her wounds, and they called the EMTs on their cell phones. Just as they were loading her into the ambulance, the whole scene was repeated with two more people needing rescue. The whole sequence continued. The friends called for help, and people responded generously. Soon an emergency tent city was set up, people brought in food and water, medical personnel volunteered their time, and organizers raised money, for the bodies kept coming, and the sturdy group of volunteers was overwhelmed by the urgent needs of the wounded and drowning people. Not everyone could be saved.

After a few weeks, a construction crew had set up a more permanent shelter with emergency medical equipment and some basic housing for the volunteers. Media crews visited to document the extraordinary tragedy and generous helping response. Some conflicts began to develop among the leadership; the people who had been on the original picnic claimed that they knew the most about the situation and should be elected as leaders of the new rescue organization. Names were suggested for the group. One evening a young man from a different town arrived to help. He immediately began running at full speed up the river. The rescue crew yelled at him to get back and help with the food preparation for the volunteers and victims. "Where the heck do you think you're going?" one of the leaders yelled. "I'm going upstream to see who's pushing all these people in the river. Come help me see what's happening and get this stopped now!" the runner replied.

As the fable illustrates, there's no reason to spend all our energy taking care of disasters. We need to find out what's causing them, then put energy into preventing further disasters.

Romances break up, families extend estrangements over years, and intractable conflicts damage peoples' enjoyment of work. Violence at home, at school, and in the wider society can be reduced by teaching people conflict resolution (Johnson and Johnson 1996). We mention "passion," which means *to suffer with*. Passionate conflict prevention involves staying with a situation long enough to make a difference rather than avoiding. Even with a wide repertoire of conflict resolution skills, most of us would rather prevent or avoid conflict than have to process it. On the international scene, conflict prevention could keep thousands or even millions of people from death or destruction. Our well-being as a globe depends on learning to prevent devastating conflict (Wenger and Mockli 2003).

Application 11.1   One Day's Newspaper Stories

Choose a newspaper from a medium to large city. Look through the entire paper and make a list of conflicts that are reported. With your small group discuss the following:

1. Which were inevitable?
2. Which might have been prevented?
3. Which might still be resolved?
4. What third party might be helpful in each instance?

One way to think about conflict prevention is to use a metaphor from earlier in the book. Conflict can be seen as a dance. To prevent crashing into each other and other dancers, you have to learn steps that allow a lot of people to dance on the floor at one time. One of the basic steps *in the conflict dance* everyone must learn is *"from out to in."* Engagement means stepping close enough to the other people in the conflict dance to touch, see, talk, and respond. Moving toward trouble, bad news, distress, or upset on another person's part remains difficult but essential to reduce and prevent further conflict. The other basic move in the dance of conflict is from *large* to *small*. Rather than making huge, grand gestures, conflict is reduced or prevented by learning to look for ways to make intensity lessen, threats vanish, and complex issues ultimately more simple.

If we want to prevent conflicts, we have to be willing to give up certain kinds of communication in favor of better ways. The skill of resolving issues "unmemorably" (Prather and Prather 1998) means we give up a certain level of intensity and drama. We have found the following values underlying practices of prevention. People holding these values often serve as catalysts for prevention of destructive conflict.

Core Values Lead to Best Practices

In the book so far, we have emphasized specific **core values** that underlie constructive and peaceful conflict resolution. In practice, some of these values may seem either self-evident or entirely too difficult to a normal human being to adopt. Yet we have seen many people who are furious, resentful, or sad or have been betrayed nevertheless use these principles to transform conflicts.

Some of the important core values are the use of *kindness, compassion, and respect* for others. Kindness flows from a genuine desire not to hurt and wound, not from a contrived sense of "being nice." Kindness as a value asks us to assume that everyone is doing the best he or she can at the moment (even though it may not seem like that effort is being made). We assume that we are all human beings together and that every human being is worthy of our compassion. We gain nothing and lose a lot when we make people into enemies, barbarians, "the other side," or "crazy." The core value of *forebearance*, discussed in chapter 10, urges us to put aside vengeance, retribution, and reactivity. When we forebear, we can then listen receptively, putting aside self long enough to comprehend the other. Honesty delivered without blame and judgment prevents indirect, misleading communication. Honesty takes courage.

Another core value instructs that we *avoid distancing and objectifying* people. We often do this by keeping people at a distance with e-mail, by avoidance, or by not being clear and plain. We exclude people, or treat them just as someone in the way. We may distance people by "acting big" or using power destructively; the same is true when we distance ourselves by withdrawing or putting ourselves down. These tactics create chasms across which communication lines fray and often break.

Application 11.2　　　　　My Core Values

1.　Decide which of the above values and practices are your "top three."

2.　Decide which of the above values and practices present the greatest challenge for you.

3.　What would you add? Together with your group or class, come up with your own core values and practices. Consider sending them to the authors for the next edition! We'd like to know what you think.

4.　Think of someone who exemplifies many of the core values. Remembering that person, or observing him/her, what do you learn about the prevention of conflict? What one or two traits would you like to incorporate into your own life?

Learn from History

Prevention depends on developing a good memory for what went wrong in the past. Anticipating what might happen in a future conflict depends on clearly remembering what happened in the past. When we revisit conversations that went wrong, we may learn something (Stone, Patton, and Heen 1999, 159ff). You might remember that you felt intense emotion, maybe anger or dread. You might recall that every time you tried to bring up an issue, your son avoided it (like talking about his grades). You might remember a reactive, "ping-pong" conversation, when you and another person at work went back and forth endlessly, arguing and not getting anywhere.

Application 11.3　　　Learning from My History

Select a conflict you have had over the recent past that did not go well. Then try to specify, as descriptively as possible:

1.　What were the communication behaviors of the other person?

2.　What were your communication behaviors?

　　a.　Make sure you describe what actually happened, describing the *event* rather than your *intent.*

　　b.　Here is a hint—if you use any negative, blaming words to describe yourself or the other person, you have not provided a clear, descriptive account. Avoid labeling.

(continued)

Application 11.3   Learning from My History

3. Then looking over this short history,

    a. What could the other person have done differently that would have a posi-
        tive impact on you?
    b. What could you have done differently that would have had a positive impact on
        the other person?

In the assessment chapter (chapter 6), we introduced you to the idea of the "third story." An excellent conflict prevention technique is to revisit a former difficult conversation by bringing it up (not avoiding it) and then talking about how to talk about it. For instance, you might say, "I wonder whether there is a better way we could address these issues?" (Stone, Patton, and Heen 1999). Or you might say, "Let's discuss this again, but both agree not to raise our voices."

Learning from your conflict history also means remembering which of the four levels of conflict—the *topic*, *relationship*, *identity*, or *process*—was most central to the conflict. If the relationship issues never were addressed, finding a way to bring up those issues will help prevent a repetitive, escalated conflict. The following example will clarify these ideas.

Application 11.4   The Communication Coach and the Supervisor

Carla is a recently graduated communication major. She has been employed at a local bank with several branches to coach the sales staff in communication skills. Julie is a new teller whose communication skills had annoyed customers and co-workers. Julie told her supervisor that she would like to train the next teller, but one of the complaints about Julie is that she had not been tactful or constructive in training new personnel or communicating with customers when she was stressed. Carla, as the communication coach, began talking with Julie about how to better meet customer needs and how to train effectively.

One day Carla took a sick day; when she returned, the atmosphere was noticeably chilly with her supervisor, Bob (who was also Julie's supervisor). Bob went to his supervisor, Brad, when Carla was at home sick, complaining that Carla was infringing on his territory by "supervising" Julie. When Carla was called in to talk with Brad, she became angry and called the manager of communication coaching, Sally, who worked at another branch. Sally called Brad and asked him not to interfere with Carla's coaching activities.

Was this conflict resolved? Not for the long term. If Carla is wise, she will talk with Bob and Brad about what each understands about her coaching role. She will ask them to talk about how they see the new activity, and she will refer to the conversation that went badly. In this way, she will be preventing future conflicts that might escalate quickly. Along the way, she will be demonstrating good communication skills as well!

Analysis of the past enables you to plan effectively for the future. Since "conflict happens," the prevention you will be putting into place will help you avoid debilitating, relationship-deflating, "same old/same old" conflicts. You will be attempting to reach the goals we discussed in the first pages of the book, to solve problems and enhance relationships for future love, friendship, or work.

One of the skills of conflict prevention involves staying aware of the communication around you, and the way you yourself are communicating. One of the characteristics of good communication is that nothing is ever "simple" when it comes to conflict. This can be a curse and a blessing. You may be one of the few people around in your family, work group, friend group, or team who notices when a cycle of conflict is beginning. You will find that this is a valuable skill and people will appreciate you having some ideas about what to do.

Recognize Cycles: Where Are You in the Big Picture?

Previously, we have written about Combs' four-stage cycle of conflict: (2004, xxi). They are:

- The appearance of conflict.
- The absence of hope.
- The occurrence of creativity.
- The emergence of stability.

Figure 11.1 illustrates a **cycle of conflict** (Combs 2004, 60).

Moving to the left on the cycle of change, notice that in *stage one,* some disruption of conflict is introduced. In one family, the brother and two sisters disapproved of the divorce of their sister and their former brother-in-law, Ted. For about a year after the divorce, their mother and all the siblings argued when they got together about whether Maya should have left "such a wonderful man." The family continued to include Ted in their family gatherings, hoping that Maya would come to her senses. Maya, understandably, was hurt and angry about what she considered a betrayal of her belonging in her family.

In *stage two,* chaos and conflict intensify if it is not resolved in stage one. Maya's family invited Ted to the wedding of Maya's brother, who in fact invited Ted to be his best man. As Maya reported, "I might have been able to live with this except all the plans were made before I was even invited. I was an afterthought. I began to think maybe I was better off without contact with my family. But I felt incredibly sad and angry."

In *stage three,* if the conflict is not resolved in stage two, some kind of change or adaptation has to happen, since most people cannot stand staying at an intolerable level of conflict. Maya wrote a letter to her family members telling them how hurt she was, and stating what she needed—"to have you give me the role I used to have as your sister and daughter, including me first in your plans, and then deciding whether to include Ted." She also asked her family to accept that she had made a final decision and she would not be re-uniting with Ted even if it cost her precious connections with her family. She asked them to respect her choice.

In *stage four,* new solutions and stability are reached if all goes well. In Maya's family, all but her brother have now accepted her choice and honored her requests. Maya

Figure 11.1 Cycle of Conflict

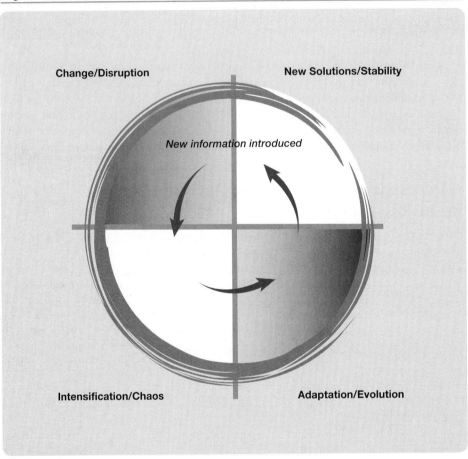

has decided to stay connected to her brother in spite of his unwillingness to honor her requests, because the relationship is so important to her. While the "stability" is not perfect, the family is no longer in active, destructive conflict. Prevention of future conflict can enter into any of the four stages of the cycle. When stage four is reached, and some degree of stability reigns for a while, people are in a wonderful place to plan ahead for prevention of another cycle of conflict. By staying aware of the big picture, future cycles will at least be new—different problems will be solved, and different challenges faced. This is one of the ways people, families, relationships, and communities grow.

❧Preventing Destructive Avoidance
When Others Avoid

People who do not avoid conflict often feel perplexed or frustrated by those who habitually avoid. They often say, "I can't deal with someone who won't speak up." Over the years, we have convened groups of self-identified "conflict avoiders" (who state they are more comfortable avoiding than confronting) and asked them, "How do you want to be treated when someone has a conflict with you?" Here is what you can do to **prevent destructive avoidance** when working with avoiders:

- *Put them at ease.* Use a nonthreatening approach—calm voice, friendly and open nonverbal actions; don't "trap" them in a car or small space; and consider sharing a meal together.

- *Provide safety.* Set ground rules ("I promise I won't raise my voice or interrupt you") and let them have time to prepare for the discussion.

- *Change the mode of communication*—if you have been using e-mails, talk face-to-face; try writing if talking in person doesn't work.

- *Frame the conversation as relationship-building.* Say, for example, "I have a suggestion for how you could help our relationship," or "Our project needs some help. Would you be willing to talk with me about our timeline?" Don't say, "We need to talk!"

When You Avoid

If you see yourself as an avoider, we hope you will want to expand your repertoire to be able to collaborate, confront, stay engaged, and even escalate when needed. You will need to find the sources of your fearful responses, be willing to take breaks when you need to, practice initiating important conversations instead of waiting for others to initiate (this gives you a sense of necessary control), and focus on what is actually happening in the interaction instead of only how you feel. You may need to ask for help, from others in the conflict or from a third party, when you feel overwhelmed. Why should you do this? Because if you stay stuck in the avoider role, others will have to (1) avoid all potentially conflicting topics to take care of you or (2) escalate to balance your avoidance. Either choice for the other sets in motion a destructive system. You may see yourself as a victim, or as the one who is right but persecuted. You can change your sense of self by adopting new, risky, but rewarding skills.

In addition to the above ways of thinking about avoidance, the following specific suggestions will help you work with your own avoidance:

Safety comes first. If you do not feel protected, you can't use productive conflict skills. If your partner shows any history or signs of physically harming you, work only with a third party.

Take breaks if you freeze when you are afraid. Be sure to tell people what is happening, such as, "This is hard for me. I need to take a break but I'll be back." You won't be seen as an avoider but as a careful person.

Learn to *initiate conversations rather than waiting.* There is magic in the power of choosing to engage.

Ask for help if you are stuck. You can ask a manager, professional third party, counselor, or even a trusted friend to help you talk about something difficult.

❧Preventing Destructive Escalation
When Others Escalate

Escalation spirals are in motion when the general climate deteriorates into ugliness or hostility. Name-calling may occur, "tit for tat" communication prevails, and sometimes people will bring up hot topics when they have been drinking or using drugs, or when they are exhausted and can't think well. Then the "state" they were in might become the "reason" for the escalation. We coach people never to talk about important, potentially conflict-laden issues when drinking or on any other substance. Alcohol and drugs decrease inhibitions and increase the possibility of verbal and physical escalation.

When the language is sarcastic and angry, you can be sure that hurt will follow. When escalation sequences are successfully short-circuited, "it is usually because one partner backs off and says something to de-escalate the argument. Often this requires the simple humility of choosing to soften your tone and put down your shield" (Markman, Stanley, and Blumberg 2001, 49). Further suggestions for de-escalating spirals are

- Set and keep ground rules for interaction.
- Limit the issues instead of expanding them.
- Look for ways to reframe the other's behavior in positive ways.
- Meta-communicate about the spiral; that is, "This isn't working for me, but I do want to work it out. We can do better, and I'd like to try."

Prevention of serious conflict depends on people of goodwill having the good sense to de-escalate. That person can be you. **Preventing escalation** depends partly on stopping spirals, which protects all of you, your future relationship, and everyone's feelings. Remember that conflict is characterized by strong emotion. If you refuse to "match" another's escalation, yet stay connected to them, your calmness will usually prevail.

You can learn to challenge yourself to change habitual avoidance and escalation patterns. When you do, you will become much more confident of your skills, and you will find that others will help you out in interactions.

When You Escalate

Recognize your escalation for what it is. If you call others names, try to overpower others, want to damage the other person, threaten, or rage at others, you are someone who escalates. You can learn to change your habit.

Referring back to chapter 7, you can learn that *anger is not a reason to escalate;* it is an internal feeling that can be recognized, worked with and learned from. Remember that fear fuels anger. Try to figure out your own fear. When you feel like *attacking,* find a way not to. You can learn to identify your **warning signs,** and then practice stopping instead of "letting it fly." Finally, you can prevent future escalation explosions by mending relationships and apologizing (see chapter 10).

❧Prevention Interventions

Much of this book has focused on giving you intervention ideas for prevention of conflict, and we will not repeat these here. We encourage you to practice new skills in the service of stepping in to prevent further escalation of conflict. You will be pleased at how effective simple interventions can be, and others will be very grateful. Employers, for instance, are "practically begging" for workers who can "think, collaborate, communicate, coordinate and create" (Kaplan-Leiserson 2004). Being an effective supervisor, parent, loving partner, family member, or friend calls upon every conflict-prevention skill you have learned. You can be part of creating a climate of support, affirmation, clarification, and inquiry in all your many roles.

Contracts Prevent Disputes

Often after a conflict, the natural inclination is to sigh deeply and forget it. But both at work and in intimate relationships, some follow-through helps greatly in preventing new conflicts. You can use the failed interactions as a guide for what to do and not do the next time you are in a similar situation. This is "learning from history," as we discussed previously. The process of clarifying with "new rules" serves to guide new expectations of behavior.

A Communication Protocol

Any agreement that can help shape future behavior will help prevent conflict. Expectations are clearly stated, highlighting both communication to do and not do. After a third-party intervenes in the workplace, usually a **"post-conflict contract"** or "protocol" is established by the participants with the facilitator guiding the conversation. Good post-conflict protocols share similarities. One example of a **communication protocol** established by a work team follows.

A Protocol at Work

1. Schedule talks—don't spring them on unsuspecting people.
2. Talk about tough topics in private, one-on-one with the person involved.
3. Be direct and specific, leaving no room for doubt.
4. Use all the skills of respect and kindness.
5. Assume the best, not the worst.
6. Only use humor when appropriate and when the other person seems up for it.
7. Offer to actively help solve the problem.
8. Thank the person for the talk.

If a couple or family seeks the help of a professional counselor, often the counselor will work out a set of agreements with the couple, for instance. Once the emotionally laden issues have been thoroughly discussed, the couple and the counselor might work out a set of written agreements. These agreements should never be imposed by the counselor but should arise from honest and open discussion with the couple. The agreements do not substitute for the discussion; they reflect the discussion. In that way, the agreements can serve as a conflict prevention device for the future. If you are in counseling, you might ask your counselor to help you with such agreements when the time is right. A warning: It never works to "gang up" on one of the partners, hoping that a set of agreements will correct his or her behavior.

A Counseling Agreement to Prevent Further Conflict

The following is a set of agreements worked out with a couple after the husband had an affair, the reasons were thoroughly understood, the hurt and betrayal were explored, the apology and trust-rebuilding work were done, and the couple agreed they wanted to stay together. The agreement helped stabilize all the hard work the couple had done in counseling:

1. Husband agrees to call wife when he is going to be later than 15 minutes from the time he agreed to meet her.
2. Husband agrees to share his e-mail password with wife until she does not want it.
3. Wife agrees not to bring up the affair in a public place (at dinner, walking, etc.).
4. Wife agrees not to talk further with her family about the affair.
5. Husband agrees to make a joint call with wife asking the former lover not to contact him, and telling her he will not contact her.
6. Both partners agree to tell the "truth under the truth" and search for new ways to communicate with each other.
7. Wife agrees not to violate husband's privacy except his e-mail account (where much of the affair was conducted).

You can easily see that the above agreements would provoke, not prevent, conflict if all the issues had not been carefully and thoughtfully discussed. The agreement anchors the choices of both parties in the counseling experience they had. The **counseling agreement** helps bind them to productive communication, limits certain freedom for the sake of the relationship, and reduces fear and uncertainty.

Problem Solving

Most communication students know the steps and sequences of problem solving. You can use these **problem-solving steps** or **sequences** in every area of your work and personal life. A review of an expanded version of problem solving is presented here since problem solving helps to prevent conflict. Look for contexts to use problem solving naturally and creatively. It is an extremely effective conflict prevention activity.

Expanded Problem Solving

1. Identify the problem (not the problem person).
2. Determine the causes and stressors.
3. Clarify everyone's perceptions of the problem and stressors.
4. Identify shared goals, needs, hopes, and desired outcomes.
5. Generate as many options as possible without editing at this stage.
6. Reduce the number of options.
7. Choose the best solution(s).
8. Develop "doables"; that is, stepping stones to specific actions.
9. Decide how to implement the solutions, the timeline, and the evaluation needed.
10. Make clear agreements that benefit everyone. (Adapted from Weeks 1992 and Kansas University Web site 2005)

❧Personal Change for Conflict Prevention

We began this book by warning you, the reader, that three approaches to change are possible: (1) *change the other person*, (2) *change the situation*, or (3) *change yourself*. We noted that whereas sometimes we can change the situation by transforming the elements of conflict, we can almost never change the other person except by triggering their reactivity (not a good thing!), but we always have the option of **personal change.** We end our study of conflict prevention by highlighting some ways in which you might choose to further change yourself. After all, each of us is a "work in progress" and we hope this course as well as all your other life experiences will bring challenging and creative ways for you to change in ways that enhance your life and the lives of those around you.

Address the Relationship and Identity Issues in Your Life

Conflict revolves around the four issues of topic, relationship, identity, and process. We have noted that the issues of relationship (*Who* are we to each other?) and identity (*Who am I* to you and to myself?) drive the *intensity* of conflicts. Conflicts are by their nature emotion-laden. Much of the emotion infusing our conflicts has to do with relationship and identity issues.

You probably have noticed that in the book we have interwoven conflict management suggestions by urging you to improve your interpersonal skills *and* your internal reactions. Both changes add to your relationship and identity repertoire. When you change both your outward communication and your internal response, you have an immediate impact on those with whom you are in conflict, and you change yourself. So much of communication is nonverbal that *congruence* (communicating in accord with genuine feelings), as Carl Rogers pointed out in the 1940s, is one of the keys of communication. If we are authentic inside, we will be able to be authentic outside. We can't really fake it. For instance, nondefensiveness needs to be genuine. When we pretend to be nondefensive, but are seething and hardened inside, people can tell.

An example of the wise recognition of this truth is Cecilia, who is the head of a large government agency. When her health communication group came under fire from the public and from a consultant hired to evaluate her agency, Cecilia was devastated to learn that her communication style was a negative focus of the report. Later, she castigated herself for not sitting up front with the other managers at the special meeting convened to receive the report. Yet, Cecilia realized that to hear the negative (and, in her view, inaccurate) feedback, and then shake hands and pretend to be "a good team member" would be even more devastating. Wisely, she chose to sit at the back, and then go to her office to recover emotionally and feel her way clear as to how to proceed. She needed to be out of the public eye. Pretending to be "a good team member" would have been a relationship lie, at that point. She was angry and dismayed and felt betrayed. She used good sense to protect herself.

Identity issues have to do with how we see ourselves, with saving face so we can continue to feel a sense of self-worth. Sometimes we have to make the hard choice to let go of a part of our identity so some greater good, like an important relationship, can be healthy and strong. For instance, Mike saw himself as independent, autonomous, and "the captain of his own ship." When he married Anna, he discovered that she saw herself in much the same way. They had a lot of conflicts in their first year of marriage over where to spend holidays, whether to move for Mike's work, when to begin to try to have a child, and how much money to save. Finally, Mike realized that his identity, "captain of my own ship," needed to change if he was to build a good partnership with Anna. He had seen compromise as losing. He began to see collaboration as a "third way," and their marriage took on excitement from adventure instead of conflict. Mike's identity changed.

Finally, Communication *Is* the Key

Conflict resolution and prevention mandate communication change—**communication is the key.** In one study from the University of Ulster (McGrane 2004), people were asked what were effective skills for dispute resolution one-on-one. Both women and men, supervisors and employees, responded:

- Gather information or advice from others.
- Initiate a conversation as opposed to avoiding it.
- Approach the other party as soon as possible without brooding.
- Employ a calm, cooperative style of communication, using an informal tone while listening.
- Treat the other party fairly and with respect.
- Maintain the privacy of the conversation.

This is an excellent summary of basic human communication skills. Emotionally intelligent people are the ones who get promoted, have happier relationships, and generally have a better life (Goleman 1995). These basic emotional intelligence skills are *self-awareness, self-regulation, motivation to use our deep values to guide us toward our goals, empathy,* and *social skills* (318).

The prevention of serious, destructive conflict, if you take on this task, will undoubtedly take your lifetime to complete. As we think about how much the world at large, and the people close by you, need you to learn these skills, we hope you will be inspired, as we have been, to keep adding to your repertoire, keep changing, stay open, and stay curious. We can attest that the more you learn about conflict resolution and prevention, the more joyful your life will be.

Summary

Conflict prevention skills help keep conflict from fully developing and becoming destructive. Core values associated with prevention were presented, and we encouraged you to examine your own history in conflict and identify what might be changed. We presented information on identifying conflict cycles as they unfold, with change options given for each stage. We discussed the warning signs for avoidance and escalation spirals, giving specific suggestions for what to do in each case. Post-conflict assessments, contracts, and agreements were presented as prevention activities. Problem solving was discussed as a further prevention technique. Making personal changes in conflict necessitates addressing habitual relationship and identity issues for yourself, and then letting go of anger and resentment.

We gave detailed communication suggestions for those who habitually avoid or escalate conflict. Finally, conflict prevention is essentially the same set of skills as excellent communication in general.

As you improve and add to your communication choices, conflict will become less negative for you and more productive when it does arise, and you will give great benefits to those around you.

Key Terms

Use the text's Online Learning Center at **www.mhhe.com/wilmot7** to further your understanding of the following terminology.

prevention 326
core values 328
learning from your conflict history 330
cycle of conflict 331
preventing destructive avoidance 333

escalation spirals 333
preventing escalation 334
warning signs 334
post-conflict contract 335
communication protocol 335
counseling agreement 336

problem-solving steps 336
problem-solving sequences 336
personal change 337
communication is the key 338

Review Questions

Go to the self-quizzes on the Online Learning Center at **www.mhhe.com/wilmot 7** to test your knowledge of the chapter concepts.

1. Define prevention.
2. Why is prevention important?
3. What was the creative move in the "rescue crew" fable?
4. What are some core values that lead to prevention of conflict? Discuss those most important to you.
5. Outline your personal conflict history and what you might change based on this history.
6. How can avoidance spirals be prevented?
7. What can you do if you habitually avoid becoming more effective in conflict?
8. What do avoiders need when they are in conflict?
9. How can escalation spirals be de-escalated or prevented?
10. What is contracting?
11. What are some forms that "contracting" takes to prevent conflict?
12. Describe a counseling agreement.
13. What are the requirements for a constructive counseling agreement?
14. Reproduce the major steps of an expanded problem-solving sequence.
15. What are the two TRIP issues that usually underlie difficult conflicts?
16. Discuss some steps to try if you continually escalate.
17. Why is communication the key feature in conflict?

Appendix

Conflict Resolution Resources on the Web

The following Web sites are good starting points for information. These tend to change, so we recommend doing a search using some of the key words at the bottom.

www.acresolution.org

The Association for Conflict Resolution is a helpful site with articles, updates, and mediator listings. The organization holds an annual conference, training events and provides extensive resources, and listings of Advanced Practitioner members in family and workplace sections.

www.mediate.com

The Mediate.com site is a privately owned site with timely articles on mediation issues and a variety of resources. It is a good source for linking to state associations. Its listing of mediators is limited to lists of those who pay a fee to Mediate.com.

www.adr.org

The American Arbitration Association site that includes all forms of ADR (alternative dispute resolution) including mediation and arbitration.

www.campus.adr.org

Tools and resources about conflict in higher education located at Wayne State University. It is a good source for listing graduate programs in conflict resolution and mediation in the United States, Canada, and Europe.

www.restorativejustice.org

Overview, resources, and links about restorative justice mediation.

Key Words to Use in a Search

Conflict management
Conflict resolution
Graduate programs in conflict
Conflict resolution in schools
Peer mediation
Peace studies

Justice studies
Mediation training
Restorative justice
Family & conciliation courts
Alternative Dispute Resolution

References

Acitelli, L. K., E. Douvan, and J. Veroff. 1993. Perceptions of conflict in the first year of marriage: How important are similarity and understanding? *Journal of Social and Personal Relationships* 10: 5–20.

Alberts, J., and G. Driscoll. 1992. Containment versus escalation: The trajectory of couples' conversational complaints. *Western Journal of Communication* 56: 394–412.

Alberts, J. K., P. Lutgen-Sandvik, and S. J. Tracy. 2005. *Bullying in the workplace: A case of escalated incivility*. To be presented at the International Communication Association Convention, New York, May.

Alper, B. S., and L. W. Nichols. 1981. *Beyond the courtroom*. Lexington, MA: Lexington Books.

Amato, P. R., and S. R. Rogers. 1999. Do attitudes toward divorce affect marital quality? *Journal of Family Issues* 20: 69–87.

Anonymous, 1993, *Getting Over*, The New Yorker.

Apfelbaum, E. 1974. On conflicts and bargaining. *Advances in Experimental Social Psychology* 7: 103–156.

Applegate, J. L. 1982. The impact of construct system development on communication and impression formation in persuasive contexts. *Communication Monographs* 49 (December): 277–286.

Argyle, M., and A. Furnham. 1983. Sources of satisfaction and conflict in long-term relationships. *Journal of Marriage and the Family* 45: 481–493.

Arnett, R. C. 1980a. *Dialogical foundations of conflict resolution*. Paper presented to the Speech Communication Association Convention, New York, November 16.

Arnold, W. E. 1977. Crisis communication. In *Communicating through behavior*, edited by W. E. Arnold and R. O. Hirsch. St. Paul, MN: West Publishing.

Association for Conflict Resolution. 2004. *Conflict resolution education: Fostering peace building in our schools*. Fall.

Augsburger, D. W. 1992. *Conflict mediation across cultures: Pathways and patterns*. Louisville, KY: Westminster/John Knox Press.

Bach, G. R., and H. Goldberg. 1974. *Creative aggression: The art of assertive living*. New York: Avon Books.

Bach, G. R., and P. Wyden. 1968. *The intimate enemy: How to fight fair in love and marriage*. New York: Avon Books.

Baillie, G. 1999. *Violence unveiled*. New York: Crossroad Publishing Company.

Ballard, S. 2004. How to handle a workplace bully: Schoolyard bullies have graduated from the classroom to the boardroom. *Jet* 106: 16–20.

Barnett, R. C., N. L. Marshall, and J. H. Pleck. 1992. Men's multiple roles and their relationship to men's psychological distress. *Journal of Marriage and the Family* 54: 358–368.

Barnlund, D. C. 1989. *Communicative styles of Japanese and Americans: Images and realities*. Belmont, CA: Wadsworth.

Baron, R. A. 1984. Reducing organizational conflict: An incompatible response approach. *Journal of Applied Psychology* 69: 272–279.

Barr, C. 2000. No borders in Spice Island clash. *The Christian Science Monitor*, January 20, 6–7.

Bartos, O. J. 1974. *Process and outcome of negotiations*. New York: Columbia University Press.

Baskin, T. and Enright, R., (2004, Winter), Intervention Studies on Forgiveness: A Meta-Analysis, *Journal of Counseling & Development*, Vol. 82, 79–90.

Bateson, G. 1972. *Steps to an ecology of mind*. New York: Ballantine Books.

———. 1980. *Mind and nature: A necessary unity*. New York: Bantam Books.

Baumeister, R. R., A. Stillwell, and S. R. Wotman. 1990. Victim and perpetrator accounts of interpersonal conflict: Autobiographical narratives about anger. *Journal of Personality and Social Psychology* 59: 994–1005.

Baxter, L. A. 1982. Conflict management: An episodic approach. *Small Group Behavior* 13, no. 1: 23–42.

Baxter, Leslie A., D. O. Braithwaite, and J. Nicholson. 1999. Turning points in the development of blended family relationships. *Journal of Social and Personal Relationships* 16: 291–313.

Bazerman, M. H., T. Magliozzi, and M. A. Neale. 1985. Integrative bargaining in a competitive market. *Organizational Behavior and Human Decision Processes* 35: 294–313.

Bazerman, M. H., and M. A. Neale. 1983. Heuristics in negotiation: Limitations to effective dispute resolution procedures. In *Negotiating in organizations*, edited by M. Bazerman and R. Lewicki. Beverly Hills, CA: Sage Publications.

Beck, A. T. 1988. *Love is never enough*. New York: Harper & Row.

Belenky, M., B. Clinchy, N. Goldberger, and J. Tarule. 1986. *Women's ways of knowing: The development of self, voice, and mind*. New York: Basic Books.

Bell, D. C., J. S. Chafetz, and L. H. Horn. 1982. Marital conflict resolution: A study of strategies and outcomes. *Journal of Family Issues* 3: 111–131.

Bell, M. L., and D. Forde. 1999. A factorial survey of interpersonal conflict resolution. *Journal of Social Psychology* 139: 369–378.

Bell, R. A., and J. A. Daly. 1984. The affinity-seeking function of communication. *Communication Monographs* 51: 91–115.

Benoit, P. J. 1983. Characteristics of arguing from a naive social actor's perspective. In *Argument in transition: Proceedings of the third summer conference on argumentation*, edited by D. Zarefsky, M. O. Sillars, and J. Rhodes, 544–559. Annandale, VA: Speech Communication Association.

———. 1992. Introduction, special issue: Interpersonal argumentation. *Argumentation and Advocacy* 29: 39–40.

Berger, C. R. 1980. Power and the family. In *Persuasion: New directions in theory and research*, edited by M. E. Roloff and G. R. Miller. Beverly Hills, CA: Sage Publications.

Bergmann, T. J., and R. J. Volkema. 1994. Issues, behavioral responses and consequences in interpersonal conflicts. *Journal of Organizational Behavior* 15: 467–471.

Bernard, M., and J. Bernard. 1983. Violent intimacy: The family as a model for love relationships. *Family Relations* 32: 283–286.

Bernstein, L. 1981. *Disarmament*. Address to Johns Hopkins University, Baltimore, MD.

Berry, W. 1992. Pray without ceasing. In *Fidelity*. New York and London: Pantheon Press.

Betz, B., and W. R. Fry. 1995. The role of group schema in the selection of influence attempts. *Basic and Applied Social Psychology* 16: 351–365.

Bingham, L. B. 2004. Employment dispute resolution: The case for mediation. *Conflict Resolution Quarterly* 22, no. 1–2: 145–174.

Bjorkqvist, K., K. Osterman, and M. Hjelt-Back. 1994. Aggression among university employees. *Aggressive Behavior* 20: 173–184.

Bjorkqvist, K., K. Osterman, and K. M. J. Lagerspetz. 1994. Sex differences in covert aggression among adults. *Aggressive Behavior* 20: 27–33.

Blake, R. R., and J. S. Mouton. 1964. *Managerial grid*. Houston, TX: Gulf Publishing.

Blake, R. R., A. Shepard, and J. S. Mouton. 1964. *Managing intergroup conflict in industry*. Houston, TX: Gulf Publishing.

Blau, P. M. 1964. *Exchange and power in social life*. New York: John Wiley & Sons.

Blood, R. O., Jr., and D. M. Wolfe. 1960. *Husbands and wives: The dynamics of married living*. Glencoe, IL: Free Press.

Bochner, A. P. 1976. Conceptual frontiers in the study of communication in families: An introduction to the literature. *Human Communication Research* 2, no. 4: 381–397.

Bochner, A. P., D. L. Krueger, and T. L. Chmielewski. 1982. Interpersonal perceptions and marital adjustments. *Journal of Communication* 32: 135–147.

Bodtker, A. M., and J. K. Jameson. 2001. Emotion in conflict formation and its transformation: Application to organizational conflict management. *International Journal of Conflict Management* 12, no. 3: 259–275.

Bolger, N., A. DeLongis, R. C. Kessler, and E. A. Schilling. 1989. Effects of daily stress on negative mood. *Journal of Personality and Social Psychology* 57: 808–818.

Borisoff, D., and D. A. Victor. 1989. *Conflict management: A communication skills approach*. Englewood Cliffs, NJ: Prentice Hall.

Boulding, K. 1962. *Conflict and defense: A general theory*. New York: Harper Torchbooks.

———. 1987. Learning peace. In *The quest for peace*, edited by R. Vayrynen. London: Sage Publications.

———. 1989. *Three faces of power*. Newbury Park, CA: Sage Publications.

Bowers, J. W. 1974. Beyond threats and promises. *Speech Monographs* 41: ix–xi.

Bowers, J. W., and D. J. Ochs. 1971. *The rhetoric of agitation and control*. Reading, MA: Addison-Wesley Publishing.

Braiker, H. B., and H. H. Kelley. 1979. Conflict in the development of close relationships. In *Social exchange in developing relationships*, edited by R. L. Burgess and T. L. Huston. New York: Academic Press.

Braithwaite, D. O., L. Olson, T. Golish, C. Soukup, and P. Turman. 2001. Becoming a family: Developmental processes represented in blended family discourse. *Journal of Applied Communication Research* 29: 221–247.

Braman, R. 1998. Teaching peace to adults: Using critical thinking to improve conflict resolution. *Adult Learning* (Winter): 30–33.

Brammer, L. M. 1973. *The helping relationship*. Englewood Cliffs, NJ: Prentice Hall.

Breggin, P. B. 1992. *Beyond conflict: From self-help and psychotherapy to peacemaking*. New York: St. Martin's Press.

Brett, J. M., Z. I. Barsness, and S. B. Goldberg. 1996. The effectiveness of mediation: An independent analysis of cases handled by four major service providers. *Negotiation Journal* 12: 259–269.

Brockner, J., and J. Z. Rubin. 1985. *Entrapment in escalating conflicts: A social psychological analysis*. New York: Springer-Verlag.

Brockriede, W. 1972. Arguers as lovers. *Philosophy and Rhetoric* 5 (Winter): 1–11.

Brown, B. R. 1977. Face-saving and face-restoration in negotiation. In *Negotiations*, edited by D. Druckman, 275–299. Beverly Hills, CA: Sage Publications.

Brown, C. T., and P. W. Keller. 1973. *Monologue to dialogue*. Englewood Cliffs, NJ: Prentice Hall.

Brown, L. D. 1992. Normative conflict management theories: Past, present and future. *Journal of Organizational Behavior* 13: 303–309.

Brown, L. M., and C. Gilligan. 1992. *Meeting at the crossroads: Women's psychology and girls' development*. Cambridge, MA: Harvard University Press.

Brown, P., and S. Levinson. 1978. Universals in language use: Politeness phenomena. In *Questions and politeness: Strategies in social interaction*, edited by E. Goody. New York: Cambridge University Press.

Browning, J., and O. Dotton. 1986. Assessment of wife assault with the conflict tactics scale: Using couple data to quantify the differential reporting effect. *Journal of Marriage and the Family* 48: 375–379.

Brutz, J., and C. M. Allen. 1986. Religious commitment, peace activism, and marital violence in Quaker families. *Journal of Marriage and the Family* 48: 491–502.

Brygger, M. P., and M. Edleson. 1984. *Gender differences in reporting of battering incidents*. Paper presented at the Second National Conference for Family Violence Researchers, University of New Hampshire, Durham.

Buber, M. 1972. *Between man and man*. New York: Macmillan.

Buitrago, Y. 1997. *Mediation through a Hispanic lens*. Paper presented to the Intercultural Communication Division of

Western State Communication Association, San Diego, California.

Bullis, C. 1983. *Conflict behavior: An inductive examination of deductive measures.* Paper presented at the Western Speech Communication Association Convention, Albuquerque, New Mexico, February.

Burggraf, D., and A. Sillars. 1987. A critical examination of sex differences in marital communication. *Communication Monographs* 54: 276–294.

Burgoon, J. K., M. L. Johnson, and P. T. Koch. 1998. The nature and measurement of interpersonal dominance. *Communication Monographs* 65, no. 4: 308–310.

Burleson, B. R., A. W. Kunkel, W. Samter, and K. J. Werking. 1996. Men's and women's evaluations of communication skills in personal relationships: When sex differences make a difference—and when they don't. *Journal of Social and Personal Relationships* 13: 201–224.

Burman, B and Margolin, G. 1992. "Analysis of the association between marital relationships and health problems: an interactional perspective" *Psychological Bulletin* v112 n1 p39(25).

Burrell, N. A., and D. D. Cahn. 1994. Mediating peer conflicts in education contexts: The maintenance of school relationships. In *Conflict in personal relationships*, edited by D. D. Cahn, 79–94. Hillsdale, NJ: Lawrence Erlbaum Associates.

Burrell, N. A., W. A. Donohue, and M. Allen. 1988. Gender-based perceptual biases in mediation. *Communication Research* 15: 447–469.

Bush, R. A. B., and J. P. Folger. 1994. *The promise of mediation: Responding to conflict through empowerment and recognition.* San Francisco: Jossey-Bass.

Buttny, R. 2000. Discursive positioning as accounting and dialogic practice. *Narrative Inquiry* 10, no. 1: 147–151.

Buunk, B. P., C. Schaap, and N. Prevoo. 1990. Conflict resolution styles attributed to self and partner in premarital relationships. *Journal of Social Psychology* 130: 821–823.

Buzzard, L. R., and L. Eck. 1982. *Tell it to the church: Reconciling out of court.* Elgin, IL: David C. Cook Publishing.

Cahill, M. 1982. *Couples' perceptions of power.* Paper for Interpersonal Communication 595: Advanced Conflict Management, University of Montana.

Cahn, D. D. 1994. *Conflict in personal relationships.* Hillsdale, NJ: Lawrence Erlbaum Associates.

Camara, K. A., and G. Resnick. 1989. Styles of conflict resolution and cooperation between divorced parents: Effects on child behavior and adjustment. *American Journal of Orthopsychiatry* 59, no. 4: 560–575.

Cameron, K. S., and D. A. Whetten. 1995. *Developing management skills.* New York: Harper Collins College Publishers.

Campbell, J. 1988. *The power of myth.* New York: Doubleday.

Canary, D. J., E. M. Cunningham, and M. J. Cody. 1988. Goal types, gender, and locus of control in managing interpersonal conflict. *Communication Research* 15: 426–447.

Canary, D. J., and W. R. Cupach. 1988. Relational and episodic characteristics associated with conflict tactics. *Journal of Social and Personal Relationships* 5: 305–322.

Canary, D. J., W. R. Cupach, and S. J. Messman. 1995. *Relationship conflict.* Thousand Oaks, CA: Sage Publications.

Canary, D. J., and B. H. Spitzberg. 1987. Appropriateness and effectiveness perceptions of conflict strategies. *Human Communication Research* 14: 93–118.

———. 1990. Attribution biases and associations between conflict strategies and competence outcomes. *Communication Monographs* 57 (June): 141–151.

Carey, C. M., and P. A. Mongeau. 1996. Communication and violence in courtship relationships. In *Family violence from a communication perspective*, edited by D. D. Cahn and S. A. Lloyd, 127–150. Hillsdale, NJ: Lawrence Erlbaum Associates.

Carkhuff, R. 1969. *Helping and human relations*, 2 vols. New York: Holt, Rinehart & Winston.

Carnes, P. J. 1981. *Family development.* Vol. 1, *Understanding us.* Minneapolis: Interpersonal Communication Programs.

Carnevale, P. J. D., and E. J. Lawler. 1986. Time pressure and the development of integrative agreements in bilateral negotiations. *Journal of Conflict Resolution* 30: 636–659.

Cate, R., J. Henton, J. Koval, R. Christopher, and S. Lloyd. 1982. Premarital abuse: A social psychological perspective. *Journal of Family Issues* 3: 70–90.

Cavanaugh, M., C. Larson, A. Goldberg, and J. Bellow. 1981a. Power. *Communication* 10, no. 2: 81–107.

———. 1981b. *Power and communication behavior: A formulative investigation.* Unpublished manuscript. Department of Speech Communication, University of Denver.

Chafetz, J. S. 1980. Conflict resolution in marriage: Toward a theory of spousal strategies and marital dissolution rates. *Journal of Family Issues* 1: 397–421.

Chanin, M. N., and J. A. Schneer. 1984. A study of the relationship between Jungian personality dimensions and conflict-handling behavior. *Human Relations* 37, no. 10: 863–879.

Chodron, T. 2001. *Working with anger.* Ithaca, NY: Snow Lion Publications.

Christiansen, A., and D. C. Nies. 1980. The spouse observation checklist: Empirical analysis and critique. *American Journal of Family Therapy* 8: 69–79.

Cissna, K. and Sieburg, E. 1981. Patterns of interactional confirmation and disconfirmation in *Rigor and Imagination*, Wilder-Mott, C. and Weakland, J. (Eds.), Praeger Publications.

Clark, R. A., L. L. O'Dell, and S. C. Willihnganz. 1985. Training fourth graders in compromising and persuasive strategies. *Communication Education* 34: 331–342.

Cloven, D. H., and M. E. Roloff. 1991. Sense-making activities and interpersonal conflict: Communicative cures for the mulling blues. *Western Journal of Speech Communication* 55: 134–158.

———. 1993a. The chilling effect of aggressive potential on the expression of complaints in intimate relationships. *Communication Monographs* 60: 199–219.

———. 1993b. Sense-making activities and interpersonal conflict. Part 2, The effects of communicative intentions on internal dialogue. *Western Journal of Speech Communication* 57: 309–329.

———. 1995. Cognitive tuning effects on anticipating communication on thought about an interpersonal conflict. *Communication Reports* 8: 1–9.

Cohen, B. 1999. *The Missoulian,* September 26, A-1.

Coleman, D. H., and M. A. Straus. 1986. Marital power, conflict, and violence in a nationally representative sample of American couples. *Violence and Victims* 1: 141–157.

Coleman, M. A., M. A. Fine, L. G. Ganong, K. M. Downs, and N. Pauk. 2001. When you're not the Brady Bunch: Identifying perceived conflicts and resolution strategies in stepfamilies. *Personal Relationships* 8: 57–73.

Combs, D. 2004. *The way of conflict: Elemental wisdom for resolving disputes and transcending differences.* Novato, CA: New World Library.

Comstock, J. 1994. Parent–adolescent conflict: A developmental approach. *Western Journal of Communication* 58: 263–282.

Comstock, J., and Strzyzewski. 1990. Interpersonal interaction on television: Family conflict and jealousy on prime time. *Journal of Broadcasting and Electronic Media* 34: 263–282.

Condon, J. C. 1985. *Good neighbors: Communicating with the Mexicans.* Yarmouth, ME: Intercultural Press.

Conflict prevention. 1996. *PC Week* 13, no. 32: E3–E4.

Coogler, O. J. 1978. *Structured mediation in divorce settlement.* Lexington, MA: D. C. Heath & Company.

Coraso, W. A., and T. A. Rizzo. 1990. Disputes in the peer culture of American and Italian nursery-school children. In *Research on Conflict Talk,* edited by A. D. Grimshaw, 21–66. Cambridge: Cambridge University Press.

Cose, E. 2004. *Bone to pick.* New York: Atria Books.

Coser, L. A. 1967. *Continuities in the study of social conflict.* New York: Free Press.

Crohan, S. E. 1992. Marital happiness and spousal consensus on beliefs about marital conflict: A longitudinal investigation. *Journal of Social and Personal Relationships* 9: 89–102.

Cromwell, R. E., and D. H. Olson. 1975. *Power in families.* Beverly Hills, CA: Sage Publications.

Cuber, J. F., and P. B. Haroff. 1955. *The significant Americans: A study of sexual behavior among the affluent.* New York: Appleton-Century.

Cupach, W. R. 1980. *Interpersonal conflict: Relational strategies and intimacy.* Paper presented to the Speech Communication Association Convention, New York.

———. 1982. *Communication satisfaction and interpersonal solidarity as outcomes of conflict message strategy use.* Paper presented at the International Communication Association Convention, May.

Cupach, W., and B. Spitzberg, eds. 1994. *The dark side of interpersonal communication.* Hillsday, NJ: Lawrence Erlbaum.

Cupach, W. R., and L. N. Olson. In press. Emotion regulation theory: A lens for viewing family conflict and violence. In *Family communication theories,* edited by D. O. Braithwaite and L. A. Baxter. Thousand Oaks, CA: Sage.

Dahl, R. A. 1957. The concept of power. *Behavioral Science* 2: 201–215.

———. 1963. *Modern political analysis.* Englewood Cliffs, NJ: Prentice Hall.

Deal, J. E., and K. S. Wampler. 1986. Dating violence: The primacy of previous experience. *Journal of Social and Personal Relationships* 3: 457–471.

Delia, J. G., and R. A. Clark. 1977. Cognitive complexity, social perception and the development of listener-adapted communication in six-, eight-, ten-, and twelve-year-old boys. *Communication Monographs* 44, no. 4: 326–345.

Deturck, M. A. 1987. When communication fails: Physical aggression as a compliance-gaining strategy. *Communication Monographs* 54: 106–112.

Deutsch, M. 1949. A theory of competition and cooperation. *Human Relations* 2: 129–151.

———. 1958. Trust and suspicion. *Journal of Conflict Resolution* 2: 265–279.

———. 1973. Conflicts: Productive and destructive. In *Conflict resolution through communication,* edited by F. E. Jandt. New York: Harper & Row.

Deutsch, M., and P. Coleman, eds. 2000. *The handbook of conflict resolution.* San Francisco, CA: Jossey Bass.

Deutsch, M., and R. M. Krauss. 1960. The effect of threat upon interpersonal bargaining. *Journal of Abnormal and Social Psychology* 61: 181–189.

DeVoe, D. 1999. Communications skills: Learn to resolve or avoid work conflicts. *InfoWorld,* no. 34 (August): 84.

Diblasio, F. 2000. Decision-based forgiveness treatment in cases of marital infidelity. *Psychotherapy* 37, no. 2: 149–158.

Dien, D. S. F. 1982. A Chinese perspective on Kohlberg's theory of moral development. *Developmental Review* 2: 331–341.

Dobash, R. E., and R. P. Dobash. 1979. *Violence against wives.* New York: Free Press.

Dollard, J., L. W. Dobb, N. Miller, O. H. Mower, and R. R. Sears. 1939. *Frustration and aggression.* New Haven, CT: Yale University Press.

Donohue, W. A. 1991. *Communication, marital dispute, and divorce mediation.* Hillsdale, NJ: Lawrence Erlbaum Associates.

Donohue, W. A., M. Allen, and N. Burrell. 1988. Mediator communicative competence. *Communication Monographs* 55: 104–119.

Donohue, W. A., L. Drake, and A. J. Roberto. 1994. Mediator issue intervention strategies: A replication and some conclusions. *Mediation Quarterly* 11: 261–274.

Donohue, W. A., and R. Kolt. 1992. *Managing interpersonal conflict.* Newbury Park, CA: Sage Publications.

Downs, T., and J. Downs. 2003. *Fight fair: Winning at conflict without losing at love.* Chicago: Moody Publishers.

Duhl, F. A., D. Kantor, and B. S. Duhl. 1973. Learning, space and action in family therapy: A primer of sculpture. In *Techniques of family psychotherapy,* edited by D. Bloch. New York: Grune & Stratton.

Dumlao, R., and R. A. Botta. 2000. Family communication patterns and the conflict styles young adults use with their fathers. *Communication Quarterly* 48, no. 2: 174–190.

Dunn, C. W., and C. M. Tucker. 1993. Black children's adaptive functioning and maladaptive behavior associated with quality of family support. *Journal of Multicultural Counseling and Development* 21: 79–87.

Edelgard, M., and W. Colsman. 2002. Conflict resolution style as an indicator of adolescents' substance use and other problem behaviors. *Addictive Behaviors* 26, no. 4: 633–648.

Eder, D., 1990. Serious and playful disputes: Variation in conflict talk among female adolescents. In *Research on conflict talk*, edited by A. D. Grimshaw, 67–84. Cambridge: Cambridge University Press.

Edwards, H. T., and J. J. White. 1977. *Problems, readings and materials on the lawyer as a negotiator.* St. Paul, MN: West Publishing.

Einarsen, S. 1999. The nature and causes of bullying at work. *International Journal of Manpower* 20: 16–27.

Einarsen, S., and E. G. Mikkelsen. 2003. Individual effects of exposure to bullying at work. In *Bullying and emotional abuse in the workplace: International perspectives in research and practice*, edited by S. Einarsen, H. Hoel, D. Zapf, and C. L. Cooper, 127–144. London: Taylor & Francis Publishers.

Eleff, L. 2001. Paper for mediation class. Arizona State University.

Elkouri, F., and E. Elkouri. 1985. *How arbitration works.* 3d ed. Washington, DC: Bureau of National Affairs.

Ellis, D. G. 1979. Relational control in two group systems. *Communication Monographs* 46, no. 3: 153–166.

El-Sheikh, M. 1994. Children's emotional and physiological responses to interadult angry behavior: The role of history of interparental hostility. *Journal of Abnormal Child Psychology* 22: 661–679.

El-Sheikh, M., and J. Cheskes. 1995. Background verbal and physical anger: A comparison of children's responses to adult-adult and adult-child arguments. *Child Development* 66: 446–458.

Emerson, R. M. 1962. Power-dependence relations. *American Sociological Review* 27: 31–41.

Enright, R. 1996. Counseling within the forgiveness triad: On forgiving, receiving forgiveness, and self-forgiveness. *Counseling and Values* 40, no. 2: 107–127.

Enright, R. D., & the Human Development Study Group. (1991). The moral development of forgiveness. In W. Kurtines & Gewirtz (Eds.), *Moral behavior and development* [Vol. 1. pp. 123–152]. Hillsdale, NJ, Erlbaum.

Enright, R., E. Gassin, and C. Wu. 1992. Forgiveness: A developmental view. *Journal of Moral Education* 21: 101.

Ertel, D. 1991. How to design a conflict management procedure that fits your dispute. *Sloan Management Review* 32, no. 4: 29–43.

Evans, P. 1992. *The verbally abusive relationship.* Holbrook, MA: Bob Adams.

Exline, J., and R. Baumeister. 2000. Expressing forgiveness and repentance. *Forgiveness, theory, research, and practice*, edited by M. McCullough, K. Pargament, and C. Thoresen. New York: Guilford Press.

Falbo, T., and L. A. Peplau. 1980. Power strategies in intimate relationships. *Journal of Personality and Social Psychology* 38: 618–628.

Felson, R. B. 1996. Big people hit little people: Sex differences in physical power and interpersonal violence. *Criminology* 34, no. 3: 433–452.

Files, L. A. 1981. The human services management task: A time allocation study. *Public Administration Review* 41: 686–692.

Fincham, F. D., and S. R. H. Beach. 1999. Conflict in marriage: Implications for working with couples. *Annual Review of Psychology.*

Fisher, L. 1982. Transactional theories but individual assessment: A frequent discrepancy in family research. *Family Process* 21 (September): 313–320.

Fisher, R. 1971. Fractioning conflict. In *Conflict resolution: Contributions of the behavioral sciences*, edited by C. Smith, 157–169. Notre Dame: University of Notre Dame Press.

———. 1972. Third party consultation: A method for the study and resolution of conflict. *Journal of Conflict Resolution* 16 (March): 67–94.

———. 1985. Beyond yes. *Negotiation Journal* 1: 67–70.

———. 1986. Dealing with conflict among individuals and nations: Are there common principles? *Psychoanalytic Inquiry* 6: 143–153.

Fisher, R., and S. Brown. 1988. *Getting together: Building a relationship that gets to yes.* Boston, MA: Houghton Mifflin.

Fisher, R., and W. Ury. 1981. *Getting to yes: Negotiating agreement without giving in.* Boston, MA: Houghton Mifflin.

Fisher, R., W. Ury, and B. Patton. 1991. *Getting to yes.* 2d ed. New York: Penguin Books.

Fiske, S. T. 1993. Controlling other people: The impact of power on stereotyping. *American Psychologist* 48 (June): 621–628.

Fletcher, J. 1999. *Disappearing acts: Gender, power, and relational practice at work.* Cambridge, MA: MIT Press.

Fogg, R. W. 1985. Dealing with conflict: A repertoire of creative, peaceful approaches. *Journal of Conflict Resolution* 29: 330–358.

Folger, J. P., and M. S. Poole. 1984. *Working through conflict: A communication perspective.* Glenview, IL: Scott, Foresman & Company.

Folger, J. P., M. S. Poole, and R. Stutman. 1993. *Working through conflict: A communication perspective.* Glenview, IL: Scott, Foresman & Company.

Folger, J. P., M. S. Poole, and R. K. Stutman. 2004. *Working through conflict: Strategies for relationships, groups, and organizations.* 5th ed. Glenview, IL: Poole, Allyn and Bacon.

Follett, M. P. 1940. *Dynamic administration: The collected papers of M. P. Follett.* Edited by H. C. Metcalf and L. Urwick. New York: Harper & Brothers.

Forte, P. S. 1997. The high cost of conflict. *Nursing Economics* 15, no. 3: 119–124.

Foss, S., and C. L. Griffin. 1995. Beyond persuasion: A proposal for an invitational rhetoric. *Communication Monographs* 62 (March): 2–18.

Frank, J. D. 1978. *Psychotherapy and the human predicament: A psychosocial approach.* New York: Schocken Books.

Freeman, S. A., S. W. Littlejohn, and W. B. Pearce. 1992. Communication and moral conflict. *Western Journal of Communication* 56: 311–329.

Frentz, T., and J. H. Rushing. 1980. *A communicative perspective on closeness/distance and stability/change in intimate ongoing dyads.* Unpublished manuscript. University of Colorado, Boulder.

Funk, J., R. Elliott, H. Bechtoldt, T. Pasold, and A. Tsavoussis. 2003. The attitudes toward violence scale: Child version. *Journal of Interpersonal Violence* 18, no. 2: 186–197.

Galtung, J. (1996). *Peace by Peaceful Means.* Oslo, Norway: International Peace Research Institute.

Galvin, K. M., and B. J. Brommel. 1982. *Family communication: Cohesion and change.* Glenview, IL: Scott, Foresman & Company.

———. 1986. *Family communication: Cohesion and change.* 2d ed. Glenview, IL: Scott, Foresman & Company.

Garber, R. J. 1991. Long-term effects of divorce on the self-esteem of young adults. *Journal of Divorce and Remarriage* 17: 131–137.

Gayle, B. M. 1991. Sex equity in workplace conflict management. *Journal of Applied Communication Research* 19: 152–169.

Gayle-Hackett, B. 1989a. *Do females and males differ in the selection of conflict management strategies: A meta-analytic review.* Paper presented to the Western Speech Communication Association Convention, Spokane, Washington, February 17.

———. 1989b. *Gender differences in conflict management strategy selection: A preliminary organizational investigation.* Paper presented to the Western Speech Communication Association Convention, Spokane, Washington, February 17.

Gelles, R. 1981. The myth of the battered husband. In *Marriage and family,* edited by R. Walsh and O. Poes. New York: Guilford Press.

———. 1987. *The violent home.* Beverly Hills, CA: Sage Publications.

Gelles, R. J. 1997. *Intimate violence in families.* Thousand Oaks, CA: Sage Publishing.

Gelles, R. J., and C. P. Cornell. 1990. *Intimate violence in families.* 2d ed. Newbury Park, CA: Sage Publications.

Gerzon, M. 1992. *A Choice of Heroes: The Changing Faces of American Manhood.* New York: Houghton Mifflin Company; Reprint edition.

———. 1994. *A choice of heroes.* Boston, MA: Houghton Mifflin.

———. Getting over. 1993. *The NewYorker:* 67, 24

Gibb, J. 1961. Defensive communication. *Journal of Communication* 11, no. 3: 141–148.

Gilligan, C. 1982. *In a different voice.* Cambridge, MA: Harvard University Press: 18–63.

Gilmore, S. K., and P. W. Fraleigh. 1992. *Style profile for communication at work.* Eugene, OR: Friendly Press.

Gire, J. T., and D. W. Carment. 1993. Dealing with disputes: The influence of individualism-collectivism. *Journal of Social Psychology* 133, no. 1: 81–96.

Glass, I. 2004. Apology. This American life. *Chicago Public Radio.* November 5.

Glick, B. R., and S. J. Gross. 1975. Marital interaction and marital conflict: A critical evaluation of current research strategies. *Journal of Marriage and the Family* 37, no. 3: 505–512.

Goffman, E. 1967. *Interaction ritual: Essays on face to face behavior.* Garden City, NY: Doubleday.

Goldberg, A. A., M. S. Cavanaugh, and C. E. Larson. 1983. The meaning of "power." *Journal of Applied Communication Research* 11, no. 2: 89–108.

Goleman, D. 1995. *Emotional intelligence.* New York: Bantam Books.

———. 1998. *Working with emotional intelligence.* New York: Bantam Books.

Goleman, D., R. Boyatzis, and A. Mckee. 2002. *Primal leadership: Realizing the power of emotional intelligence.* Cambridge: Harvard Business School Press.

Goodpaster, G. 1992. Lawsuits as negotiations. *Negotiation Journal* 8, no. 3: 221–239.

Goodrich, D. W., and D. S. Boomer. 1963. Experimental assessment of modes of conflict resolution. *Family Process* 2: 15–24.

Goodrich, T. J. 1991. Women, power, and family therapy: What's wrong with this picture? In *Women and power: Perspectives for family therapy,* edited by T. J. Goodrich, 3–35. New York: W. W. Norton & Company.

Gottman, J. and N. Jacobsen. *When Men Batter Women: New Insights into ending abusive relationships.* New York, NY: Simon and Schuster, 1998.

Gottman, J., C. Notarius, J. Gonso, and H. Markman. 1976. *A couple's guide to communication.* Champaign, IL: Research Press.

Gottman, J. M. 1982. Emotional responsiveness in marital conversations. *Journal of Communication* 32, no. 8: 108–120.

———. 1994. *What predicts divorce? The relationship between marital processes and marital outcomes.* Hillsdale, NJ: Lawrence Erlbaum Associates.

———. 1999. *The marriage clinic: A scientifically based marital therapy.* New York: W. W. Norton and Co.

Gottman, J. M., and L. J. Krokoff. 1989. Marital interaction and satisfaction: A longitudinal view. *Journal of Consulting and Clinical Psychology* 57: 47–52.

Gray, B. 1989. *Collaborating: Finding common ground for multiparty problems.* San Francisco, CA: Jossey-Bass.

Gray, F., P. S. Graubard, and H. Rosenberg. 1974. Little brother is changing you. *Psychology Today* (March): 12–16.

Gray-Little, B. 1982. Marital quality and power processes among black couples. *Journal of Marriage and the Family* 44, no. 3: 633–646.

Gray-Little, B., and N. Burks. 1983. Power and satisfaction in marriage: A review and critique. *Psychological Bulletin* 93, no. 3: 513–538.

Greene, K., and M. Bogo. 2002. The different faces of intimate violence: Implications for assessment and treatment. *Journal of Marital and Family Therapy* 28, no. 4: 455–467.

Greer, C. 1998. Without memory there is no healing. Without forgiveness there is no future. *Parade Magazine*, January 16, 4–6.

Grimshaw, A. D., ed. 1990. *Conflict talk: Sociolinguistic investigations of arguments in conversations*. Cambridge: Cambridge University Press.

Grych, J. H., and F. D. Fincham. 1990. Marital conflict and children's adjustment: A cognitive conceptual framework. *Psychological Bulletin* 108: 267–290.

Gudykunst, W., and S. Ting-Toomey. 1988. *Culture and interpersonal communication*. Beverly Hills, CA: Sage Publications.

Gudykunst, W. B., and Y. Yun Kim. 2002. *Communicating with strangers: An approach to intercultural communication*. New York: McGraw-Hill.

Guerin, P. J., Jr., L. F. Fay, S. L. Burden, and J. G. Kautto. 1987. *The evaluation and treatment of marital conflict: A four-stage approach*. New York: Basic Books.

Guggenbuhl-Craig, A. 1971. *Power and the helping professions*. Translated by M. Gubitz. Dallas, TX: Spring Publications.

Gulliver, P. H. 1979. *Disputes and negotiations: A cross-cultural perspective*. New York: Academic Press.

Haferkamp, C. J. 1991–92. Orientations to conflict: Gender, attributions, resolution strategies, and self-monitoring. *Current Psychology: Research and Reviews* 10: 227–240.

Haley, J. 1959. An interactional description of schizophrenia. *Psychiatry* 22: 321–332.

Hall, J. 1969. *Conflict management survey*. Conroe, TX: Teleometrics.

Hample, D., and M. Dalinger. 1995. A Lewinian perspective on taking conflict personally: Revision, refinement, and validation of the instrument. *Communication Quarterly* 43: 297–319.

Han, G., and B. Park. 1995. Children's choice in conflict: Application of the theory of individualism-collectivism. *Journal of Cross-Cultural Psychology* 26: 298–313.

Hanh, T. N. 2001. *Anger: Wisdom for cooling the flames*. New York: Riverhead Books.

Hanson, T. L., S. S. McLanahan, and E. Thomson. 1996. Double jeopardy: Parental conflict and stepfamily outcomes for children. *Journal of Marriage and the Family* 58: 141–154.

Hargrave, T. D. 1994. *Families and forgiveness*. New York: Brunner/Mazel.

Harrar, S. 2002. How grudges hurt you: Learn to forgive—for your health's sake. *Prevention* 54, no. 2: 38–39.

Harre, R. 1974. Some remarks on "rule" as a scientific concept. In *Understanding other persons*, edited by T. Mischel. Oxford: Basil Blackwell.

Harrell, W. A. 1990. Husband's masculinity, wife's power, and marital conflict. *Social Behavior and Personality* 18: 207–216.

Harris, L. M., K. J. Gergen, and J. W. Lannamann. 1986. Aggression rituals. *Communication Monographs* 53: 252–265.

Harrison, T. R., and C. Morrill. 2004. Ombuds processes and disputant reconciliation. *Journal of Applied Communication Research* 32, no. 4: 318–342.

Harsanyi, J. C. 1962a. Measurement of social power in n-person reciprocal power situations. *Behavioral Science* 7: 81–91.

———. 1962b. Measurement of social power, opportunity costs, and the theory of two-person bargaining games. *Behavioral Science* 7: 67–80.

Hart, R. P., and D. M. Burks. 1972. Rhetorical sensitivity and social interaction. *Speech Monographs* 39, no. 2: 75–91.

Hartje, J. H. 1984. Lawyer's skills in negotiations: Justice in unseen hands. *Missouri Journal of Dispute Resolution*: 119–192.

Hatfield, E., M. K. Utne, and J. Traupmann. 1979. Equity theory and intimate relationships. In *Social exchange in developing relationships*, edited by R. L. Burgess and T. L. Huston. New York: Academic Press.

Hathaway, W. 1995. A new way of viewing dispute resolution training. *Mediation Quarterly* 13: 37–45.

Hawes, L. C., and D. Smith. 1973. A critique of assumptions underlying the study of communication in conflict. *Quarterly Journal of Speech* 59: 423–435.

Hayakawa, S. I. 1978. *Language in thought and action*. 4th ed. New York: Harcourt Brace Jovanovich.

Haynes, J. M. 1983. The process of negotiations. In *Dimensions and practice of divorce mediation*, edited by J. A. Lemmon. *Mediation Quarterly*, no. 1. San Francisco: Jossey-Bass.

Hedeen, T. 2004. The evolution and evaluation of community mediation: Limited research suggests unlimited progress. *Conflict Resolution Quarterly* 22, no. 1–2: 101–133.

Heer, D. M. 1963. The measurement and bases of family power: An overview. *Marriage and Family Living* 25: 133–139.

Heilbrun, C. 1988. *Writing a woman's life*. New York: Ballantine Books.

Heim, P., and S. K. Galant. 1993. *Smashing the glass ceiling: Tactics for women who want to win in business*. New York: Simon and Schuster.

Heitler, S. 1990. *From conflict to resolution: Skills and strategies for individual, couple, and family therapy*. New York: W. W. Norton & Company.

Henderson, M. 1999. The road to forgiveness. *The Christian Science Monitor*, November 24, 11.

Hermone, R. H. 1974. How to negotiate and come out the winner. *Management Review* 1: 19–25.

Hijuelos, O. 1995. *Mr. Ives' Christmas*. New York: Harper Collins.

Hilgerman, R. H. 1994. *Goal management at work*. New York: McGraw-Hill.

Hirschman, A. O. 1970. *Exit, voice, and loyalty: Responses to decline in firms, organizations, and states*. Cambridge, MA: Harvard University Press.

———. 1974. Exit, voice and loyalty: Further reflections and a survey of recent contributions. *Social Science Information* 13: 7–26.

Hocker, J. L., and B. W. Bach. 1981. *Functions of metaphor in couples' descriptions of conflicts*. Unpublished paper. University of Montana.

Hoffman, L. 1981. *Foundations of family therapy: A conceptual framework for systems change*. New York: Basic Books.

Holloway, S., and G. Brager. 1985. Implicit negotiations and organizational practice. *Administration in Social Work* 9: 15–24.

Holmes, M. E. 1992. Phase structures in negotiation. In *Communication and negotiation*, edited by L. L. Putnam and M. E. Roloff, 83–105. Newbury Park, CA: Sage Publications.

Holmgren, M. 1993. Forgiveness and the intrinsic value of persons. *American Philosophical Quarterly* 30: 4.

Huang, B., H. R. White, R. Kosterman, R. F. Catalano, and J. D. Hawkins. 2001. Developmental associations between alcohol and interpersonal aggression during adolescence. *Journal of Research in Crime and Delinquency* 38, no. 1: 64.

Ilich, J. 1981. *Power negotiating: Strategies for winning in life and business*. Boston, MA: Addison-Wesley Publishing.

Infante, D. A., K. C. Hartley, M. M. Martin, M. A. Higgins, S. D. Bruning, and G. Hur. 1992. Initiating and reciprocating verbal aggression: Effects on credibility and credited valid arguments. *Communication Studies* 43: 182–190.

Infante, D. A., S. A. Myers, and R. Buerkel. 1993. *Argument and verbal aggression in constructive and destructive family and organizational disagreements*. Paper presented at Speech Communication Association Convention, Miami.

Infante, D. A., B. L. Riddle, C. L. Horvath, and S. A. Tumlin. 1992. Verbal aggressiveness: Messages and reasons. *Communication Quarterly* 40: 116–126.

Infante, D. A., and C. J. Wigley III. 1986. Verbal aggressiveness: An interpersonal model and measure. *Communication Monographs* 53: 61–69.

Irving, H. H., and P. E. Bohm. 1978. A social science approach to family dispute resolution. *Canadian Journal of Family Law* 1, no. 1: 39–56.

Ivy, D. K., and P. Backlund. 2003. *Genderspeak: Personal effectiveness in gender communication*. New York: McGraw-Hill.

Jacobson, N. S., and J. M. Gottman. 1998. Anatomy of a violent relationship. *Psychology Today* 3, no. 2: 60–69.

Jaffrey, Z. 1998. Desmond Tutu. *The Progressive* 62: 18–21.

Jamieson, D. W., and K. W. Thomas. 1974. Power and conflict in the student-teacher relationship. *Journal of Applied Behavioral Science* 10: 321–333.

Jamieson, K. H. 1995. *Beyond the double bind: Women and leadership*. New York: Oxford University Press.

Jandt, F. E., ed. 1973. *Conflict resolution through communication*. New York: Harper & Row.

Jaycox, L. H., and R. L. Repetti. 1993. Conflict in families and the psychological adjustment of preadolescent children. *Journal of Family Psychology* 7: 344–355.

Jennings, A. M., C. J. Salts, and T. A. Smith Jr. 1991. Attitudes toward marriage: Effects of parental conflict, family structure, and gender. *Journal of Divorce and Remarriage* 17: 67–79.

Johnson, A. J. 2002. Beliefs about arguing: A comparison of public issue and personal issue arguments. *Communication Reports* 15, no. 2: 99–112.

Johnson, B. 1977. *Communication: The process of organizing*. Boston, MA: Allyn & Bacon.

Johnson, C., and R. Ford. 1996. Dependence power, legitimacy, and tactical choice. *Social Psychology Quarterly* 59, no. 2: 126–141.

Johnson, D. W. 1996. *Reaching out: Interpersonal effectiveness and self-actualization*. Englewood Cliffs, NJ: Prentice Hall.

Johnson, D. W., and R. T. Johnson. 1996. Reducing school violence through conflict resolution training. *NAASP Bulletin* 80, no. 579: 11–19.

Johnson, D. W., R. Johnson, B. Cotten, D. Harris, and S. Louison. 1995. Using conflict managers to mediate conflicts in an inner-city elementary school. *Mediation Quarterly* 12: 379–390.

Johnson, P. 1976. Women and power: Toward a theory of effectiveness. *Journal of Social Issues* 32: 99–110.

Jones, D. C. 1992. Parental divorce, family conflict and friendship networks. *Journal of Social and Personal Relationships* 9: 219–235.

Jones, T. S. 1988. Phase structures in agreement and no-agreement mediation. *Communication Research* 15: 470–495.

———. 2004. Conflict resolution education: The field, the findings, and the future. *Conflict Resolution Quarterly* 22, no. 1–2: 233–267.

Jones, T. S. and A. M. Bodtker. 2001. Mediating with heart in mind: Addressing emotion in mediation practice. *Negotiation Journal* 17, no. 3: 217–244.

Jordan, J. S. 1984. Empathy and self-boundaries. In *Work in progress*. Stone Center Working Paper Series. Wellesley, MA: Stone Center, Wellesley College.

———. 1990. Courage in connection: Conflict, compassion, creativity. In *Work in progress*. Stone Center Working Paper Series. Wellesley, MA: Stone Center, Wellesley College.

———. 1992. Relational resilience. In *Work in progress*. Stone Center Working Paper Series. Wellesley, MA: Stone Center, Wellesley College.

Jordan, J., S. Kaplan, J. Miller, I. Stiver, and J. Surrey. 1991. *Women's growth in connection*. New York: Guilford Press.

Jouriles, E. N., W. J. Bourg, and A. M. Farris. 1991. Marital adjustment and child conduct problems: A comparison of the correlation across subsamples. *Journal of Consulting and Clinical Psychology* 59: 354–357.

Jouriles, E. N., and A. Farris. 1992. Effects of marital conflict on subsequent parent-son interactions. *Behavior Therapy* 23: 355–374.

Kalmuss, D. S., and M. A. Straus. 1982. Wife's marital dependency and wife abuse. *Journal of Marriage and the Family* 44: 277–286.

Kaplan-Leiserson, E. 2004. "Workforce of tomorrow: How can we prepare all youth for future work success?" *Training and Development*, April v58 i4 p12(3).

Kaplan, R. E. 1975. Maintaining interpersonal relationships. *Interpersonal Development* 6: 106.

Karrass, C. 1974. *Give and take: A complete guide to negotiating strategies and tactics*. New York: Thomas Y. Crowell.

Kaschak, E. 1992. *Engendered lives: A new psychology of women's experience*. New York: Basic Books.

Katz, L. F., and J. M. Gottman. 1993. Patterns of marital conflict predict children's internalizing and externalizing behaviors. *Developmental Psychology* 29: 940–950.

Kaufman, S., and G. T. Duncan. 1988. The role of mandates in third party intervention. *Negotiation Journal* 4, no. 4: 403–412.

Keene, F. 1995. The politics of forgiveness. *On the Issues*, Fall: 107–109.

Keeping the Peace. 1995. *Entrepreneur* 23, no. 3: 60–62.

Kellermann, K., and B. C. Shea. 1996. Threats, suggestions, hints and promises: Gaining compliance efficiently and politely. *Communication Quarterly* 44: 145–165.

Kelley, D. 1998. The communication of forgiveness. *Communication Studies* 49: 255–271.

Kelly, J. 2004. Family mediation research: Is there empirical support for the field? *Conflict Resolution Quarterly* 22, no. 1–2: 3–35.

Keltner, J. (Sam). 1983. *You are the mediator*. Unpublished guide. Department of Speech Communication, Oregon State University.

Keltner, J. W. 1987. *Mediation: Toward a civilized system of dispute resolution*. Annandale, VA: Speech Communication Association.

——. 1994. *The management of struggle: Elements of dispute resolution through negotiation, mediation and arbitration*. Cresskill, NJ: Hampton Press.

Kenkel, W. W. 1957. Influence differentiation in family decision making. *Sociology and Social Research* 43: 18–25.

Keough, C. M. 1992. Bargaining arguments and argumentative bargainers. In *Communication and negotiation*, edited by L. L. Putnam and M. E. Roloff, 109–127. Newbury Park, CA: Sage Publications.

Kiecolt-Glaser, J. K., Newton, T, Cacioppo, J. T., CacCallum, R. G., Glaser, R. and Malarkey, W. B., 1996. "Marital conflict and endocrine function: are men really more physiologically affected than women?" *Journal of Consulting and Clinical Psychology* v64 n2 p324(9).

Kiersey, D. 1998. *Please understand me*. Del Mar, CA: Prometheus Nemesis.

Kilmann, R., and K. W. Thomas. 1975. Interpersonal conflict-handling behavior as reflections of Jungian personality dimensions. *Psychological Reports* 37: 971–980.

Kim, J., and C. Emery. 2003. Marital power, conflict, norm consensus, and marital violence in a nationally representative sample of Korean couples. *Journal of Interpersonal Violence* 18, no. 2: 197–220.

Kim, S. H., and R. H. Smith. 1993. Revenge and conflict escalation. *Negotiation Journal* 9, no. 1: 37–43.

Kimmel, M. J., D. G. Pruitt, J. M. Magenau, E. Konar-Goldband, and P. J. D. Carnevale. 1980. Effects of trust, aspiration, and gender on negotiation tactics. *Journal of Personality and Social Psychology* 38: 9–22.

King, A. 1987. *Power and communication*. Prospect Heights, IL: Waveland Press.

King, M. L., Jr. 1989. *Strength to Love*. Augsburg Fortress Press.

Kipnis, D. 1976. The *powerholders*. Chicago: University of Chicago Press.

Kipnis, D., S. Schmidt, and I. Wilkerson. 1980. Intraorganizational influence tactics: Explorations in getting one's way. *Journal of Applied Psychology* 65: 440–452.

Kirka, D. 1999. Mob killing prompts West to watch Kosovo. *The Missoulian*, December 6, A–8.

Kluwer, E. S., J. A. M. Heesink, and E. van de Vliert. 1996. Marital conflict about the division of household labor and paid work. *Journal of Marriage and the Family* 58, no. 4: 958–970.

Knapp, M. L., L. L. Putnam, and L. J. Davis. 1988. Measuring interpersonal conflict in organizations: Where do we go from here? *Management Communication Quarterly* 1: 414–429.

Knox, D., C. Schacht, J. Turner, and P. Norris. 1995. College students' preference for win-win relationships. *College Student Journal* 29: 44–46.

Knudson, R. M., A. A. Sommers, and S. L. Golding. 1980. Interpersonal perception and mode of resolution in marital conflict. *Journal of Personality and Social Psychology* 38, no. 5: 751–763.

Kochan, T. A., and T. Jick. 1978. The public sector mediation process: A theory and empirical examination. *Journal of Conflict Resolution* 22, no. 2: 209–240.

Koerner, A. F., and M. A. Fitzpatrick. 2002. You never leave your family in a fight: The impact of family of origin on conflict-behavior in romantic relationships. *Communication Studies* 53, no. 3: 234–252.

Kohlberg, L. 1976. Moral stages and moralization: The cognitive development approach in Licrona. In *Moral development and behavior: Theory, research and social issues*. New York: Holt Reinhart.

Kolb, D. M. 1983. Strategy and the tactics of mediation. *Human Relations* 36, no. 3: 247–268.

——. 1987. Dealing with organizational conflict: Implications from theory. *Negotiation Journal* 3: 123–125.

Kolb, D., and L. Putnam. 1992. The multiple faces of conflict in organizations. *Journal of Organizational Behavior* 13: 311–324.

——. 1997. Through the looking glass: Negotiation theory refracted through the lens of gender. In *Frontiers in dispute resolution in industrial relations and human resources*, edited by S. Gleason, 231–257. East Lansing, MI: Michigan State University Press.

Kolb, D., and B. Sheppard. 1985. Do managers mediate, or even arbitrate? *Negotiation Journal* 1: 379–388.

Korabik, K., G. L. Baril, and C. Watson. 1993. Managers' conflict management style and leadership effectiveness: The moderating effects of gender. *Sex Roles* 29, no. 5/6: 405–418.

Kornfield, J. 2001. *After the ecstasy, the laundry*. New York: Bantam Press.

Kottler, J. 1994. Taking responsibility without blaming. In *Beyond blame: A new way of resolving conflicts in relationships*. San Francisco, CA: Jossey-Bass.

Kowalski, K. M. 1998. Peer mediation success stories: In nearly 10,000 schools nationwide, peer mediation helps teens solve problems without violence. *Current Health* 25, no. 2: 13–16.

Kressel, K., N. Jaffee, B. Tuchman, C. Watson, and M. Deutsch. 1980. A typology of divorcing couples: Implications for mediation and the divorce process. *Family Process* 19, no. 2: 101–116.

Kritek, P. B. 1994. *Negotiating at an uneven table: A practical approach to working with difference and diversity.* San Francisco: Jossey-Bass.

Krokoff, L. J., J. M. Gottman, and A. K. Roy. 1988. Blue-collar and white-collar marital interaction and communication orientation. *Journal of Social and Personal Relationships* 5: 201–221.

Kubler-Ross, E. 1970. *Death and dying.* New York: Macmillan.

Kuhn, T., and M. S. Poole. 2000. Do conflict management styles affect group decision making? Evidence from a longitudinal study. *Human Communication Research* 26, no. 4: 558–591.

Kurdek, L. A. 1994. Areas of conflict for gay, lesbian, and heterosexual couples: What couples argue about influences relationship satisfaction. *Journal of Marriage and the Family* 56: 923–935.

———. 1995. Predicting change in marital satisfaction from husbands' and wives' conflict resolution styles. *Journal of Marriage and the Family* 57: 153–165.

Laing, R. D., H. Phillipson, and A. R. Lee. 1966. *Interpersonal perception.* Baltimore, MD: Perennial Library.

Lakoff, G., and M. Johnson. 1980. *Metaphors we live by.* Chicago: University of Chicago Press.

Lamott, A. 1999. *Traveling mercies.* New York: Anchor Books.

Lampman, J. 2000. Middle East peace among grieving parents. *The Christian Science Monitor,* January 5, 1, 10.

Lampman, J., (January 4, 2005), The civil rights movement must water its spiritual roots, *The Christian Science Monitor,* Boston, 14.

Lande, J. 2004. Commentary: Focusing on program design issues in future research on court-connected mediation. *Conflict Resolution Quarterly* 22, no. 1–2: 89–100.

Lange, J. I. 1993. The logic of competing information campaigns: Conflict over old growth and the spotted owl. *Communication Monographs* 60: 239–257.

Langhinrichsen-Robling, J., P. Neidig, and G. Thorn. 1995. Violent marriages: Gender differences in levels of current violence and past abuse. *Journal of Family Violence* 10: 159–176.

Larson, C., and F. LaFasto. 1989. *Teamwork.* Newbury Park, CA: Sage Publications.

Lawrence, P. R., and J. W. Lorsch. 1969. *Organization and environment.* Homewood, IL: Irwin.

Lax, D., and J. Sebenius. 1986. *The manager as negotiator.* New York: Free Press.

Layton, M. 1999. Apology not accepted. *Utne Reader,* March–April, 45–50.

Leas, S., and P. Kittlaus. 1973. *Church fights: Managing conflict in the local church.* Philadelphia: Westminster Press.

Lederer, W. J., and D. D. Jackson. 1968. *Mirages of marriage.* New York: W. W. Norton & Company.

Legge, N. J., and W. K. Rawlins. 1992. Managing disputes in young adult friendships: Modes of convenience, cooperation and commitment. *Western Journal of Communication* 56: 226–247.

Lenton, R. L. 1995a. Power versus feminist theories of wife abuse. *Canadian Journal of Criminology* 37: 305–330.

———. 1995b. Feminist versus interpersonal power theories of wife abuse revisited. *Canadian Journal of Criminology* 37, no. 4: 567–574.

Lerner, H. 1985. *The Dance of Anger.* New York: Harper and Row.

———. 1989. *The dance of intimacy.* New York: Harper & Row.

Levy, J. S., and T. C. Morgan. 1984. The frequency and seriousness of war. *Journal of Conflict Resolution* 28: 731–749.

Lewicki, R. J., and J. A. Litterer. 1985. *Negotiation.* Homewood, IL: Irwin.

Lewicki, R. J., S. E. Weiss, and D. Lewin. 1992. Models of conflict, negotiation and third party intervention: A review and synthesis. *Journal of Organizational Behavior* 13: 209–254.

Leymann, H. 1990. Mobbing and psychological terror at workplaces. *Violence and Victims* 5: 119–126.

Lilly, E. R. 1989. The determinants of organizational power styles. *Educational Review* 41: 281–293.

Lim, T., and J. Bowers. 1991. Face-work: Solidarity, approbation, and tact. *Human Communication Research* 17: 415–450.

Lindbergh, A. 1955. *Gift from the sea.* New York: Pantheon.

Lloyd, S. A. 1987. Conflict in premarital relationships: Differential perceptions of males and females. *Family Relations* 36: 290–294.

———. 1990. A behavioral self-report technique for assessing conflict in close relationships. *Journal of Social and Personal Relationships* 8: 265–272.

———. 1996. Physical aggression, distress and everyday marital interaction. In *Family violence from a communication perspective,* edited by D. D. Cahn and S. A. Lloyd, 177–198. Hillsdale, NJ: Lawrence Erlbaum Associates.

Lloyd, S. A., and R. M. Cate. 1985. The developmental course of conflict in dissolution of premarital relationships. *Journal of Social and Personal Relationships* 2: 179–194.

Lloyd, S. A., and B. C. Emery. 1994. Physically aggressive conflict in romantic relationships. In *Conflict in personal relationships,* edited by D. D. Cahn, 27–46. Hillsdale, NJ: Lawrence Erlbaum Associates.

Lord, R. 1991. Do I have to forgive? *The Christian Century* 108: 902–903.

Lulofs, R. S. 1994. *Conflict: From theory to action.* Scottsdale, AZ: Gorsuch Scarisbuck Publishers.

Lulofs, R., and D. Cahn. 2000. *Conflict, from theory to action.* Boston: Allyn and Bacon: 317–325.

Lutgen-Sandvik, P., S. Tracy, and J. Alberts. 2005. *Burned by bullying in the American workplace: A first time study of U.S. prevalence and delineation of bullying "degree."* Presented at the

Western States Communication Convention, February, San Francisco, California.

Ma, R. 1992. The role of unofficial intermediaries in interpersonal conflicts in the Chinese culture. *Communication Quarterly* 40: 269–278.

MacDonald, G., M. P. Zanna, and J. G. Holmes. 2000. An experimental test of the role of alcohol in relationship conflict. *Journal of Experimental Social Psychology* 36, no. 2: 182–194.

Mace, D. R. 1987. *Close companions: The marriage enrichment handbook.* 1982. Reprint. New York: Continuum.

Mack, R. M., and R. C. Snyder. 1973. The analysis of social conflict—toward an overview and synthesis. In *Conflict resolution through communication,* edited by F. E. Jandt. New York: Harper & Row.

Mackey, R. A., and B. A. O'Brien. 1998. Marital conflict management: Gender and ethnic differences. *Social Work* 43, no. 2: 128–132.

Macoby, E. E., and C. N. Jacklin. 1974. The psychology of sex differences. Stanford, CA: Stanford University Press.

Madanes, C. 1981. *Strategic family therapy.* San Francisco: Jossey-Bass.

Mager, R., and P. Pipe. 1970. *Analyzing performance problems: Or you really oughta wanna.* Belmont, CA: Fearon Publishers.

Marano, H. E. 1996. A saga of spouse abuse. *Psychology Today,* May/June, 56–77.

Margolin, G. 1981. Behavior exchange in distressed and nondistressed marriages: A family cycle perspective. *Behavior Therapy* 12: 329–343.

Marin, M. J., J. C. Sherblom, and T. Shipps. 1994. Contextual influences on nurses' conflict management strategies. *Western Journal of Communication* 58: 201–228.

Markham, H. J., S. M. Stanley, and S. L. Blumberg. 2001. *Fighting for your marriage.* San Francisco: Jossey-Bass.

Marks, M. A. 1981. *The suing of America.* New York: Seaview Books.

Marshall, L. L. 1994. Physical and psychological abuse. In *The dark side of interpersonal communication,* edited by W. R. Cupach and B. H. Spitzberg, 281–311. Hillsdale, NJ: Lawrence Erlbaum Associates.

Martin, B. 1990. The transmission of relationship difficulties from one generation to the next. *Journal of Youth and Adolescence* 19: 181–199.

Martin, G. E., and T. J. Bergmann. 1996. The dynamics of behavioural response to conflict in the workplace. *Journal of Occupational and Organizational Psychology* 69, no. 4: 377–390.

Martin, M. M., C. M. Anderson, and G. L. Horvath. 1996. Feelings about verbal aggression: Justifications for sending and hurt from receiving verbally aggressive messages. *Communication Research Reports* 13: 19–26.

Martin, M. W., and R. T. Denton. 1998. Defining forgiveness: An empirical exploration of process and role. *American Journal of Family Therapy* 26, no. 4: 281–292.

Marwell, G., and D. Schmidt. 1967. Dimensions of compliance-gaining behavior: An empirical analysis. *Sociometry* 39: 350–364.

May, R. 1972. *Power and innocence: A search for the sources of violence.* New York: Dell Publishing.

Mayer, P. 2002. *Earthtown square.* Stillwater, MN: Blue Boat Publishing.

McCall, M. W., Jr. 1979. Power, authority, and influence. In *Organizational behavior,* edited by S. Kerr. Columbus, OH: Grid Publishing.

McClelland, D. C. 1969. The two faces of power. *Journal of International Affairs* 24: 141–154.

McCorkle, S., and J. Mills. 1992. Rowboat in a hurricane: Metaphors of interpersonal conflict management. *Communication Reports* 5, no. 2: 57–66.

McCready, V., J. E. Roberts, D. Bengala, H. Harris, G. Kingsley, and C. Krikorian. 1996. A comparison of conflict tactics in the supervisory process. *Journal of Speech and Hearing Research* 39, no. 1: 191–200.

McCullough, M., K. Pargament, and C. Thoresen. 2000. *Forgiveness, theory, research and practice.* New York, London: Guilford Press.

McCullough, M. E., E. L. Worthington, and K. C. Rachal. 1997. Interpersonal forgiving in close relationships. *Journal of Personality and Social Psychology* 73: 321–336.

McDonald, G. W. 1980. Family power: The assessment of a decade of theory and research. *Journal of Marriage and the Family* 42, no. 4: 841–854.

McEwan, I., 2001, *Atonement,* New York, Anchor Books.

McFall, L. 1991. What's wrong with bitterness? In *Feminist ethics,* edited by C. Card. Lawrence: University Press of Kansas.

McGillicuddy, N. B., G. L. Welton, and D. G. Pruitt. 1987. Third-party intervention: A field experiment comparing three different models. *Journal of Personality and Social Psychology* 53: 104–112.

McGillis, D. 1981. Conflict resolution outside the courts. *Applied Social Psychology Annual* 2: 243–262.

McGinnis, K., and J. McGinnis. 1981. *Parenting for peace and justice.* Maryknoll, NY: Orbis Books.

McGonagle, K. A., R. C. Kessler, and I. H. Gotlib. 1993. The effects of marital disagreement style, frequency, and outcome on marital disruption. *Journal of Social and Personal Relationships* 10: 385–404.

McGonagle, K. A., R. C. Kessler, and E. A. Schilling. 1992. The frequency and determinants of marital disagreements in a community sample. *Journal of Social and Personal Relationships* 9: 507–524.

McGrane, F. 2005. The skillful process of one-to-one dispute resolution in the workplace. Dissertation. University of Ulster, Northern Ireland.

Meierding, N. R. 1993. Does mediation work? A survey of long-term satisfaction and durability rates for privately mediated agreements. *Mediation Quarterly* 11: 157–170.

Menkel-Meadow, C. 1986. The transformation of disputes by lawyers: What the dispute paradigm does and does not tell us. *Missouri Journal of Dispute Resolution:* 25–44.

Menzel, K. E. 1991. Judging the fairness of mediation: A critical framework. *Mediation Quarterly* 9, no. 1: 3–20.

Merriam, G. 2004. Author tells docs: Learn and use the word "sorry." *The Missoulian*.

Merrill, D. M. 1996. Conflict and cooperation among adult siblings during the transition to the role of filial caregiver. *Journal of Social and Personal Relationships* 13: 399–413.

Metcoff, J., and C. A. Whitaker. 1982. Family microevents: Communication patterns for problem solving. In *Normal family processes*, edited by F. Walsh. New York: Guilford Press.

Metts, S. 1994. Relational transgressions. In *The dark side of interpersonal communication*, edited by W. R. Cupach and Brian H. Spitzberg, 217–239. Hillside, NJ: Lawrence Erlbaum Publishers.

Metz, M. E., B. R. S. Rosser, and N. Strapko. 1994. Differences in conflict-resolution styles among heterosexual, gay, and lesbian couples. *Journal of Sex Research* 31: 293–308.

Mikkelsen, E. G., and S. Einarsen. 2002. Relationships between exposure to bullying at work and psychological and psychosomatic health complaints: The role of state negative affectivity and generalized self-efficacy. *Scandinavian Journal of Psychology* 43, no. 5: 397–406.

Mikula, G., K. R. Scherer, and U. Athenstaedt. 1998. The role of injustice in the elicitation of differential emotional reactions. *Personality and Social Psychology Bulletin* 24, no. 7: 769–783.

Millar, F. E., and L. E. Rogers. 1987. Relational dimensions of interpersonal dynamics. In *Interpersonal processes: New directions in communication research*, edited by M. E. Roloff and G. R. Miller, 117–139. Vol. 14 of *Sage Annual Reviews of Communication Research*. Newbury Park, CA: Sage Publications.

———. 1988. Power dynamics in marital relationships. In *Perspectives on marital interaction*, edited by O. Noller and M. A. Fitzpatrick, 78–97. Clevedon, UK: Multilingual Matters.

Miller, G., F. Boster, M. Roloff, and D. Siebold. 1977. Compliance-gaining message strategies: A typology and some findings concerning effects of situational differences. *Communication Monographs* 44: 37–54.

Miller, G. R., and M. Steinberg. 1975. *Between people: A new analysis of interpersonal communication*. Chicago: Science Research Associates.

Miller, J. B. 1986. What do we mean by relationships? *In Work in progress.* Stone Center Working Paper Series, no. 22. Wellesley, MA: Stone Center, Wellesley College.

———. 1991. Women's and men's scripts for interpersonal conflict. *Psychology of Women Quarterly* 15: 15–29.

Miller, S., D. Wackman, E. Nunnally, and C. Saline. 1981. *Straight talk*. New York: New American Library.

Minuchin, S. 1974. *Families and family therapy*. Cambridge, MA: Harvard University Press.

Mishler, E. G., and N. E. Waxler. 1968. *Interaction in families: An experimental study of family processes and schizophrenia*. New York: John Wiley & Sons.

Miura, S. Y. 1999. The mediation of conflict in the traditional Hawaiian family: A collectivist approach. *Communication Quarterly* 47: 19.

Moffitt, T. E., A. Caspi, R. F. Krueger, L. Magdol, P. A. Silva, R. Sydney, and G Margolin. 1997. Do partners agree about abuse in their relationship? *Psychological Assessment* 9, no. 1: 47–57.

Moore, C. 1986. *The mediation process*. San Francisco, CA: Jossey-Bass.

———. 1996. *The mediation process*. 2d ed. San Francisco, CA: Jossey-Bass.

Moos, R. H., and B. S. Moos. 1976. A typology of family social environment. *Family Process* 15: 357–371.

Moran, R. T., J. Allen, R. Wichman, T. Ando, and M. Sasano. 1994. Japan. In *Global perspectives on organizational conflict*, edited by M. A. Rahim and A. A. Blum, 33–52. Westport, CT: Praeger Publishing.

Murphy, C. M., and T. J. O'Farrell. 1994. Factors associated with marital aggression in male alcoholics. *Journal of Family Psychology* 8 no. 3: 321–336.

Murray, J. A. 1986. Understanding competing theories of negotiation. *Negotiation Journal* 2 (April): 179–186.

Napier, A., and C. Whitaker. 1978. *The family crucible*. New York: Harper & Row.

Neale, M., and M. Bazerman. 1985. When will externally set aspiration levels improve negotiator performance? A look at integrative behavior in a competitive market. *Journal of Occupational Behavior* 6: 19–32.

Neff, K., and S. Harter. 2002. The authenticity of conflict resolutions among adult couples: Does women's other-oriented behavior reflect their true selves. *Sex Roles: A Journal of Research*, November, 403–421.

Neill, J. R., and D. P. Kniskern. 1982. *From psyche to system: The evolving therapy of Carl Whitaker*. New York: Guilford Press.

Neimeyer, G. J., and R. A. Neimeyer. 1985. Relational trajectories: A personal construct contribution. *Journal of Social and Personal Relationships* 2: 325–349.

Newman, Richard S. 2004. When elementary school students are harassed by peers: A self-regulative perspective on help seeking. *Elementary School Journal* 103: 339–357.

Newmark, L., A. Harrell, and P. Salem. 1995. Domestic violence and empowerment in custody and visitation cases. *Family and Conciliation Courts Review* 33: 30–62.

Nicolotti, L., M. el-Sheikh, and S. M. Whitson. 2003. Children's coping with marital conflict and their adjustment and physical health: Vulnerability and protective functions. *Journal of Family Psychology* 17, no. 3: 315–326.

Noller, P., J. A. Feeney, D. Bonnell, and V. Callan. 1994. A longitudinal study of conflict in early marriage. *Journal of Social and Personal Relationships* 11: 233–252.

O'Brien, A. 1998. Marital conflict management: gender and ethnic differences. *Social Work* 43, no. 2: 128–143.

O'Leary, K. D., J. Barling, I. Arias, A. Rosenbaum, J. Malone, and A. Tyree. 1989. Prevalence and stability of physical aggression between spouses: A longitudinal analysis. *Journal of Consulting and Clinical Psychology* 57: 263–268.

Olson, D. H., and C. Rabunsky. 1972. Validity of four measures of family power. *Journal of Marriage and Family* 34, no. 2: 224–233.

Olson, D. H., and R. G. Ryder. 1970. Inventory of marital conflict (IMC): An experimental interaction procedure. *Journal of Marriage and the Family* 32: 443–448.

Olson, D. H., D. H. Sprenkle and C. Russell. 1979. Circumplex model of marital and family systems. Part 2. Cohesion and adaptability dimensions, family types and clinical applications. *Family Process* 18: 3–28.

Olson, D. H., and M. A. Strauss. 1972. A diagnostic tool for marital and family therapy: The SIMFAM technique. *Family Coordinator* 21: 251–258.

Ortony, A. 1975. Why metaphors are necessary and not just nice. *Educational Theory* 25, no. 1: 45–53.

Pace, R. C. 1988. Communication patterns in high and low consensus discussions: A descriptive analysis. *Southern Speech Communication Journal* 53: 184–202.

Palmer, J. 1997. Finding a way to forgive: Reclaiming power and wholeness. *Prism: A Theological Forum for the UCC*, Spring, 89–99.

Papa, M. J., and E. J. Natalle. 1989. Gender, strategy selection and discussion satisfaction in interpersonal conflict. *Western Journal of Speech Communication* 53: 260–272.

Papa, M. J., and E. A. Pood. 1988a. Coorientational accuracy and differentiation in the management of conflict. *Communication Research* 15: 400–425.

———. 1988b. Coorientational accuracy and organizational conflict: An examination of tactic selection and discussion satisfaction. *Communication Research* 15: 1, 3–28.

Papp, L. M., Cummings, E. M., and Goeke-Morey, M. C., 2002. "Marital conflicts in the home when children are present versus absent." *Developmental Psychology* v38 i5 p774(10).

Papp, P. *Family Therapy*. 1978. New York, NY: John Wiley & Sons.

Papp, P., O. Silverstein, and E. Carter. 1973. Family sculpting in preventive work with "well" families. *Family Process* 12, no. 1: 197–212.

Parker, A. O. 1981. A comparison of divorce mediation versus lawyer adversary processes and the relationship to marital separation factors. In *Compilation of unpublished research about divorce*. Corte Madera, CA: Center for the Family in Transition.

Paul, J., and M. Paul. 1983. *Do I have to give up me to be loved by you?* Minneapolis, MN: CompCare Publications.

———. 1987. *If you really loved me*. Minneapolis, MN: CompCare Publications.

Pearson, J. 1981. The Denver custody mediation project. In *Compilation of unpublished research about divorce*. Corte Madera, CA: Center for the Family in Transition.

Pearson, J., N. Thonnes, and L. Vanderkooi. 1982. The decision to mediate profiles—individuals who accept and reject the opportunity to mediate contested child custody and visitation issues. *Journal of Divorce* 6 (Winter): 17–35.

Pearson, J. C., L. H. Turner, and W. Todd-Mancillas. 1991. *Gender and communication*. 2d ed. Dubuque, IA: William C. Brown Communications.

Percival, T. Q., V. Smitheram, and M. Kelly. 1992. Myers-Briggs type indicator and conflict-handling intention: An interactive approach. *Journal of Psychological Type* 23: 10–16.

Pervin, L. A. 1982. The stasis and flow of behavior: Toward a theory of goals. In *Nebraska symposium on motivation*, edited by M. E. Page, 1–51. Lincoln, NE: University of Nebraska Press.

Peterson, C. C., and J. L. Peterson. 1990. Fight or flight: Factors influencing children's and adults' decisions to avoid or confront conflict. *Journal of Genetic Psychology* 151: 461–471.

Phillips, G. M., and N. Metzger. 1976. *Intimate communication*. Boston, MA: Allyn & Bacon.

Pike, G. R., and A. L. Sillars. 1985. Reciprocity of marital communication. *Journal of Social and Personal Relationships* 2: 303–324.

Planalp, S. 1999. *Communicating emotion: Social, moral and cultural processes*. Cambridge: Cambridge University Press.

Popple, P. R. 1984. Negotiation: A critical skill for social work administrators. *Administration in Social Work* 8: 1–11.

Portello, J. Y., and C. Long. 1994. Gender role orientation, ethical and interpersonal conflicts, and conflict handling styles of female managers. *Sex Roles* 31: 683–701.

Prather, H., and G. Prather. 1998. How to resolve issues unmemorably. In *A book for couples*. New York: Doubleday Publishing.

Pruitt, D. G. 1981. *Negotiation behavior*. New York: Academic Press.

———. 1983a. Achieving integrative agreements. In *Negotiating in organizations*, edited by M. H. Bazerman and R. Lewicki. Beverly Hills, CA: Sage Publications.

———. 1983b. Strategic choice in negotiation. *American Behavioral Scientist* 27: 167–194.

———. 1986. Trends in the scientific study of negotiation and mediation. *Negotiation Journal* 2: 237–244.

Pruitt, D. G., and D. F. Johnson. 1970. Mediation as an aid to face saving in negotiation. *Journal of Personality and Social Psychology* 14, no. 3: 239–246.

Putnam, L. L. 1986. *Negotiation of intergroup conflict in organizations*. Lecture delivered at Baylor University, Waco, Texas, October 21.

———. 1988a. Communication and interpersonal conflict in organizations. *Management Communication Quarterly* 1: 293–301.

———. 1988b. *Reframing integrative and distributive bargaining: A process perspective*. Revised manuscript. Lafayette, IN: Purdue University, Spring.

———. 1996. *A gendered view of negotiation*. Address to Communication Studies Department, University of Montana, Missoula, September 26.

Putnam, L. L., and J. P. Folger. 1988. Communication, conflict, and dispute resolution: The study of interaction and the development of conflict theory. *Communication Research* 15: 349–359.

Putnam, L. L., and T. S. Jones. 1982a. Reciprocity in negotiations: An analysis of bargaining interaction. *Communication Monographs* 49: 181–191.

———. 1982b. The role of communication in bargaining. *Human Communication Research* 8: 162–280.

Putnam, L. L., and M. S Poole. 1987. Conflict and negotiation. In *Handbook of organizational communication: An interdisciplinary perspective*, edited by F. M. Jablin, L. L. Putnam, K. H. Roberts, and L. W. Porter. Newbury Park, CA: Sage Publications.

Putnam, L. L., S. A. Van Hoeven, and C. A. Bullis. 1991. The role of rituals and fantasy themes in teachers' bargaining. *Western Journal of Speech Communication* 55: 85–103.

Putnam, L. L., and C. E. Wilson. 1982. Communicative strategies in organizational conflicts: Reliability and validity of a measurement scale. In *Communication yearbook*. Vol. 6. Edited by M. Burgoon. Beverly Hills, CA: Sage Publications, International Communication Association.

Rahim, M. A. 1983. A measure of styles of handling interpersonal conflict. *Academy of Management Journal* 26: 368–376.

———. 1986. *Managing conflict in organizations*. New York: Praeger.

Rahim, M., and G. Buntzman. 1989. Supervisory power bases, styles of handling conflict with subordinates, and subordinate compliance and satisfaction. *Journal of Psychology* 123: 195–210.

Rahim, M. A., and N. R. Magner. 1995. Confirmatory factor analysis of the styles of handling interpersonal conflict: First-order factor model and its invariance across groups. *Journal of Applied Psychology* 80: 122–132.

Raiffa, H. 1982. *The art and science of negotiation*. Cambridge, MA: Harvard University Press, Belknap Press.

Rancer, A. S., R. L. Kosberg, and R. A. Baukus. 1992. Beliefs about arguing as predictors of trait argumentativeness: Implications for training in argument and conflict management. *Communication Education* 41: 375–387.

Rands, M., G. Levinger, and G. D. Mellinger. 1981. Patterns of conflict resolution and marital satisfaction. *Journal of Family Issues* 2, no. 3: 297–321.

Raush, H. C., W. A. Barry, R. Hertel, and M. A. Swain. 1974. *Communication, conflict and marriage*. San Francisco: Jossey-Bass.

Raven, B. H., and J. R. P. French Jr. 1956. A formal theory of social power. *Psychological Review* 63: 181–194.

Raven, B. H., and A. W. Kruglanski. 1970. Conflict and power. In *The structure of conflict*, edited by P. Swingel, 69–109. New York: Academic Press.

Ray, L., ed. 1982. *Alternative dispute resolution: Bane or boon to attorneys?* Washington, DC: Special Committee on Alternative Means of Dispute Resolution of the Public Services Division, American Bar Association.

Reese-Weber, M., and S. Bertle-Haring. 1998. Conflict resolution styles in family subsystems and adolescent romantic relationships. *Journal of Youth and Adolescence* 27 (December): 735–746.

Renwick, P. 1977. The effects of sex differences on the perception and management of superior-subordinate conflict: An exploratory study. *Organizational Behavior and Human Performance* 19: 403–415.

Richardson, D. R., G. S. Hammock, T. Lubben, and S. Mickler. 1989. The relationship between love attitudes and conflict responses. *Journal of Social and Clinical Psychology* 8: 430–441.

Richmond, V. P., L. M. Davis, K. Saylor, and J. C. McCroskey. 1984. Power strategies in organizations: Communication techniques and messages. *Human Communication Research* 11: 85–108.

Ridley, C. A., and C. M. Feldman. 2003. Female domestic violence toward male partners: Exploring conflict responses and outcomes. *Journal of Family Violence* 18, no. 3: 157–171.

Robert, M. 1982. *Managing conflict from the inside out*. Austin, TX: Learning Concepts.

Rodman, H. 1967. Marital power in France, Greece, Yugoslavia, and the United States: A cross-national discussion. *Journal of Marriage and the Family* 29: 320–325.

———. 1972. Marital power and the theory of resources in cultural context. *Journal of Comparative Family Studies* 3: 50–69.

Rogan, R. G., and R. Hammer. 1994. Crisis negotiations: A preliminary investigation of facework in naturalistic conflict discourse. *Journal of Applied Communication Research* 22: 216–231.

Rogers, L. E., A. Castleton, and S. A. Lloyd. 1996. Relational control and physical aggression in satisfying marital relationships. In *Family violence from a communication perspective*, edited by D. D. Cahn and S. A. Lloyd, 218–239. Hillsdale, NJ: Lawrence Erlbaum Associates.

Rogers, L. E., and R. Farace. 1975. Analysis of relational communication in dyads. *Human Communication Research* 1, no. 3: 222–239.

Rogers, M. F. 1974. Instrumental and infra-resources: The bases of power. *American Journal of Sociology* 79: 1418–1433.

Rogers-Millar, L. E., and F. E. Millar. 1977. *A transactional definition and measure of power*. Paper presented to the Speech Communication Association, Washington, DC.

Rollins, B. C., and S. Bahr. 1976. A theory of power relationship in marriage. *Journal of Marriage and the Family* 38 (November): 619–627.

Roloff, M. E. 1976. Communication strategies, relationships, and relational change. In *Explorations in interpersonal communication*, edited by G. R. Miller. Newbury Park, CA: Sage Publications.

———. 1996. The catalyst hypothesis: Conditions under which coercive communication leads to physical aggression. In *Family violence from a communication perspective*, edited by D. D. Cahn and S. A. Lloyd. Hillsdale, NJ: Lawrence Erlbaum Associates.

Roloff, M. E., and D. H. Cloven. 1994. When partners transgress: Maintaining violated relationships. In *Communication and relational maintenance*, edited by D. J. Canary and L. Stafford, 23–24. New York: Academic Press.

Rosen, K. H. 1996. The ties that bind women to violent premarital relationships: Processes of seduction and entrapment. In *Family violence from a communication perspective*, edited by D. D. Cahn and S. A. Loyd. Hillsdale, NJ: Lawrence Erlbaum Associates.

Ross, M., and D. Holmberg. 1992. Are wives' memories for events in relationships more vivid than their husbands' memories? *Journal of Social and Personal Relationships* 9: 585–604.

Rossi, A. M., and W. R. Todd-Mancillas. 1987. Male and female differences in managing conflicts. In *Communication, gender, and sex roles in diverse interaction contexts*, edited by L. P. Stewart and S. Ting-Toomey. Norwood, NJ: Ablex.

Rouhana, N., and D. Bar-Tal. 1998. Psychological dynamics of intractable ethnonational conflicts. *American Psychologist* 53: 761–770.

Roush, G., and E. Hall. 1993. Teaching peaceful conflict resolution. *Mediation Quarterly* 11: 185–191.

Rowe, M. P. 1990a. People who feel harassed need a complaint system with both formal and informal options. *Negotiation Journal* 6: 61–172.

———. 1990b. Helping people help themselves: An ADR option for interpersonal conflict. *Negotiation Journal* 6, no. 3: 239–248.

Rowland, R. C., and J. K. Barge. 1991. On interactional argument. *Argumentation and Advocacy* 28: 24–34.

Rubin, J. Z. 1980. Experimental research on third party intervention in conflict: Toward some generalizations. *Psychological Bulletin* 87: 379–391.

———. 1996. Proliferation process in conflict. Address to faculty and students. University of Montana, Missoula, May.

Rubin, J. Z., and B. R. Brown. 1975. *The social psychology of bargaining and negotiation*. New York: Academic Press.

Rubin, J. Z., D. G. Pruitt, and S. H. Kim. 1994. *Social conflict: Escalation, stalemate and settlement*. 2d ed. New York: McGraw-Hill.

Ruhly, S. 1976. *Orientations to intercultural communication*. Palo Alto, CA: SRA.

Rummel, R. J. 1976. *Understanding conflict and war: The conflict helix*. Vol. 2. New York: Sage Publications.

Rusbult, C. E. 1987. Responses to dissatisfaction in close relationships. In *Intimate relationships: Development, dynamics and deterioration*, edited by D. Perlman and S. Duck, 209–237. Newbury Park, CA: Sage Publications.

Rusbult, C. E., D. J. Johnson, and G. D. Morrow. 1984. Impact of couple patterns of problem solving on distress and nondistress in dating relationships. *Journal of Personality and Social Psychology* 50: 744–753.

———. 1986. Determinants and consequences of exit, voice, loyalty and neglect: Responses to dissatisfaction in adult romantic relationships. *Human Relations* 39, no. 1: 45–64.

Rusbult, C. E., I. Zembrodt, and L. K. Gunn. 1982. Exit, voice, loyalty and neglect: Responses to dissatisfaction in romantic involvements. *Journal of Personality and Social Psychology* 43: 1230–1242.

Rushing, J., and T. Frentz. 1995. *Projecting the shadow: The cyborg hero in American film*. Chicago: University of Chicago Press.

Rushing, J. H. 1983. *Rhetorical criticism as analogic process*. Paper presented at the Speech Communication Association/American Forensic Association Summer Conference on Argumentation, Alta, Utah, July.

Ryder, R. G., and D. W. Goodrich. 1966. Married couples' response to disagreement. *Family Process* 5: 30–42.

Sabourin, T. C. 1995. The role of negative reciprocity in spousal abuse: A relational control analysis. *Journal of Applied Communication Research* 23: 271–283.

Sabourin, T. C., and G. H. Stamp. 1995. Communication and the experience of dialectical tensions in family life: An examination of abusive and nonabusive families. *Communication Monographs* 62: 213–242.

Sadker, M., and D. Sadker. 1994. *Failing at fairness: How American schools cheat girls*. New York: Macmillan Press.

Safilios-Rothschild, C. 1970. The study of family power structure: A review 1960–1969. *Journal of Marriage and the Family* 32, no. 4: 539–549.

Sander, F. E. A. 1977. *Report on the national conference on minor disputes resolution*. Washington, DC: American Bar Association Press.

Satir, V. 1967. *Conjoint family therapy*. Palo Alto, CA: Science and Behavior Books.

———. 1972. *Peoplemaking*, Palo Alto, CA: Science and Behavior Books.

Scanzoni, J. 1979. Social processes and power in families. In *Contemporary theories about the family*, edited by E. Burr. New York: Free Press.

Schechter, S. 1982. *Women and male violence: The visions and struggles of the battered women's movement*. Boston, MA: South End Press.

Schelling, T. C. 1960. *The strategy of conflict*. Cambridge, MA: Harvard University Press.

Schmidt, S. M., and T. A. Kochan. 1972. Conflict: Toward conceptual clarity. *Administrative Science Quarterly* 17: 359–370.

Schnake, M. E., and D. S. Cochran. 1985. Effect of two goal-setting dimensions on perceived intraorganizational conflict. *Group and Organization Studies* 10: 168–183.

Schuetz, J. 1978. Communicative competence and the bargaining of Watergate. *Western Journal of Speech Communication* 41: 105–115.

Schutz, W. C. 1966. *The interpersonal underworld*. Palo Alto, CA: Science and Behavior Books.

Schwartz, G. E. 1989. *How people change: A systems perspective on integrating psychotherapies*. Invited address, Society for Exploration of Psychotherapy Integration, Berkeley, California.

Scott, M. B., and S. Lyman. 1968. Accounts. *American Sociological Review* 33: 46–62.

Sheldon, A. 1992. Conflict talk: Sociolinguistic challenges to self-assertion and how young girls meet them. *Merrill-Palmer Quarterly* 38: 95–117.

Sherif, M., and C. W. Sherif. 1956. *An outline of social psychology*. Rev. ed. New York: Harper & Brothers.

Shimanoff, S. B. 1980. *Communication rules: Theory and research*. Beverly Hills, CA: Sage Publications.

Shockley-Zalabak, P. 1981. The effects of sex differences on preference for utilization of conflict styles of managers in a work setting: An exploratory study. *Public Personnel Management Journal* 10: 289–295.

Shriver, D. 1995. *An ethic for enemies, forgiveness in politics*. New York: Oxford University Press.

Siders, C. T., and C. A. Aschenbrener. 1999. Conflict management checklist: A diagnostic tool for assessing conflict in organizations. *Physician Executive* 25, no. 4: 32–38.

Siegel, S., and L. E. Fouraker. 1960. *Bargaining and group decision making: Experiments in bilateral monopoly*. New York: McGraw-Hill.

Siegert, J. R., and G. H. Stamp. 1994. "Our first big fight" as a milestone in the development of close relationships. *Communication Monographs* 61: 345–360.

Sillars, A. L. 1980. Attributions and communication in roommate conflicts. *Communication Monographs* 47: 180–200.

———. 1981. Attributions and interpersonal conflict resolution. In *New directions in attribution research*. Vol. 3. Edited by J. H. Harvey, W. Ickes, and R. F. Kidd. Hillsdale, NJ: Lawrence Erlbaum Associates.

———. 1986. *Procedures for coding interpersonal conflict* (revised). Unpublished manuscript. Department of Interpersonal Communication, University of Montana.

———. 1998. (Mis)understanding. In *The dark side of close relationships*, edited by B. H. Spitzberg and W. R. Cupach, 73–102. Mahwah, NJ: Lawrence Erlbaum Associates.

———. 2002. For better or worse: Rethinking the role of communication and "misperception" in family conflict. B. Aubrey Fisher Memorial Lecture, Department of Communication, University of Utah.

Sillars, A. L., S. F. Coletti, D. Parry, and M. A. Rogers. 1982. Coding verbal conflict tactics: Nonverbal and perceptual correlates of the "avoidance-distributive-integrative" distinction. *Human Communication Research* 9, no. 1: 83–95.

Sillars, A. L., and D. Parry. 1982. Stress, cognition, and communication in interpersonal conflicts. *Communication Research* 9: 201–226.

Sillars, A. L., L. Roberts, T. Dun, and K. Leonard. 2000. Stepping into the stream of thought: Cognition during marital conflict. In *Attribution, communication behavior and close relationship*, edited by V. Manusov and J. H. Harvey. Cambridge: Cambridge University Press.

Sillars, A. L., and J. Weisberg. 1987. Conflict as a social skill. In *Interpersonal processes: New directions in communication research*, edited by M. E. Roloff and G. R. Miller, 140–171. Newbury Park, CA: Sage Publications.

Simmel, G. 1953. *Conflict and the web of the group affiliations*. Translated by K. H. Wolff. New York: Free Press.

Simons, H. 1972. Persuasion in social conflicts: A critique of prevailing conceptions and a framework for future research. *Speech Monographs* 39: 227–247.

Sinclair, A. 1992. The tyranny of a team ideology. *Organization Studies* 13: 611–626.

Slaikeu, K. A. 1989. Designing dispute resolution systems in the health care industry. *Negotiation Journal* 5: 395–405.

Soloman, L. 1960. The influence of some types of power relationships and game strategies upon the development of interpersonal trust. *Journal of Abnormal and Social Psychology* 61: 223–230.

Some, S. 2003. *Falling out of grace: Meditations on loss, healing and wisdom*. El Sobrante, CA: North Bay Books.

Sprey, J. 1972. Family power structure: A critical comment. *Journal of Marriage and the Family* 33 (May): 722–733.

Stets, J. E., and D. A. Henderson. 1991. Contextual factors surrounding conflict resolution while dating: Results from a national study. *Family Relations* 40: 29–36.

Stevens, A. 1989. *The roots of war: A Jungian perspective*. New York: Paragon House.

Stewart, J. 1978. Foundations of dialogic communication. *Quarterly Journal of Speech* 64: 183–201.

Stewart, J., K. Zediker, and S. Witteborn. 2005. *Together: Communicating interpersonally a social construction approach*. Los Angeles, CA: Roxbury Publishing Company.

Stewart, J. Ed., 2002, *Bridges Not Walls*, New York, McGraw-Hill.

Stone, D., B. Patton, and S. Heen. 1999. *Difficult conversations: How to discuss what matters most*. New York: Penguin Books.

Strachan, C. E., and D. G. Dutton. 1992. The role of power and gender in anger responses to sexual jealousy. *Journal of Applied Social Psychology* 22: 1721–1740.

Straus, M. A. 1978. Wife beating: Causes, treatment and research needs. In *Battered women: Issues of public policy*. U.S. Commission on Civil Rights, Washington, DC, January 30–31.

———. 1979. Measuring intrafamily conflict and violence: The conflict tactics (CT) scales. *Journal of Marriage and the Family* 41: 75–88.

———. 1987. Forward. In *The violent home*, edited by R. Gelles. Beverly Hills, CA: Sage Publications.

Straus, M. A., and R. J. Gelles. 1986. Societal change and change in family violence from 1975 to 1985 as revealed by two national surveys. *Journal of Marriage and the Family* 48: 465–479.

Straus, M. A., R. J. Gelles, and S. K. Steinmetz. 1980. *Behind closed doors: Violence in the American family*. Garden City, NY: Doubleday.

Straus, M. A., S. L. Hamby, S. Boney-McCoy, and D. B. Sugarman. 1996. The revised conflict tactics scale (CTS2): Development and preliminary psychometric data. *Journal of Family Issues* 17: 283–316.

Straus, M. A., and S. Sweet. 1992. Verbal/symbolic aggression in couples: Incidence rates and relationships to personal characteristics. *Journal of Marriage and the Family* 54: 346–357.

Strodtbeck, F. L. 1951. Husband-wife interaction over revealed differences. *American Sociological Review* 16: 468–473.

Stuart, R. B. 1980. *Helping couples change: A social learning approach to marital therapy*. New York: Guilford Press.

Stulberg, J. 1987. *Taking charge/Managing conflict*. New York: D. C. Heath & Company.

Sugarman, A. B., and G. T. Hotaling. 1989. Rating violence: Prevalence, context, and risk markers. In *Violence in dating relationships*, edited by M. A. Pirog-Good and J. E. Stets, 3–32. New York: Praeger.

Sun, I. Y., and B. K. Payne. 2004. Racial differences in resolving conflicts: A comparison between black and white police officers. *Crime and Delinquency* 50, no. 4: 516–541.

Survivors of abuse Web site. 2004.

Szinovacz, M. E. 1983. Using couple data as a methodological tool: The case of marital violence. *Journal of Marriage and the Family* 45: 633–644.

Tannen, D. 1990. *You just don't understand: Women and men in conversation*. New York: William Morrow.

———. 1994. *Gender and discourse*. New York: Oxford University Press.

Tavris, C. 1989. *Anger: The misunderstood emotion*. 1982. Reprint. New York: Simon & Schuster/Touchstone.

Taylor, W. R. 1979. Using systems theory to organize confusion. *Family Process* 18: 479–488.

Tedeschi, J. T. 1970. Threats and promises. In *The structure of conflict*, edited by P. Swingle. New York: Academic Press.

Thomas, K. 1976. Conflict and conflict management. In *Handbook of industrial and organizational psychology*, edited by M. D. Dunnette. Chicago: Rand McNally.

Thomas, K. W., and R. Kilmann. 1977. Developing a forced-choice measure of conflict-handling behavior: The MODE instrument. *Educational and Psychological Measurement* 37: 390–395.

Thomas, K. W., and L. R. Pondy. 1977. Toward an "intent" model of conflict management among principal parties. *Human Relations* 30: 1089–1102.

Ting-Toomey, S. 1981. Conflict communication styles in blacks and whites. In *Interethnic communication: Current research*, edited by Y. Yunkim. Beverly Hills, CA: Sage Publications.

Tinsley, C. A. 2001. How negotiators get to yes: Predicting the constellation of strategies used across cultures to negotiate conflict. *Journal of Applied Psychology* 86, no. 4: 583.

Tjosvold, D. 1990. The goal interdependence approach to communication in conflict: An organizational study. In *Theory and research in conflict management*, edited by M. A. Rahim, 15–27. New York: Praeger.

Tournier, P. 1978. *The violence within*. Translated by E. Hudson. New York: Harper & Row.

Tracy, K., and J. Naughton. 1994. The identity work of questioning in intellectual discussion. *Speech Monograph* 61: 281–302.

Tracy, S. J., P. Lutgen-Sandvik, and J. K. Alberts. 2004. *Is it really bad? Exploring the emotional pain of workplace bullying through narratives, drawings and metaphors*. Paper presented at the annual convention of the National Communication Association, Chicago, Illinois (November).

Trapp, R. 1981. Special report on argumentation: Introduction. *Western Journal of Speech Communication* 45: 111–117.

———. 1989. Interpersonal argumentation: Conflict and reason-giving. *Communication Reports* 2: 105–109.

Triandis, H. C. 1980. *Handbook of cross cultural psychology*. Boston, MA: Allyn & Bacon.

Trubisky, P., S. Ting-Toomey, and S-L. Lin. 1991. The influence of individualism-collectivism and self-monitoring on conflict styles. *International Journal of Intercultural Relations* 15: 65–83.

Turk, J. L., and N. W. Bell. 1972. Measuring power in families. *Journal of Marriage and Family* 34, no. 2: 215–222.

Turner, C. M. and Barrett, P. M. 1998. "Adolescent adjustment to perceived marital conflict." *Journal of Child and Family Studies* v7 i4 p499(1).

Tutu, D. 1999. 2004. *No future without forgiveness*. New York: Doubleday.

Tutzauer, F., and M. E. Roloff. 1988. Communication processes leading to integrative agreements: Three paths to joint benefits. *Communication Research* 15: 360–380.

Tyler, T. R. 1987. The psychology of disputant concerns in mediation. *Negotiation Journal* 3: 367–374.

Umbreit, M. S. 1995. *Mediating interpersonal conflicts*. West Concord, MN: CPI Publishing.

Umbreit, M., R. B. Coates, and B. Vos. 2004. Victim-offender mediation: Three decades of practice and research. *Conflict Resolution Quarterly* 22, no. 1–2: 279–303.

University of Kansas Web site. 2005.

Ury, W. L. 1990. Dispute resolution notes from the Kalahari. *Negotiation Journal* 6: 229–238.

———. 1995. Conflict resolution among the Bushmen: Lessons in dispute systems design. *Negotiation Journal* 11: 379–389.

Ury, W., J. Brett, and S. Goldberg. 1988. *Getting disputes resolved*. San Francisco: Jossey-Bass.

———. 1989. Dispute systems design: An introduction. *Negotiation Journal* 5: 357–358.

Van de Vliert, E. 1981. Siding and other reactions to a conflict. *Journal of Conflict Resolution* 25, no. 3: 495–520.

———. 1985. Escalative intervention in small-group conflicts. *Journal of Applied Behavioral Science* 21: 19–36.

Van den Broucke, S., W. Vandereycken, and H. Vertommen. 1995. Conflict management in married eating disorder patients: A controlled observational study. *Journal of Social and Personal Relationships* 12: 27–48.

Vangelisti, A. 1994. Messages that hurt. In *The dark side of interpersonal communication*, edited by W. R. Cupach and B. Spitzberg. Hillsdale, NJ: Lawrence Erlbaum Publisher.

Van Goozen, S. H. M., N. H. Frijda, M. Kindt, and N. E. van de Poll. 1994. Anger proneness in women: Development and validation of the anger situation questionnaire. *Aggressive Behavior* 20: 79–100.

VanLear, C. 1992. Marital communication across the generations: Learning and rebellion, continuity and change. *Journal of Social and Personal Relationships* 9: 103–123.

Vinacke, W. E., and A. Arkoff. 1957. An experimental study of coalitions in a triad. *American Sociological Review* 22: 406–414.

Vincent, J. P. 1972. *Problem-solving behavior in distressed and nondistressed married and stranger dyads.* Unpublished doctoral dissertation. University of Oregon.

Vissing, Y., and W. Baily. 1996. Parent-to-child verbal aggression. In *Family violence from a communication perspective*, edited by D. D. Cahn and S. A. Lloyd, 85–107. Hillsdale, NJ: Lawrence Erlbaum Associates.

Vivian, D., and J. Langhinrichsen-Rohling. 1994. Are bidirectionally violent couples mutually victimized? A gender-sensitive comparison. *Violence and Victims* 9: 107–124.

Volkema, R. J., and T. J. Bergmann. 1989. Interpersonal conflict at work: An analysis of behavioral responses. *Human Relations* 42: 757–770.

Vroom, P., D. Fassett, and R. A. Wakefield. 1981. Mediation: The wave of the future? *American Family* 4, no. 4: 8–15.

———. 1982. Winning through mediation: Divorce without losers. *Futurist* 16 (February): 28–34.

Vuchinich, S. 1986. On attenuation in verbal family conflict. *Social Psychology Quarterly* 49: 281–293.

Waldron, V. 1991. Achieving communication goals in superior-subordinate relationships: The multifunctionality of upward maintenance tactics. *Communication Monographs* 58: 289–306.

Walker, G. B. 1988. Bacharach and Lawler's theory of argument in bargaining: A critique. *Journal of the American Forensic Association* 24: 218–232.

Wall, J. A., Jr. 1981. Mediation: An analysis, review, and proposed research. *Journal of Conflict Resolution* 25, no. 1: 157–180.

———. 1985. *Negotiation: Theory and practice.* Glenview, IL: Scott, Foresman & Company.

———. 1993. Community mediation in China and Korea: Some similarities and differences. *Negotiation Journal* 9: 141–153.

Wall, J. A., and R. R. Callister. 1995. Ho'oponopono: Some lessons from Hawaiian mediation. *Negotiation Journal* 11: 45–53.

Wall, V. D., Jr., and G. Galanes. 1986. The SYMLOG dimensions and small group conflict. *Central States Speech Journal* 37: 61–78.

Waller, W. 1938. *The family: A dynamic interpretation.* New York: Gordon.

Waln, V. 1981. *Interpersonal conflict interaction: An examination of verbal defense of self.* Paper presented to Speech Communication Association Convention, Anaheim, California.

Walsh, F. 1984. *Normal family processes.* New York: Guilford Press.

Walton, R. E. 1969. *Interpersonal peacemaking: Confrontation and third party consultation.* Reading, MA: Addison-Wesley Publishing.

Walton, R. E., and R. B. McKersie. 1965. *A behavioral theory of labor negotiations: An analysis of a social system.* New York: McGraw-Hill.

Warner, C. T., and T. D. Olson. 1981. Another view of family conflict and family wholeness. *Family Relations* 30, no. 4: 493–504.

Watson, C. 1994. Gender versus power as a predictor of negotiation behavior and outcomes. *Negotiation Journal* 10: 117–127.

Watzlawick, P. 1966. A structured family interview. *Family Process* 5: 256–271.

Watzlawick, P., J. H. Beavin, and D. D. Jackson. 1967. *Pragmatics of human communication: A study of interaction patterns, pathologies and paradoxes.* New York: W. W. Norton & Company.

Weeks, D. 1992. *The eight essential steps to conflict resolution.* New York: Jeremy T. Tarcher/Putnam Publishing.

Wehr, P. 1979. *Conflict regulation.* Boulder, CO: Westview Press.

Weick, K. E. 1969. *The social psychology of organizing.* Reading, Mass.: Addison-Wesley Publishing.

———. 1979. *The social psychology of organizing.* 2d ed. New York: Addison-Wesley Publishing.

Weider-Hatfield, D., and J. D. Hatfield. 1995. Relationships among conflict management styles, levels of conflict, and reactions to work. *The Journal of Social Psychology* 135, no. 6: 687–710.

———. 1996. Superiors' conflict management strategies and subordinate outcomes. *Management Communication Quarterly* 10: 189–208.

Weiss, R., and G. Margolin. 1977. Marital conflict and accord. In *Handbook for behavioral assessment*, edited by A. R. Ciminero, K. S. Calhoun, and H. E. Adams. New York: John Wiley & Sons.

Weiss, R. L., H. Hops, and G. R. Patterson. 1972. A framework for conceptualizing marital conflict: A technology for altering it, some data for evaluating it. In *Behavior change: Methodology, concepts and practice* (The Fourth Banff International Conference on Behavior Modification), edited by L. A. Hammerlynck, L. C. Handy, and E. J. Mash. Champaign, IL: Research Press.

Wenger, A., and D. Mockli. 2003. *Conflict prevention: The untapped potential of the business sector.* Boulder, CO: Lynne Rienner Publishers.

Weschler, L. 1993. Getting over. *The New Yorker*, April: 173–236, 281–284.

Whitchurch, G. G., and J. L. Pace. 1993. Communication skills training and interspousal violence. *Journal of Applied Communication Research* 21: 96–102.

White, J. B., R. Tynan, A. D. Galinsky, and L. Thompson. 2004. Face threat sensitivity in negotiation: Roadblock to agreement and joint gain. *Organizational Behavior and Human Decision Processes* 94, no. 2: 102–125.

White, J. W., and J. A. Humphrey. 1994. Women's aggression in heterosexual conflicts. *Aggressive Behavior* 20: 195–202.

Wiesenthal, S. 1998. *The sunflower.* New York: Schocken Books.

Wilhelm, R., trans. 1977. *The I Ching*. Princeton, NJ: Princeton University Press.

Williams, R., and V. Williams. 1994. *Anger kills: Seventeen strategies for controlling the hostility that can harm your health*. New York: Harper Perennial.

Wilmot, W. W. 1976. *The influence of personal conflict styles of teachers on student attitudes toward conflict*. Paper presented to Instructional Communication Division, International Communication Association Convention, Portland, Oregon, April 15.

———. 1987. *Dyadic communication*. 3d ed. New York: McGraw-Hill.

———. 1994. Relational rejuvenation. In *Communication and relational maintenance*, edited by D. J. Canary and L. Stafford, 257–273. New York: Academic Press.

———. 1995. *Relational communication*. New York: McGraw-Hill.

Wilmot, W. W., and R. H. Andes. 2004. *Better bargains*. Unpublished manuscript.

Wilson, C., and P. Gross. 1994. Police-public interactions: The impact of conflict resolution tactics. *Journal of Applied Social Psychology* 24: 159–175.

Wilson, S. R. 1992. Face and facework in negotiation. In *Communication and negotiation*, edited by L. L. Putnam and M. E. Roloff, 176–205. Newbury Park, CA: Sage Publications.

Wissler, R. L. 2004. The effectiveness of court-connected dispute resolution in civil cases. *Conflict Resolution Quarterly* 22, no. 2: 55–88.

Witteman, H. 1992. Analyzing interpersonal conflict: Nature of awareness, type of initiating event, situational perceptions, and management styles. *Western Journal of Communication* 56: 248–280.

Witteman, H., and M. A. Fitzpatrick. 1986. Compliance-gaining in marital interaction: Power bases, processes, and outcomes. *Communication Monographs* 53: 130–143.

Womack, D. F. 1988. Assessing the Thomas-Kilmann conflict MODE survey. *Management Communication Quarterly* 1: 321–349.

Wood, J. T. 1994. *Gendered lives: Communication, gender, and culture*. Belmont, CA: Wadsworth Publishing.

———. 1997. *Gendered lives: Communication, gender and culture*, 2d. ed. 1997. Belmont, CA: Wadsworth Publishing Co.

Worthington, E. L. and D. Drinkard. 2000. Promoting reconciliation through psychoeducational and therapeutic interventions. *Journal of Marital and Family Therapy* 26: 1.

Yankelovich, D. 1999. *The magic of dialogue: Transforming conflict into cooperation*. New York: Simon and Schuster.

Yarbrough, E. 1977. *Rules of observation*. Unpublished monograph. Department of Communication, University of Colorado.

Yarbrough, E., and W. Wilmot. 1995. *Artful mediation: Constructive conflict at work*. Boulder, CO: Cairns Publishing.

Yelsma, P. 1984. Functional conflict management in effective marital adjustment. *Communication Quarterly* 32, no. 1: 56–61.

———. 1995. Couples' affective orientations and their verbal aggressiveness. *Communication Quarterly* 43: 100–114.

Yexley, M., and I. Borowsky. 2002. Correlation between different experiences of intrafamilial physical violence and violent adolescent behavior. *Journal of Interpersonal Violence* 17, no. 7: 707–721.

Young, O. R. 1972. Intermediaries: Additional thought on third parties. *Journal of Conflict Resolution* 16 (March): 51–65.

Young-Eisendrath, P. 1993. *You're not what I expected: Love after the romance has ended*. New York: Morrow Press.

———. 2000. Self and transcendence: A postmodern approach to analytical psychology in practice. *Psychoanalyic Dialogues* 10, no. 3: 427–428.

Zediker, K., and J. Stewart. 2002. Dialogue's basic tension. In *Bridges not walls*. 8th ed. New York: McGraw-Hill.

Zehr, H. 1985. *Retributive justice, restorative justice*. Akron, PA: Mennonite Central Committee.

———. 2001. *Transcending: Reflections of crime victims*. Intercourse, PA: Good Books.

Zietlow, P. H., and A. L. Sillars. 1988. Life-stage differences in communication during marital conflicts. *Journal of Social and Personal Relationships* 5: 223–245.

Name Index

Subject Index